For Reference

Not to be taken from this room

BUT BLOT 96 008

BUTLER'S
LIVES OF THE SAINTS

NEW
FULL EDITION

AUGUST

BUTLER'S
LIVES OF THE SAINTS

NEW FULL EDITION

Patron
H. E. CARDINAL BASIL HUME, O.S.B.
Archbishop of Westminster

BUTLER'S LIVES OF THE SAINTS

NEW
FULL EDITION

AUGUST

Revised by
JOHN CUMMING

BURNS & OATES

THE LITURGICAL PRESS
Collegeville, Minnesota

First published 1998 in Great Britain by
BURNS & OATES
Wellwood, North Farm Road,
Tunbridge Wells, Kent TN2 3DR

First published 1998 in North America by
THE LITURGICAL PRESS
St John's Abbey, Collegeville,
Minnesota 56321

ISBN 0 86012 257 3   Burns & Oates
ISBN 0-8146-2384-0   The Liturgical Press

The emblems appearing at the foot of some pages are taken from W. Ellwood Post,
Saints, Signs and Symbols: A Concise Dictionary. © Copyright 1962, 1974 by
Morehouse Publishing, with the permission of the publishers.

Library of Congress Catalog Card Number: 95-81671

Typeset by Search Press Limited
Printed in the United States of America

CONTENTS

(Entries in capital letters indicate that the saint or feast is commemorated throughout the Roman Catholic Church with the rank of Solemnity, Feast, Memorial or Optional Memorial, according to the 1969 revised Calendar of the Latin [Roman] Rite of the Catholic Church, published in the Roman Missal of 1970, or that the saint is of particular importance for the English-speaking world. These entries are placed first on their dates. All others are in chronological order, by date of death. The paragraph at the end of each day headed "*R.M.*" lists those those saints and blessed who appear in the new draft Roman Martyrology but are not given an entry in this volume.)

Contents

Contents

PREFACE

In his diary, *Journal of a Soul*, Pope John XXIII recalls the day of his ordination: "I visited the churches to which I was most devoted, the altars of my most familiar saints, the images of Our Lady. They were very short visits. It seemed that evening as if I had something to say to all those holy ones and as if every one of them had something to say to me. And indeed it was so."

The best one can hope of a volume like this is that a reasonable number of its entries may prompt similar dialogues.

Essentially, the form is time-honoured. It is biographical and keeps to the structure of a beginning, a middle, and an end, unless reliable information is lacking and all we have is two or even one of the elements—in too many cases just an end. In the case of saints, however, their "reception" over the centuries, what they have meant to people and how that meaning has been constructed and conveyed, is often more important than even the ascertainable facts of who they were and what they did. Therefore possible psychological motives, social influences, and so forth, are also suggested: with regard not only to the saints' behaviour but to their making—by the Church diffusing knowledge of them, and by feedback from the faithful in that strange, more potent dimension where the popular will confirms their sanctification. Similarly, for the best-known saints, I have listed some of the most powerful images (and their locations) that have helped to make their subjects what they mean to us.

The important thing about most of the people in this volume is that they belong to us in this moment. They are living now. Antipathy toward what is new can be serious indeed, but: "The inability to keep the past alive," says Ortega y Gasset, "is the truly reactionary feature.... If the past falls dead within our memories the very recesses of our souls are infected."

Often the very remoteness of the saints' times makes that difficult to understand, however many references are made to "background" suasions. But August holds a number of exceptional witnesses to truth and compassion before the most obvious evils of our own times. Edith Stein (19th), Jakob Gapp and Otto Neururer (13th), and Maxmilian Kolbe (14th), for instance, were people of courage who by their behaviour and unwavering resolution proclaimed the dignity of truth and of truth as compassion. Their witness forces on us the relevance of similar situations every day now in some part of the world but also shocks into immediacy the lives of earlier victims, from the Roman persecutions through the Elizabethan and Jacobean martyrs to the missionaries of the nineteenth century, who appear in this volume. Jakob Gapp's refusal to say the system was right and Maximilian Kolbe's defiance of cruelty help us to appreciate the tenacity of Maximus the Confessor (13th), the steadfastness of Edward Bamber, John Woodcock, and Thomas Whitaker (7th), and the fatal kindness of Margaret Ward (30th) to one of the most maverick of maverick priests. An unwavering decision to say Yes to truth and No to untruth unites many of these brave men and women over the centuries.

Not only unusual courage stands out in this volume. Considered attentively, in their social or personal aspects, all people are complex, irrational, and odd. The saints are no different, yet when they pour feeling into ordinariness they add a special defiance to their uniqueness. Many of them resist all tendencies to appropriate or eliminate the sacred in favour of some tedious local cause or supreme formula.

Some of August's people are delightful—even when not utterly so. Radegund (13th) in her country retreat receiving elegant verse epistles and exchanging gifts of delicacies with her equally refined "holy troubadour," Venantius Fortunatus, is unique, of course. Nevertheless, there are similar moments in the lives of, say, Clare (11th), as when she tucks the other Sisters up in bed; and of Louis of France (25th), as when he disconcerts his retinue by suddenly sitting on the ground. Such minor epiphanies bring a place and time very much to light, as when the kindly Blaan (10th) strikes sparks from his fingers to light the candles in a dark Scots kirk. Then we have the holy irony and sheer cheek (even if due to inspired accretions) of so many martyrs' dialogues with their persecutors. August seems replete with these. On occasions, to be sure, they approach black comedy, as when Laurence (10th) assures his persecutors that he has been done to a turn and advises them to try a slice.

Many of this month's saints remind us of the importance of being a person. The destruction of outer as well as inner quiet has always been a threat to the development of saints, but a special kind of menace arrived with the Industrial Age. Changes come ever faster in the latest, electronic phase of the era of technology. The cultivation of the unique viewpoint has almost disappeared with the peace needed to refine it. The loss of a secure order and of obedience to rules of perspective in almost every sense may have freed people to choose their own ways of seeing and thinking, but it has also deprived them of the framework for contemplation that makes that choice possible. The examples of those who have accepted, or forced, a space in the rapidity of things in order to consider the nature of those things are precious substitutes for contexts that seemed automatically to supply such refuges. The very constraints the saints were subject to should encourage us in our own lostness, even if they seem willful or bizarre in asserting their individuality: the "unspeakable stress of pitch" of their self-hood (Hopkins). Only by knowing who we are can we know the "exquisite, determining, selfmaking, power" (Hopkins again). We deduce the existence, the "whatness" of God from our own and others' particularity. Major figures in this sense are Augustine (28th), that great psychoanalyst *avant la lettre*, as he examines previous relationships in the light of the transcendental meeting he has always looked for. But there are also Clare, Edith Stein, Maximus, and even Dominic (8th) and Bernard (20th), in spite of their busyness in the world. There are many others, for all but the most summary of these lives proclaim this principle of selfhood, especially, perhaps, in their denial of self-importance.

August also contains the usual batch of case-histories of saints whose pious and particularly self-denying or self-punitive practices make them seem quite or very sick. This is not so noticeable when the person in question has a lot more to him or her than penitential enthusiasm, but it is difficult, for instance, to accept Rose of Lima's (23rd) singing duets with birds and insects as compensation for her attempts to disfigure herself—the "neurotic excoriations" that for the dermatologist-cum-psychiatrist may express not humility but aggression or inappropriate submissiveness. Ours is a very sadistic and masochistic age, yet we flinch in a particularly modern way from the verminous hairshirts, dolorous couches, and quaint diets of the saints. But, even when they seem pathological by modern standards, these aspects of certain saints' behaviour remain significant features of their lives and must be subjects for informed inquiry. Nevertheless, apart from those who are—as we know them—little more than inhabitants of a folk-tale, the saints worth knowing are not saints because of their psychic wounds but, from our viewpoint, in spite of them. We must often ask whether precisely the most distasteful of these voluntary punishments, with all the accretions of their recounting over the centuries, do not represent a form of self-knowledge, and even of protest against the cruelties of social circumstance. This seems an obvious aspect when the saint had to fight family pressures to marry instead of opting for the religious life, or had to survive a disadvantaged upbringing, misguided direction, or envy. Such aspects of the lives of Clare, John Vianney (4th), and several others deserve careful study.

Some August people will seem dull and the virtues for which they were originally recommended to us unimpressive. That may be the fault of the scant evidence that has come down to us or of our time-bound preference for what seems singular and intense. Perhaps some saints, even John Berchmans (13th) and Stanislaus Kostka (15th), will seem vital to a different age with different insights. Archbishop Lanfranc's classic strictures on the excessive number of Anglo-Saxon saints whose merits were unproven apply to almost all ages and places. But this volume is also a reference-book; many of those who consult a book about the saints seek neither an intercessor nor a thaumaturge; and the nuts and bolts of even suspect dates and places serve many purposes.

To be sure, we cannot avoid a mild demythologization of the saints, if not of sanctity itself. To some extent we have to reinterpret myths, narratives, complexes of symbolism, and the understandings that have grown up about them and in which they are conveyed to us. "Many ingenious lovely things are gone

/ That seemed sheer miracle to the multitude" (Yeats). Yet, in that sense again, the reported lives of the saints, which also means their legends, may be their own best interpreters and should not be wholly excised. The miraculous, Karl Rahner reminds us, may be an invitation and challenge to share the uniqueness of the specific situation of a particular human being, which is never a neutral objective world uniformly accessible and meaningful to all of us in exactly the same way.

There are also the supposedly "simple" saints. The late nineteenth-century cult of simplicity has tended to obscure its real importance: how it was experienced, which has its own message for us. It is very difficult nowadays both to avoid excessive adulation of "simple faith," and to bring out the nature of such figures as the Curé d'Ars, who tried to make himself seem even more simple than he was by various strategies, such as assuming a peasant accent for important visitors. Some wonderfully stalwart characters emerge from the ranks of these "ordinary" people: the remarkable Joan Delanoue (17th) (and her fairy-tale visitor), say, or the indefatigable illiterate Mary Baouardy (26th), who, against terrible odds, outshone all her persecutors and superiors.

Pious monarchs are another group well represented here. With Oswald of Northumbria (5th), Stephen of Hungary (16th), and Louis of France (25th), for example, it is necessary to suggest divisions between commendations for establishing and fortifying Christianity and the Church and national myths derived from their zeal as rulers which may have been culpably misused in modern times.

Then we have the beatified or canonized popes. Clearly even short versions of their lives demand some reference to the burgeoning historical scholarship and to the commentaries on the political and personal influences that often coloured their policies. Innocent XI (12th) was a major actor on the political stage; Pius X's (21st) attitude to the development of Christian democracy, to Catholics' understanding of their political responsibilities, and especially to freedom of thought within the Church, remains variously effective. As with the martyrs for truth, attention to the problems and self-understanding of these popes of modern times helps us to understand the actions of such predecessors as Pontian (13th).

I am grateful to many who helped me with facilities, information, comments, and corrections: to the librarians of the National Library of Scotland, the *Institut catholique* of Paris, the diocesan library at Nîmes, the municipal and university libraries of Montpellier, the *Musée d'art sacré du Gard* at Pont Saint-Esprit, and the *Mediathèque* of Uzès; to Prof. Kathleen Jones, Rev. Dr Lukas Vischer, Dom Henry Wansbrough, O.S.B., Dom Alberic Stacpoole, O.S.B., Dom Eric Hollas, O.S.B., Fr Simon Tugwell, O.P., Dr John Stephens, and D. H. Farmer; to the biographers, hagiographers, commentators, and research-workers acknowledged in the bibliographies, whose findings and insights I have cribbed and, I hope, traduced only moderately; and to Paul Burns in so many respects, above all for his sorely-tried patience. And may all those good men and women, from Augustine whose plain anxieties are ours reverberating among his complexities to Maximilian who must touch your heart too, forgive me for trying to put them in these nutshells.

I am not responsible for the articles on Bd Edmund Ignatius Rice (29th), Bd Ildefonsus Schuster (30th), and Bd Mary MacKillop (8th). The first was kindly contributed by Br Donal Blake, C.F.C., who compiled the documentary case for his beatification; the second is the joint work of Paul Burns and the team responsible for the Italian edition of this work; the last is by David Hugh Farmer, and taken from the May volume, where the entry appeared on the basis of mistaken information.

---

14 August 1997, Feast of St Maximilian Kolbe, martyr

John Cumming

Abbreviations and Short Forms

A.A.S.	*Acta Apostolicae Sedis, Commentarium Officiale.* Rome, 1908-.
AA.SS.	*Acta Sanctorum.* 64 vols. Antwerp, also Rome and Paris, 1643- . (Page and volume numbers vary in different editions.)
Anal.Boll.	*Analecta Bollandiana* (1882-).
Anstruther	G. Anstruther, O.P. *The Seminary Priests.* 4 vols. Ware, Ushaw, and Great Wakering, 1968-77.
A.S.E.	*Anglo-Saxon England* (1972-).
Bede, *H.E.*	The Venerable Bede. *Historia Ecclesiastica.* Various editions.
B.H.L.	Society of Bollandists. *Bibliotheca Hagiographica Latina.* 2 vols. Brussels, 1898-1901.
Bibl.SS.	*Bibliotheca Sanctorum.* 12 vols. Rome, 1960-70; Suppl. 1, Rome, 1987.
B.T.A.	H. Thurston and D. Attwater (eds.). *Butler's Lives of the Saints.* 4 vols. London and New York, 1953-4. The previous edition of this work.
C.M.H.	H. Delehaye, P. Peeters, *et al* (eds.). *Commentarius Perpetuus in Martyrologium Hieronymianum.* In *AA.SS.*, vol. 64, 1940.
D.A.C.L.	F. Cabrol and H. Leclercq (eds.). *Dictionnaire d'archéologie chrétienne et de liturgie.* Paris, 1907-36.
D.C.B.	W. Smith and H. Wace (eds.). *Dictionary of Christian Biography.* 4 vols. London, 1877-87.
D.H.G.E.	A. Baudrillart *et al.* (eds.). *Dictionnaire d'histoire et de géographie écclésiastique.* Paris, 1912- .
D.N.B.	L. Stephens and S. Lee (eds.). *Dictionary of National Biography.* 63 vols. London, 1885-1900.
D.N.H.	F. Holböck. *Die neuen Heiligen der katholische Kirche.* 3 vols. Stein am Rhein, 1991-4.
D.T.C.	A. Vacant, A. Mangenot, and E. Amann (eds.). *Dictionnaire de théologie catholique.* 15 vols. Paris, 1903-50.
Duchesne, *Fastes*	L. Duchesne. *Fastes épiscopaux de l'ancienne Gaule.* 3 vols. 4th ed., Paris, 1908.
E.H.D.	D. C. Douglas *et al.* (eds.). *English Historical Documents.* London, 1953- .
Eusebius, *H.E.*	Eusebius of Caesarea. *Historia Ecclesiastica.*Various editions.

Gillow   J. Gillow (ed.). *A Literary and Biographical History, or Bibliographical Dictionary of the English Catholics from the Breach with Rome in 1534 to the Present Day.* 5 vols. London and New York, 1881-1903 (plus Index vol. added by J. Bevan, 1985).

H.C.S.   H. Bouyer *et al.* (eds.). *A History of Christian Spirituality.* Eng. trans. of *Histoire de la spiritualité chrétienne.* 3 vols. London and New York, 1963-8.

H.S.S.C.   F. Chiovaro *et al.* (eds.). *Histoire des saints et de la sainteté chrétienne.* 12 vols. Paris, 1972-88.

Jedin-Dolan   H. Jedin and H. Dolan (eds.). *History of the Church.* Eng. trans. of *Handbuch der Kirchengeschichte.* 10 vols. London and New York, 1965-81.

J.T.S.   *Journal of Theological Studies* (1900-).

K.S.S.   A. P. Forbes (ed.). *Kalendars of Scottish Saints.* Edinburgh, 1872.

L.E.M. 1   Bede Camm (ed.). *Lives of the English Martyrs*, first series. 2 vols. London, 1904-5.

L.E.M. 2   E. H. Burton and J. H. Pollen, *Lives of the English Martyrs*, second series, on the martyrs declared Venerable 1583-8. London, 1915.

Liber Pontificalis   L. Duchesne (ed.). *Liber Pontificalis.* Paris, 1886.

M.G.H.   G. Pertz *et al.* (eds.) *Monumenta Germaniae Historiae, Scriptores.* 64 vols. Hanover, 1839-1921. Sub-series include *Auctores Antiquissimi, Epistolae Selectae*, and *Scriptores Rerum Merovingicarum.*

M.M.P.   R. Challoner. *Memoirs of Missionary Priests.* New ed. by J. H. Pollen. London, 1924.

N.C.E.   *New Catholic Encyclopaedia.* 14 vols. New York, 1967.

N.D.T.   J. A. Komonchak, M. Collins, and D. A. Lane (eds.). *The New Dictionary of Theology.* New York and Dublin, 1987.

N.S.B. 1   Thierry Lelièvre. *100 Nouveaux saints et bienheureux de 1963 à 1984.* Paris, 1983.

N.S.B. 2   Thierry Lelièvre. *Nouveaux saints et bienheureux de 1984 à 1988.* Paris, 1989.

O.D.P.   J. W. Kelly (ed.). *The Oxford Dictionary of Popes.* Oxford, 1986.

P.L.   J. P. Migne (ed.). *Patrologia Latina.* 221 vols. Paris, 1844-64.

Plummer	C. Plummer. *Vitae Sanctorum Hiberniae.* 2 vols. Oxford 1910, rp. 1968.
Procter	J. Procter (ed.). *Short Lives of the Dominican Saints.* New ed., London, 1900.
Riv.A.C.	*Rivista di arceologia Cristiana* (1924-).
R.S.	Rolls Series: *Rerum Britannicum Medii Aevi Scriptores.* London, 1858- .
Theodoret, *H.E.*	Theodoret. *Historia Ecclesiastica.* Various editions.
Z.K.T.	*Zeitschrift für Katholische Theologie* (1877-).

1

ST ALPHONSUS DE' LIGUORI, *Bishop, Doctor, and Founder*
(1696–1787)

Alfonso Maria de' Liguori was born near Naples in 1696. His parents were Don Giuseppe de' Liguori, captain of the royal galleys, and Donna Cavalieri. His father wanted his first child to be well educated, so Alphonsus was instructed by tutors from an early age. He was thirteen when he began to study law, and at sixteen, four years before the usual time, he became a doctor of Naples University in civil and canon law. He is said (with exaggeration) never to have lost a case in eight years of practice as a barrister. In 1717 Don Giuseppe arranged a marriage for his son, but it came to nothing. The older Lives say that for a year or two his religious enthusiasm was rather slack and that, though not a serious sinner, he was overfond of "society life," fashionable amusements, and the music of the Neapolitan theatre, almost certainly to an extent now thought to be quite compatible with holiness. During Lent 1722 he went into retreat with the Lazarists; in Lent 1723 he decided privately not to marry and to practise law only while the inner mentor he thought of as God's voice told him to.

A few months later a Neapolitan nobleman sued the grand-duke of Tuscany for a valuable estate. Alphonsus was briefed in the case, but the judgment went against his client. The point was whether the estate was held under Lombard or Angevin law. Alphonsus had overlooked a clause that made the issue clear. He interpreted his failure as a sign of God's will. Though his father was indignant, Alphonsus refused to remain a barrister or to consider another possible wife. When he visited the patients in the hospital for incurable diseases he twice heard his inner voice say, "Leave the world and give yourself to me." He went to the church of Our Lady of Ransom, put his sword on the altar, and asked to join the priests of the Oratory. Don Giuseppe tried to dissuade his son but eventually let him become a priest on condition that he did not join the Oratory but stayed at home. Alphonsus agreed on the advice of his spiritual director, the Oratorian Fr Pagano.

He began studying theology at home and in 1726 was ordained priest. He spent two years in missionary work throughout the kingdom of Naples and earned a reputation as an unaffected preacher and an effective confessor, avoiding both pomposity and Jansenist rigorism. "It is a pleasure to hear your sermons. You forget yourself and preach Jesus Christ," he was told. He treated his penitents as souls to be saved, not as criminals to be punished or frightened.

He is said never to have refused anyone absolution. But some people found his approach suspect. He organized the *lazzaroni*, or layabouts and unemployed of Naples, into groups which met for Christian instruction. He reproved one of the members for overzealous fasting, and another priest added: "God wants us to eat to live. If you are given cutlets, eat them and be thankful. They will do you good." The remark went the rounds and was twisted to discredit Alphonsus. The clubs were said to be secret societies of Epicureans or Quietists, even to belong to a new sect called "Cutlets." Some members were arrested, and Alphonsus had to explain what had happened. The archbishop told him to be careful and the "Cutlet clubs" continued undisturbed. (They developed into the Association of the Chapels, which by the twentieth century numbered thousands of workingmen meeting daily for prayer and instruction in the confraternity chapels.)

In 1729, when he was thirty-three, Alphonsus left his father's house to become chaplain to a college training missionaries to China. There he met Thomas Falcoia, a priest twice his own age, who became a close friend. Falcoia had spent years trying to set up a new religious Institute after a vision he claimed to have had in Rome. He had succeeded only in founding a convent of nuns at Scala, near Amalfi, which followed his version of the Visitandine Rule. But one of the nuns, Sister Mary Celeste, said the Rule the nuns ought to follow had been revealed to her privately. Falcoia was pleased to discover that its provisions resembled those revealed in his own vision twenty years before. In 1730 he interested Alphonsus in the matter. About the same time Falcoia was appointed bishop of Castellamare. This left him free to associate himself with the Scala convent again. He asked Alphonsus to give a retreat to the nuns.

Alphonsus gave the retreat and investigated Sister Mary Celeste's revelation with legal if not scientific precision. He decided that it was not a hallucination but from God and that the convent should be reorganized in accordance with the vision. The bishop of Scala agreed. In 1731 on the feast of the Transfiguration the nuns put on their new red and blue habit and began a strictly enclosed and penitential life. This was the beginning of the Redemptoristines, who still flourish in various countries. Alphonsus himself expanded the new Rule and made it more explicit. Bishop Thomas suggested that he should establish a new Congregation of missionaries to work particularly among the peasants, at that time an original and daring enterprise, especially in absolutist Bourbon Naples. Alphonsus agreed but had to face a storm of opposition. In November 1732 he left Naples for Scala, where the Congregation of the Most Holy Redeemer was founded on the 9th of the month. Its first home was in a small house belonging to the nuns. There were seven postulants under Alphonsus, with Falcoia as an informal superior general. From the start there were arguments, mainly about who was in overall authority. One group opposed the bishop and Alphonsus; both houses were divided. Sister Mary Celeste left to found a convent at Foggia. After a month Alphonsus was alone except for one lay brother. But other postulants arrived, a larger house was needed, and in autumn 1733 successful missions were given in the diocese of Amalfi. The next January a second foundation was made at Villa degli Schiavi, where Alphonsus went to live and conducted missions. From 1726 to 1752 he preached up and down the kingdom of Naples, especially in villages and hamlets, with great success. His confessional was crowded, many hardened sinners returned to the sacraments, enemies were reconciled, and family feuds were healed. He also started the practice of returning some months after a mission to consolidate its work.

In 1734, however, Spain re-asserted its authority over Naples. It was thought that missions to the neglected poor might presage the spread of dangerous political ideas such as egalitarianism. In 1737 a rogue priest spread evil rumours about the establishment at Villa, armed men attacked the community, and it was thought best to close the house. In the following year Scala had to be abandoned. Nevertheless, Cardinal Spinelli, archbishop of Naples, made Alphonsus head of a general mission throughout his diocese. For two years he organized and conducted it until Falcoia's death recalled him to the work of the Congregation. A general chapter was held and elected Alphonsus rector major (or superior general). Vows were taken and Constitutions drawn up. They were now a duly-constituted religious Congregation. In the next few years they made several new foundations in spite of the local and official opposition of the anticlerical faction.

With experience the former lawyer and lucid, sympathetic preacher became a leading moral theologian. The first edition of Alphonsus' *Moral Theology* took the form of annotations to the work of Busenbaum, a Jesuit theologian. It was published at Naples in 1748, and the second edition, properly the first of his own complete work, in 1753-5. It was approved by Pope Benedict XIV and was immediately successful. It emphasized God's mercy and steered a middle course between the rigorism of Jansenism and undue laxity. There were seven more editions in the author's lifetime. Since the publication of this work the name of Alphonsus has been associated with probabilism, the system in moral theology which holds that if one of two opinions insists that in certain circumstances a law is binding, whereas the other holds that in these circumstances it is not, we may follow an opinion favouring liberty if it is truly and solidly probable, even though the opinion favouring the law is more probable.

Alphonsus eventually preferred what he called "equiprobabilism," which insists that the law must be obeyed unless the opinion favouring liberty is at least almost equally probable with that favouring the law, though there would seem to be little practical difference between the two systems when summarized thus. The Church has allowed moral theologians to apply either system. Attempts have been made to impugn the morality of Alphonsus' teaching about lying, although he held that all lies are intrinsically wrong and illicit, and this is what the Church teaches. When reduced to simple propositions, as in the foregoing, highly-nuanced arguments developed over many pages can seem like mere equivocation; and the ex-jurist Alphonsus, scrupulous in his pursuit of the exact truth, has often been accused of just that. He also attacked the Jansenist notions that Holy Communion can be received worthily only very rarely and that devotion to Our Lady is a useless superstition. He emphatically rejected the second contention in *The Glories of Mary* (1750). For a long time this was a popular work of devotion, influencing a tradition in Marian spirituality that lasted throughout the nineteenth century.

After Bishop Falcoia's death in 1743 Alphonsus' life was most industrious. He guided his Congregation through external and internal troubles. He tried to have it authorized by the king, and he ministered to individuals, conducted missions all over Naples and Sicily, wrote hymns, composed music, and painted pictures. After 1752 his health was failing, his missionary vigour decreased, and he spent more time writing. A prebendary of Naples expressed a general opinion when he said, "If I were pope I would canonize him without process." "He most perfectly fulfilled," said Fr Mazzini, "the divine precept of loving God above all things, with his whole heart and with all his strength, as all could see and as I saw better than anyone during the long years I spent with him." Alphonsus was strict but tender and compassionate. Since he often suffered acutely from scrupulosity he was particularly kind to the overscrupulous.

When Alphonsus was sixty-six, Pope Clement XIII made him bishop of Sant' Agata dei Goti, between Benevento and Capua. When the apostolic nuncio's messenger arrived at Nocera, greeted Alphonsus as "Most illustrious Lord," and handed over the letter announcing the appointment, he read it and gave it back saying, "Please do not return with any more of your 'Most illustrious.' It would be the death of me." But the pope would accept no refusal, and Alphonsus was consecrated in the church of the Minerva at Rome. Sant' Agata numbered thirty thousand people with seventeen religious houses and four hundred secular priests, some of whom did no pastoral work at all but lived on the proceeds of an easy benefice. Others were not only slack but evil-living. After nearly thirty years of neglect the laity were in a similar situation. After setting up his own modest household, the new bishop sent out a band of priests on a general mission throughout the diocese. They were recruited from all Orders and Institutes in Naples except, for reasons of tact and prudence, his own Redemptorists. Alphonsus told his missioners to be plain in the pulpit and charitable in the confessional. When one priest neglected the advice, Alphonsus said: "Your sermon kept me awake all night. . . . If you wanted to preach yourself rather than Jesus Christ, why come all the way from Naples to Ariola to do it?" He began to reform the seminary and the careless way in which benefices were granted. Some priests said their Mass in fifteen minutes or less. Alphonsus suspended them until they changed their ways, and he wrote a treatise on the subject: "'The priest at the altar,' says St Cyprian, 'stands for Jesus Christ in person.' But so many people today are just mountebanks earn-ing their livelihood by their antics. It is particularly distressing to see religious, even some in reformed Orders, say Mass so fast and destructively that even pagans would be scandalized. . . . 'Truly the sight of Mass celebrated in this way is enough to make one lose the faith.'"

After he had been at Sant' Agata a short time, famine and plague broke out. Alphonsus had often predicted this in the previous two years, but nothing had been done to prevent it. Thousands were starving, so he sold everything to buy food for the suffering, including his carriage and mules and his uncle's episcopal ring. The Holy See allowed him to use the see's endowment for the same purpose, and he ran up many debts in his efforts at relief. When the mob wanted to kill the mayor of Sant' Agata, who was unjustly accused of withholding food, Alphonsus braved their fury, offered his own life for that of the mayor, and then distracted them by distributing the rations for the next two days.

As bishop Alphonsus was very concerned about public morality. He began with kindness, but when there was no promise of amendment or when relapse occurred he took strong measures and asked the civil authorities to help. This made him many enemies, and his life was often in danger from those of high rank and others against whom he instituted proceedings. The courts usually banished hardened offenders, whether public vagabonds or private sinners, and this must have made things very difficult for the districts to which they went. Presumably the bishops of neighbouring dioceses were not very pleased when the bishop of Sant' Agata said: "Each must look after his own flock. When these people find themselves turned out everywhere, in disgrace and without food or shelter, they will come to their senses and give up their sinful lives." Judged by some late-twentieth-century notions of saintly forbearance, Alphonsus' attitude may seem harsh. But his conscientious scrutiny of the real ends and applications of moral law and his unremitting search for the best outcome for the general as well as the religious community in the conditions of his time and place, including the *ancien régime* under which he lived, make him a saint for all times.

In June 1767 Alphonsus was attacked by severe rheumatic fever. It became so unremitting that he was not expected to recover. He received the Last Sacraments, and preparations were begun for his funeral. After twelve months his life was saved, but he was left with a permanent and incurably bent neck, which can be seen in portraits of him. Until the surgeons succeeded in straightening it a little, the pressure of the chin caused a raw wound in his chest, and he could not celebrate Mass, though he managed to do so later with the aid of a chair at the Communion.

Alphonsus lived at a time of increasing secularization. He had to face not only attacks on his moral theology but an accusation that the Redemptorists were merely carrying on the Society of Jesus, which had been suppressed in the Spanish dominions in 1767. An anti-Redemptorist action, begun but adjourned some time before, was revived in 1770. The case dragged on for another thirteen years before it was decided in Alphonsus' favour on all counts. In 1775 Alphonsus asked the new pope, Pius VI, to allow him to resign his see. Clement XIII and XIV had refused similar requests, but his physical condition was now taken into account, and the aged bishop retired to his cell at Nocera, hoping to end his days in peace.

In 1777 the Redemptorists were attacked again, for their humane sympathies continued to offend an excessively authoritarian ruler and government. Alphonsus made another effort to get the royal sanction for his Rule. By now the Congregation had four houses in Naples, one in Sicily, and four others in the Papal States. Alphonsus agreed with the royal almoner, Mgr Testa, to waive any request to be allowed to hold property in common but otherwise to submit the Rule unchanged, and the almoner was to put it before the king. Testa betrayed him. He altered the Rule in vital respects, even abolishing the vows of religion. The altered Rule, in minute handwriting and with many erasures, was presented to Alphonsus, old, crippled, deaf, and with poor eyesight. He read the familiar opening lines and signed the document. The king approved the Rule, and it became legally binding. Only then did the Redemptorists discover its provisions. Alphonsus was told, "You founded the Congregation and you have destroyed it." He reproached himself: "It was my duty to read it myself, but you know I find it difficult to read even a few lines."

To refuse to accept the Rule now would mean a royal suppression of the Redemptorists. To accept it would mean suppression by the pope, for the Holy See had already approved the original Rule. Alphonsus tried to consult the pope, but the Redemptorists in the Papal States had immediately denounced the new Rule and placed themselves under the protection of the Holy See. Pius VI forbade them to accept the Rule and took them out of Alphonsus' jurisdiction. He provisionally recognized those of the Papal States as the only true Redemptorists and named Fr Francis de Paula their superior general. In 1781 the fathers of Naples accepted the Rule with a slight modification to which the king had agreed, but this was not acceptable at Rome, and the provisional decree was made final. Alphonsus thus was excluded from the Order he had founded.

He bore the humiliation inflicted by a loved and respected authority with patience and accepted as God's will the apparent end of all his hopes. During 1784-5 he went through a terrible "dark night of the soul" and is said to have suffered temptations against every article of faith and virtue. He was attacked by scruples, groundless fears, and illusions he described as diabolical. They lasted for eighteen months with intervals of lucidity. This period was followed by one of frequent ecstasies, when prophecy and even miracles are said to have replaced inward trials. Contemporary reports of the experiences of the sick and aged Alphonsus presented them as an exemplary struggle between good and evil inclinations, but it is impossible now to assess them in terms of modern geriatric medicine, though the onset of several diseases may be described as a contest between darkness and light.

Alphonsus died on the night of 31 July–1 August 1787, within two months of his ninety-first birthday. In 1796 Pius VI, the pope who had condemned him under a misapprehension, decreed the introduction of his cause. In 1816 he was beatified, in 1839 canonized, and in 1871 declared a Doctor of the Church. Alphonsus predicted that the separated houses in the Papal States would prosper and spread the Redemptorist Congregation, but the reunion did not occur until after his death. In 1785 St Clement Hofbauer (15 Mar.) established the Congregation beyond the Alps. In 1793 the Neapolitan government recognized the original Rule, and the Redemptorists were again united. Today they are established as missioners throughout Europe and America and in several other parts of the world.

The full edition of Alphonsus' *Opere Ascetiche* was published in 1933-60. The most exhaustive biography remains the French work by Fr Berthe (1900), which was improved and corrected in Harold Castle's English translation (2 vols., 1905). Other worthwhile accounts are the biography by D. F. Miller and L. X. Aubin (1940) and the exhaustive work in Spanish by R. Tellería, *San Alfonso M. de Ligorio* (2 vols., 1950-1). More contemporary viewpoints are available in F. M. Jones, *Alphonsus de Liguori: the Saint of Bourbon Naples* (1992), and H. F. G. Swanston, *Celebrating Eternity Now: A Study in the Theology of St Alphonsus de Liguori* (1995). A recent Spanish study is M. Vidal, *La familia en la vida y en la obra de Alfonso de Ligorio (1696-1787)* (1995). On probabilism and equiprobabilism see *N.D.T.*, pp. 801-3; B. Häring, *Free and Faithful in Christ, General Moral Theology*, 1 (1978); on the spiritual teaching of Alphonsus, see P. Pourrat, *La spiritualité chrétienne*, 4 (1947), pp. 449-91; and on an example of its effects, J. Guerber, *Le ralliement du clergé français à la morale liguorienne* (1973).

There is a fascinating, and apparently contemporary, portrait by an unknown hand in the Redemptorist House at Pagant. It conveys the physical and mental concentration and suffering of the saint.

St Exsuperius, *Bishop (c. 412)*

He was probably born at Arreau in the High Pyrenees in France, where a chapel dedicated to him is a place of pilgrimage. He succeeded to the see of Toulouse on the death of St Silvius about the year 405 and completed the great church of St Saturninus (or Sernin, 29 Nov.), begun by his predecessor. Generosity is said to have been his outstanding quality. It was needed at home in his time, for Gaul was overrun by the Vandals, but Exsuperius believed in supranational relief work and even sent gifts to the monks of Egypt and Palestine. St Jerome (30 Sept.) heard through the monk Sisinnius of the ascetical monastic movements in Toulouse and Marseilles and dedicated his commentary on Zechariah to Exsuperius. Jerome also wrote of him: "To relieve the hunger of the poor he suffers it himself. His pale face shows how rigorously he fasts, but the hunger of others grieves him. He gives everything he has to Christ's poor. . . . His charity is unlimited, looking for worthy causes in the most distant places; even the hermits benefit from it."

Exsuperius wrote to Pope Innocent I for advice on discipline and the canon of scripture. Innocent was determined to make Roman custom the binding norm throughout the Church. He sent Exsuperius a list of the authentic books of the Bible as then received in Rome (which was the same as today, including the deuterocanonical books—for churches of the Reformation, the Apocrypha). It is not known where and when Exsuperius died, but he seems to have been exiled first. St Paulinus of Nola (22 June) called him one of the most illustrious bishops of the Church in Gaul, and by the mid-sixth century the church of Toulouse held him in equal honour with St Saturninus.

Strange to say, Exsuperius, whose fame had reached Rome and Palestine, is not in the *Hieronynianum. AA.SS.*, Sept., 7, collects what has been recorded about him. *D.T.C.*, 5, 2022-37, contains a full notice. See also Duchesne, *Fastes*, 1, p. 307.

His emblem is a sword, and he wears a cope, as in the painting (National Gallery, London) by a member of the circle of the Master of Liesborn, where he appears with Ambrose and Jerome.

St Aled, *Martyr* (Sixth Century)

Aled (also Eiluned) has been retained in the new draft Roman Martyrology, though almost everything related about her is legendary. Nevertheless, her well-attested cult is of considerable interest and may stand as a case-history for a multitude of similar British saints.

The *Itinerary through Wales* of Giraldus Cambrensis (or Gerald of Wales) tells us:

Not far from Brecon is the church called St Aledha's, after the holy maiden who refused an earthly husband, was joined to the Eternal King, and triumphed there in a happy martyrdom. A solemn feast is held in her honour every year on 1 August and many people come from far and wide. Those suffering from various diseases receive the health they desire through the merits of the blessed maiden. I find some things which happen at this anniversary quite remarkable. In the church or in the churchyard, during the dance which is led round the churchyard with a song, you see men and girls suddenly fall to the ground as in a trance. Then, as if frenzied, they jump up and with their hands and feet mime for the people whatever work they have done unlawfully on great feasts. You see one man put his hand to the plough, and another seemingly goad on the oxen, lightening their labour with the usual uncouth song. One imitates the trade of a cobbler, another that of a tanner. You see a girl with a distaff drawing out the thread and winding it again on the spindle. Another arranges the threads for the web as she walks along, and yet another throws the shuttle and seems to weave. When they enter the church and are led to the altar with their offerings, you will be astonished to see them suddenly come to their senses again. In this way, by the divine mercy which rejoices not at the death of sinners but at their conversion, many people, though convicted by their own actions, are corrected and amended on these feast days.

Gerald was archdeacon of Brecon from 1175 for over twenty years and lived only a couple of miles away at Llanddew, which had been the centre of a Celtic Christian community, or *clas*. He was well placed to verify the details of the behaviour he describes, which seems to have its remotest origins in the dancing and mimetic play of a pre-Christian fertility ritual. The custom of dancing in churchyards not only at weddings but at feasts and revels, though on the north side, where burials were less frequent, is recorded throughout Wales well into the nineteenth century. The identity and story offer valuable evidence of the intertwining of pious and extra-religious legends with the traditional veneration (as historically respectable as many others) of a Celtic hermit of exceptionally holy life. Gerald himself gives Aled a prime mythical lineage when he says that she was a daughter of the legendary King Brychan, a prolific progenitor of Celtic saints, and a figure with the marks of a pagan divinity. But her names appears only in some lists of these children and, oddly, while she figures in at least one Latin calendar, she is unknown to the Welsh ones.

As current in the seventeenth century, her legend, with its threefold curse, fairytale elements and miraculous water-source, has a suspicious resemblance to the story of St Winifred (3 Nov.), herself a fascinating quasi-legendary figure with a folkloristic pedigree. While still young, Aled is said to have dedicated herself completely to God. When a young prince, supported by her family, urged her to marry him, she fled in disguise to Llanddew. Here she was so badly treated that she withdrew to Llanfillo, and then again to Llechfaen, where she had to sleep in the street as nobody would give her a bed. So she took refuge in the wood on Slwch Tump, near Brecon itself, where the lord of the place helped her to build a cell. She settled down there, prophesying that "a chastisement would rest on the village of Llanddew for the injuries done to her; that the village of Llanfillo would be plagued with thieves . . . and Llechfaen with envy" (Hugh Thomas, *c*. 1698).

It is not recorded that Aled also foretold her own misfortunes, but very soon her princely suitor is said to have discovered her in her retreat. When she saw him she ran down the hill. He followed, caught her up, and in rage cut off her head with his sword. Where Aled's head fell, a spring of water welled up from the rock. Thereafter she was venerated as a saint and martyr. William of Worcester says that "St Elevetha" was buried at Usk, but other writers agree that it was in her cell, which became the first St Aled's chapel on Slwch hill and in turn a small church of some importance in the Middle Ages. By 1698 it was roofless and disused, and the site is now almost unidentifiable.

The legend appears in a late-seventeenth-century manuscript of Hugh Thomas, the Breconshire herald (Harleian MS. 4181). See *Archaeologia Cambrensis* for 1883, pp. 46-7, 168, and for 1903, pp. 214-23; Gerald of Wales, *Itinerary through Wales*, bk 1, ch. 2; Jones, *History of Brecknock*, vol. 1, pp. 43-4 (edition of 1909); Cressy, *Church History of Brittany* (i.e. Britain, published at Rouen in 1668); F. Jones, *The Holy Wells of Wales* (1954); E. G. Bowen, *The Settlements of the Celtic Saints in Wales* (1956).

St Ethelwold, *Bishop* (984)

Ethelwold (or Aethelwold) was a native of Winchester. He spent his youth as a courtier of King Athelstan (924-39) but then applied to St Alphege the Bald, bishop of Winchester (12 Mar.), to accept him for the priesthood. Alphege ordained him at the same time as St Dunstan (19 May), who was about his age. When Dunstan became abbot of Glastonbury in 940 and introduced the strict Benedictine observance there, Ethelwold entered the Order. He was made one of the deans of the house, then prior. He would never sleep after Matins and generally led so austere a life that Dunstan had to order him even to eat meat once every three months. He worked as a cook, as a mason, but above all as a bell-founder; he was also an enthusiastic scholar. He wanted to go to France to study the reform at Cluny, but about 954 King Edred appointed Ethelwold abbot of Abingdon in Berkshire, which had been a great abbey but had fallen into disrepair. Monks from Glastonbury helped him to make the defunct abbey a model of regular discipline. He built a new, double-rotunda church and recruited a master of church music from Corbie. He sent his disciple Osgar to Fleury, a monastery noted for its strict observance and its possession of St Benedict's relics, to learn its discipline for the benefit of Abingdon, which could then become a model of Continental practice for England. After the Danish incursions English monasticism was somewhat weakened, and in spite of King Alfred's reforms, the education of young people was inadequate. Dunstan, Ethelwold, and Oswald of Worcester (28 Feb.) worked to restore and extend monasticism and scholarship.

In 963 Dunstan consecrated Ethelwold bishop of Winchester, the largest town in Wessex. A major monastic reform began. Ethelwold dismissed the canons of Winchester cathedral with the approval of King Edgar, whose tutor he had been, and replaced them with monks from Abingdon, thus constituting the first monastic cathedral—an institution found only in England. Ethelwold imposed stringent monastic vows on the collegiate clergy. The alternative was expulsion, and he did not hesitate to invoke secular help to enforce his reforms. Three of the former canons took the monastic habit and continued to serve in the same church. The connection between the foundation and the nearby court presaged the royal support that was to be so important for Ethelwold's reforms. Next year Ethelwold expelled the secular priests from the Newminster monastery at Winchester and replaced them with Benedictines under an abbot, sent monks to Chertsey, and restored the monastery at Milton, in Dorset. In 965 he repaired the nunnery dedicated to our Lady in Winchester and in 970 bought from the king the lands and ruins of the great nunnery of St Ethelreda in the isle of Ely, which the Danes had burned a century before; he established an abbey of monks on the same spot. He also bought the ruins of Thorney in Cambridgeshire, which he restored about 972, bulding a church with an apse at either end. He directed and helped Aldulf to buy the ruins of Peterborough Abbey, which after flourishing for two hundred years had been destroyed by the Danes in 870. He rebuilt it (966) and recruited monks for the foundation. Aldulf, King Edgar's chancellor, had lost his only son, so he gave his entire estate to this house, became a monk there, and was chosen the first abbot.

Peterborough was one of the first districts to win the status of an ecclesiastical franchise, so that the reformed monasteries, not Edgar, controlled the local courts and received their profits. Ethelwold also built the finest organ in the country at Winchester; it had four hundred pipes and thirty-six bellows. He developed an elaborate liturgical practice and the first English polyphony (the Winchester Troper) and introduced a style of manuscript illumination peculiar to Winchester and his other foundations, which won a reputation beyond England. In 971 he presided over the translation of the relics of St Swithun of Winchester (2 July). The consecration of Winchester cathedral in 980 was a major event. There he also encouraged the proficient translation into English, largely for the secular clergy, of Latin texts, and it became a centre of vernacular writing and scholarship. In religious practice and celebration, church governance, letters, and many other areas the monastic reforms introduced and overseen by Ethelwold were immensely influential throughout the pre-Norman period. The majority of English bishops before the Norman Conquest came from the monasteries of the reform initiated by Dunstan and Ethelwold.

At times, however, Ethelwold's determined reforms, especially the replacing of slack canons with strict monks, were fiercely opposed, and his dour, unrelenting, and commanding approach won him the name "Boanerges," or "son of thunder." Nevertheless, many found him benevolent, "more gentle than a dove." He was called the "father of monks" and was known for his humility and charity. He was an effective royal counsellor. He died on 1 August 984 and was buried in Winchester Cathedral. Miracles were said to have been worked through his intercession, and his body was exhumed and solemnly buried under the altar by St Alphege, his immediate successor and kinsman. Several written works are credited to Ethelwold including a translation into English of the *Rule of St Benedict*, which Edgar is said to have rewarded with the grant of a considerable estate in East Suffolk. Ethelwold probably also wrote and certainly promoted, at the congress he summoned in about 970, the *Regularis Concordia*, or general Rule, for his thirty reformed monasteries in southern England, which was formerly attributed to Dunstan.

There is a fair amount of historical material for the life of Ethelwold. Aelfric's biography appears in the *Chronicon Monasterii de Abingdon* (R.S., 1858). There are two contemporary Lives: one by Wulfstan, the other derived from it by Aelfric. Both are printed with full introduction in M. Lapidge and M. Winterbottom, *Wulfstan of Winchester: the Life of St Ethelwold* (1991), completing M. Winterbottom, *Three Lives of English Saints* (1972). See also B. Yorke (ed.), *Bishop Ethelwold: His Career and Influence* (1988), and D. Parsons (ed.), *Tenth-century Studies* (1975). Ethelwold's account of the monastic revivlal is in *E.H.D.*, 1, pp. 846-51. See D. Knowles, *The Monastic Order in England* (1949), pp. 38-59; T. Symons, *Regularis Concordia* (1954); E. John, "The Beginnings of the Benedictine Reform in England," in *Orbis Britanniae* (1966). For his importance to art, language, and music see

F. Wormald, *The Benedictional of St Ethelwold* (1958); H. Gneuss, "The Origin of Standard Old English and Aethelwold's School at Winchester," *A.S.E.* 1 (1972), pp. 63-83; M. Gretsch, "Ethelwold's translation of the Regula Sancti Benedicti and its Latin Exemplar," *A.S.E.* 3 (1974), pp. 125-52; W. H. Frere, *The Winchester Troper* (1894); and J. Handschin, "The Two Winchester Tropers," *J.T.S.* 36 (1936), pp. 34-9, 156-72.

Bd John of Rieti (*c.* 1350)

Giovanni Bufalari was born about the beginning of the fourteenth century at Castel Porziano in Umbria. He was the brother of Bd Lucy of Amelia (27 July). Little is known of his life except that it was uneventful. Early in life he joined the Hermits of St Augustine (the Austin friars) at Rieti. He was always helpful to others, especially the sick and strangers, and was pleased to wait on guests at the monastery. He spent many hours in contemplation and was an ardent altar server in the friary church. He wept not only for his own faults but for those of others. When walking in the garden he would say: "You just have to weep. All round us we see trees and grass and flowers and plants germinating, growing, producing their fruit, and dying back again into the earth as their Maker's laws demand, yet human beings, to whom God has given a reasoning mind and the promise of a transcendent reward, are always doing the opposite to what he wants." The exact date of John's death is unknown, but his holy life and the miracles reported at his tomb encouraged a cult which persisted and was formally confirmed in 1832.

See Torelli, *Secoli Agostiniani*, vol. 2; and P. Seeböck, *Die Herrlichkeit der Katholischen Kirche* (1900), pp. 299-300.

Bd Peter Favre (1506-46)

Peter Favre (Faber) was the senior of St Ignatius of Loyola's first companions. Ignatius (31 July) thought as highly of him as of St Francis Xavier (3 Dec.), and he was the first Jesuit to assess the Reformation proficiently. He was a Savoyard, born to a farming family in 1506. While still a shepherd boy he longed to study and eventually did so, first with a priest at Thônes, then at a local college. In 1525 he went to Paris and entered the college of Sainte-Barbe. He shared a lodging with a Navarrese student, Francis Xavier, and met an undergraduate from Salamanca, Ignatius of Loyola. The three became firm friends. In 1530 Favre received his degree on the same day as Xavier but took some time to decide on a profession. Medicine, law, and teaching, by turns, seemed attractive. Finally he decided to follow Ignatius. He was ordained priest in 1534 and on 15 August in the same year celebrated the Mass at Montmartre at which the seven first Jesuits took their vows, promising poverty, chastity, a pilgrimage to Jerusalem if possible, and a life of apostolic service. He was in charge of the little company that met Ignatius at Venice early in 1537 only to find that the Turkish war prevented them from leaving as missionaries to the Holy Land. At the end of the year Favre accompanied Ignatius and Laynez to Rome, where they were appointed mission preachers. For a time he was a professor at the university.

When the emperor Charles V convoked a series of conferences, or "diets," of Catholic and Protestant leaders to resolve the religious troubles in Germany, Pope Paul III appointed Favre to go to the Diet of Worms, in 1540. After this abortive meeting he was at the equally unsuccessful Diet of Ratisbon (Regensburg) in the following year. Favre decided that Germany did not need discussions with Protestants but a reformation of the life and discipline of the Catholic clergy and laity. His views would support the now well known thesis that the Protestant and Catholic Reformations were in many ways two aspects of an attempt to re-Christianize, thoroughly instruct, and even educate an uneducated and effectively half-converted Europe. Favre was shocked by lay and clerical lethargy and ill living and devoted himself to preaching in Speyer, Regensburg, and Mainz. In the last-named place Peter Canisius (21 Dec.), then a layman, made the Spiritual Exercises under his direction and became a Jesuit. Favre was very successful in Cologne, where the archbishop, Herman von Wied, had been a Protestant, and he helped to found the first Jesuit residence there. He then went to Portugal and to Spain. When travelling through France he was imprisoned for seven days, and he vowed to accept no stipends for celebrating Mass or preaching whenever he could refuse them without injustice to others. In Spain and elsewhere he gave retreats to laypeople and clergy. He used the *Spiritual Exercises* and translated them into Latin for the Cologne Carthusians. Among those in Spain whose life was permanently influenced by Favre was Francis Borgia (10 Oct.), then duke of Gandia.

Pope Paul III wanted Favre as his theologian at the Council of Trent. Peter made a resolution of obedience, confirmed by the archbishop of Mainz's request that he should accompany him and by the pope's summons in 1546. He was sick, it was a hot summer, and the journey and the strain of his work exhausted him. He died in the arms of Ignatius soon after his arrival in Rome.

In his *Memoriale* Favre left a detailed, almost day-to-day account of his spiritual life over a long period. This is a characteristic entry: "One day I went to the palace to hear the sermon in the prince's chapel. The porter did not know me and would not let me in. I stopped outside and considered how often I had allowed my soul to entertain vain thoughts and evil imaginings, while refusing entry to Jesu knocking at the door. I reflected how the world receives him badly everywhere. I prayed for myself and the porter that the Lord would not make us wait long in Purgatory before admitting us to heaven. I had many other good thoughts at that time and I felt very kindly toward the porter who had been the occasion for me of so much devotion." Peter Favre had what would now be termed an ecumenical frame of mind and was opposed to coercion when dealing with Protestants. He had little faith in diets and formal conferences but, if necessary, would meet such opponents as Bucer and

Melanchthon in face-to-face discussions. Set against the intransigence of his day, his attitude seems conciliatory. He felt it was much more important to change people's hearts, amend their lives, and lead them to Christ and his Church. "It is necessary," he wrote, "for anyone who wants to help heretics in the present age to hold them in great affection and love them very truly, excluding all thoughts and feelings tending to discredit them. One must also win their good will and love by friendly discussion and conversation about matters on which we do not differ, taking care to avoid all controversial subjects that lead to bickering and mutual recrimination. The things that unite us ought to be the very basis of our approach, not the things that keep us apart."

A contemporary said that Peter Favre's "lovable and pleasing manner earned everyone's good-will and affection and won all who met him to the love of God. When he spoke of divine things he seemed to have the keys of human hearts on his tongue, so powerfully did he move and attract them." His cult was confirmed in 1872.

Since the publication by the Spanish Jesuits of the *Monumenta historica Societatis Jesu*, an immense amount of material regarding the activities of Ignatius' first companions has been available. A special volume of nearly 1,000 pages, *Fabri monumenta*, contains a critically revised text of his *Memoriale*, and of the beatification documents. Modern Lives include that by Fr Boero, trans. into English for the Quarterly Series; a French biography by A. Maurel; one in German by R. Cornely; and one in Spanish by F. Maruri. Three Lives in French appeared in 1931-5, by F. Pochat-Baron, L. Buffet, and J. Guitton. See also J. Brodrick, S.J., *The Origin of the Jesuits* (1940); *idem, Saint Ignatius Loyola: The Pilgrim Years* (1957).

Bd Thomas Welbourn, *Martyr* (1605)

Challoner tells us the little that is known of this martyr: "Thomas Welbourn was a schoolmaster, a native of Kitenbushel [Hutton Bushel], in Yorkshire, and John Fulthering was a layman of the same county, who being zealous Catholics, and industrious in exhorting some of their neighbours to embrace the Catholic faith, were upon that account arraigned and condemned to suffer as in cases of high treason; as also was William Brown, a native of Northamptonshire, convicted of the same offence. They were all executed according to sentence [by hanging, drawing, and quartering]; Mr Welbourn and Mr Fulthering at York, 1 August 1605; Mr Brown at Ripon, 5 September, the same year." Welbourn and Brown were beatified in 1929.

M.M.P., p. 280.

St Peter Julian Eymard, *Founder* (1811-68)

Pierre-Julien Eymard was born in 1811 at La Mure d'Isère, a small town in the diocese of Grenoble in France. His father was a cutler, and Peter Julian worked at the same trade and in an oil press until he was eighteen. In his spare time he studied Latin and was instructed by a Grenoble priest for whom he worked for a time. In 1831 he entered the seminary at Grenoble, where he was ordained priest in 1834. For the next five years he ministered at Chatte and Monteynard. When Eymard wanted to become a Marist, his bishop said, "A sign of how highly I think of that Congregation is that I allow a priest like you to enter it." After his novitiate he became spiritual director of the Belley junior seminary and in 1845 provincial of his Congregation at Lyons. His life revolved around the Blessed Sacrament. One Corpus Christi Sunday, when carrying the Host in procession, he had an overwhelming experience of faith and love for Jesus in the Blessed Sacrament: "Those two hours seemed a moment. I laid the Church in France and throughout the world, everybody, myself, at our Lord's feet. My eyes filled with tears. My heart seemed under the wine-press."

In 1851 Eymard made a pilgrimage to Notre-Dame de Fourvières: "One idea haunted me: Jesus in the Blessed Sacrament has no religious Institute to glorify his mystery of love, to the sole service of which it is consecrated. . . . I promised Mary to devote myself to this end." His superiors advised him to think again, and he spent four years at La Seyne, receiving encouragement from Pope Pius IX and from Venerable John Colin, founder of the Marists. In 1856, with the approval of the Marist superior general, he submitted a scheme for an Institute of priest-adorers of the Blessed Sacrament to Archbishop de Sibour of Paris, who approved it and put a house at his disposal, where Eymard resided with a single companion. On 6 January 1857 the Blessed Sacrament was exposed in its chapel for the first time, and Eymard preached to a large assembly.

The first members of the Congregation of Priests of the Most Blessed Sacrament, or Blessed Sacrament Fathers, were Fr de Cuers and Fr Champion. They began with exposition three times a week. Vocations were slow. They had to leave their first house and in 1858 obtained a small chapel in the Faubourg Saint-Jacques. The following year Pope Pius IX gave the Congregation a laudatory Brief; a second house was opened in Marseilles and in 1862 a third in Angers. By then a regular novitiate could be established, and the Congregation expanded rapidly. The priests recited the divine office in choir and performed all other duties of the clergy, subordinate to their chief duty of maintaining perpetual adoration of the Blessed Sacrament exposed, in which they were assisted by lay brothers. In 1357 Eymard planned the Pious Union of Priest Adorers, under the spiritual direction of his Congregation, and drafted its statutes a year before he died. They were approved in 1878 and formally passed by Pope Leo XIII in 1881. In 1858 Eymard established the Servants of the Blessed Sacrament, Sisters also engaged in perpetual adoration and spreading the love of Our Lord. He also founded the Priests' Eucharistic League, formally approved in Rome in 1905, and made an arch-association the year after, whose members pledged themselves to spend as far as possible about an hour a day in prayer before the tabernacle. In his Work for Poor Adults Eymard showed his Congregation the need to prepare for First Communion all adults no longer of an age or unable to attend parish catechism classes. He also organized the Archconfraternity of the Blessed Sacrament, which was no mere echo but rather an expansion of similar confraternities in existence since the fifteenth century. It eventually came under the spiritual guidance of the Dominicans. The 1917 Code of Canon Law desired that a branch should be founded in every parish, an aim which was largely achieved by the mid-twentieth century and owed much to Eymard's work. He also wrote several formerly very popular, now forgotten, books on the Eucharist, which were translated into a number of languages.

One difficulty Eymard faced in his new foundation was adverse criticism because he had left the Society of Mary. He excused detractors of his work: "I know well it must be persecuted. Was not Our Lord persecuted throughout his life?" In spite of this and other difficulties final approval of his Congregation was confirmed by the Holy See in perpetuity in 1895.

Eymard's spirit of devotion was exemplary, but its emphases were interestingly characteristic of certain tendencies in nineteenth-century European Catholicism. Particularly in France, with its many changes of régime from pro- to anti-Catholic and back again, pious practices, devotion to the Blessed Sacrament and to the Sacred Hearts of Jesus and Mary, and a multitude of confraternities and sodalities were firmly encouraged to counteract the growing paganism or indifference not only of the peasantry but especially of the urban working class and its political movements as well as state anticlericalism and repeated anti-ecclesiastical measures. The widespread nature of the trend in Europe is shown by a short list of organizations with similar aims: the Confraternity for Nocturnal Adoration of the Blessed Sacrament (1809); the Archsodality of Perpetual Adoration of the Blessed Sacrament and of Work for Poor Churches (1848); the Pious Union of the Blessed Sacrament (1859, which came under the spiritual guidance of Eymard's Congregation); the Pious Union of Daily and Universal Adoration of the Blessed Sacrament (1870); and the Adorers of the Blessed Sacrament (1887).

A developing understanding of the Eucharist as a sacrificial meal, to which exposition was secondary and, in the years before Vatican II, the dialogue Mass movement, and afterwards the stress on active participation in a vernacular liturgy, reduced the over-emphasis on a static conception of the Eucharist that could result from Eymard's type of piety. Yet he is important as one of a number of resolute individuals (such as Louis Dupont or Claude Colin, and to a lesser degree St John-Baptist Vianney, the Curé d'Ars [4 Aug.]), who similarly influenced the style of the nineteenth- and early-twentieth-century Church. He had a considerable influence on what may justly be called a spiritual renewal after 1848—the "year of revolutions." It was based on a christocentric (if also Marian) piety, an emphasis on the humanity of Jesus evident not only in a new kind of Eucharistic devotion but in a renewed interest in the cult of the Sacred Heart, the Child Jesus, the Holy Family, or the "Holy Countenance" and in the rapid spread of practices such as the Stations of the Cross. Moreover, although adoration of the Blessed Sacrament may be thought to have encouraged an individualistic form of Christian practice, Eymard wanted his Congregations of "true and perpetual adorers" to become authentic apostles of the social reign of Christ, and for evening adoration, as certainly happened among his female Congregations, to show such practical fruits as charitable works, teaching, and so on, during the day.

In his lifetime Eymard was spoken of as a saint and was even credited with such supernatural gifts as an ability to divine the thoughts of absent persons, read souls, and exercise prophetic prevision.

During the last four years of his life Eymard suffered from rheumatic gout and insomnia, and the difficulties suffered by the Congregation made him visibly depressed. In July 1868 he broke down, went to La Mure by coach in extreme heat, and arrived in a state of collapse and partial paralysis. He died on 1 August. Miracles were said to have taken place at his tomb before the end of that year. He was beatified in 1925 and canonized during the Second Vatican Council, in 1962.

There is a short sketch by Lady Herbert, *The Priest of the Eucharist* (1898); a Life by J. M. Lambert in the series Les Saints (1925); a full biography in French by F. Trochu (1949); and one in Italian by P. Fossati (1925). See also A. Bettinger, *Pierre-Julien Eymard et sa méthode d'Adoration* (1927); P. Pierrard, *Les pauvres, l'Evangile et la Révolution* (1977); François Lebrun (ed.), *Histoire des Catholiques en France du XVe Siècle à nos Jours* (1980), pp. 337-46.

R.M.

St Secundinus, martyr (? second/fourth century)
St Felicius, martyr under Diocletian (fourth century)
SS Leontius, Attus, Alexander, Minnaus, and their fifteen Companions, martyrs (fifth century)
St Leo of Montefeltro, hermit (fifth/sixth century)
St Severus (*c.* 500)
St Bandaricus, bishop of Soissons (545)
St Arcadius, bishop of Bourges (before 549)
Ss Friardus and Secundellus, deacons and hermits of Nantes (seventh century)
St Timothy, bishop in the Hellespont (seventh century)
St Ionatus, abbot of Cambrai (*c.* 690)
St Mary the Consolatrix, of Verona (*c.* 770)
Bd Varmundus, bishop of Ivrea (*c.* 1010)
St Thomas of Rimini, Augustinian friar (*c.* 1300)
Bd Emericus de Quart, bishop (1313).
SS Dominic Nguyen Van Hanh (Dieu) and Bernard Guyen Vu Van Due, martyrs (1838)—see "Martyrs of Vietnam," 2 Feb.

2

ST EUSEBIUS OF VERCELLI, *Bishop* (371)

Eusebius was born on the island of Sardinia. His father is said to have died in chains as a Christian martyr. His widowed mother took her infant son and daughter to Rome, where Eusebius was brought up and ordained lector. He served so well at Vercelli, in Piedmont, that clergy and people chose him to govern the church. He is the first bishop of Vercelli whose name we know. St Ambrose (7 Dec.) says that he was the first in the West to unite monastic and clerical disciplines and that he lived in community with some of his clergy. Therefore he is specially venerated by the canons regular, or Austin Canons, as almost their co-founder together with St Augustine (28 Aug.). His formation of a zealous clergy led other churches to recruit his disciples as bishops. He was also a very effective teacher and preacher.

In 354 Eusebius was called to the work of the Church at large. In the same year Pope Liberius asked him, with Lucifer of Cagliari, to persuade the emperor Constantius to assemble a council to end the disputes between Catholics and Arians. Constantius agreed, and a council (or synod) met at Milan in 355. Though the Catholic bishops were more numerous, Eusebius thought that the greater power of the Arians would prevail, and he refused to attend until Constantius himself pressed him. When the bishops were asked to sign a condemnation of Athanasius (2 May), Eusebius refused, put the Nicene Creed on the table, and insisted on everyone signing that before Athanasius' case was considered. Confusion followed, and the emperor sent for Eusebius, Dionysius of Milan, and Lucifer of Cagliari and asked them to condemn Athanasius. They insisted that he was innocent, that he could not be condemned without a hearing, and that secular force should not be used to influence ecclesiastical decisions. The emperor threatened to put the bishops to death but banished them instead. Eusebius was exiled first to Scythopolis (Beisan) in Palestine, where the Arian bishop, Patrophilus, was put in charge of him.

At first he stayed with St Joseph of Palestine (22 July) in the only orthodox household in the town and was visited by Epiphanius and others, including the deputies of his church at Vercelli, who brought money for his keep, but after Count Joseph died the Arians insulted Eusebius, dragged him half-naked through the streets, and shut him in a small room to make him conform. They would not let his deacons and other fellow-confessors see him, so he wrote to Bishop Patrophilus as "Eusebius, the servant of God, with other servants of God who suffer with him for the faith, to Patrophilus the jailer, and to his officers." He described his sufferings, asked that the deacons should be allowed to visit him, then went on a virtual hunger strike. When he had spent four days without food, the Arians sent him back to his lodging. Three weeks later they broke in, stole his goods and provisions, ejected his attendants, and dragged him away. All this Eusebius described in a letter to his flock. Later he was moved from Scythopolis to Cappadocia and then to the Upper Thebaid in Egypt. There he wrote to Bishop Gregory of Elvira to praise him for resisting enemies of the faith.

When Constantius died toward the end of 361, Julian allowed the banished bishops to return to their sees. Eusebius went to Alexandria to discuss ways of remedying the trouble in the Church. He took part in a council there, then travelled to Antioch to carry out the council's wish that Meletius (12 Feb.) should be recognized as the local bishop and the Eustathian schism healed. But he found that Lucifer of Cagliari had made things worse by ordaining the Antiochene presbyter Paulinus bishop for the Eustathians. Resenting Eusebius' reproofs, Lucifer broke off communion with him and with all those who, together with the Council of Alexandria, received the ex-Arian bishops. This was the origin of the Luciferian schism.

Eusebius then travelled over the East and through Illyricum to reassure the wavering and reconvert those who had gone astray. In Italy he met St Hilary of Poitiers (13 Jan.) and with him opposed the Arianizing Auxentius of Milan. We know that Vercelli was pleased to see the bishop after a long absence but nothing of Eusebius' last years except that he is said to have died on 1 August 371. He is sometimes referred to as a martyr, but he was so only by his sufferings and not by the way in which he died. Vercelli Cathedral has a manuscript codex of the Gospels formerly said to have been written by Eusebius, but this is very doubtful. It was covered with silver plates by order of King Berengarius when it seemed to be wearing out over a thousand years ago. This is the earliest codex of the Old Latin version in existence. Eusebius is also one of the several people who have been credited with the composition of the Athanasian Creed and other works of uncertain authorship, but three authentic letters survive. He is known to have made a now-lost Latin translation of Eusebius of Caesarea's commentary on the psalms. He is mainly venerated as an indefatigable supporter of orthodoxy.

There is no proficient early biography of Eusebius. We depend on his own (three surviving) letters (see the critical edition, with other material, by V. Bulhart in *C.C., Series Latina*, 9, [1957], pp. 1-205; and *P.L.*, 12, 947-54, and 62, 237-88), a notice in *Viri illustres* of St Jerome, and the controversial literature of the period. See also V. C. De Clercq in *D.H.G.E.*, 25 (1963), pp. 1477-83. The main incidents of his life are part of general ecclesiastical history. See, for example, Hefele-Leclercq, *Histoire des Conciles*, 1, pp. 872ff. and 961ff.; Duchesne, *Histoire ancienne de l'Eglise*, 2, pp. 341-50; Bardenhewer, *Geschichte der altkirchlichen Literatur*, 3, pp. 486-7; and especially Savio, *Gli antichi vescovi d'Italia*, 1, pp. 412-20, 514-44; *Q.D.C.C.* (1970), pp. 482-3.

St Stephen I, *Pope* (257)

Stephen was born a Roman and was a priest when he succeeded Pope St Lucius I (14 Mar.) in 254. The little known of him personally is mostly gathered from the writings of those who disagreed with him. He intervened in doctrinal disputes in Gaul (the Novatianist heresy) and Spain (the Decian persecution), but the main event of his short pontificate was a controversy on Baptism as administered by heretics. St Cyprian (16 Sept.) and the bishops of Africa, and three councils there said such Baptism was null and void and that anyone so baptized had to be baptized again on becoming a Catholic. Many bishops in Asia supported this view. Stephen taught that, other things being equal, Baptism given by heretics is valid. Firmilian of Caesarea in Cappadocia fiercely opposed him for this view. The pope would allow no innovation, said that tradition should be observed, and refused to receive the delegates of the African synod that supported Cyprian (who otherwise acknowledged the chronological pre-eminence of the Bishop of Rome). Stephen threatened those who dissented with excommunication, but, Augustine says, "Charity persuaded him that it was better to stay in union. The peace of Christ triumphed in their hearts." Nevertheless, the disagreement was not yet resolved. In spite of a decisive rupture with the North African church, which ended only in the pontificate of Dionysius and therefore after his death, Stephen resolutely maintained the traditional primacy of the Bishop of Rome in the Church as a whole.

The Valerian persecution began in the year of Stephen's death. A once-popular *passio* says that he was taken prisoner while celebrating Mass, which led to his veneration as a martyr, but the earliest relevant sources say nothing about this. The original Roman tradition seems to be that he died in peace.

In his edition of the *Liber Pontificalis* (1, p. 154), and in his *Histoire ancienne de l'Eglise* (1, pp. 419-32), Duchesne has established the main points of interest. Other authorities are Eusebius, *H.E.*, 7; and the letters of St Cyprian (*Epistolae*, 68-75), Firmilian, and St Dionysius of Alexandria. A larger fragment of a letter of Dionysius to this pope was recovered from an Armenian source by F. C. Conybeare and reproduced in the *English Historical Review* 25 (1910), pp. 111-3. See also *D.T.C.*, 5, 970-3; *C.M.H.*, pp. 412-3; *AA.SS.*, Aug., 1, pp. 112-46; *O.D.P.*, pp. 20-1; J. Ernst, *Forschungen zur christlichen Literatur- und Dogmengeschichte*, 5, no. 4 (1905); *Z.K.T.* 29 (1905), pp. 258-98.

St Syagrius, *Bishop* (600)

Syagrius is said to have been a Gallo-Roman by birth. He became bishop of Autun in about 560. He was influential at councils and in Christian formation. He tried to settle a dispute at the Convent of the Holy Cross at Poitiers, where two nuns rebelled against their abbess, but the task was too much for him and other bishops, and a synod had to excommunicate the rebels. This made him overcareful, for some years later Pope St Gregory the Great (3 Sept.) reproved him for not preventing the marriage of a nun (named, strange to say, Syagria) who had been abducted from her cloister. The pope nevertheless showed his respect for Syagrius and, when he sent Augustine and missionaries to England, recommended them to Syagrius, who entertained them on their journey. Though only a bishop, Syagrius was allowed to wear the *pallium*, at the instance of Queen Brunhilda. King Gontran asked him to accompany him to Clotaire III's Baptism at Nanterre in 591.

AA.SS., Aug., 6; Duchesne, *Fastes,* 2, p. 173.

Bd Joan of Aza (*c.* 1190)

The little we are told of St Dominic's mother is not based on very sound evidence. The most interesting details are wholly legendary but notably recurrent in art and, to a certain extent, literature. She is said to have been born in the castle of Aza, near Aranda de Duero in Old Castile. Nothing is known of her childhood, but she was probably married when very young, as was usual. Her husband was Felix, perhaps de Guzman, warden of the small town of Calaruega in the province of Burgos. They had four children: Antony, who became a canon of St James and sold everything to serve the poor and sick in a hospital; Bd Mannes (30 July), who followed his younger brother, Dominic; and a daughter, whose two sons became preaching friars. When Antony and Mannes were grown up, Joan prayed for another son in the abbey church of Silos. She is said to have had a vision of St Dominic of Silos (20 Dec.) in her sleep. The saint told her that she would have a son who would be a shining light to the Church. Accordingly she decided to baptize him Dominic.

When pregnant, so it is said, Joan dreamed she had a black and white dog in her womb that broke away from her with a burning torch in its mouth to set the world aflame. This dog became a symbol of the Dominican Order, and in later ages it gave rise to the pun *"Domini canes,"* "the watch-dogs of the Lord." Some of the many legends about Dominic's infancy say that Dominic's godmother (or Joan) had another dream in which the baby had a shining star on his forehead enlightening the world, and a star duly appears in some images of the saint. Dominic remained with his mother until he was seven, at which point he was sent for instruction to his uncle, the parish priest of Gumiel d'Izan.

Not many saints' mothers have been beatified. Joan, "as beautiful of soul as of body," is said to have achieved this by her own and not her children's virtues, and some commentators have claimed that her cult dates from the moment of her death. A hermitage at Uclés, where she visited the commandery of the Knights of St James, and a chapel in the cemetery at Calaruega were named after her. The cult was confirmed in 1828 at the request of King Ferdinand VII. Nevertheless, its real origin lies in the remarkably early popular devotion to St Dominic, who is clearly the focus of the retrospective legends about Joan.

21

See Ganay, *Les Bienheureuses Dominicaines*, pp. 13ff.; R. Castaño, *Monografía de Santa Joanna* (1900); Procter, pp. 215-9; for primary sources, F. C. Lehner, *Saint Dominic: Biographical Documents* (1964); and standard lives of St Dominic.

St Thomas of Dover (1295)

Thomas of Hales (or de la Hale) was a monk of the Benedictine priory of St Martin at Dover, a cell of Christ Church, Canterbury. On 2 August 1295 the French raided Dover from the sea, and the monks fled, with the exception of the aged Thomas, who followed the Rule in taking his midday siesta. The raiders, guided by some local men to the dormitory where the treasure was thought to be hidden, found Thomas on his bed and demanded the whereabouts of the church plate and other valuables, such as charters. He refused to tell them, so they killed him immediately. Miracles were reported at his tomb, and Simon Simeon, an Irish friar who made a pilgrimage to the Holy Land about 1322, mentions the honour given to Thomas as a martyr "at the Black Monks, under Dover Castle." King Richard II asked Pope Urban VI to canonize Thomas.

Indulgences for visiting his tomb were issued from Winchester and Canterbury, and a process was begun with papal approval in 1380-2 but never carried out, perhaps because of a lack of financial support or the necessary enthusiasm from the Dover community. There was a considerable popular cult of Thomas locally, and an altar before which he was buried came to be ascribed to the Bd Thomas de Halys. He is represented among the paintings of martyrs in the English College at Rome, but to call him a saint is an almost entirely modern practice. He appears in the revised Roman Martyrology.

There is a Life and *passio* in *B.H.L.*, 2, 8248 b, and a summary of it and of some miracles in *B.H.L.* 2, 8249; texts in C. Horstman, *Nova Legenda Angliae* (1901), vol. 2, pp. 555-8 and 403; trans. in C. R. Haines, *Dover Priory* (1930). In *Anal. Boll.* 72 (1954), pp. 167-91, P. Grosjean documents his discussion of all that is known of Thomas de la Hale.

Bd Ceferino Jiménez Malla, *Martyr* (1861-1936)

Ceferino Jiménez Malla (nicknamed "El Pelé") was an illiterate Spanish gypsy horsetrader. He was converted to Catholicism late in life. During the early days of the Spanish Civil War, when seventy-five years of age, he was arrested at Barbastro in the Huesca province of Aragon (probably by the Government police or forces, or an associated militia, though there is some doubt about this) for helping a young priest. He insisted on saying the rosary in gaol and was taken out to be shot on 2 August 1936, with his beads still in his hands.

On 4 May 1997 four thousand gypsies attended a ceremony in St Peter's at which he was beatified by Pope John Paul II as a martyr to the faith. The pope noted his devotion, concern for the poor, and attempts to resolve conflicts among Romanies and between gypsies and others, and recommended him as an example of the "presence of Christ in different peoples."

Osservatore Romano, 4 May 1997.

R.M.

St Rutilius, martyr (third century)
St Centolla, martyr in Spain (? third century)
St Auspicius, bishop of Apt in Provence (? third century)
St Betharius, bishop of Eichstätt (*c.* 623)
Bd Gundecharius, bishop (1075)
St Peter of Osma, bishop (1109)
Bd Walter, disciple of St Francis of Assisi (*c.* 1258)

3

St Lydia (First Century)

Lydia is described in the Acts of the Apostles (16:13ff.) as a dealer in purple dyed fabrics. The dye usually originated, in Old Testament times, in the dye-production centres on the Phoenician coast. In the New Testament period, Asia Minor was a major centre of dye manufactures. There were two kinds, red and violet purple, and the place Lydia came from, Thyatira in the province of Lydia (in what is now western Turkey), was famous for the red dye. Her name is an *ethnicon*, deriving from her place of origin.

She was a Jewish prosylete who became the first person whom the apostle Paul (25 Jan., 29 June) baptized in Philippi. She offered the apostles hospitality in her house: "On the Sabbath day we went outside the city gate by the riverside, where we thought there would be a place of prayer, and sat down and talked to the women who had gathered there. One of them named Lydia, a dealer in purple fabric from the city of Thyatira, who was a worshipper of God, was listening and the Lord opened her heart to respond to what Paul said. She was baptized, and her household with her, and then she said to us: 'If you have judged me to be a believer in the Lord, I beg you to come and stay in my house.' And she insisted on our going." Nothing more is said about her.

This brief passage, however, is enough to give her, as the feminist exegetes who have done so much in recent decades to uncover the "hidden" history of women in the New Testament have shown, "a central position in the Acts of the Apostles. She . . . is one of the few women in Luke's work who has a chance to speak. She does speak. And what she says is theologically significant" (Ivoni Richter Reimer).

She is the first person with whom Paul came into contact in what is now Europe and the first "European" Christian convert. She is the first person in the region who gathers a house church around her. The first significant point in her story is that it is a group of women who have gathered in a "place of prayer," or synagogue. The word used for "gather" may express a deliberate gathering for religious purposes: Luke regularly uses the word in the context of discipleship and shared work. When the missionaries are said to "sit down," this may also imply a formal process of teaching and explaining the scriptures. So the passage can be understood as suggesting that the missionaries are spending the sabbath with these women in the same way as they usually participated in Jewish worship. There was, then, a gathering of women at the synagogue, and the missionaries sat down and interpreted the scriptures for them. Acts 16:13-14 then attests to women's presence at Jewish worship services.

If such a brief pasage can be shown to reveal so much about the situation of women in general in relation to Judaism, what can it tell us about the one woman specifically named in it? Lydia is called "a worshipper of God," which suggests that she was one of a large group known as "god-fearers," sympathizers with Judaism, believers in the one God, but who had not yet become "proselytes" or taken the final steps to conversion to Judaism. Lydia is described simply as a dealer in purple cloth. This is not expanded, suggesting that the occupation was sufficiently known (or that Luke has no further interest). This statement has generally been taken to mean that Lydia was a wealthy woman, since the material was costly, but other speculations are possible. Thyatira, the city she came from, is known from inscriptions to have had workers organized into guilds, including one for dyers—not "purple dyers" but just "dyers," suggesting that other dyes were also worked with there. The region was known for the production of dyed wool and woollen clothing—an activity usually associated with women. The dye used in Thyatira (famed more for its red shade) was probably extracted from plants, mainly madder roots, rather than from the sea snails that produced the most prized violet shade of purple. This may argue against the supposition that Lydia was a wealthy woman. She may well have been involved in selling as well as in producing purple cloth, and this could have been the reason for her presence in Philippi. Work with dyes was regarded as "dirty work" (Cicero, Pliny), and this again argues against the idea of Lydia being a woman of high social standing. It was certainly not one of the "liberal" professions. Work with textiles was often done by slaves and freed persons. There is no direct evidence that Lydia had once been a slave, but the fact that her name is her place of origin rather than a personal name suggests this as at least a possibility.

Acts states that Lydia's "home" (*oikos*) was baptized with her. There are a number of meanings possible in the use of this term, including "household," but it is impossible to determine from the text who might have been comprised in Lydia's household. The fact that there is no mention of a man has been used to deduce that she was a widow, but this has been challenged as a patriarchal interpretation. The term *oikos* here could be applied to a group of women (and possibly also of men) engaged together in the purple cloth business and travelling together to sell their product. It is most likely that this group consisted largely if not exclusively of freed women, of whom Lydia may have been the leader. The production was on a small household scale, and there is no compelling reason to regard her as a wealthy businesswoman; the work probably earned a subsistence living for the household, no more. Lydia and her circle were, in addition, immigrants from the East, then—as now—despised by the upper classes of the Roman Empire.

On the other hand, Luke is status-conscious, and Lydia's house was obviously large enough for the missionaries to stay in and to accomodate her "household." She is evidently a person with enough authority to put pressure on the missionaries to stay at her house, to "insist" that they do so: the term used is a strong one, implying the exercise of authority. So Lydia, who makes such a brief appearance in the New Testament, can be seen as a highly significant figure. She sheds light on the relationship of women to Jewish worship; she indicates that women, in Judaism as well as in the "Jesus movement," could be heads of household; and she suggests that the very beginnings of Christianity in Europe belong among the working rather than the upper classes.

Baronius included her name in the Roman Martyrology, but she was formally canonized by the Eastern Church in Constantinople only in 1982.

Acts 16:13-15. The above interpretation is derived largely from I. Richter Reimer, *Women in the Acts of the Apostles: A Feminist Liberation Perspective* (Eng. trans., 1995): see esp. "Lydia and Her House," pp. 71-149, and bibliog., pp. 273-90. See also C. Ricci, *Mary Magdalen and Many Others: Women who Followed Jesus* (1994), p. 70, and bibliog., pp. 213-25; E. M. Tetlow, *Women and Ministry in the New Testament: Called to Serve*; S. Heine, *Women and Early Christianity: A Reappraisal* (Eng. trans., 1988). On the trade in purple cloth see M. Besnier, "Purpura (Porfuvra)," in *Dict. des antiquités grecques et romaines* (1877ff.), pp. 769-78; K. Schneider, "Purpura, porfuvra," in *Paulys Real-Encyclopädie der klassischen Althertumswissenschaft* 46 (1959), 2000-20; J.-P. Waltzing, *Etude historique sur les corporations professionelles chez les Romains* (4 vols., 1895-1900, rp. 1970), 3, pp. 47ff.

St Martin (*c*. 580)

The new draft Roman Martyrology today mentions Martin, a solitary in Campania in Italy, and refers to his famous deeds chronicled by St Gregory the Great (3 Sept.). Gregory says that many of his friends knew Martin personally and had observed his miracles and that he had heard much of him from his predecessor, Pope Pelagius II.

Martin lived alone in a small cave on Mount Marsicus (Mondragone). He is said miraculously to have overcome the lack of water; to have suffered the company of the devil in the form of a serpent every day for three years; and, when first in the cave—like a lesser though voluntary Prometheus—to have chained his ankle to the rock so that he would not leave on mere impulse. St Benedict (11 July) at Monte Cassino, where Martin was possibly a monk, heard of this last practice and sent a message: "If you are God's servant, be held by Christ's chain, not by any chain of iron." Accordingly, when his followers complained about a faulty bucket-rope in the well, Martin, heedful of criticism but sensibly economical, removed the chain and gave it to them.

The *Dialogues* of St Gregory (3, 16) are our only source of information: see the critical edition by A. de Vogué in *S.C.* (1978-80).

Bd Augustine of Lucera, *Bishop* (*c*. 1260-1323)

Augustine Gazotich was born at Trogir in Dalmatia about 1260. Before he was twenty he joined the Friars Preachers. He went to Paris to study at the university, but he and a fellow-Dominican, Brother James, were attacked while travelling through Pavia. James was killed, and Augustine recovered only after some weeks' nursing. He preached successfully in his own country and established several new houses. After missions in Italy and Bosnia he was sent to Hungary, a country in a miserable and irreligious state after continual civil wars. There he met Cardinal Nicholas Boccasini, the papal legate, who in 1303 became pope as Benedict XI, sent for Augustine, and consecrated him bishop of Zagreb in Croatia.

The clergy and diocese needed reform. Augustine held disciplinary synods whose canons he enforced by frequent visitations. He encouraged learning and biblical studies by founding a Dominican priory in his cathedral city. He was present at the General Council of Vienne in 1311-2 and on his return was persecuted by Miladin, governor of Dalmatia, against whose tyranny he had protested.

It was said that Augustine had the the gift of healing, that he had cured of rheumatism the hands that anointed him at his consecration, and that when people flocked to him for cures, he rebuked them by planting a lime tree, saying that its leaves would be more efficacious than his hands. The tree worked wonders; even the invading Turks respected it.

After fourteen years in Zagreb, Augustine became bishop of Lucera in the province of Benevento, where he tried to eradicate the religious and moral corruption following the departure of most of the Saracens and the rather uncertain conversion of the remaining Muslims in 1300. King Robert of Naples endowed a Dominican monastery to help him. He was said to have changed the situation in five years. Augustine was respected for his charity and zeal by all, from the royal family downward. When he died on 3 August 1323, a cult began which was formally confirmed in 1702.

The main source seems to be a Latin Life written as late as the seventeenth century by Thomas Marnavich, bishop of Bosnia. Here the family name is Gozottus. It appears in *AA.SS.*, Aug., 1. See also Taurisano, *Catalogus Hagiographicus O.P.*, pp. 27-8.

R.M.
St Asprenatis, first bishop of Naples (second-third century)
SS Dalmatius (*c.* 440) and Faustus (fifth century)
St Euphronius, bishop (after 475)
Bd Benno of Einsiedeln, bishop (940)
St Peter, bishop of Anagni (1105)
St Gaufridus, bishop of Le Mans (1255)
Bd Conrad, O.Cist. (1270)

4

ST JOHN VIANNEY (1786-1859)

Jean-Marie Vianney was born into a peasant family at Dardilly, near Lyons, on 8 May 1786. He was to become the model priest of the nineteenth century, but he now seems an oddly contradictory figure. When he was three the Revolution began. Two years later a "constitutional priest," or one who had made an accommodation with the new régime (which did not mean a villainous turncoat, for many such acted in good faith), was imposed on Dardilly. John and his parents assisted in secret at the Masses of fugitive priests loyal to Rome and, probably—as the revolutionaries became more anticlerical—the *ancien régime* of the Bourbons. John was raised to be conservative but courageous during one of the most unsettling sequences of forms of rule in European history. His resistance to the contagion of change suited the general attitude of the French Church in the nineteenth century. During the Terror he was learning to be a herd boy on Matthieu Vianney's farm. He was quiet, well-behaved, and religious. He would rather play "at church" than games, with the exception of quoits because he was good at it, which perhaps shows that he was not so much priggish as aware of his abilities and limitations. He made his First Communion secretly when he was thirteen. Not long after, Mass could be celebrated again in public at Dardilly.

Five years later John told his father he wanted to be a priest. But Matthieu, with other members of the family to provide for and a farm to look after, could not afford to educate his son (he spent only a short time at the village school when he was nine) or spare him. Only when he was twenty could John leave for the neighbouring village of Ecully, where Fr Balley ran a "presbytery-school." He was not a natural scholar, found Latin very difficult, and became discouraged. In the summer of 1806 he made a pilgrimage on foot of over sixty miles, begging his food and shelter, to the shrine of St John Francis Regis (16 June) at La Louvese to ask God's help. His studies were no easier but he felt more confident. He was confirmed in the following year and took the name Baptist. In error he was not entered on the list of exempt ecclesiastical students, so he was called up for the army and had to report to the Lyons depot on 26 October 1809. He was taken ill two days later and sent to hospital. His draft left without him. On 5 January he was ordered to report again but went into a church to pray and arrived when the draft had gone. He set out to catch up with the troop but made very slow progress. He was resting at a mountain approach when a stranger picked up his knapsack and told him to follow. He soon reached an isolated hut and discovered that the stranger was one of many deserters from the army. After a few days John reported to the sympathetic local mayor, who pointed out that he had already compromised himself as a deserter and offered his own cousin's house as a refuge. For fourteen months John taught the children, worked on the farm, and tried to study. In March 1810 Napoleon declared an amnesty, and early the next year (when his brother volunteered early as a substitute) John returned home a free man.

In 1811 he received the tonsure and at the end of the next year was sent to study philosophy at a minor seminary. In autumn 1813 he went to the major seminary at Lyons, where the usual severe discipline ruled, but he made no headway, for instruction was in Latin. At the end of the first term he left to be coached privately by Fr Balley but broke down during the examination for the priesthood. At first the examiners refused to accept him and recommended a less exacting diocese. Nevertheless, the intellectual level of very many French curés at the time was scarcely higher than that of their parishioners; Vianney was interviewed privately, and the case of "the most unlearned but the most devout seminarian in Lyons" came before the vicar general. He asked, "Is M. Vianney good?" "He is a model of goodness," was the reply. "Very well. Then let him be ordained. The grace of God will do the rest." On 2 July 1814 John received the minor orders and subdiaconate and returned to study at Ecully. In June 1815 he became a deacon and on 12 August a priest. He was made curate to Fr Balley. Both priest and curate led very austere lives.

A few months after his appointment to Ecully he received his faculties to hear Confession. His unusual mixture of high seriousness and empathy made him a popular confessor at a time when examination of conscience and Confession were often the essentials of Christian practice. Later, hearing Confessions was to take up three-quarters of his time. In 1817 Fr Balley died and Vianney was made parish priest of the remote Ars-en-Dombes, a depressing place that would usually have been assigned one of the many ill-educated French priests, reluctant to proselytize and able to preach only a few set-piece and therefore doctrinally safe sermons. To his superiors Vianney seemed a suitable choice.

The new priest was hostile to the tendencies of the age but not content to minister to the faithful few. He redoubled his austerities, especially the use of a discipline. For the first six years he lived on almost nothing but potatoes, trying to make himself a sacrifice for the inadequacies of his "feeble flock" in their dead-end village. When he had visited every household and set up a regular catechism class for the children, he began his great plan: the total conversion of Ars to a religious life. He worked by unremitting personal example, by contact with each individual, by long hours of scrutiny and direction in the confessional, and by well-prepared sermons delivered naturally but so forcefully that one parishioner said they were "long ones, and always on Hell. . . . Some people say there's no Hell. He certainly thought there was!" To a large extent popular Christianity was still a religion of fear, and remnants of a once-fashionable Jansenism in his own instructors probably encouraged Vianney's strictness. Moreover, there was the supreme example of Pope Leo XII, who, when he took over in Rome in 1823, closed the wine shops and banned waltzing at the carnival. Vianney decided that too much money was spent in the village taverns. (Throughout Europe at that time, many cottages in tiny villages were also occasional dram shops for a few cronies or regulars.) First the two near the church were closed for lack of business, then two more; seven new ones were opened in succession, but each had to close. He waged war against bad language and even used the offensive words in the pulpit so that there could be no mistake—an indication of his peasant verve and psychological acumen. He demanded modest dress. For eight years he fought for Sunday observance, not merely to get everyone to Mass and Vespers but to abolish unnecessary Sunday labour. He was utterly opposed to cabarets and to dancing, which he saw as an occasion of sin to dancers and onlookers. He refused absolution to those who persisted, waged this battle for twenty-five years, and is said to have won in the end. Over the arch of St John the Baptist's chapel in the parish church he had painted: "His head was the price of a dance!" From the standpoint of the late twentieth century John could seem an unsympathetic killjoy, and many in his own lifetime thought he was a disagreeable fanatic. Still, as the English Methodists found, anti-alcoholism and strict religious practice were sometimes the only practical means of helping large families to move from near-destitution to respectable poverty. As for dancing, until the mid-twentieth century many French clergy saw it as the major instrument of dechristianization.

In 1821 the Ars district was made a succursal parish and in 1823 part of the revived diocese of Belley. In spite of slanderous attacks on the reformist Vianney the new bishop came to trust him. He was asked to give several parochial missions. He sent two young village women to a convent for training, and in 1824 under his guidance they opened a free school for girls at Ars. Three years later this became the famous *La Providence*, run on alms, and a free shelter for orphans and other homeless children from which no one was turned away. The two women and their helpers received no salary. At times Vianney had to provide for sixty people there. Miracles of supply, such as an unexpected wheat-filled loft and a multiplication of loaves, were reported. As often, such exaggerations may be taken as signs of a growing reputation for sanctity.

At the same time, by night and day for over thirty years from 1824, Vianney experienced unpleasant phenomena which he interpreted as evidence of persecution by the devil. He (and occasionally other observers) reported such things as noises, voices, personal violence, and the unexplained burning of his bed. He came to accept the attacks as inevitable. Possible explanations of Vianney's "poltergeists" and "diabolical infestations" range from paranoia aroused by resistance to his reforms, through self-delusion in a state of heightened religiosity, to symbolic manifestations of his brother priests' repeated criticisms of the "ill-judged zeal," "ambition," and "presumption" of a "quack" and "impostor." "Poor little Curé d'Ars!" he commented, "What don't they make him do and say! They are preaching on him now and no longer on the gospel." They also delated him to the bishop, who refused to take any action. When a priest called Vianney mad, the bishop said at the annual clergy retreat, "Gentlemen, I wish all my clergy had a small grain of the same madness."

Vianney developed an intense devotion to "dear little St Philomena," the name given in error to a supposed virgin martyr in 1802 when the entombed bones of a young girl were found in a Roman catacomb. The cult that grew up around the imaginary martyr was encouraged by Popes Gregory XVI and Pius IX and suppressed only in 1960. It fitted the Church's increasing promotion throughout the century of the image of the simple but devout girl, a model of unquestioning piety, that reached its culmination in Bernadette of Lourdes and Thérèse of Lisieux. Vianney set up a shrine to Philomena and, out of modesty, attributed to her the alleged cures and other unusual phenomena associated with his own extraordinary charisma. Ars became a place of pilgrimage. From as early as 1827 a steady stream of penitents from afar began to seek his spiritual direction in the confessional. This upset his envious clerical critics. From 1830 to 1845 the daily visitors averaged over three hundred. At Lyons railway station a special booking office was opened for Ars, and eight-day return tickets issued to ensure a consultation. For Vianney this meant no less than eleven or twelve hours in the confessional every day in winter and anything up to sixteen in summer. For the last fifteen years of his life he also gave instruction every day in the church at eleven o'clock. Rich and poor, simple and learned, lay and cleric, bishops, priests, and religious, came to kneel in the confessional. Vianney gave only a few words of advice but they had the authority of holiness, and it was often reported that they showed supernatural knowledge of the penitent's life. "What a pity! What a pity!" he would murmur at each accusation and weep at the tale of sin. To some extent Vianney's special acuteness—and wit—can be estimated from his recorded remarks, which would fill several volumes (see, *e.g.*, Nodet, below). They range from the pithy "The greatest temptation is not to have any" to the acerbic reply (to a future Daughter of Charity who asked him for some relics): "Make them yourself!"

At first he treated outsiders with the same rigour as his parishoners, but with advancing years and deeper insight into all sorts and conditions of people, he became a more subtle mentor of souls whose cures depended on the total authenticity of his own personality. He also recommended the rosary, the Angelus, ejaculatory prayer, and the Church's liturgy. "Private prayer," he would say, "is like straw scattered here and there: if you set it on fire it makes a lot of little flames. But gather these straws into a bundle and light them and you get a mighty fire, rising like a column into the sky: public prayer is like that."

Vianney was often credited with the gift of prophecy and an ability to know the hidden past and future. Yet his kind of insight had to do not with public

31

events but with the psychology and consolation of individuals. He was said to work miracles of physical healing, but the schoolmaster of Ars saw that "the most difficult, extraordinary and amazing work that the Curé did was his own life." After each noon Angelus, when he left the church for the presbytery to eat the food brought from *La Providence*, it took him up to twenty minutes to cross the dozen yards. The sick in soul, mind, and body knelt to ask his blessing and prayers and even tore pieces from his cassock. "What misguided devotion!" he exclaimed. Throughout his forty-one years at Ars he would have preferred to become a Carthusian or Cistercian. He left the village three times, "ran away," in fact, and in 1843, after a serious illness, the bishop and others had to persuade him to return.

In 1852 the bishop of Belley made him an honorary canon, yet he never again put on his *mozzetta* but sold it eventually for charity. Three years later he was made a knight of the Imperial Order of the Legion of Honour. He refused to be invested and would never wear the imperial cross. "What if, when I die, I turn up with these toys and God says to me: 'Get lost! You've had your reward'?" In 1853 Vianney made his last attempt at flight from Ars, but the bishop would not let him resign. He devoted himself to his ministry more assiduously than ever. In 1858-9 over one thousand pilgrims visited Ars each week. He was now seventy-three, and the strain was too much. On 18 July he knew he was soon to die, and on the 29th he said: "It's my poor end. You must send for the priest from Jassans." Even then he asked several penitents to kneel by his bed and finish their Confessions. People flocked to Ars. Twenty priests accompanied the abbé Beau with the Last Sacraments. "It is sad to receive holy communion for the last time," murmured Vianney. He died gently during a thunderstorm on 4 August.

He was a loving man who cared what happened to people and who fostered a natural ability to chat helpfully with them. But he was also a simplistic moralist whose mentality reflected the restrictive, populist, and sentimental emphases of nineteenth-century Ultramontanist strategy. Threats to papal rights during the Second Empire, more virulent anticlericalism after its collapse, then ecclesiastical resistance to Gallicanism, liberalism, and Modernism in the Church and, above all, to rapid social change helped to mould the image of the Curé d'Ars into one of rigour, obedience, and simple devotion. It has been remarked that many people certainly came to seek a confessor, but nostalgia brought just as many to see an exceptional phenomenon: a parish of practising Catholics in mid-nineteenth-century France that recalled a golden age otherwise lost for ever. That Vianney stands for more than that is shown by his effect on his contemporaries across denominational boundaries and by his continuing power to change individual lives.

In 1925 St John Mary Baptist Vianney was canonized by Pius XI, who in 1929 made him principal patron saint of the parochial clergy throughout the world.

F. Trochu's *Life of the Curé d'Ars* is based on the evidence for beatification and canonization (Eng. trans., 1927). Earlier biographies by A. Monnin (1861) and J. Vianney (1911) reveal contemporary attitudes. A. M. Zecca's *Ars e il suo curato* (1929) records the impressions of a pilgrim to Ars. A good but slighter sketch is that of H. Ghéon (1928), trans. F. J. Sheed, *The Secret of the Curé d'Ars* (1929). See also Trochu, *L'âme du Curé d'Ars* (1929), *L'Admirable Vie du Curé d'Ars* (1932; Eng. trans., 2 vols., 1932-4), and *Autour du Curé d'Ars* (1950); L. C. Sheppard, *Curé d'Ars: Portrait of a Parish Priest* (1958); other Lives by M. Trouncer (1959) and D. Pézeril (1959; Eng. trans., 1961); the saint's sermons, edited in four volumes by M. A. Delaroche (1925); and *L'Enigme des Sermons du Curé d'Ars* (1961). H. Nodet, *Jean-Marie Vianney, Curé d'Ars: sa pensée—son coeur* (5th ed., 1960), is a marvellous collection of his recorded sayings. On the French clergy see Abbé Lagoutte, *Du prêtre et de la société présente* (1868); J. Rogé, *Le Simple Prêtre* (1965); P. Pierrard, *Le Prêtre français* (1969); P. Rémond, *L'anticléricalisme en France de 1815 à nos jours* (1976); T. Tackett, *Priest and Parish in Eighteenth Century France* (1977). On Philomena see O. Marucchi, "Osservazioni archeologiche sulla iscrizione di S. Filomena," in *Miscellanea di Storia ecclesiastica e di Studi ausiliari*, vol. 2 (1904), pp. 365-86; idem, "Studio archeologico sulla celebre iscrizione di Filumena scoperta nel cimitero di Priscilla," in *Nuovo Bulletino di Archeologia cristiana* 12 (1906), pp. 253-300; and F. Trochu, *La "Petite Sainte" du curé d'Ars* (1924).

St Ia, *Martyr* (*c.* 360)

The Christians in Persia were granted complete freedom under King Sapor (Shapur) I. When they sympathized with the newly Christian Roman Empire under Constantine, the Sassinid monarchy changed its attitude to Christianity. The persecution of Christians under Sapor II from about 314 to 389 was unusually cruel. Tradition says that the victims included not only Ia but numerous companions in suffering (once said to number nine thousand but omitted from the revised Roman Martyrology). According to her quite unreliable *passio* she was a Greek and had converted a number of Persian women. The details of her ordeal, which involved torture sessions with long and short intervals of imprisonment before she was finally beheaded, though quite possible are lingeringly exact.

The best text of the passio is that edited by H. Delehaye in the *Patrologia orientalis*, vol. 2, pp. 453-73, fasc. 4. It also appears in *AA.SS.*, Aug., 1. On pious exaggerations of persecutions and martyrdom in the early centuries of Christianity see A. Mandouze, "Les Persécutions à l'origine de l'Eglise," in *Histoire vécue du peuple Chrétien*, vol. 1, ed. J. Delumeau (1979), pp. 49-74.

St Molua, *Abbot* (608)

Molua (or Lughaidh, Lugaid, and other forms) was possibly the son of Carthach of the Hy Fidhgente of Limerick County, Ireland, and his mother came from Ossory. His late Life claims that he was a herd boy until, having worked miracles, he was sent to be a monk under St Comgall (11 May) at Bangor in Wales. He was ordained priest and eventually despatched by his abbot to found monasteries elsewhere. The most important was at Clonfertmulloe, now

Kyle, in the Slievebloom Mountains between Leix and Offaly, which had a very large community. He is said to have gone to Rome and to have submitted to Pope St Gregory the Great (3 Sept.) the typically arduous Rule he had drawn up for his monasteries, of which the pope remarked: "The holy man who drew up this Rule has laid a hedge round his family which reaches to Heaven." Molua addressed his monks from his death-bed, urging them to culivate their land industriously: ". . . that you may have sufficient food, drink and clothing. For where there is sufficient there is stability. Where there is stability, there is true religion. And the end of true religion is everlasting life." Flannan, his main disciple, succeeded him. It is also said that Molua became a hermit and that the now submerged oratory on Friars' Island was his. The legend says that he never killed a living thing and that the birds wept when he died. This affinity between saints and the natural world, especially animals, often occurs in Celtic hagiography and mythology, which stress the unity of creation more than any other group of saints' Lives before the split noticeable in Renaissance and post-Renaissance spirituality and religious writing.

There is some confusion between this Molua and others of the same name. Killaloe (Cill da Lua) may get its name from him or from another called "the Leper," or they may both be the same person.

There are three Latin recensions of the life of St Molua. One appears in *AA.SS.*, Aug., 1; another in De Smedt's edition of the *Codex Salmaticensis*; and the third has been printed by C. Plummer in *V.S.H.*, 2, pp. 206-25. See also H. G. Leask in *J.R.S.A.I.* 60 (1930), pp. 130-6. See also Sr M. Donatus, *Beasts and Birds in the Lives of Early Irish Saints* (1934).

BB Cecilia Cesarini and Amata (1290)

In 1222 Bd Jordan of Saxony (15 Feb.) persuaded the powerful d'Andalo family of Bologna to found a small convent for Dominican nuns. Bd Diana d'Andalo (9 June), whose vow of virginity had been received by St Dominic himself, and four companions, all inexperienced in the religious life, were installed there. To help them four nuns were brought from the convent of San Sisto in Rome. Two of these, Cecilia and Amata, are always associated with Diana. They were buried in her tomb and beatified with her in 1891.

Nothing else is known of Amata, but Cecilia was a member of the noble Roman family of the Cesarini. When she was seventeen and in the convent at the Trastevere before its removal to San Sisto, she had been the first of the nuns to respond to Dominic's efforts to reform them, and she persuaded the abbess and sisters to submit to his Rule. She was said to be the first woman to receive the Dominican habit and was well fitted to govern the convent of St Agnes at Bologna in its early days. Jordan's letters reveal his fears that the nuns were too austere and would injure their health. When she was very old, Cecilia dictated her reminiscences of St Dominic.

There is a Latin biography of Bd Diana in H. M. Cormier, *La bienheureuse Diane d'Andalo* (1892). Bd Jordan's letters were re-edited in 1925 by B. Altaner, *Die Briefe Jordans von*

Sachsen, and there is a French translation of the letters written to Bd Diana produced by M. Aron (1924; Eng. trans., *To Heaven with Diana,* 1939). See also M. C. de Ganay, *Les Bienheureuses Dominicaines* (1913), pp. 23-48; Procter, pp. 168-70; and N. Georges, *Bd Diana and Bd Jordan* (1933).

Bd William Horn, *Martyr* (1540)

William Horn(e) was the last in time of the English Carthusian martyrs who refused to adhere by oath to the Act of Succession under Henry VIII, or the Act of Supremacy, which declared it was high treason to deny that the king was the sole and supreme head of the Church. The Carthusians had been required to take the Oath of Succession in 1534. Three priors, SS William Houghton, Robert Lawrence, and Augustine Webster (all 25 Oct.), were executed at Tyburn on 4 May 1535. On 18 May 1537 the prior and nineteen of the monks of the London charterhouse agreed to take the oath. A heroic minority of ten continued in staunch resistance. One was the lay brother William Horn. For a time he and the others were kept alive in the Marshalsea, where they had been tied up and left to starve and rot. St Thomas More's adopted daughter, disguised as a milkmaid, fed them by putting food in their mouths. The gaoler refused her admission when the king heard of the Carthusians' survival. The others died, but Horn lived and was removed to the Tower. Three years later he was attainted, condemned for denying the royal supremacy, and hanged, drawn, and quartered at Tyburn on 4 August 1540 (some sources say 4 November 1541). He was beatified in 1886 by papal decree on the feast of St Thomas of Canterbury, 29 December.

See the state papers in Record Office and elsewhere, all calendared in *Letters and Papers, Foreign and Domestic: the Reign of Henry VIII*; Dom M. Chauncy, *Historia aliquot nostri saeculi Martyrum*: Eng. trans. by G. W. S. Curtis, *The Passion and Martyrdom of the Holy English Carthusian Fathers* (1935), esp. pp. 123-9; L. Hendriks, *The London Charterhouse* (1889). See also E. M. Thompson, *The Carthusian Order in England* (1930).

Bd Frederick Jansoone (1838-1916)

Frédéric Jansoone, Franciscan priest and missionary, was born at Ghyvelde, in the diocese of Lille, France, on 19 November 1838. His father died early, and Frederick had to leave his theology course to look after the family until his mother's death. As a layman he was an outstanding student at the Institute of Our Lady of the Sands but was attracted by the Franciscan ethos. He entered the Franciscan novitiate at Amiens in 1864, took his vows on 18 July 1865, and was ordained priest on 17 August 1870. He served as a military chaplain during the Franco-Prussian War. When the war was over, he founded a Franciscan convent at Bordeaux. Then he was sent to Paris in connection with the work of the Order in the Holy Land, where he was transferred in 1876 and stayed until 1881. He was mainly concerned with the Franciscan guardianship of the Holy Places but also worked assiduously to obtain funds for poor Palestinian Christians and for Christian interests there, including the encouragement and care of pilgrims. He was a highly effective preacher and conducted the Way of the Cross through Jerusalem. He also became known as a proficient contemplative in the Franciscan tradition, uniting in his prayer all sorts and conditions of people, everyday events, and the various aspects of creation.

In 1881, after the promulgation of the papal Bull asking for universal Christian support for Christians in Jerusalem and the Holy Land, he was sent to Trois Rivières in French-speaking Canada to encourage such efforts and raise funds. There he was noted not only for this work and for the example he gave of contemplative prayer but for his ability to inspire devotion to the ideals of the Franciscan Third Order in the family and at work. He organized missions, edited various religious journals, and looked after the shrine of Our Lady at Notre-Dame du Cap. He died in Montreal, Canada, on 4 August 1916. He was beatified by Pope John Paul II on 25 September 1988.

F. Holböck, *Die neuen Heiligen der Katholischen Kirche*, 3 (1994), pp. 64-5.

R.M.

St Aristarchus of Thessalonica; SS Justin and Crescentius, martyrs in Rome (258)

St Eleutherius, martyr in Tarsus (third century)

SS Atom, Nerseh, Varaiavor, and Manachir, martyrs (421)

St Euphronius, bishop (567)

St Rainerius, bishop and martyr (1180).

5

ST OSWALD, *Martyr* (642)

Oswald was the son of Ethelfrith, king of Northumbria. He fled to Scotland when King (St) Edwin (12 Oct.), then a pagan, took the throne. Edwin was baptized by Paulinus of York (10 Oct.) in 627/8 but died in battle against Penda and Cadwallon in 633. Paulinus abandoned any further attempt to spread Christianity in Northumbria and went to Kent with Queen Ethelburga. Edwin's nephew Oswald was now, unlike his brothers, a resolute Christian, having been converted by St Columba's monks at Iona, and tried to win back both parts of Northumbria. In 634 a battle was fought at Rowley Burn, later called Heavenfield, south of Hexham. The night before, so the story goes, Oswald erected a great wooden cross; he called on his largely pagan army to pray to the true God, and they all obeyed him. Later that night Oswald had a vision of the protection of St Columba of Iona (9 June). Cadwallon was killed and his forces defeated. Chips of the cross were later claimed to have a curative effect, and a church was built on the site.

Oswald set about converting his dominions. He asked for a bishop and assistants from Scotland. After an unsuccessful attempt by a too-rigorous bishop, Oswald chose the Irish abbot St Aidan (31 Aug.), from Iona, and gave him the island of Lindisfarne as his episcopal see and monastery. The king himself is said to have been his interpreter before he learned English. Aidan and his missionaries established Christianity in Northumbria, where many churches and monasteries were built.

Oswald's kingdom extended to the Firth of Forth, and other English kings recognized his nominal overlordship of Britain. He married Cyneburga, daughter of Cynegils, the first Christian king of Wessex, and was his sponsor at Baptism. They had one child, Ethelwald, who became king of Deira.

After some years war broke out with the pagan Penda of Mercia, who allied himself with the Welsh. A decisive battle was fought at Maserfield (probably Oswestry in Shropshire). Oswald's forces were inferior and he was killed in the battle on 5 August 642, aged thirty-eight. His last prayer when surrounded became a catchphrase: "O God, have mercy on their souls, as Oswald said when he fell." Penda mutilated the body and put the fragments on stakes as a sacrifice to his god Woden. The arms were cut off in the process. The right one is said to have remained at Bamburgh and to have stayed incorrupt, at least till the time of Simeon of Durham (d. *c.* 1135), when it was kept at Peterborough Minster, having been stolen by a monk there; it later went to Ely. Both

Durham and Gloucester claimed to have an arm. His head was put in St Cuthbert's coffin on Lindisfarne in 875 and discovered at Durham in 1827, though another head (or fragment) was venerated at Echternach, and yet another (or fragment) is still in an early twelfth-century casket at Hildesheim. Commentators suggest that the Durham head has the best claim to authenticity. Relics of the first and second classes were widely distributed, and Bede reports their miraculous effects. A monastery in Flanders claimed to have the "complete" body, but Iconoclasts destroyed this marvellously reconstituted whole (or torso—the accounts are unclear) in 1558. The situation is complicated both by the practice of of putting only a part of the head, arm, or leg in a reliquary and by its use then as a safe receptacle for relics of other saints.

Oswald, undaunted by early defeat by a usurper, winning battles against a tyrant's superior forces, and finally vanquished by an unfairly brutish pagan—but not in spirit and, so it seems, not even in body—was well suited to become the typical English hero he remained for centuries. As always with such warrior-saints, it is impossible to disentangle the threads of regionalist (and later nationalist) merit from those of ecclesiastical virtue and to say at what point tribal wars become meritorious Christianization. Certainly, by means then considered licit and praiseworthy, Oswald consistently supported Christianity in his kingdom and elsewhere, for instance in Wessex. He is also said to have been a devout monarch who was especially generous to the sick and poor. St Adamnan (23 Sept.) says that one Easter day he sent a large silver dish of meat to the poor outside and ordered the metal to be broken and divided among them. Aidan took him by the right hand, saying, "May this hand never perish." For centuries Oswald remained an almost magical and glamorous figure with strong folklore elements in addition to the feats that caused seventy churches to be dedicated to him. He was also venerated in Scotland, Ireland, Portugal, northern Italy, Bohemia, the Netherlands, southern Germany, Austria, and Switzerland, where he is patron of Zug. Initially St Willibrord (7 Nov.) was responsible for the continental European cult, which three devout aristocratic women, assisted by the relics, helped to spread later.

We know little of Oswald beyond the record (which does not describe him as a martyr) in Bede's *Ecclesiastical History*, 3, but Plummer in his edition gives (2, 1896, p. 161, and notes) a list of subsequent Lives. That by Drogo (eleventh century) is in *AA.SS.*, Aug., 2; and that by Reginald of Durham in T. Arnold's edition of Simeon of Durham (R.S., 1882), 1, pp. 326–85. See the notes on Bede's text in the edition of Mayor and Lumby (1881) and more recent editions. For the general cult see Plummer *et al.*; for the Swiss version see E. P. Baker's article in *Archaeologia* 93 (1949), pp. 103–23; for northern Italy, *idem*, in *Archaeologia* 94 (1951), pp. 167–94. See also B. Colgrave in C. F. Battiscombe (ed.), *The Relics of St Cuthbert* (1956), pp. 116–8; W. Bonser, "The Magic of St Oswald," *Antiquity* 9 (1935), pp. 418–23; R. Folz, "St Oswald, roi de Northumbrie," *Anal. Boll.* 98 (1980), pp. 49–74.

Oswald appears in a number of paintings. The most famous is probably the altarpiece painted by Tiepolo (1696-1770) for a church in Padua, in which he is shown with St Maximus Vitalianus, second bishop of the city (there is another version in the National Gallery, London). Oswald's cult was long established in the Veneto.

SS Addai and Mari, *Bishops* (? *c.* 180)

The Acts of the Apostles say that some people from Mesopotamia were present when St Peter and his companions preached at Pentecost, but we do not know exactly when Christianity was introduced there. There is evidence of a Christian colony at Edessa in the second century, but it was probably not until the Sassanid dynasty that Christianity began to spread from there through Mesopotamia, Adiabene, and Persia. Local ecclesiastical tradition ascribes the evangelization of these areas to the apostle Thomas, and more particularly to Addai, Aggai, and Mari. A delightful account of how they came to Edessa is found in Eusebius and in a Syriac document called *The Doctrine of Addai* (probably written *c.* 400 from older sources and the main foundation of Eusebius' report), which had some influence on later Christian art and narrative. Only a bare summary of the legend and a few of its now rather homely details (clearly the embellishments of oral tradition) can be given here.

In the lifetime of Christ, King Abgar the Black ruled at Edessa. He suffered from an incurable disease. He heard of Jesus' healing powers, wrote to say he knew Jesus was divine, and asked him to visit Edessa and cure him. Jesus wrote back politely to say that he could not accept the invitation as he was about to return to his Father but would send a disciple later. The Syriac document also says that the messenger, Abgar's servant, made a portrait of our Lord and returned with it. This is one of the legendary origins of the Holy Mandylion. After the Ascension Thomas fulfilled the Master's promise by sending one of the seventy-two disciples, Addai (whom Eusebius identifies with Thaddaeus). He healed Abgar and converted him and many of his people, including the royal jeweller, Aggai, whom he made a bishop and who was later martyred. All this is very engaging, but the most that can be said of Addai is that he was perhaps a missionary in Edessa before the end of the second century. Burkitt opines that he is the second-century Tatian and that the tradition of a first-century Addai is of later date.

The story of Mari is also pleasingly quaint, and he seems entirely apocryphal. Nevertheless, he appears with Addai in the revised Roman Martyrology, possibly out of tact because he holds so secure a place in Middle Eastern Christianity. According to his late Acts he was a disciple of Addai, who sent him to Nisibis, where he preached and then took up the work of the prophet Jonah at Nineveh. He died near Seleucia-Ctesiphon after consecrating as its bishop Papa bar Aggai, a historical personage and the first *katholikos* of the East Syrian churches but who lived at the beginning of the fourth century. Mari is credited with quite prodigious feats of conversion, temple destruction, church building, and monastic foundation. Nevertheless, from early times the nebulous SS Addai and Mari have been venerated as evangelists of the lands around the Tigris and Euphrates and still are by their successors, the Catholic Chaldeans and the Nestorians of Iraq and Kurdistan. They are referred to as "the Holy Apostles," and the main anaphora of the Eucharistic liturgy of those

Christians (presumably composed *c*. 200) is known as the Liturgy of Addai and Mari.

The two primary sources are Eusebius, *H.E.*, 1, 13, and *The Doctrine of Addai*, Syriac text with Eng. trans., ed. G. Philips (1876). See L. J. Tixeront, *Les Origines de l'Eglise d'Edesse et la légende d'Abgar* (1888), pp. 20-159; B. Altaner, *Patrologie* (rev. by A. Stuiber, 1966), p. 139; B. D. Spinks, *Addai and Mari: the Anaphora of the Apostles* (1980); *The Teaching of Addai* (1981); "Letters of Christ and Abgar," in J. K. Elliott, *Apocryphal New Testament* (1993).

St Emydigius, *Bishop and Martyr* (304)

St Emygdius (Emidius) is greatly honoured in Italy, mainly as patron against earthquakes. For the same reason his cult in later years has been extended to San Francisco and Los Angeles in the United States. His true history is unknown, but his legend is preserved in his Acts. He is described as a German convert to Christianity who left his native Trier for Rome during the pontificate of Pope Marcellus I. The zealous Emygdius is said to have entered a temple and dashed a statue of Aesculapius, hero and god of healing, to the ground. Pope Marcellus had to protect him from the angry pagans by ordaining and consecrating him and sending him to evangelize the region of Ascoli Piceno, where he made many converts. He was beheaded during the Diocletian persecution with three companions, SS Eupolus, Germanus, and Valentinus. However, since Marcellus was not pope until 308, he could not have ordained Emygdius. Perhaps a careless scribe substituted the name Marcellus for that of Marcellinus, his predecessor.

Though the supposed *passio* of Emygdius appears in *AA.SS.*, Aug., 2, 1, the Bollandists regard it as wholly untrustworthy. Inhabitants of Ascoli and others have written uncritical accounts of their patron.

St Nonna (374)

Nonna was born toward the end of the third century and was brought up as a Christian. She married and converted a member of the Hypsistarians, a Judaic-pagan sect. Her husband (for the clergy were allowed to marry) became a priest, then a bishop, and is venerated as St Gregory Nazianzen the Elder. Their three children were saints. The eldest, St Gregory Nazianzen the Divine (2 Jan.) became a Doctor of the Church and in his writings often mentions his mother's virtuous life. St Gorgonia (9 Dec.) married and had three children. St Caesarius (25 Feb.) became a physician. Nonna heard funeral sermons preached for Gorgonia and Caesarius by Gregory the Younger. She survived her husband by a few months and died at a considerable age. The ever-spreading sanctity of the family has been cited as evidence of the beneficial effects of a married priesthood.

AA.SS., Aug., 2; *D.C.B.*, 4, p. 50.

St Margaret the Barefooted (*c.* 1395)

She was born into a poor family at San Severino, Ancona, Italy, in the mid-fourteenth century and was married when fifteen to a husband who ill treated her. He was particularly enraged by the nickname people gave her because she wore no shoes in order to be like the beggars she helped. Margaret bore his opposition patiently for years until he died and she could spend the rest of her life in prayer and alms-deeds. Her body is entombed in the church of St Dominic at San Severino. Cardinal Baronius added her to the Roman Martyrology.

A brief Life and a fragment of an account by a contemporary, Pompilio Caccialupo, are in *AA.SS.*, Aug., 2.

R.M.

St Memmius, bishop (third-fourth century)

St Paridis, bishop (fourth century)

St Cassian, bishop (fourth century)

St Venantius, bishop of Viviers (*c.* 544)

SS Vardan and companions, martyrs under the Persians (451)

St Viator, hermit (sixth century)

St Abel, archbishop of Reims and Benedictine monk (*c.* 750)

St Euthymius, bishop of Constantinople (917)

6

SS Justus and Pastor, *Martyrs* (304)

These two brothers are said while schoolboys to have heroically opposed the rage of Dacian, governor of Spain under Diocletian and Maximian. Their Acts relate that in his progress through the province in search of Christians Dacian came to Complutum, now Alcalá de Henares, and began to torture followers of Christ. Justus and Pastor, one thirteen, the other nine, were at the city's public school and wanted to share in the victims' glory. They ran from their books to the scene and showed they were Christians. The judge was furious to see children defying his authority and had them severely whipped to curb their enthusiasm. To the spectators' astonishment they encouraged each other and still defied Dacian, who ordered them to be beheaded. Their relics are enshrined at Alcalá, and they are the patrons of that city and of Madrid.

Though their Acts (*AA.SS.*, Aug., 2) are doubtful, their cult is genuine and ancient. St Paulinus of Nola had his little son buried close beside them at Alcalá. Prudentius numbers them among the most glorious martyrs of Spain. Their names appear in the *Hieronymianum* on 25 August.

St Hormisdas, *Pope* (523)

Hormisdas, himself a Campanian by birth and the son of one, named Justus, nevertheless bore the Persian name of the Zoroastrian god of light and goodness, which has led to speculation that Justus was a Persian convert. Hormisdas was a deacon of the Roman church when he showed his diplomatic gifts by helping to reconcile the followers of Pope Symmachus and the antipope Lawrence, a division which rested to some extent on the splitting of allegiance between the Gothic rulers and the Eastern emperor, brought in issues of orthodoxy and heresy, such as Arianism and Monophytism, and resulted in bitter street fights and counter-condemnations and dispossessions.

Hormisdas became pope two days after the death of Symmachus in 514. Almost his entire pontificate was devoted to dealing with the complex division between East and West since 484, known as the Acacian schism, caused by Acacius of Constantinople's attempt to placate the Monophysites. The emperor Anastasius I prevented an attempted solution in 515 by refusing to accept the pope's demands for a reconciliation that included the condemnation of Acacius, his followers, the Monophysites, and other heretics, the acceptance of Chalcedon, and recognition of the pope's supremacy. In 519 under the pro-

Chalcedonian emperor Justin I, Hormisdas resolved the schism by the confession of faith that bears his name, the Formula of Hormisdas. On 28 March 519 the emperor and the patriarch of Constantinople (and later many Eastern bishops) accepted the Formula and thus the condemnation of Acacius and his teachings, the Chalcedonian Definition of 451, which restates the definitions of Nicaea and Constantinople, the Tome of Leo (or the Christological Epistle of Pope Leo I to Flavian of Constantinople, 449), and to a considerable degree the authority of the see of Rome. There was still strong opposition to this submission from a number of Eastern bishops, and without the emperor's insistence they would not have accepted the Formula, which was cited at the First Vatican Council as evidence of the acknowledgment of papal authority in the first six centuries. There were various attempts to sabotage the new unity, particularly by the exiled Severus of Antioch in Egypt and by Metropolitan Doretheus of Thessalonica. There is a Roman epitaph which praises Hormisdas for closing the Roman schism and reconciling the Greeks.

Hormisdas carried on a detailed correspondence with the Spanish bishops, which stressed the vital connection of the Spanish church with Rome. Nothing is recorded of Hormisdas' less public life, though he was obviously sagacious and a man of peace. He severely rebuked some quarrelsome African monks and some Scythian monks from Constantinople who were excessively enthusiastic anti-Nestorians and wanted the pope to allow the use of a formula which said that one person of the Trinity suffered. Hormisdas also negotiated with the Goths regarding ecclesiastical affairs. During his last days the Vandal persecution in Africa came to an end.

See the *Liber Pontificalis*, ed. L. Duchesne (1886-92), with notes to vol. 1, pp. 272-4, *AA.SS.*, Aug., 2, for his public activities; the substantial article in *O. D. P.* (1985), pp. 52-4, with ref. to J. Richards, *The Popes and the Papacy in the Early Middle Ages* (1979); A. Dvornik, *The Idea of Apostolicity in Byzantium* (1958), pp. 124-34; J. Chapin, *N.C.E.*, 7, p. 148, *s.v.* For Hormisdas' letters see the critical edition by O. Guenther in *C.S.E.L.*, 35, 2 (1898).

R.M.

Bd Octavain, bishop of Savona, brother of Pope Callistus II (1132)

Bd Schecelinus, hermit of Luxembourg (*c.* 1138)

7

SS SIXTUS II, AGAPITUS, FELICISSIMUS, and COMPANIONS, *Martyrs* (258)

Sixtus (or Xystus), who succeeded Pope St Stephen I (2 Aug.) in 257, is a figure somewhat less shadowy than other early popes, largely because he died at a time of internal changes in the Roman Empire that portended major external threats to its traditions and security. He is best known as a title-figure of one of the most celebrated works of art in Western history.

In three letters St Dionysius of Alexandria consulted Sixtus about the dispute begun under Stephen (see p. 20, above) and advised him to be patient with the African and some Asiatic Churches when reproving them for their insistence that Baptism by heretics was invalid. Sixtus heeded the advice, renewed relations with St Cyprian and those Churches, and tactfully ignored the Asiatic practice of baptizing converts from heresy. Pontius, Cyprian's biographer, called Sixtus a "good and peaceable priest."

In 257, the fourth year of his reign, the hitherto friendly emperor Valerian issued his first decree against the Christians. His minister, Macrianus, possibly advised this course in the hope of confiscating rich Christians' property and thus helping to balance the imperial books, which were very much in the red. Perhaps Valerian genuinely believed that his empire was troubled by the Persians and other formidable foes without, and by financial, social, and ideological dissension within, because the gods were angry about the Christians and his tolerance of them. Then he would merely have reverted to the old Roman suspicion that the Christian body was politically dangerous: "Christians were considered mathematici and magi, and these were the secret intriguers against established government, the resort of desperate politicians, the enemies of the established religion, the disseminators of lying rumours, the perpetrators of poisonings and other crimes" (in Newman's memorable words).

Since by Valerian's time the practice of the state religion among the eminent was more pragmatic than fervent, it is also possible that, like other autocratic rulers in different eras, he was trying to avoid a threatened coup by deflecting discontent on to easily identifiable scapegoats. Yet the emperor and his advisers knew well that many influential pillars of the state were Christians, and Valerian's edict was expressly addressed to *egregii viri* and *equites Romani*: senators, knights, and high officials. They were not required to renounce their beliefs but only to demonstrate their loyalty by open sacrifice to the gods. A few laypeople compromised, but most of them and the clergy remained steadfast. Given such recalcitrance, the persecution soon became an attempt to eradicate Christianity by destroying its leaders and bases of power and influence. Higher ecclesiastics in important centres such as North Africa, Egypt, and, of course, Rome were essential targets.

In 257, liturgical worship and use of the cemeteries were forbidden; bishops, priests, and deacons had to sacrifice to the gods or go into exile; and Sixtus was consecrated in secret. There were martyrs among the higher and lower clergy throughout the empire. There were many more the next year, when the clergy could be executed without trial, and the leading laity were also subject to the death sentence. In Africa, Cyprian (16 Sept.), who was to perish in the same persecution, told his fellow-bishops that Sixtus and four deacons had died on 6 August. During persecutions Christians met in the underground caverns to celebrate Mass, though this was forbidden, and Sixtus was killed in a cemetery (that of Praetextatus). He was seized while seated addressing the assembly and was said to have refused a chance to escape, for he wanted to prevent a massacre of the congregation. He was either beheaded immediately or taken to court for sentence, then brought back for execution. He was buried across the road in the cemetery of St Callistus on the Appian Way. A century later Pope St Damasus (11 Dec.) wrote an inscription for his tomb.

Four deacons, SS Januarius, Vincent, Magnus, and Stephen, were seized with Sixtus and executed with him. Two others, SS Felicissimus and Agapitus, were probably martyred on the same day and were buried in the cemetery of Praetextatus. The seventh deacon of the city, St Laurence (10 Aug.), followed them four days later. The persecution came to an end in 259 with Valerian's death in Persian captivity. His son, Gallienus, published an edict in favour of the Christians.

Sixtus was the most highly venerated of the popes martyred after St Peter. His relics were said to be preserved with those of St Barbara in the conventual church of the Black Friars, St Sixtus in Piacenza, by tradition the pope's birthplace. He is portrayed with St Laurence in a well-known sixth-century mosaic in the church of S. Apollinare Nuovo, Ravenna, Italy. He also appears in one of the most famous and most often copied and reproduced paintings in the world, the *Sistine Madonna*, or *Our Lady and Child with SS Sixtus II and Barbara*, by Raphael (1483-1520), now in the Dresden Art Gallery, Germany. Either Pope Julius II or Cardinal Grassi commissioned the work for the altar of the church at Piacenza to commemorate that city's incorporation in the Papal States after Julius' victory over the French in 1512. (The church of S. Sisto sold it to Augustus III, elector of Saxony and king of Poland in 1754.) In deference to his patron, Raphael gave Sixtus the features of the aging Julius; he also placed an acorn on the tiara and the oak tree of the pope's family coat-of-arms on the cope. Sixtus is shown pointing to the faithful (the spectators), whom he recommends to our Lady's protection, and this is thought to refer partly to Julius' unremitting defence of the pope's authority as a temporal ruler

45

and arbiter. Then the earlier pope's refusal to defer to state coercion would be interpreted as a symbolic and actual precedent for the behaviour of the combative and indeed, unlike Sixtus, very warlike Julius. The curtains drawn back (and blown forward by a divine wind) in the painting were designed to give the illusion of a window in the choir through which Mary and Jesus, whom she carries like a prince, were to be seen in glory on a bank of clouds raised above mundane reality. The central figure of the otherwise static picture (which might well be titled *The Vision of St Sixtus*) is the apparently mobile, indeed descending, Mary as the Queen of Heaven, a notion scarcely current in Sixtus' period, but the pope is the privileged communicator between the sacred and the profane. The picture's fame, shared with a few others such as Raphael's *Madonna della Sedia* and Leonardo's *Last Supper* and *Mona Lisa*, dates only from the eighteenth century, when many copies were made and circulated and the spate of reproductive engravings began.

There is early and conclusive evidence that Sixtus suffered on 6 August and was buried in the catacomb of Callistus. See *C.M.H.*, pp. 420-1, for a summary. A misinterpretation of one of Damasus' inscriptions led Prudentius to think that Sixtus was crucified, but he was probably put to death by the sword. The *Liber Pontificalis* (followed in this by the new draft Roman Martyrology) is wrong in stating that the "four deacons" as well as Felicissimus and Agapitus were buried in Praetextatus. See Duchesne's notes, 1, pp. 155-6; P. Franchi de' Cavalieri in *Studi e Testi*, 6, pp. 147-78. The *Passio S. Sixti*, in all recensions, is historically worthless. See also Cyprian, *Ep.* 80, 1; *AA.SS.*, Aug., 2; J. H. Newman, *An Essay on the Development of Christian Doctrine* (1846), pp. 206-42; *Anal. Boll.* 51 (1933), pp. 43-9; P. Kereszetes, "The Imperial Roman Government and the Christian Church," in *Archiv für neue Religionswissenschaft* 2, 23, 1 (1979), pp. 247-315, 375-86; Jedin-Dolan, 1, pp. 226-7.

ST CAJETAN, *Founder* (1480-1547)

Tommaso de Vio Cajetan (Gaetano), co-founder of the Theatine Clerks Regular, was born in Vicenza in 1480. His parents were Caspar, count of Thiene, and Maria di Porto. He was known for his long hours of devotion when studying theology and law at Padua. He became a senator of Vicenza and received the tonsure, as he wished to become a priest. In 1506 he went to Rome, where Pope Julius II soon made him a protonotary in the Curia, with a benefice. On Julius' death in 1513, Cajetan resigned his office and spent three years preparing for the priesthood. He was ordained in 1516 and returned to Vicenza in 1518.

In Rome he had re-founded a clerical confraternity, the Oratory of the Divine Love. At Vicenza he entered the Oratory of St Jerome, which included only men from the lowest stations of life. His friends interpreted this as an insult to his family's honour. Cajetan served the sick and poor and cared for the least appealing patients in the hospital for incurables. He said that in his Oratory they tried to serve God by worship, but "in our hospital we can say that we actually find him." He founded another Oratory at Verona. In 1520 he went for three years to the new hospital in Venice and became its main benefactor.

The dissolute lives and indifference of many priests shocked Cajetan. In 1523 he went to Rome to discuss means of renewing the spiritual life of the clergy with his friends of the Oratory of Divine Love. They decided to found an Order of regular clergy on the model of the apostles' lives and the Augustinian Rule. His first associates were John Peter Caraffa, later Pope Paul IV but then bishop of Theate (Chieti); Paul Consiglieri, of the Ghislieri family; and Boniface da Colle, a gentleman of Milan. Clement VII approved the Institute, and Caraffa was made the first provost general. The term "Theatines" came from his episcopal name. On 14 September 1524 the four original members discarded their prelatical robes and were professed in St Peter's. They wanted to preach sound doctrine, help the sick, restore frequent use of the sacraments, and bring the clergy back to a committed and regular way of life with an emphasis on poverty, sacred studies (especially the Bible), preaching, pastoral care, and properly conducted worship. The Order would have no set income and own no buildings or land. It would rely not on begging but on divine Providence.

In 1527 the army of the emperor, Charles V, sacked Rome, the Theatines' house was nearly demolished, and its members fled to Venice. In 1530 Cajetan replaced Caraffa as superior. He worked heroically to relieve sufferers during a plague and the subsequent famine.

After three years Caraffa became superior again, and Cajetan was sent to Verona, where clergy and laity resisted the bishop's reforms. Shortly after, he went to Naples to establish the Order there. The Count of Oppido gave him a large house and offered him a landed estate, which Cajetan refused. He is said to have improved the religious life of Naples and successfully opposed three apostates, a layman, an Augustinian, and a Franciscan, respectively Socinian, Calvinist, and Lutheran, who were influencing the people, though it is not clear whether their eloquence or their way of life had this effect. His reputation for sternness, along with the close association with the grimly austere Caraffa (exceptionally reformist and authoritarian yet oddly nepotistic as Paul IV, and in his later years as pope both fiercely anti-Spanish and virulently anti-Protestant) and the extraordinary spread of the Jesuits rather than the Theatines, to some extent obscured Cajetan's real achievements. In the last years of his life, together with Bd John Marinoni (13 Dec.) he set up the "benevolent pawn-shops" (or *montes pietatis*) sanctioned by the Fifth Lateran Council. Worn out trying to reduce civil strife in Naples and disappointed by the suspension of the Council of Trent, he took to his sick-bed in summer 1547. He refused a mattress and preferred hard boards in emulation of Christ's suffering on the cross. He was canonized in 1671.

Cajetan was an outstanding figure of the pre-Tridentine Catholic Reformation with his exemplary Institution of priests bound by vows and living in community but engaged in active pastoral work. The Order flourished in Italy under Paul IV, and by the end of the seventeenth century houses were established in Prague, Salzburg, Munich, and elsewhere, but it has now been reduced to small bodies. Thomas Goldwell, bishop of Saint Asaph from 1555 to 1559, in the reign of Queen Mary, and last survivor of the old hierarchy of England and Wales was a Theatine; he entered their Neapolitan house in the year of Cajetan's death.

There is no biography by anyone who actually knew him. That in *AA.SS.*, Aug., 2, by A. Caracciolo was written sixty years after Cajetan's death. Probably Cajetan's close association with Caraffa and the extreme unpopularity of the latter's pontificate (he became pope eight years after Cajetan's death) made the early history of the Theatines a delicate subject to handle. In more recent times L. von Pastor, G. M. Monti, and O. Premoli have revealed much that was formerly obscure in this connection. The sketch by Premoli, *S. Gaetano Thiene* (1910), is the most reliable picture of Cajetan, but for his earlier career see Pio Paschini, *S. Gaetano . . . e le origini dei . . . Teatini* (1929). R. de Maulde la Clavière's Life can be recommended only with reservations: see reviews in *Anal. Boll.* 22, p. 119, and 24, p. 419. See *Bibl.SS.*, 5, 1345-9, and biographies in Italian by P. Chiminelli (1948, long), L. Ruiz de Cardenas (1947, short); in Spanish by A. Veny Ballester (1950); and in English, P. H. Hallett, *Catholic Reformer* (1959).

St Afra, *Martyr* (304)

Diocletian's persecution of Christians continued with great cruelty under Maximian in the provinces he controlled when the empire was divided. At Augsburg, in Rhaetia (now Germany), according to her Acts, the officers arrested Afra, a former prostitute. A later addition to the legend says that she was converted by (St) Narcissus, bishop of Gerona in Spain, of whom nothing is known for certain. The judge told her to sacrifice to the gods rather than die in torment. She refused to add to her already great sins. He reminded her that she had been a prostitute and unacceptable to the Christian God. Afra said that Jesus forgave a sinful woman and that she was willing for her sinful body to suffer rather than ruin her soul. She was tied to a stake on an island in the river Lech and suffocated with the smoke of burning vine leaves (a suspiciously symbolic detail). Her mother and three of her servants who had led similar lives and been converted carried away her body for burial. The judge sent soldiers to demand that they offer sacrifice. When they refused they were roasted alive in the vault.

The existence of a martyr named Afra who suffered at Augsburg is credible and referred to by Venantius Fortunatus, but her Acts are of doubtful value. Some commentators hold that the trial and martyrdom are an expanded version of an earlier historical narrative, whereas her harlotry and conversion and the execution of her mother and servants are inventions of the Carolingian era.

The two most important Latin texts were edited by B. Krusch in *M.G.H., Scriptores Merov.*, 3, pp. 55-64, and 7, pp. 192-204. Krusch says, against Duchesne, that the original text of the Acts is not a Merovingian document but elaborated from a terse notice in the *Hieronymianum*. Bigelmair, Poncelet, and Riedner support Krusch. See *C.M.H.*, p. 423, for an opposite view.

St Donatus, *Bishop* (*c.* 656)

This Donatus was bishop of Besançon, France. In emulation of the Rules of SS Benedict (11 July), Columban (23 Nov.), and in particular Caesarius of Arles (27 Aug.), who wrote one for a nunnery there, he composed a Rule for nuns. He is not to be confused with Donatus, possibly the second bishop of Arezzo and formerly but erroneously considered to be a martyr and commemorated on the same day (but since 1969 only in local calendars, though still recorded in the new draft Roman Martyrology), or with Donatus, bishop of Euroea in Epirus.

For all that is known of Donatus see Jonas' *Vita Columbani*, critically ed. by B. Krusch in *M.G.H., Scriptores Merov.*, 4, pp. 1–56, and the seemingly authentic text of the *Regula ad Virgines* in *P.L.*, 87, 273 ff.

St Victricius, *Bishop* (*c.* 407)

Victricius of Rouen is said to have been a bishop of great wisdom and holiness, but we know less about him than about other famous fourth-century bishops. His exact date of death is uncertain. He was probably born near the river Scheldt about 330. His father or near ancestor was in a Roman legion called Victrix. When seventeen he became a soldier and not long afterwards a Christian. Many Christians thought it unlawful to bear arms, and Victricius asked for a discharge before his period of service had expired. He was flogged and sentenced to death for desertion but, with some Christian comrades, was released and discharged. Paulinus of Nola (22 June) calls the intervention miraculous.

We next hear of Victricius as bishop of Rouen, where he was elected about 386. He converted many pagans in his diocese, but progress was slow among country people (and remained so for another two centuries). Victricius introduced a form of monasticism to Rouen. He founded some rural parishes and preached in Artois, western Flanders, Hainault, and Brabant; but the fifth-century barbarian invasions largely undid his work and destroyed his religious foundations. St Ambrose of Milan (7 Dec.) sent him some relics of the saints, and he preached or wrote *On Praise of the Saints*, a panegyric and thesis on the cult of the saints. About 396 the British bishops asked him to settle some differences. Their nature is not known, but Victricius' description of his reaction has acquired quasi-proverbial status: "I inspired the wise with love of peace; I taught it to the teachable; I explained it to the ignorant; and I imposed it on the obstinate."

Toward the end of his life Victricius went to Rome and succeeded in clearing himself of a charge of heresy. In 404 he received from Pope Innocent I, who was anxious to impose Roman customs and papal rule as the norm in the Gallic church, a famous decretal on disciplinary matters, including the reference of important cases from local bishops to the Holy See.

There is no early Life. We rely on the letters of St Paulinus of Nola: *Epistolae*, 27 (ed. W. Hartel, *C.S.E.L.*, 29 [1894], pp. 128-37, and 37, pp. 316-23). For Innocent's letter see *P.L.*, 20, 469-81. See the study by E. Vacandard in the series "Les Saints" (1903). Cf. also E. de Moreau, *Histoire de l'Eglise en Belgique*, vol. 1 (1945); G. Bardy, in *D.T.C.*, 15, 2 (1950), 2954-6; and S. Prete in *Bibl. SS.*, 12 (1969), 1310-5. For his influence on St Patrick see P. Grosjean in *Anal. Boll.* 64 (1946), pp. 94-9.

St Albert of Trapani (*c*. 1307)

His biography is late and contains many impossible and dubious details. Also called "of Sicily," he is said to have been born at Trapani on that island to long-childless parents who vowed to dedicate a male child to Our Lady of Mount Carmel in her Order. He became a Carmelite and after ordination was sent to the priory of Messina, where he was a successful preacher and added voluntary austerities to those of his Rule. During the last years of his life he lived as a hermit near Messina. He was never formally canonized, but his cult was approved in 1476.

For the early fifteenth-century Latin Life see *Anal. Boll.* 17 (1898), pp. 317 ff. See also B. Zimmerman, *Monumenta historica Carmelitana*, pp. 259, 422, etc.

BB Agathangelo and Cassian, *Martyrs* (1638)

Fr Joseph Leclerc du Tremblay of Paris directed the first Capuchin mission in the Levant in the seventeenth century. Early in 1629 five Capuchins landed at Alexandretta, among them Fr Agathangelo (François Noury) of Vendôme in France.

He was born there in 1598, became a Capuchin when twenty-one, and was ordained in 1625. When sent to Aleppo in Syria, he ministered to French and Italian traders and others while learning Arabic. He cultivated the society of Muslims and non-Latin Christians and won the good will and respect of the leading imam and of many others. Even though public preaching to Muslims was forbidden by the Congregation for the Propagation of the Faith, he explained Christianity to the Turks and awakened their tolerance and interest.

In 1633 Agathangelo was sent to Cairo to take charge of a hitherto unsuccessful mission. He was joined by three missionaries from Marseilles, including Cassian of Nantes (born Gundisalvo da López-Nato), a Frenchman of Portuguese parentage who became Agathangelo's right-hand man. By conciliation and discussion they tried to inspire a reunion of the local Coptic church with the Holy See. A measure of their respect and tact is Patriarch Matthew's opening of the churches to Agathangelo, who celebrated Mass, preached, and taught there. There were some individual reconciliations. In 1636 Agathangelo and Fr Benedict of Dijon made a long journey to the important Dair Antonios Monastery in the Lower Thebaid in an attempt to gain influence among the Coptic monks from whom the bishops were chosen. They were well received and reconciled two members of the community, whom they left there in the hope that they would persuade the others to do the same. At this time, Catholic laypeople were allowed to attend Coptic churches and priests to celebrate Mass in them, but when Propaganda abruptly prohibited this, the missionaries in Palestine and Egypt disagreed with the Roman action. Agathangelo wrote to the Holy Office and presumably obtained a favourable decision, for the practice continued for some time.

When the synod of the Coptic patriarch met in 1637 to discuss reunion, one counsellor denounced the proposal because of the scandalous lives of prominent Catholics in Cairo: "The Roman Church in this country is a brothel." Agathangelo, who was present, could not deny this. He wrote to the cardinal prefect of Propaganda to complain about the refusal of his many requests, over three years, for excommunication of the worst offenders.

A few days later he left for Ethiopia (Abyssinia) with Cassian, who had been learning Amharic, and now took the leading place. Catholic Portugal had helped Ethiopia to defeat a Muslim threat in the early sixteenth century and the first Jesuit missionary had reached the country in 1555. For some time Catholic missionaries were well received, but Ethiopia, with its ancient Christian church (the non-Chalcedonian Ethiopian Orthodox Church dates its foundation to 332), was understandably hostile to Catholic attempts to propagate Latin Christianity. Such ventures were usually pursued under the aegis of a colonialist power granted a sphere of influence by the pope. Portugal played this part until the nineteenth century.

A Lutheran physician named Peter Heyling is said to have exacerbated matters when the Capuchins arrived. The friars were arrested at Dibarua in early summer 1638, put in manacles, and taken to Gondar. They were brought before the *negus*, or king, Basilides (or Fasilidas), and his court. Cassian said they were in Ethiopia to ask Christians there to reunite with the Roman Church. He cited his letter of introduction from the Coptic patriarch of Alexandria to the newly elected *abuna*, or primate, Mark, of the Ethiopian church (appointed by the patriarch). But Mark, who had been friendly with Agathangelo in Cairo, refused to see the missionaries, said they intended only straightforward conversion, called Agathangelo evil, and recommended hanging. Basilides was inclined to banish them, but others disagreed. The Capuchins were offered their lives if they abjured their beliefs. They refused, were hanged with the cords of their Franciscan habits, but died by stoning. Local Catholics are said to have buried them secretly. Other Capuchins and Franciscans who tried to enter the country and proselytize in the seventeenth and eighteenth centuries were expelled or put to death. A native bishop was consecrated in Rome in 1788 but had to escape to Cairo in 1797. In the nineteenth century a small Uniate church developed under Italian influence.

Changes in ecclesiastical and secular politics over four centuries have obscured Agathangelo's interestingly conciliatory attitude. By now it is impossible to elicit the true story of his and his companions' work and the reasons for

51

their execution. The whole complex of problems attached to official Catholic thinking on the Coptic Church and its alleged Monophysitism and on Uniate Churches of local and Latin rites, which were allowed certain disciplinary concessions in return for accepting obedience to Rome as their ultimate unifying principle, encouraged a one-sided attitude to Catholic martyrs in Ethiopia. This was confirmed by Italian dreams of an African empire and by actual aggression in Libya, Eritrea, and Ethiopia in the early to mid-twentieth century with varying degrees of church approval, complicated by the Church's desire to take advantage of territorial gains by a Catholic country and the simultaneous dispute between the papacy and the kingdom of Italy, which was resolved only by the Concordat and Lateran Treaty of 1929. In 1882 Italy established the colony of Eritrea, and in 1894 Leo XIII created an apostolic prefecture there. In 1889 the Treaty of Ucciali implied an Italian protectorate over Ethiopia, withdrawn in 1896 after an Italian defeat by the Treaty of Addis Ababa. Pope Pius X followed up a difficult correspondence on behalf of Ethiopian Uniates (and Italian prisoners) between Leo XIII and the highly resistant emperor Menelik II. In 1905 Pius X beatified Agathangelo and Cassian; in 1906 he made a formal appeal to the emperor for tolerance of the Uniates. In 1911 Libya became an Italian colony. In 1936 Italy annexed Ethiopia, and Catholic missionaries arrived in force.

With due regard to the dates and origins of these accounts see Ladislas de Vannes, *Deux martyrs capucins* (1905); Antonio da Pontedera, *Vita e martirio dei BB. Agatangelo e Cassiano* (1904). Cf. also T. Somigli, *Etiopia francescana nei documenti dei secoli XVII e XVIII*, 2 vols (1928-48); G. Van Winsen, "L'Eglise Catholique en Ethiopie," *Nouvelle revue des sciences missiologiques* 21 (1965), pp. 118-31; F. Heyer, *Die Kirche Äthiopiens* (1971); M. Singleton, *Ethiopia Tikdem—Ethiopia First: The Shades of Things Past and the Shape of Things to come for Roman Catholic Christianity in Southern Ethiopia* (1977).

BB Edward Bamber, John Woodcock, and Thomas Whitaker, *Martyrs* (1646)

Edward Bamber, also known under the assumed name Reding or Reading, was born at his family's ancient manor house, The Moor, Poulton-le-Fylde, Lancashire. He studied at the English College at Valladolid or at Douai, was ordained priest, and sent on the English mission. He was immediately detected by the governor of Dover Castle and banished but then returned to England. He was noted for zeal and courage in pastoral work and in instructing and disputing with non-Catholics in the very difficult Civil War period. He was arrested and escaped imprisonment twice before his final capture and three years in gaol in Lancaster Castle. He is said to have made one escape dressed only in a shirt while his gaolers were drunk—but one source attributes this feat and other events to Whitaker. Two former Catholics appeared as witnesses against Bamber by confirming that he had administered Baptism and performed marriages and was thus a priest. While being drawn to the place of execution, he is said to have converted and publicly absolved a felon named Croft. On the scaffold he threw a handful of money among the people, saying with a smile, "God loves a cheerful giver." He was hanged only a short time and butchered while still alive. He died aged forty-six.

John Woodcock, O.F.M. (alias John Farringdon and Thompson, and in religion Fr Martin of St Felix), was born at Clayton-le-Woods, near Preston, Lancashire, in 1603. His father was an Anglican and his mother a Catholic. He studied at St Omer and at the English College in Rome. He joined the English Franciscans at Douai and was clothed there in 1631. For some time he lived as a chaplain and confessor to a Mr Sheldon at Arras. He became a zealous worker on the English mission for many years but suffered from continual sickness and eventually retired to the convent at Douai. On hearing a French Capuchin's sermon on martyrdom he asked leave to return to England. He was arrested the first night after arriving in Lancashire and was gaoled for two years in Lancaster Castle. At his trial in August 1646 he freely confessed he was a Franciscan and praised God for his sentence for high treason. The sheriff interrupted him when he tried to address the people before his execution. He was half-hanged and butchered while alive. He died aged forty-four.

Thomas Whitaker was a secular priest born at Burnley, Lancashire. His father was a free-school master. A neighbouring Catholic family paid for him to study abroad and at the English College at Valladolid, where he was ordained priest, and he was sent on the English mission in 1638. He laboured for five years before imprisonment at Lancaster. He escaped through a window while stripped to his shirt (though see above, under Bamber) and was eventually rescued by a Catholic whose whereabouts in a nearby field were revealed to him in an opportune dream while resting from exhaustion. He was arrested again in 1643 by a gang of priest-catchers who clubbed him. He spent six weeks of his three years' gaol in solitary confinement. As the youngest priest in the gaol he helped the sick and aged among his fellow-prisoners. He refused a pardon and died, after encouragement from Bamber, aged thirty-three.

Bamber, Woodcock, and Whitaker were hanged, drawn, and quartered at Lancaster on 7 August 1646. They were beatified by Pope John Paul II on 22 November 1987.

See *M.M.P.*, pp. 481-9; Gillow, 1, pp. 120-2.

Bd Nicholas Postgate, *Martyr* (*c.* 1597-1679)

Nicholas Postgate (or Posket) was a secular priest. He was born at Kirkdale House, Egton (Eyton) Bridge, Yorkshire, about 1597. Both his parents were staunch Catholics. He went to Douai on 11 July 1621, studied at the English College under the alias of Whitmore, and was ordained priest in 1628. He was sent on the English mission on 29 June 1630. He worked diligently in Yorkshire for some fifty years. He lived with the Hungates at Saxton, became chaplain to Lady Dunbar, and served the seats of the Saltmarsh and Meynell families and others. He also lived on Blackamoor, five miles from Whitby. He was said to have brought about the conversion of almost a thousand people. He was betrayed for a £20 reward by an excise-man (who is said never to have received it) at the house of one Matthew Lythis, with whom he was gaoled at York. He was examined by Sir William Calley, who left a detailed account:

> Nicholas Postgate, about the age of fourscore years saith that about 40 years since he lived at Saxton with the lady Hungate until she died. And since he hath lived with the old lady Dunbar but how long it is since he knoweth not. Of late he hath had no certain residence but hath travelled about among his friends. Being demanded whether he be a popish priest or no he saith "Let them prove it" and would give no other direct answer. Being demanded how he came by and what use he made of the books, wafers and other things that were found with him, and which he owned, he saith that some of them were given him by Mr Goodrick, a roman catholic, and some by one Mr Jowsey, a supposed romish priest, both of which are dead. . . . Being demanded why he named himself at the first Watson [another alias he used], he saith that he hath been sometimes so called, his grandfather on his father's side being so called and he being like that kindred.

He died at York in his eightieth year, and his quartered body was given to his friends and buried. One of his hands is said to be preserved at Douai College. Nicholas Postgate was beatified by Pope John Paul II on 22 November 1987.

See Gillow, 5, pp. 347-8.

R.M.
St Donation, bishop, at Châlons-sur-Marne, France (fourth century)
St Hypersechius, monk in Egypt (forth century)
Bd Jordan Fozaté, abbot of Santa Justina, Padua (*c.* 1248)
St Conrad Nantwein, pilgrim, unjustly condemned to death (*c.* 1280)
St Albert of Ancona, Camaldolese monk (1350)
Bd Vincent of Aquila, Franciscan lay brother (1504)

ST DOMINIC (facing page)
In a pun on his name, the Dominicans became known as "watchdogs of the Lord" (Domini canes). Gray dog, brown torch, red flames with white tips, on black and white field.

8

ST DOMINIC, *Founder* (*c.* 1170–1221)

Dominic, founder of the Order of Preachers, or Black Friars, left no writings. Narratives are based on tradition and evidence from variously reliable sources. Many fascinating legends and works of art but also the ascription to him of others' reasons and actions have produced pseudo-Dominics with their own valuable histories. Much is now known about the extraordinary early growth of his Order, yet in some way Dominic is a vague figure, for his exact motives, loyalties, attitudes, and conduct, especially with regard to conversion and to the ideal of poverty and the need for mendicancy, remain uncertain. Recent accounts insist that he must be seen not alone but as part of a larger whole of groups and individuals. Some of these, by precept and example, inspired; whereas others were affected by his wish to spread enlightenment both intellectual and spiritual. From all this a consistent image emerges of an essentially loving man increasingly determined to realize his vision throughout Christendom and beyond. When asked which books he had read most often, he replied: "I have studied the book of charity more than any other, for it teaches us all things."

Dominic was born soon after 1170 at Caleruega, then Calaroga, in Old Castile, Spain, not far from the Benedictine abbey of (St) Dominic of Silos (20 Dec.), after whom he may have been named. His father, Felix, warden of the town, possibly belonged to the Guzmán family; his mother was Bd Joan of Aza (2 Aug.).

Dominic's parents wanted him to dedicate his life to the Church. He was suitably devout and is said to have slept on the ground when a child. He was about fourteen when he left the care of his uncle, archpriest of Gumiel d'Izan, to enter Palencia University, where he specialized in theology. He was a hardworking though far from melancholy student. Unusually, he owned his books. He sold these and other things to help the needy during a severe famine in Palencia. Others followed his example. Partly because of this, while still a student he was made a canon of Osma Cathedral (*c.* 1197) by the reforming bishop Martin of Osma, or by the prior, and after ordination took up his duties there with enthusiasm. The reformed chapter lived a community life under the Rule of St Augustine. Dominic spent much time in study, public worship, and private prayer through many of the night hours. He was sacristan by 1199 and subprior by the end of 1200. When Diego de Azevedo was made bishop of Osma on 27 July 1201, Dominic became his friend and succeeded him as prior of the chapter.

In late 1203 Alfonso VIII, king of Castile, sent Diego to the north of Germany, or to Denmark, to negotiate a marriage for his son. Diego took Dominic with him on what proved a successful venture. Two years later they returned to complete the arrangements, but the prince's future wife had decided to become a nun. On both occasions they passed through the Languedoc, in southern France, where Cathar (*Cathari*=perfect ones), or Albigensian, heretics were strong. They stayed in a Cathar's house at Toulouse. Dominic is said to have spent the night disputing with him and the man to have abjured his errors at morning light. After their second embassy Diego and Dominic (with a lifelong passion to convert non-Christians) went to Rome to ask Pope Innocent III's permission to preach the gospel to the pagan Cumans (probably in Hungary), for in 1203 they had seen the destruction caused by Cuman mercenaries in German lands. Diego wanted to resign his see. The pope asked them instead to use their zeal against heresy in the West. He was not unsympathetic to more orthodox evangelical movements but determined to fight heresy and any "alternative" church. In around 1140 St Bernard (20 Aug.) and the Cistercians had conducted an unsuccessful mission against the heretics in southern France. At the end of May 1204 the pope appointed three pontifical legates for a new campaign under the abbot of Cîteaux. Since heresy was a crime, they were not only to preach but to hand over heretics to the secular power for banishment and confiscation of property. One legate, Bd Peter of Castelnau (15 Jan.), earnestly approved of this aspect of their work and was feared and hated in the south. Yet the authorities were often reluctant to cooperate, and the local clergy were ineffectual. In spring 1206 the legates met in Montpellier to decide whether to abandon the mission. On their way back Dominic and Diego visited Cîteaux, for Diego wanted the Cistercians to make a foundation in his diocese. They also passed through Montpellier, where they met the legates, who asked Diego for advice. He soon realized why orthodoxy had failed.

The origins of the Catharism that had spread in France since the beginning of the eleventh century are much disputed. An amalgam of pre-Christian and Christian elements, it offered revelation and salvation, appealed to the New but shunned the Old Testament, and claimed to practise the ascetic purity of the early Church. "Catharism or Albigensianism was a Christian heresy: there is no doubt on this point at least. Its supporters considered and proclaimed themselves 'true Christians'" (E. Le Roy Ladurie). It was a minimally intellectual but consistent culture identified with regional aspirations and vernaculars. Popular knowledge of the Catholic faith was neither profound nor widespread; it was identified with the alien, oppressive power of the north. Catharism also won adherents because influential supporters controlled certain areas. It was organized in communities with travelling ministers compelled to earn a living. Its main attractions were a simple if inflexible system of thought, demanding yet eventually self-limiting ascetic conduct, a social practice adapted to specific groups, an opportunity for all to achieve the highest status in this life, and on death redemption from an illusory world. Roughly summarized, it was based on a belief in two opposing principles, good and evil. God allowed the evil power to sustain matter as a deceptive emanation. Generally, however, this amounted to a Manichaean opposition between two gods with power over their own realms. In effect, this was no different from the "more or less conscious, more or less summary Manichaeism of God on the one hand and the Devil on the other that dominated the mind and conduct" of the general run of medieval humanity, Catholics and heretics alike (J. Le Goff). The Bible was interpreted allegorically. Christ was an angel and never participated in an evil world. Hell, purgatory, the resurrection of the body, and the Catholic sacraments were rejected (though bread was blessed at meals). The "Perfect" received the unique sacrament (the *consolamentum,* or imposition of hands, administered to ordinary believers in danger of death). For this inner circle, attainable human perfection demanded a very restrained diet and abstinence from sex. Rank-and-file Cathars admired those leading a more austere life than that of the local clergy and of such outsiders as the missioners. The ascetic behaviour of other, much smaller dissident groups of orthodox believers also impressed the populace. Even a reasonable use of material things by the missioners seemed inappropriate in the circumstances. Although Diego saw the intellectual poverty of Catharism and the dangers of its pessimistic view of creation, he acknowledged its followers' sincerity. He advised the legates to imitate their rivals by abandoning legally required, even sensibly cautious travel with horses and retinues, and the use of good inns. They should walk, have no money, and beg for food and other necessities. We do not know what Dominic thought, but his attitude on other occasions suggests that he also approved of the association of preaching with radical poverty and of peaceful discussion, not threats. This seems to have been his own method, though we cannot know how he dealt with the loyalties of virtually another nation, with those who rejected his teaching, or with relapsed converts.

The papal legates agreed to try the austere way. They asked Diego to supervise them. He dismissed his retinue, kept only Dominic, and became a poor preacher. After a trial period only one legate, Raoul, stayed with Diego and Dominic. Conferences with the Cathars influenced some ordinary people, especially at Servian, where the authorities had to protect the heretics, but had little effect on the leaders. There were discouraging experiences at Béziers and Carcassonne. Soon Diego had to go back to Osma, but he eventually returned with a few clerics. Some considerable successes demanded well-founded, long-drawn-out argument. The Cistercian general chapter approved the campaign. In November 1206 the pope gave Raoul the right to choose volunteer preachers from among monks anxious to join the mission. Diego saw the importance of women in propagating Catharism, for it offered them functions and a status as "Perfects" unobtainable in Catholicism, and many girls were educated in Cathar convents, sometimes out of poverty or the lack of an alternative. With a ruined church as the base, he founded and funded a monastery for women volunteers at Prouille, near the Cathar centre of Fanjeaux. Nearby was a house for his helpers. Nine convert nuns joined the community. When Diego departed for Spain in early 1207, he left Dominic in charge of a small but recognized centre where he could train preachers, educate some girls, house some converts, and maintain a permanent house of prayer. In 1211 nineteen convert nuns were still living in the house. After Dominic's death the number had risen to fifty.

In April 1207 Diego returned for a major two-week debate with the Cathars at Montréal, near Carcassonne. Dominic provided one of the main written depositions. The Catholic party is said to have proved superior and to have made fifty converts. Soon afterwards twelve Cistercian priests and some monks arrived under Abbot Arnaud, who took charge of the campaign, which proved unsuccessful. Diego returned to Osma, and Raoul died in July. Before the year's end most of the Cistercians had retired, leaving Dominic and a few others to continue the mission. Diego returned and suggested the use of a band of full-time preachers. He also took part in a major debate not only with Cathars but with dissident Catholics led by Durand of Osca (who later submitted to the pope and obtained permission for his party to lead an apostolic life, from which they became known as the "Poor Catholics").

In November 1207 Innocent III wrote to the French king asking him to quell the obdurate heretics. Diego died on 30 December and Dominic remained effectively in charge of preaching. In 1208 a servant of the Cathar count of Toulouse, Raymund VI, assassinated the papal legate, Peter of Castelnau. This and other actions not only invited the usual harsh punishment but in July 1209 prompted a savage crusade against the Cathars led by Simon IV de Montfort, *de iure* Earl of Leicester. Motivated mainly by royal territorial ambitions and by ecclesiastical centralism, it became a civil war in which "Christian" forces tortured and massacred opponents declared heretics by the Church. At Minerve in 1210 Abbot Arnaud of Cîteaux shocked the crusaders when he insisted on giving the few heretics prepared to convert the chance of escaping the flames. The Cathars, led by the count of Toulouse, reacted accordingly. Toulouse was besieged in 1211 (Dominic was there with Simon de Montfort) and fell in 1214. Dominic continued to preach when possible. He was associated with the orthodox forces, operated from their fortresses, and became a close friend of Simon de Montfort, who funded the preachers and the Prouille establishment. In 1213-14 Dominic was vicar general to the bishop of Carcassonne when he preached the crusade in the north. At Easter 1214 Dominic moved to Fanjeaux, where he was helped by Bishop Fulk. There is no indication that Dominic took part in the crusade itself.

Tradition presents Dominic as a man of unusual integrity in an age when integrity seemed to demand brutal intolerance. He thought heresy was obnoxious, for it obscured the fullness of revelation and barred essential means of access to grace. Heretics had to be shown the truth and saved. Yet he seems never to have agreed to the execution of anyone for his or her faith. He is said to have rebuked his ex-troubadour supporter, Fulk, bishop of Toulouse, when he went on a visitation with soldiers, servants, and supply mules: "You cannot defeat the enemies of the faith like that. Arm yourself with prayer, not a sword. Wear humility, not fine clothes!"

Dominic is said to have followed Diego's example, to have preached tactfully, and to have travelled, eaten, slept, and prayed so rigorously that Cathars were ready to hear his message. Like Diego, he is said to have found military force an improper and ineffective means of imposing orthodoxy. A heretic whom he saved from execution is said to have recalled Dominic's sympathetic method when he become a Dominican twenty-five years later. Nevertheless, Dominic was severe with converts, as with a Perfect who was reconciled only after being whipped along the roadway for three feast-days and on condition that he follow a lifelong régime in conformity with his Cathar austerity. Eventually, however, he returned to Catharism. An unknown number of converts relapsed, as some testified at the Inquisitions of the 1240s. The superior authorities found Dominic's earnest approach slow-acting and embarrassing. Obviously, Dominic had nothing to do with the establishment, from 1233, of Inquisitions in conjunction with the civil authorities leading to the burning, life-imprisonment, or forced collaboration of men and women. (The Dominicans unwillingly received charge of the Inquisitions, which they conducted effectively. In 1243 they unsuccessfully petitioned Pope Innocent IV to be relieved of the duty.)

Three times Dominic was invited to become a bishop. He always refused. He had spent ten years preaching in Languedoc as leader, without canonical status, of a small band of special preachers, beginning his special contribution to a process of religious instruction from the highest social levels downward, now seen as essential to the internalization of piety throughout thirteenth-century Christian society. His long acquaintance with the Cathar way of life probably influenced his conception of a religious Order. He wore the habit of a regular Augustinian canon and followed that Rule. He now planned to form a body of men who would supplement contemplation with sacred studies and pastoral functions, especially preaching. In late 1214 or early 1215 the new papal legate made him head of the preaching mission with headquarters in Toulouse. Fulk wanted to found a permanent Institute of preachers in the diocese. One candidate gave Dominic a house in the town. Alexander of Stavensby, at the cathedral school, taught the preachers theology. Fulk provided another house for women converts and attendant Brothers. In 1215 the embryonic though not formal Order received an episcopal charter. A few months later Dominic accompanied Fulk to the Fourth Lateran Council, called for November 1215.

One of the council's emphases was on heresy and preaching. Fulk and Dominic went to Rome in October to stress the need for something more effective than a diocesan Institute of preaching. Innocent III drew up a decree, the tenth canon of the council, to enforce the obligation of preaching by bishops and priests and the choice of pastors effective in example and preaching. Yet the same council forbade the multiplication of new religious Orders. Nevertheless, the pope wanted duly-constituted apostolic foundations to reduce heresy and ignorance outside southern France too. At last he gave word-of-mouth approval and asked Dominic to decide on an appropriate Rule for a religious Order. The Brothers met at Prouille some time in 1216 and chose the Rule of St Augustine. Dominic added some Constitutions, including borrowings from the Cistercian-inspired and less flexible Order of Prémontré. A missing second volume on the preachers' way of life was not supplied until the second general chapter. In general, the right method would be established empirically. The cathedral chapter gave Dominic formal possession of Saint-Romain's church. He was prior and master but no longer canon of Osma. The first Dominican community began its common life under vows at Toulouse. In the same year Bertrand de Garrigues was chosen as superior of the monastery. Dominic remained in charge of preaching.

Innocent III died on 18 July 1216. Dominic left for Rome after the beginning of October. In December a Bull from Pope Honorius III confirmed the new Order's papal protection. In January 1217 the first of several Bulls on the new foundation invited theologians from Paris to teach at Toulouse. Another confirmed the Brothers of Saint-Romain as "preachers on the territory of Toulouse" and thus their official function as preachers of the word. Yet another allowed them to leave the monastery without the prior's permission. Dominic stayed in Rome until perhaps the end of March, cultivating friendships with Cardinal Ugolino (later Pope Gregory IX) and possibly even with Francis of Assisi (4 Oct.). He also met a young cleric, William of Montferrat, who was to study theology in Paris before leaving with Dominic for a mission among Prussian and other northern non-Christians.

Simon de Montfort had been recognized as the new count of Toulouse. In 1216 his position was weak, for Catharism was regaining ground in the area. It seemed that Count Raymund would retake the town with the support of many citizens. Dominic was afraid of the risks for a higher teaching faculty and proposed to disperse the Brothers. On 15 August 1217 the Friars Preachers met, probably at Prouille. Dominic sent the friars in many directions. Four were despatched to Spain and seven in two groups to Paris, which could be a centre of advanced studies if Toulouse was threatened. Two returned to Toulouse; two stayed at Prouille. There was some dissension when it became clear that Dominic's insistence on a mendicant life did not fit the style demanded of canons travelling outside their own diocese. He also had to settle an argument about an increased share for the Dominicans of the diocesan allotment for the poor. Count Raymund was soon enthusiastically received in the city, even—

out of patriotism—by Catholics. On 1 October Simon de Montfort besieged Toulouse. The following December Dominic met him there, then left for Rome. He obtained copies of the first of a new series of Bulls recommending the Brothers of the Order of Preachers. This gave them a universal status.

In early 1218, after good reports from Paris, Dominic secured a papal letter prompting the university to assign a property to the Brothers. In March Dominicans from Spain reported Simon de Montfort's inability to take Toulouse, and the continuing threat to the official house there. Dominic asked the pope to reconfirm Prouille's status. Four Brothers had been sent to Bologna; the two Spaniards went to join them. A famous Dominican house was established there under Bd Reginald of Orleans (17 Feb.). The university towns of Paris and Bologna were to be key bases for the Order's development.

In mid-April Dominic heard that Saint-Romain was almost deserted. With a small group he headed for southern France through Catalonia. In August the Paris Dominicans were provisionally accorded a church and a building for their monastery. Dominic recalled Bertrand de Garrigues from Paris to the south, where Simon de Montfort's son had abandoned the siege a month after his father's death, and the monastery could start anew. A foundation was made later at Lyons. In the meantime Dominic made for Spain, where he established a house under his brother Bd Mannes (30 July) at Madrid and another at Segovia.

The old problem of incompatible life styles arose in Paris, where the community had to obey the laws governing canons regular and had found a source for the money and horses they needed when travelling. Dominic did not approve of this. He was unsuccessful in his plan to ensure that lay brothers saw to temporal affairs so that clerics could concentrate on preaching and study.

Dominic eventually crossed the Alps on foot (his usual practice). Possibly at the end of summer 1219 he arrived in Bologna and met many of the Brothers for the first time. The town became his ordinary residence until the end of his life. The major community with its own church there had established houses in Milan, Bergamo, and possibly Florence. Within a year or so there were others at Verona, Piacenza, and Brescia. The developing international scope of the Order was evident from the profession of three Scandinavian students and a Hungarian teacher. This rekindled Dominic's urge to preach to non-Christians, especially the Cumans. In the meantime, acquisition of the church at Bologna had proved difficult. It required the permission of the bishop and the lay proprietor. Diana d'Andalo, the latter's grand-daughter, was impressed by the friars' preaching and persuaded him to surrender the church to the Dominicans and to sell them the adjoining land. She told Dominic she wanted to see a women's Order associated with his and made her profession to him without more ado. Dominic asked a commission of friars to discuss the founding of an Order of nuns as a matter of urgency. The bishop's refusal to approve a site delayed the project. However, a rich man had presented a valuable property to the friars, but this represented an income and Dominic had the contract destroyed. Reginald, a major influence on the growth of the Bologna community, was sent to Paris to encourage development there; his preaching brought Bd Jordan of Saxony (15 Feb.), Dominic's eventual sucessor as master into the Order.

Toward the end of 1219 Dominic and William visited the pope in Viterbo to obtain Bulls of recommendation. Two were sent to the Church in Spain and Italy. The pope told Dominic of the restored church of St Sixtus in Rome and his inherited plan to establish nearby a new reformed monastery for nuns. The Gilbertines seemed to have abandoned the project and Dominic was given St Sixtus. He selected the few with authentic vocations from dispersed groups of nuns in the city, many of whom led what amounted to a secular life, imposed a strictly enclosed Rule, and gave them St Sixtus. Almost all the nuns from the poverty-stricken Santa Maria in Tempulo joined the new reformed house, but the community was very small. In December 1219 in a new Bull the pope effectively revised the tenth canon of the Fourth Lateran Council by characterizing the ministry of the Order as "necessary." Now bishops were called on to cooperate with the Dominicans, acknowledged to be a mendicant Order dependent on charity. Dominic sent copies of the Bull to Bologna and to Paris to convince the friars there of the Order's essential commitment.

In 1220 Honorius confirmed Dominic as master general, and the first general chapter was held at Pentecost. Dominic asked to be relieved of his direction of the Order. The friars refused, but Dominic insisted that the chapter as a body, not he, should make the essential decisions. Reluctantly, he accepted the title of Master for the head of the Order. The final Constitution was drawn up for a religious Order in the modern sense, in which the Order and not the house is the unit and all members are subject to one superior general. The Order's commitment to begging was confirmed. The first part of the 1216 laws governing its way of life now applied only when the Dominicans were in their monasteries, not when they were travelling. A new flexibility allowed superiors to dispense friars from observances that might frustrate the aims of pastoral work, preaching, conversion, scholarship, and so on. A new section on the duties of the novice-master was added to the Constitution: he was to encourage not just study but the permeation of the friars' lives at all times by what they read. Temporary superiors and "peripatetic" friars could be sent from house to house and could preach anywhere without consultation. Their presence in universities became an essential aspect of Dominican life. The basic element of the Order was a duly-constituted group of at least twelve Dominicans, not necessarily already possessing a house or church but with a prior and master, ensuring the instruction of novices and local clergy and effective preaching to the laity.

Dominic preached wherever he travelled and stressed the ministry of the word above all other methods. His friars had to prepare by prayer, humility, self-denial, and obedience for a vocation that was educational in two senses: their houses were to be centres of learning and inquiry, and in all personal encounters they were to "hand on to others the fruits of contemplation." A favourite saying of Dominic's was: "Whoever governs the passions is master of the world. We must either rule them, or be ruled by them. It is better to be the hammer than the anvil." He taught his missionaries to address the heart, though learning, biblical studies, and teaching were always of prime importance and the emphasis was on intellectual, not manual, labour. The Dominicans were to exist by begging and to own only their monasteries and churches. Dominic himself maintained this discipline inflexibly (Pope Sixtus IV revoked the rule of corporate poverty in 1475).

After the chapter Dominic went to Milan, a centre of heresy, where he fell ill. When he returned to Bologna in 1220 he found the friars' convent being built in what he thought was a stately way, inconsistent with poverty. He stopped the work (which was resumed after his death). In fact, the roof level had been raised to give the friars more room in their cells. Dominic was overjoyed when Diana d'Andalo took the habit at Ronzano monastery, then saddened to hear that she had been captured and was sick and a prisoner in her father's house. Dominic managed to correspond with her clandestinely.

In Rome, toward the end of 1220, Dominic asked the pope for Bulls of recommendation to help establish the Order in, for example, Catalonia. In February 1221 he went to Santa Maria in Tempulo, where the would-be nuns had been dissuaded from their vocation. Dominic persuaded at least some of them to return, and St Sixtus was opened before the end of the month with nuns from Prouille strengthening the community. For his friars he accepted Honorius' gift of a house of the Savelli, on the Aventine, with the church of St Sabina, and left only a few Brothers at St Sixtus, which he inspected regularly. After a month in Rome he obtained another Bull addressed to all prelates of the Church. This would enable him to share in the great work of converting those outside the Christian world. In April Bishop Fulk of Toulouse arrived in Rome and presented the Order with the church of Fanjeaux. In May Dominic obtained another Bull recommending the Dominicans to King Waldemar of Denmark as preachers and as missionaries to non-Christians in Livonia, a project that he probably intended to oversee himself. In the event, the Danish Brother Salomon was sent, with a personal letter to Archbishop Sunesen, to put the Order on a sound footing in Scandinavia.

Expansion was the main topic at the second general chapter in Bologna in June 1221. The Order's growth had been centred on major houses, such as Bologna, Paris, and Toulouse. Dominic had taken change of the work in Italy; otherwise priors were responsible for "dependent" territories. The same system began to operate in Italy. Soon the Order had some sixty friaries divided into eight provinces. Friars were in Poland, Scandinavia, Germany, Hungary, Palestine, and Morocco; and the conversion of the Cumans, Muslims, and others was a major aim. Brother Gilbert with twelve others founded houses in Canterbury, London, and Oxford. Within a few centuries the Order's missions and houses were to spread across Asia and South and North America.

After the second general chapter Dominic visited Trevisa, going on to see Cardinal Ugolino in Venice. He left some friars there to start a new foundation and went back to Bologna with the new prior, Ventura. Dominic was tired from the heat and the journey but insisted on working. He prayed through the night. The next day he was very sick and was put to bed. He made a general Confession, saying that he had always been celibate yet preferred to talk to young women rather than listen to old ones. To escape the heat he was taken to the country to the church of St Mary in the Hills, but he knew he was dying: "My dear sons, these are my bequests: practise charity in common; remain humble; stay poor willingly." He was about fifty-two when, on the evening of 6 August 1221, after a last sermon to the prior and twenty friars, he was taken to the monastery. He told the friars round his bed that he would be more useful after his death than living, asked them to pray for him, and died in the poverty of which he had recently spoken "in Brother Moneta's bed because he had none of his own; in Brother Moneta's habit, because he had no other to replace the one he had worn for so long." As Bd Jordan of Saxony wrote in Dominic's lifetime: "Nothing disturbed his equanimity except a lively sympathy with any suffering. A person's face shows whether he or she is really happy. Dominic's was friendly and joyful. You could easily see his inward peace."

After his death Dominic's brethren, attentive to the saint's prayers and the work he had inspired rather than to any cult, paid no great attention to his relics. The tomb they constructed was not grand. It was left in the open when work started on a new church at Bologna in 1228. Pope Gregory IX authorized the solemn translation of Dominic's body to the new church only in 1233, when the saint's cult was gathering strength. In 1234 the pope signed the decree of canonization for his friend, called him a "man of the gospel in the footsteps of his Redeemer," and said that he no more doubted the sanctity of Dominic than that of St Peter or St Paul. Dominic's brother Bd Mannes founded a church in the saint's honour in the house of his birth. The best monument to Dominic is the work today of some 6,600 friars in 51 provinces, 38,000 contemplative and apostolic nuns in 150 congregations, 4,400 enclosed nuns in 250 monasteries, and 70,000 lay members in seventy fraternities. His Order has produced countless superlative preachers, missionaries, adminstrators, and scholars and many saints and restless spirits with something of Dominic's relentless determination. It produced the great philosopher Thomas Aquinas (28 Jan.) but also Torquemada, the Grand Inquisitor, and the ascetic reformer Savanarola, who was burned at the stake.

Popular devotion to Dominic soon spread, and many tales were composed about his childhood and supposed miracles. He did not invent the use of the rosary, with which he has been credited. The origins of the practice are lost to us. Perhaps it came to Christianity by way of Islam. Alan de Rupe, a fifteenth-century Dominican, founded a confraternity of Our Lady and St Dominic at Douai, France, and made saying the rosary a condition of membership, as did Jacon Weyts, prior of the friary at Haarlem, in the Netherlands (where the first Confraternity of the Rosary there was started in 1478), and the Dominican prior of Cologne, Jacob Sprenger, who established one at Rome (with the special attraction of indulgences from Pope Sixtus IV to all who used the devotion). Within a few years hundreds of similar confraternities strengthened the rosary's association with the Order. The Dominican pope, St Pius V (30 Apr.), established the feast of the Holy Rosary to commemorate its supposed significance in the battle of Lepanto (1570).

There is much relatively early biographical material, beginning with the Life by Bd Jordan of Saxony. For the more important elements, see *AA.SS.*, Aug., 1; *Scriptores O.P.*, by Quétif and Echard; M. H. Laurent (ed.), *Monumenta O.F.P. Historica*, 15 and 16 (1933-5); F. Balme and P. Lelaidier, *Cartulaire ou histoire diplomatique de St Dominique* (3 vols., 1893-1901); M. H. Vicaire, *Saint Dominique de Caleruega d'après les documents du XIIIe siècle* (1955; Eng. trans, 1964; 2d ed. as *Saint Dominique, La Vie Apostolique*, 1965); and *Saint Dominique et ses frères. Evangile ou croisade?* (1967); E. C. Lehner, *Saint Dominic: Biographical Documents* (1964). Still useful but, like the foregoing, requiring correction in terms of more recent research is P. Mandonnet and M. H. Vicaire, *S. Dominique, l'idée, l'homme et l'oeuvre* (2 vols., 1937-8), with an English abridgement of the biography in vol. 1 (1944). Other Lives in English are B. Jarrett (1924), V. J. Koudelka, *St Dominic* (1997); in German, B. Altaner (1922) and H. C. Scheeben (1927); and in French, Lacordaire (1840), H. Petitot (1925), M. S. Gillet (1942); and, incorporating major findings in an easy narrative, S. Tugwell, O.P. (1996). See also Jedin-Dolan, 4, pp. 173-7; *H.S.S.C*, 6, pp. 112-23.

See also A. Mortier, *Histoire des maîtres généraux O.P.*, 1; G. R. Galbraith, *The Constitution of the Dominican Order*, 1216-1360 (1925); and for recent research, S. Tugwell, in *Archivum Fratrum Praedicatorum* 65 (1995), 66 (1996), other articles forthcoming; G. Kaftal, *St Dominic in Early Tuscan Painting* (1948); W. A. Hinnebusch, *The History of the Dominican Order* (1966); *idem.*, "Dominican Spirituality" in *N.C.E.*, 4 (1967), pp. 971-82; *La Prière au Moyen Age*, Sénéfiance series 10 (1981); H. van Os, *The Art of Devotion in the Late Middle Ages in Europe, 1300-1500* (1995); *H.C.S.*, 2, pp. 315-27.

On the Cathar period and Catharism see J. Le Goff, *La Civilisation de l'Occident Médiéval* (1965), pp. 169-248; *Saint Dominique en Languedoc*, intro. M. H. Vicaire (Cahiers de Fanjeaux, 1; 1966); W. A. Wakefield and A. P. Evans, *Heresies of the High Middle Ages* (1969); E. LeRoy Ladurie, *Montaillou, Village Occitan* (1975; abridged Eng. trans., 1982); J. Duvernoy, *La Religion des Cathares*, 1 (1976); M. Roquebert, *L'Epopée cathare*, 5 vols. (1979-95); A. Brenon, *Le Vrai Visage du Catharisme* (1989); M. Lambert, *Medieval Heresy* (2d ed., 1992).

From the Legend of the Rosary of St Dominic, after Geertgen tot Sint Jans (Leipzig, Germany, Museum der bildenden Künste), is among early paintings that associate the saint with the devotion, but the relative severity of this and similar works is less attractive than the early baroque simplicity of Dominic's portrayal in, say, Cerano's *The Virgin of the Rosary* in the Brera, Milan. There is a vast number of images of Dominic in Western art. He generally appears in the Dominican habit and may be shown with the rosary, a dog with a flaming torch in its mouth, a star on his forehead or on his halo (said to have appeared on his forehead during Baptism), a loaf of bread (a reference to an angelic miracle of supply when the monastery was out of food), a lily (for purity) or a book (for sacred learning), and any combination of these. Among the finest portraits showing him with lily and book are

Bellini's (1515; National Gallery, London) and the lovely *Tabernacle with St Dominic* by Cosimo Rosselli (1439-1507; Rijksmuseum, Amsterdam). Pisano's tomb at Bologna and Fra Angelico's paintings at Fiesole and Florence are among the best known of the vast number of works of art inspired by Dominic's actual and legendary life. An impressive fresco in the former library of S. Maria di Castello, Genoa, illustrates the relatively late legendary account of the meeting of SS Dominic and Francis. Cosimo Tura's fifteenth-century portrait in the Uffizi, Florence, is an unforgettably dramatic, almost sculptural interpretation of the ascetic, meditative Dominic. There is a wonderfully simple fifteenth-century marble statue at Caleruega. Guido Reni's sixteenth-century version of the saint (also in the Uffizi) is more realistic, yet here too his gaze and spirit are directed heavenwards. The late-seventeenth-century fresco ceiling, "The Apotheosis of St Dominic" by Domenico Maria Canuti and Enrico Haffner in the church of SS Dominic and Sixtus, Rome, portrays him in glory with a splendid late baroque exuberance and even extravagance that now seem inappropriate to Dominic's own precepts and show how far visual as well as written hagiography can depart from recorded fact. Though based on a legend, *St Dominic Resuscitating a Child* by Alessandro Tiarini (1612-3; S. Domenico, Bologna) celebrates Dominic's charity and commitment as well as his spiritual intensity. A dramatically effective painting by Hyacinthe Besson, O.P. (1815-61), in the chapter room of S. Sisto Vecchio, Rome, shows SS Peter and Paul appearing to Dominic.

SS Cyriacus, Largus, Smaragdus, and Companions,

Martyrs (? Early Fourth Century)

The *Depositio Martyrum* of 354 seems to show that Cyriacus was an authentic martyr, honoured in Rome on this day from an early date. He is said to be buried close beside the seventh milestone on the road to Ostia together with Largus, "Ixmaracdus," Crescentianus, Memmia (?), and Juliana. This Cyriacus has been confused with another, the founder of a place of worship, the *titulus Cyriaci*, and a romance about his life and sufferings under Maximian was evolved later. It is best known as an episode in the spurious Acts of Pope St Marcellus (16 Jan.).

See Delehaye in *C.M.H.*, pp. 190, 425, 431-3, and Duchesne in *Mélanges d'archéologie et d'histoire*, 36, pp. 49-56.

An early baroque southern German statue of Cyriacus in painted limewood (Landesmuseum, Stuttgart, Germany) shows him in a deacon's tunicle and with attendant angels.

St Altman, *Bishop* (1091)

Altman was born at Paderborn, Germany, in the first quarter of the eleventh century. He studied at Paris. After ordination he became canon and master of the cathedral school at Paderborn, then provost of the chapter at Aachen and chaplain to Emperor Henry III, and confessor and counsellor to the dowager empress Agnes. In 1064 he joined a pilgrimage to the Holy Land, which is said, improbably, to have numbered seven thousand persons. They were attacked by Saracens in Palestine and besieged in a deserted village. A friendly emir saved them from massacre. They reached Jerusalem but no other Holy Places; only half the pilgrims returned home.

On his return Altman became bishop of Passau and proved an energetic diocesan organizer. He founded an abbey of Augustinian canons at Göttweig, replaced secular canons with the same at Sankt Pölten, and introduced the Cluniac reform at Kremsmünster. In 1074 Pope St Gregory VII renewed the pontifical decrees against simony and married clergy. There was uproar when Altman read out the letter in his cathedral. His provost led the opposition to celibacy. The Augustinians supported Altman; the rebels sought the emperor's help. Altman excommunicated the provost and, when the pope forbade lay investiture, opposed Henry, was driven from his see, and fled to Rome. He had scruples about holding his see simoniacally, as he had obtained it by the empress Agnes' favour, but Gregory confirmed him in it and made him apostolic delegate for Germany.

Altman returned to his see in 1081 but was soon expelled. He spent the rest of his life in exile but retained influence in the eastern part of his diocese. Though without revenues he remained charitable to the poor and, during a famine, sold his furniture for the suffering. He was important in the early history of canons regular, whom he also instituted at Sankt Florian, at St Nicholas' in his cathedral city, and elsewhere. His cult was approved by Pope Leo XIII.

See *AA.SS.*, Aug., 1, for two Lives; the older (re-edited in *M.G.H., Scriptores*, 12, pp. 226-43) was written some fifty years after Altman's death by a canon of Göttweig; the second fills some gaps in the narrative toward the end. For an annotated German version of the first, see A. Fuchs, *Der heilige Altmann* (1929). See also H. Hirsch "Die Vita Altmanni" in *Jahrbuch für Landeskunde von Nieder-Österreich*, 15, 16, pp. 348-66; and A. Stonner, *Heilige der deutschen Frühzeit*, 2 (1935).

Bd John Felton, *Martyr* (1570)

On 25 February 1570 Pope St Pius V (30 Apr.) exercised a deposing power by then in fact a dead letter, and thus added to the already considerable difficulties of devout but loyal Catholics in England. As part of his ill-conceived encouragement of Philip of Spain to invade England and depose Elizabeth in favour of the imprisoned Mary, Queen of Scots, the Catholic claimant to the throne, he published the Bull *Regnans in excelsis* against Queen Elizabeth, ostensibly still a Catholic. He not only ignored the anti-Spanish feeling of most English Catholics but played into Cecil's hands by allowing the enactment in the next Parliament of new statutes with cruel penalties against Catholics. Pius declared Elizabeth excommunicate, deprived of her kingdom, and all her subjects discharged from their allegiance because she claimed headship of the Church in England, sheltered heretics, oppressed Catholics, and coerced her subjects into heresy and repudiation of the Holy See, contrary to her coronation oath. The Bull was published in some secrecy, and no Catholic monarch was notified directly of it. Nevertheless, it was posted in the Dutch seaports. The governor general of the Spanish Netherlands sent Roberto Ridolfi, a

Florentine banker resident in London, six printed copies. Next 25 May, on the feast of Corpus Christi, one of these appeared on the door of the bishop of London's house, by St Paul's Cathedral. It was possibly obtained from the Spanish ambassador's chaplain and had been put there late the previous night by John Felton, a Catholic gentleman with considerable property. He came from Norfolk but lived at Bermondsey Abbey, Southwark. His temper was said to be almost uncontrollable when the interests of his religion were at stake.

A copy of the Bull was found in the chambers of a well-known Catholic lawyer, who was arrested and racked. He confessed that Felton had given it to him. Felton was seized at Bermondsey when five hundred halberdiers surrounded his house early in the morning. He admitted the action and was imprisoned for three months. He was racked three times in the hope that he would confess to political intrigue with the Spaniards, with no result. He refused to implicate any accomplices, and when brought to trial at the Guildhall on 4 August he pleaded guilty to posting the Bull and asserted the supremacy of the Holy See. Four days later he was dragged to St Paul's churchyard. He overcame his initial fear at the scaffold, pointed at the bishop's door, and said: "The supreme pontiff's letters against the pretended queen were by me exhibited there. Now I am ready to die for the Catholic faith." Though he called the queen "the Pretender" on the scaffold, he sent her a valuable diamond ring from his finger as a token of good will, knelt, said the *Miserere*, and was hanged but cut down alive. As his heart was torn out his daughter heard him utter the name of Jesus twice. His valuable plate and jewels were seized for the queen's use.

Felton's action was foolhardy and increased the embarrassment of Catholics anxious to define their loyalties as nicely as possible. But it scarcely justified his execution, though this was also part of a programme of public warnings against plots and rebellion. That summer there was a big invasion scare when a great Spanish fleet was sent to Antwerp to escort Philip II's fourth bride. Yet even quite late that year, Elizabeth, though openly defiant, was secretly trying through Emperor Maximilian II to have the papal sentence reversed. In childhood Felton's wife had been a personal friend and companion of the queen, who after her husband's death licensed her to have a priest as chaplain in her house for her own use and that of her family for as long as she lived. Such inconsistencies betray the existence of much larger ironies and possible reversals of policy and allegiance. As ideological assurance fades and period antagonisms recede, it becomes clear that Felton was a victim in many different ways.

He was beatified by Pope Leo XIII's decree of 1886, ratifying the traditional English Catholic view that he was a martyr.

See the full account in *L.E.M.*, 2 (1905), pp. 1–13; cf. also the introduction, pp. xviii–xx; and see further J. H. Pollen in *The Month*, February 1902. On the Bull see P. Hughes, *The Reformation in England*, vol. 3 (1954), and C. Haigh, *English Deformations* (1993), pp. 257–61.

BB John Fingley and Robert Bickerdike, *Martyrs* (1586)

John Fingley (or Finglow) was a secular priest, the son of John and Elizabeth Fingley, born at Barmby-in-the-Marsh (or Barneby) in the East Riding of Yorkshire. He studied at Caius College, Cambridge, and earned his keep there by working as a butler. He went to the English College at Reims in 1580, was ordained priest on 25 March 1580, and sent on the English mission in April 1581. He worked zealously in Yorkshire and was arrested and imprisoned in York. A young recusant, Frances Webster, in the cell above his dark dungeon, opened a grating to let in some light. Fingley was condemned for high treason as a Roman priest and for reconciling the queen's subjects to Rome.

Robert Bickerdike (or Bickendike) was a gentleman born at Low Hall or near Knaresborough, Yorkshire, who lived in the city of York. He was arrested for being reconciled to Rome and for treasonable opinions. The magistrate asked him whether, if the pope or his agent, the king of Spain, should invade England he would take the queen's part or the pope's. He said that "if any such thing happened he would then do as God should put him in mind." He was found not guilty by one jury, but—at the judge's command—was re-tried by another and condemned.

Fingley and Bickerdike were hanged, drawn, and quartered at York in 1586 and beatified by Pope John Paul II on 22 November 1987.

See *M.M.P.*, pp.115-6, 120; Anstruther, 1, p. 117.

Bd Mary Margaret Caiani, *Foundress* (1863)

Mary Margaret, foundress of the Order of nuns known as the Institute of Franciscan Minims of the Sacred Heart, was born Maria Anna Rosa Caiani in Poggio a Caiano, near Florence, on 2 November 1863. From an early age she said that she wished to become a nun but for some years could not decide which Order best fitted her conception of the ideals of prayer and commitment to people in need, especially children, the sick, and the aged. Eventually she settled on the Sisters of St Maximus at Campi Bisenzio and entered the convent. It proved inadequate so she left, convinced that the only way to find a Sisterhood that was precisely what she wanted was to found one herself. In 1894, relying on her family's resources, she and two friends opened a school for neglected and abandoned children. On 15 December 1902 she established her community with five members, living a religious life in a house that was also a chapel dedicated to the Sacred Heart. She took the name Mary Margaret in memory of Margaret Mary Alacoque (16 Oct.). The Order grew and spread to Milan, Florence, Leghorn, Lodi, Arezzo, and Genoa. In October 1915 at the first general chapter she was elected superior of the Order. She founded twelve houses herself, and the Order now has some five hundred members in fifty-four houses with five missionary houses in Egypt, Israel, and Brazil. Bd Mary Margaret died in Florence on 8 August 1921. She was beatified by Pope John

Paul II on 23 April 1989. The pope singled out her unassuming dedication to the poor and unfortunate people of Tuscany, to unwanted children and wounded soldiers, and her ability to inspire the same commitment in the members of her Order.

C. Rijon, *La Madre Margherita Caiani* (1945); *Bibl.SS.*, Suppl. 1, 235-6.

Bd Mary MacKillop, *Foundress* (1842-1909)

Mary is Australia's first native-born blessed. Her parents were both Scottish, but they first met in Australia. Her father had been a seminarist in Rome and proved somewhat unreliable. Her mother's faults also tended to make their marriage unhappy, as witnessed by Mary herself. In 1860 she went to be a governess at Penola (South Australia), where she met Fr Julian Tenison Woods, a gifted and well-educated priest and geologist. He became her director and later co-founder of the Sisters of St Joseph of the Sacred Heart (Josephites), which it was Mary's principal life work to found and to rule. Mary had thought of joining one of the older Congregations, but Fr Woods, much concerned with the lack of education for Catholics in those pioneering days, encouraged her to meet this urgent need. The new Congregation obtained episcopal approval in 1868. Its purpose was to provide for schools, particularly for poor children, as well as for orphanages and other works of charity. Its early history was turbulent; there were repeated clashes with the local bishops including excommunications, depositions, and dispensations from vows, but Mother Mary won through. By 1981 her Sisters numbered as many as 1,790 in 289 convents in Australia, New Zealand, and Peru.

Mary had a better education than most girls in Australia then, partly through the influence of her father. This, together with her courage and perseverance, enabled her to become teacher and educator, social worker, and carer for the most unfortunate. In 1867 Fr Woods drew up the first Rule for the Sisters, and Mary made her profession the same year. In 1869 she took final vows and left for a foundation in Brisbane. The following years were critical. Some Australian bishops were in Rome for the First Vatican Council when troubles arose in Adelaide. Fr Woods had indiscreetly encouraged some visionaries among the Sisters, and several clergy wished him to be removed from his post of director of education because of his over-insistence on poverty and refusal of all state aid. In 1871 Bishop Sheil of Adelaide returned from Rome. Mary also went back to Adelaide, but Fr Woods left Adelaide permanently and in 1873 was removed from the direction of the Sisters.

By 1871 there were thirty-four schools and 127 Sisters in South Australia. The bishop wanted to keep everything concerning the Order in his own hands. He was now a very sick man who relied on others' advice—and also, it was said, on alcohol. He excommunicated Mary, supposedly for disobedience, and dispensed about fifty Sisters from their vows. The following year, mortally ill, he absolved the excommunicated and apologized for being misled by bad (clerical) advisers. He died in March 1872. The habits were restored to the Sisters, and the Holy See appointed a commission to investigate the state of the diocese with particular reference to this incident.

The three points at issue were the desirability of having a general superior, the unreal insistence on the Order owning no property (not even the motherhouse where novices could be trained), and Fr Woods' position as the spiritual director of the Order. In 1873 Mary went to Rome with an effective introduction. Cardinal Barnabo and later Pius IX received her kindly. The disputed questions were resolved by their approving the general superior's post and modifying the poverty rule. Like other teaching Sisters, they were encouraged to own (and not just rent) their own convents. The central government concept was approved in 1874, and at the general chapter of 1875 the Constitutions were accepted and Mary elected superior general. Meanwhile, she had travelled in England, Ireland, and Scotland seeking, with some success, both funds and postulants. At about this time education was becoming free, secular, and compulsory throughout Australia. In her efforts to provide a truly Catholic education for the children under her care, Mary obtained support from the new archbishops of Sydney, Vaughan and Moran, but bishops in Queensland and South Australia were again hostile.

These ecclesiastical disputes attracted much attention in spite of Mary's correct attitude. They should not obscure the excellent work of her Sisters, chronicled by contemporary journalists. Some Protestants especially appreciated the Sisters' social work in their hostels, homes, refuges, and orphanages. Those they helped were simply the poor, of all denominations or none. Their work was compared to that of the Salvation Army. When they begged for funds, donors were readily found, not least because the Sisters were unsalaried and their standard of comfort was poor. Their sincerity was impressive, and they offered excellent value for money to their supporters. Moreover, they did not try to proselytize the people they helped. Visitors could see for themselves how austere the living conditions of the Sisters were.

In 1885 there was more trouble. Bishop Reynolds of Adelaide was determined to regain diocesan control of the Sisters, even though Rome had decided otherwise. The Australian plenary council of bishops voted against central government for the Congregation, but in 1887 Rome excluded this decision from the approved decrees of the council. Once again the Holy See had supported the Institute but found that Mary's term of office had expired before her re-election, so a new superior general was appointed in her place. In 1888 the Holy See again approved the Josephite Sisters as a Regular Congregation with its motherhouse in Sydney. Diocesan Congregations were to be distinct, with alterations of habit. Mother Bernard was confirmed as general for ten years; meanwhile Mary became assistant to Mother Bernard and spent much of her time visiting the different houses of the Congregation in New South

Wales, Victoria, South Australia, and New Zealand. In 1898 Mother Bernard died, and Mary was again elected general almost unanimously. In 1905 she was elected yet again. She died on 8 August 1909 after a severe stroke and after suffering crippling rheumatism and other illnesses for many years. These problems, not to mention the more serious internal conflict and external differences with certain bishops, whose arrogance and high-handedness appear so blameworthy, gave her an opportunity to practise the heroic virtue recognized in her cause in 1973. She was beatified by Pope John Paul II in Australia in 1995. The beatification and other ceremonies were presented as celebrations for all Australians, not just the Catholic populace, and fittingly had a strong ecumencal flavour (to the extent, in fact, that intercommunion was widespread, as an administrative error led the invited guests from other churches to believe they were invited to receive Communion, which they did).

Some today see Mary as a feminist pioneer because of her courageous leadership and patient perseverance, particularly in the face of mistreatment at the hands of some of the local church hierarchy. Many photographs of her reveal an attractive face and penetrating eyes. Mary's only major written work was a biography of her co-founder Fr Woods, which Cardinal Moran would not allow published. About one thousand of her letters also survive, written in her own hand.

There are several Lives, the most authoritative by P. Gardiner, S.J. (1993); see also L. O'Brien, *Mary MacKillop Unveiled* (1994); D. Lyne, *Mary MacKillop: Spirituality and Charisms*. An annotated editon of Mary's biography of Fr Wooods has been published as *Julian Tenison Woods: A Life*, ed. Margaret Press, R.S.J. (1997). For an account of the Congregation's foundation see M. T. Foale, R.S.J., *The Josephite Story: Mary MacKillop and the Sisters of St Joseph 1866-1893* (1989).

Mary, a feature film docudrama of MacKillop's life, directed by Kay Pavlou, was produced in 1994.

R.M.

SS Secundus, Carpophorus, Victorinus, and Severianus, martyrs (? third century)

St Marinus of Tersoos in Cilicia, martyr, beheaded (*c*. 303-11)

St Eusebius, bishop of Milan (*c*. 462)

St Mummolus, abbot of Fleury-sur-Loire (678)

St Emilian, bishop of Cyzicus, on the island of Arctonnesus in the Hellespont (ninth century)

St Famian, O.Cist., hermit (*c*. 1150)

St Hugolina, recluse of Vercelli (*c*. 1300)

Bd Paul Keye-T'ing Chou, martyr in the Boxer uprising in China (1900)

St Romanus, *Martyr* (258)

According to the *Liber Pontificalis* Romanus was a door keeper of the Roman church who suffered martyrdom at the same time as St Laurence (10 Aug.). His unreliable Acts state that he was a soldier in Rome at the time of Laurence's martyrdom. He was said to have observed Laurence's joy and constancy and to have asked him to instruct and baptize him in prison. Romanus confessed what he had done and was arraigned, condemned, and beheaded the day before Laurence's execution. He was buried in the cemetery on the road to Tivoli, and seventh-century itineraries give that as the site of his grave.

Duchesne's note in his edition of the *Liber Pontificalis*, 1, p. 156, gives all available information; see also *C.M.H.*, p. 428.

SS Nathy and Felim, *Bishops* (? Sixth Century)

Though not associated with each other so far as is known, these two saints are celebrated throughout Ireland by a common feast on this day. St Felim (Fedlimid) was said to be the son of Dediva, a lady who was married four times and had several saints among her children, including Dermot, abbot of Inin Clothrann, half-brother to Felim. We have no particulars or even legends of St Felim, but he is traditionally venerated as the first bishop of Kilmore. He was possibly a regionary bishop in the Breffney country.

St Nathy (Nath Í) Cruimthir, that is, "the Priest," was a native of the Luighne district in Sligo and is mentioned in the very late life of St Attracta (9 Feb.), who was probably his contemporary. He is said to have been placed at Achonry by St Finnian of Clonard (12 Dec.) in the sixth century, though the name by which he was known makes it unlikely that he was a bishop.

No biography either in Latin or Irish seems to be available in either case. Nathy is commemorated under this day in the *Félire* of Oengus. See *L.I.S.*, 8.

Bd John of Salerno (*c.* 1242)

John Guarna was born at Salerno, Italy, about 1190. While studying at Bologna he met St Dominic and received the habit of the new Order. In 1219 thirteen friars were sent to preach in Etruria, and John, though the youngest, was made superior. They were given a house near Ripoli and visited the whole neighbourhood, especially Florence, where John preached in the streets. The community moved to San Pancrazio, adjoining the city walls.

John was known as a very perceptive confessor, and the legend offers in his favour a reasonably credible version of the age-old theme of the temptation of holy or eminent men by the ever-wily feminine—common to hagiography and to picaresque and other popular tales. The sources are lost to us, and they are most familiar in the reworked versions of such framework narratives as the *Arabian Nights* and the *Decameron*. In sacred versions the sage is triumphantly resistant; in secular narratives he succumbs. A woman infatuated with John pretended to be sick, went to bed, and sent for him to hear her Confession. When she tried to take advantage of the situation, he rebuked her, but with no result, so he left and prayed for her. Eventually she repented and apologized to him.

In 1221 John's community was turned out of the church where they had sung the divine office. He soon re-established them at Santa Maria Novella. Florence was affected at the time by a group called the Patarenes, by analogy with the members of the Pataria, the eleventh-century Milanese reform party, largely lay, partly clerical. The doctrine of the Patarenes of Milan was orthodox, though they were unjustly accused of heresy; they were certainly radically anti-authoritarian and dangerous to established church order yet to some extent favoured by the papacy. They had drawn on like-minded priests in Florence and the reform movement of St John Gualbert (12 July). By 1184, with the papal Bull against heresy, *Ad abolendam*, the term "Paterenes" applied to heretics, whether Speronists, Waldensians, or Cathars. The thirteenth-century Patarenes were in fact urban Cathars (for an account of Catharism, see St Dominic; 8 Aug.), often artisans and merchants but also wealthy people and aristocrats, inside and outside the walls of many Italian towns, who provided safe houses for the peddlers and other mobile Cathar Perfects. In John's lifetime Italy was a relatively safe refuge for Catharism. Many communes tolerated and even supported them for a mixture of social, anticlerical, and political reasons. The struggle between Emperor Frederick II and the popes guaranteed them a certain immunity, for though the papacy had secured potentially effective anti-heretical legislation from the State it was reluctant to implement it effectively for fear of losing allies in the cities. For some years both Frederick and Pope Gregory IX played an outward antiheretical game while remaining relatively inactive in fact. An alliance with the influential Ghibelline faction also protected the Cathars for some time. Nevertheless, they seemed to be dangerously in the ascendant in Italy though seriously weakened in France when Pope Gregory IX commissioned John to preach against them. An exemplary Dominican, he did so vigorously and, it is claimed, made many converts.

The Cathars lost their support only after John's and, more importantly, Frederick's death and with the rise of the conservative Guelf party in the cities and the disappearance of the papacy's need for allies. Cathar Perfects were being burned in great numbers in Italy in the 1270s. Many of those in Florence submitted during the Inquisition conducted by Brother Salomone da Lucca in 1282. As elsewhere, unrelenting repression was more successful than preaching.

John's cult was approved in 1783.

A life by John Caroli appears in *AA.SS.*, Sept., 3; the lacunae have been made good from a recovered text and are in *Anal. Boll.* 7 (1888), pp. 85-94. Mortier mentions John in his *Histoire des maîtres généraux O.P.*, 1, pp. 106ff. See also Procter, pp. 226-8. For the Patarenes see M. Lambert, *Medieval Heresy* (2d ed., 1992), pp. 36-8, 80, 105-46; J. N. Stephens, "Heresy in Medieval and Renaissance Florence," *Past and Present* 54 (1972), pp. 25-60; E. Duffy, *Saints and Sinners: A History of the Papacy* (1997), p. 92.

Bd Richard Bere, *Martyr* (1537)

Richard Bere (or Beer), a Carthusian priest of the London charterhouse, was one of the heroic minority of ten who on 18 May 1537 still refused to take the Oath of Allegiance to King Henry VIII. With the others, he was tied to a post in the Marshalsea and died of starvation and neglect, though for a time his hunger was secretly relieved by St Thomas More's adopted daughter, Margaret Clement, disguised as a milkmaid. The cult of the Carthusian martyrs was recognized by Pope Leo XIII in 1886.

See *Letters and Papers, Foreign and Domestic: the Reign of Henry VIII*; M. Chauncy, *Historia aliquot nostri saeculi Martyrum*; L. Hendriks, *The London Charterhouse* (1889); V. Doreau, *Henri VIII et les Martyrs de la Chartreuse* (1890).

St Teresa Benedicta of the Cross (Edith Stein),
Martyr (1891-1942)

She was born Edith Stein at Breslau, then in Germany (now Wroclaw, Poland), on 12 October 1891, the eleventh child of a Jewish family. Her mother was especially devout. As a schoolgirl and as a student Edith herself was a convinced atheist whose belief that there was no God nevertheless became her way to faith. When she was fifteen she decided never to pray again. But she was always in search of truth and subjected every issue to an intense intellectual scrutiny. As she recalled later, "My quest for truth was my only prayer."

At the universities of Göttingen and Freiburg she studied psychology, German literature, and history, but above all philosophy. She came under the influence of the phenomenological school and especially the thought of Edmmund Husserl (1859-1938), one of her professors and himself of Jewish ancestry though baptized a Christian when a young man. Husserl was a profoundly serious and austere thinker who developed and refined his ideas under criticism; one of his pupils was the philosopher Heidegger (1889-1976), a former Jesuit novice and a major influence on thinkers as disparate as the philosopher Sartre and the theologian Karl Rahner but one who, not only by his magisterial welcome for Hitler as a regenerative force but in the shifts and paradoxes of his philosophy, has been said to have misled and confused a whole generation of young German scholars. It might be said that some germs of that confusion were already present in Husserl's phenomenology. Almost inevitably, traces of the early Heidegger's existentialism, of his approach to the human location in nature, to human anguish faced with being and death, and to the necessity of using freedom of choice responsibly and creatively are to be found in Edith Stein's own writings. At Göttingen, Edith was also impressed by the ideas of Max Scheler (1874-1928), for some time a Catholic, and an interestingly wayward disciple of Husserl's concerned with the study of emotions as well as reason. Scheler encouraged Edith to share his interest in the eliciting of ultimate, eternal, and religious values as a prime philosophical task. He introduced her to the importance of contemporary Catholic thought: "Suddenly the barriers of my rationalist prejudices, which I had never doubted as they developed in me, were lifted to reveal the world of faith."

She found the autobiography of St Teresa of Avila (15 Oct.) in a friend's house and read it at a sitting until the sun rose. Whereas the effect of that great self-analysis on another woman atheist of vast intellectual and ethical integrity and similar high seriousness, the English novelist George Eliot, had been to confirm not only her sense of duty and vocation but her atheism, Edith as she closed the book told herself, "This is the truth!" She was baptized a Catholic on 1 January 1922. She was acutely aware of how this hurt her mother and later accompanied her to the synagogue and read the psalms with her. But Edith did not see her adoption of Christianity as a rejection of the Jewish people: "I had ceased to practise my religion at the age of fourteen. Once I had cast off what bound me to God I no longer felt that I was Jewish." Now she felt joined to Christ not only "spiritually but by blood."

She was already drawn to the Carmelites, but it was ten years before she entered the Order. She taught philosophy at Speyer and Münster and consciously tried to lead her students along the ways of knowledge to Christ. Immersing herself in the works of St Thomas Aquinas (28 Jan.), she learned the "practice of scholarship as a form of divine office." After her conscientious study of Thomism, which took her far from the often-barren version of it that passed at that time for the official "philosophy" of Catholicism in many seminaries, and her grounding in phenomenology (in the primary sense of the detection and elucidation of essential meanings present to the mind without inferences and assumptions) and in varieties of mystical thought that tempered the aridities of her teachers, she herself became a profound thinker and mystic. Her writings testify to her constant exploration of the notions of love and sacrifice as concomitants of knowledge.

Edith finally joined the Carmelites at Cologne on 12 October 1933, after Hitler had been voted into power and become chancellor and thereby dictator of Germany. She told her superior: "Human action cannot help us but only the sufferings of Christ. My aspiration is to share them." She made her final profession in 1938 and had printed on the commemorative card some words of St John of the Cross (14 Dec.): "Henceforth my only vocation will be constantly to love all the more." In one of her letters she compared herself to Queen Esther in exile at the Persian court: "I believe that the Lord has called me on behalf of all my people. I cannot help thinking of Queen Esther who was taken from her people precisely so that she could defend them before a king. I am a very poor and powerless Esther, but the King who has chosen me is infinitely great and merciful."

Again and again Edith Stein, now Sr Teresa Benedicta of the Cross, referred to her increasing understanding of the destiny of the people of Israel in the light of the cross and to her personal sense of her task of expiation. As Hitler and his followers raised the historical and scarcely latent anti-Semitism of the German people, approximately fify per cent of whom were Catholics, to the level of a national duty, harsh and terrible sufferings once again became the unjust fate of the Jewish people of Europe, but to a degree and on a scale hitherto unknown in the history of racial and religious persecution. Sr Teresa became convinced that "my people's destiny was also my own." She often referred to her sense of encounter with Christ in the mystery of the cross. In one of her prayers she says that she knows that it is the cross of Christ that the Jewish people must bear and that anyone who realizes this must willingly agree to carry it on behalf of all: "I wanted to bear it. All he had to do was to show me how." She said that she knew that her prayer was answered.

As a person of Jewish ancestry and birth, Sr Teresa came under the 1936 racist Nuremberg Laws, which tore families apart, deprived people of their citizenship, and sought to reduce human beings to the level of creatures without status. They were devised for the Nazi regime by the Catholic jurist Hans Globke, who later, when he served the postwar Catholic chancellor, Adenauer, excused the precise categories of these wholly despicable regulations used to implement the Nazi programme of insane eugenics, relentless persecution, and mass murder with the claim that if he had not done so someone else would have drawn up a much worse set. Sr Teresa left Cologne to protect her Sisters in religion from Nazi persecution and went to the Carmelite house at Echt, in the Netherlands, determined to share the suffering of Christ. There she wrote her major work, *The Knowledge of the Cross*. There, once again, her Jewishness subjected her to the barbaric anti-Semitic laws applied during the German occupation with the assistance of enthusiastic Dutch Nazis and other collaborators, even though baptized Jews were at first exempted from deportation and, therefore, extermination.

Unlike the episcopates of other countries occupied by or allied to the Germans, where the policy of racial murder was generally enforced (with a few courageous though variously partial exceptions, as in Denmark), the Catholic bishops of the Netherlands issued a pastoral letter unambiguously protesting against the deportations. The occupiers were indifferent to any local reactions this might arouse, for they ruthlessly punished any courageous demonstrations of sympathy by workers and students. In the absence of any similar letter from the German bishops and of any unambiguous general encyclical, letter, or broadcast to the same effect from Pope Pius XII, the Germans ordered that Christians of Jewish descent or converted from Judaism and resident in the

Netherlands should be rounded up and despatched to the East for "resettlement," that is, to Poland. Accordingly, Sr Teresa, together with her sister Rosa, who had also taken refuge with the Echt Carmelites, was arrested on 2 August 1942. As they left the convent, Edith took her sister's hand and said, "Come on—we are on our way to our own people." After the usual unspeakable experience of transport in a cattle truck, she was murdered on 9 August 1942 in the gas chambers of the German extermination camp at Auschwitz (Oswiecim), Poland, for no reason other than that she was one of Christ's own people.

An original religious thinker whose synthesis of mysticism and philosophy owes more to Judaism than has been acknowledged, a great Jewish and Christian model of virtue, self-denial, and heroism, Sr Teresa entered and walked as a loving person through the most terrible absence of mercy and compassion in recorded history, believing that "sufferings endured with the Lord are his sufferings, and bear great fruit in the context of his great work of redemption." She was beatified by Pope John Paul II at Cologne on 1 May 1987 and canonized by him in 1998.

Her works in German are available as: *Edith Steins Werke*, ed. L. Gelber and R. Leuven, vols. 1-11 (1983-87). See also Sr Teresa de Spiritu Sancto, *Edith Stein* (1948; Eng. trans. 1952); H. C. Graef, *The Scholar and the Cross: The Life and Work of Edith Stein* (1955); U. T. Mannshausen, *Die Biographie der Edith Stein* (1984); Christian Feldmann, *Liebe, die das Leben kostet* (1987).

R.M.

St Antoninus, martyr at Alexandria (? third/fourth century)

St Miro, bishop on the island of Crete (fourth century)

SS Julian, Marcian, John, James, Alexius, Demetrius, Leontius, Photius, Peter, and Mary, martyred at Constantinople for venerating images (*c.* 729)

St Hathumarus, first bishop of Paderborn (815)

St Sabba, priest of Bulgaria (ninth century)

Bd John Elisaeus, Franciscan hermit in Tuscany (1312)

Bd Falcus, hermit in Calabria (forteenth century)

ST LAURENCE (facing page)
Black gridiron on silver field.

10

ST LAURENCE, *Martyr* (258)

Laurence is one of the most celebrated saints in the history of the Church. His extraordinary fame is based mainly on fiction: on a quaint mixture of sacred irony (or sheer cheek) and miracle, of the kind found in the *Fabliaux* and *Gesta Romanorum*, and on his main attribute—the gridiron on which he is said to have been cooked, but painlessly, because of his holy enthusiasm. His life and sufferings became a subject so immensely attractive to the patrons of religious artists that several volumes would be needed merely to represent the main variations on the theme.

Laurence was one of the seven deacons of the Roman church. This was a post of great trust as it involved caring for the church's goods and giving alms to the poor. In 257 the emperor Valerian published edicts against Christians, and Pope St Sixtus (6 Aug.) was arrested the next year and executed. On the fourth day after that, Laurence also became a martyr. That is all that is known for certain of his life and death. One tradition says that he was born at Huesca in Aragon. Details supplied by St Ambrose (7 Dec.), Prudentius, and others have embellished historically unreliable accounts of incidents such as Laurence's dispersal of the church's goods and the way in which he died. These have entered into Christian legend, art, and devotion and deserve to be mentioned.

Sixtus (so the story goes) told Laurence he would follow him in death in three days. Laurence quickly sold the sacred vessels to increase the money he had in his keeping and gave it all to the poor, widows, and orphans. The prefect of Rome heard of this, sent for Laurence, and told him that no tortures were contemplated but that the emperor needed gold and silver to maintain his forces. He advised Laurence to follow Jesus by rendering unto Caesar what was Caesar's: to hand over the cash and be rich in words. Laurence asked for time to make an inventory of the church's valuables. He was given three days.

Laurence ransacked Rome for the poor supported by the Church. On the third day he assembled the decrepit, blind, lame, cripples, lepers, orphans, widows, and maidens and invited the prefect to inspect the Church's real treasure. The prefect said that this insult showed that Laurence wanted to die but that he would perish not immediately but by inches. Laurence was stripped and put on a gridiron with glowing coals below. He was slowly roasted, with distasteful results—but only for pagan onlookers: for believers he was surrounded by a beautiful light and gave off a sweet smell. The martyr wanted to be with Christ so much that he felt no pain. After broiling for some time, he asked to be turned so that the other side could be done. His would-be tormentors obliged until he said: "Now it's done to a turn You can start eating." Then he prayed for the conversion of Rome and died. Some senators became Christians on the spot and buried the martyr's body on the Via Tiburtina. Laurence's death put an end to idolatry in the city, and very soon the conversion of all Rome showed the power of his prayers.

St Laurence has been one of the most venerated martyrs of the Roman church since the fourth century. He was probably beheaded, like Sixtus, and certainly buried in the cemetery of Cyriaca on the Via Tiburtina, where Constantine built the first chapel on the site of the present church of St Laurence-outside-the-Walls, the fifth patriarchal basilica of the city, enlarged by Pelagius II (579-90); four other basilicas are dedicated to him. The narrative of the gridiron seems to have been taken from the Acts of St Vincent of Saragossa (22 Jan.). The origin of the story is lost to us, but it may have a Phyrgian source. Ultimately, it relies on ancient notions of testing by ordeal, of baptism by fire, and of fire as a divine gift that declares its nature if abused. Laurence's legend spread rapidly throughout the Christian world, supported by the writings of Prudentius, Ambrose, and Augustine. Spain and North Africa were major locations of his cult in the patristic age. In the seventh century King Oswy of Northumbria received relics of the saint from Pope Vitalian. Numerous churches were named in honour of Laurence; the Bradford-on-Avon church is among a number of early English dedications to him, and there were many early examples in Scandinavia. A Benedictine community of St Laurence established in France moved in 1824 to Ampleforth in Yorkshire, where a supposed relic of his forearm is venerated in the abbey church. The popularity of the cult throughout Europe is attested to by many additional legends and superstitions, such as that once common in the Low Countries, where St Laurence's help was invoked with a special prayer while lighting the fire in the morning.

Over the centuries Laurence's legend elicited representations both humble and magnificent, and some of the greatest masters of the Renaissance were inspired by it. Their achievements show how certain sacred fictions about saints can rise to the power of myth and reverberate like the central images and events of the Christian faith, which indeed they mirror. Some legends that in one context or medium seem tawdry or banal enclose kernels of profound mystery that only the private sympathies of individuals or the highest creative sensibilities can effectively disclose. As with so many other saints, the vitality of St Laurence is revealed not in the few scraps of his life remaining after scholarly debate but in the evidence of its reception. Nearly all the great museums possess a number of inspired images of Laurence. They testify to the former strength of a cult that has faded in an age without similar monuments to its own terrible martyrdoms.

The document purporting to be the Acts of St Laurence is only an item in a series of similar narratives. See *B.H.L.*, n. 6884, as compared with nn. 7801 and 4753. Prudentius' poem, given in Ruinart's *Acta sincera*, offers a relatively clear statement from which the above account is drawn, but it is improbable that this represents an oral tradition or lost documents. St Ambrose (see, *e.g.*, his *De Officis*, 1, 41) believed the martyr was roasted, and so did other early Fathers. Franchi de' Cavalieri, in *Römische Quartalschrift* 4 (1900), pp. 159-76; *Note agiografiche*, 5 (1915), pp. 65-82, and Delehaye, in *Anal.Boll.* 29, pp. 452-3 (see also 52, pp. 49-58, and *C.M.H.*, pp. 431-2), reject the gridiron tradition; but for defenders see H. Leclercq in *D.A.C.L.*, 47, 1827-31, and 8, 1917-47). See also J. P. Kirsch, *Die römische Titelkirchen in Altertum*, pp. 80-4; Huelsen, *Le Chiese di Roma nel medio evo*, pp. 280-97; Duchesne, "Le Sanctuaire de S. Laurent," in *Mélanges d'archéologie* 39 (1921), pp. 3-24; and W. Frankl, E. Josi, and R. Krautheimer, "Le esplorazioni nella basilica di S. Lorenzo nell'Agro Verano," in *Riv.A.C.* 29 (pt. 2; 1929), 1917-61. For a modern study, especially of the contributions of Ambrose and Prudentius, see *H.S.S.C.*, 2, pp. 202-10. For the Valerian persecution see the entry on Sixtus II (7 Aug., above).

Laurence may be represented as a deacon, sometimes in a fiery tunicle. He wears an extremely rich and elaborate tunic in Bernardo Strozzi's (1581-1644) *St Laurence Giving the Treasures of the Church to the Poor* (New York, Kress Collection) and in Paolo Veronese's (1528-88) *Madonna and Child with SS Laurence, Agnes, and Anthony Abbot* (New Orleans, Isaac Delgado Museum of Art). He sometimes swings a censer but more often carries a cross or a palm to indicate his martyrdom, or a dish filled with gold and silver coins or a purse of money, to recall his distribution of the supposed treasures of the church. Usually, however, the gridiron—another cross and therefore a symbol of a symbol—is his distin-guishing mark. At a fairly early stage it is associated with him in the fifth-century Ravenna mosaics (in the Mausoleum of Galla Placidia), in the ninth-century cycle of frescoes in the church of St Vincent at Volturno, Italy, and in Fra Angelico's detailed, stylized paintings of his life for the Vatican chapel of Nicholas V (1447-50), in which he is ordained deacon, distributes alms, appears before the emperor, and so on. In *St Laurence Prepared for Martyrdom* by Adam Elsheimer (1578-1610; London, National Gallery) the gridiron is ready in the background, but the prominent statue of a deity in the foreground implies that Laurence suffered for refusing to worship false gods. Zurbarán's *St Laurence* (1636; Leningrad, Hermitage) shows him standing, ecstatic in a very heavy baroque tunicle; another by the same artist (1637-9; Cadiz, Provincial Museum of Fine Arts) portrays him in formal baroque prayer; in both cases Laurence holds or embraces a clean and shimmer-ing gridiron. One of the most graphic portrayals of the poor of Rome and the outraged prefect is a canvas by the Master of the St Ursula Legend (late-fifteenth–early-sixteenth century; London, National Gallery) from a probable series of eight.

   Among the most noteworthy *Martyrdoms of St Laurence* is Titian's of 1564-7, sent to Philip II of Spain for the high altar of the old church in the Escorial, the monastery of St Laurence, where it remains. Here Laurence, from among a tumultuous throng of torturers in contemporary military dress, through a terrible darkness lit by blazing coals and sinister torches, looks up to the faint, clouded moonlight of heaven that only he can perceive as hope and promise of a greater light. Titian's other version in the church of the Jesuits, Venice (started in 1548 and placed by Elisabetta Querini on her husband Lorenzo's tomb in 1557-9), is equally dramatic but has an intentionally antique setting in which the light from above shines down on Laurence, displaying him more surely to initiates than the intermediate torches and fire below. Tintoretto's *Martyrdom* (1570-80; Christ Church, Oxford) is derived from Titian's Escorial version of the subject and subordinates the figures to an overall rhythm with a fervent, mystical, and yet somehow intimate treatment. Another important version is Daddi's (1312-48) in Santa Croce, Florence.

St Blaan, *Bishop* (? *c.* 590)

The chronology of this Scottish bishop, also called Blane, who was born in Bute, is very uncertain. He is said to have spent seven years in Ireland under the instruction of St Comgall (10 May) and St Canice (11 Oct.) and presumably became a monk there. He then returned to the isle of Bute ("in a boat without oars") and put himself under the discipline of his uncle St Cathan, who ordained him. He devoted himself to apostolic work in Scotland. He eventually became a bishop and is said to have gone on pilgrimage to Rome, returning on foot through England. He died and was buried at Kingarth, Bute. The cathedral of Dunblane was built on the site of his monastery and is said still to contain his bell. Devotion to St Blaan became popular at an early date. He was said to be able to rekindle the church lights, extinguished during the night office, by striking fire from his fingernails. Since antiquity the emission of a sacred flame has been the sign of celestial fire in an individual's heart, and of his or her ability to communicate with the power that bestowed it. Blaan's gift could signify sparks struck from Christ's fire and a readiness to emulate Christ's burning desire. More exactly, however, it calls to mind a dreich Scottish kirk on a cold and windy night. The lamp has gone out and a monk is desperately trying to find tinder and begin the long process of coaxing it into flame. This and other curious miracles ascribed to Blaan testify to the harsh conditions of the age and place, and to what, under them, was an appropriately exceptional achievement; they deserve investigation by folklorists. His cult was confirmed in 1898.

The account in *AA.SS.*, Aug., 2, is taken mainly from the lessons of the *Aberdeen Breviary*; but see rather *K.S.S.*, pp. 280-1. St Blaan is mentioned in the *Félire* of Oengus and the *Aberdeen Martyrology*.

R.M.

St Auctoris, bishop of Metz (fifth century)

St Arigius, bishop of Lyons (after 614)

St Hugh, bishop of Auxerre (*c.* 1136)

Bd Augustine Ota, Japanese catechist, martyr (1622)—see "The Martyrs of Japan," 6 Feb.

ST CLARE OF ASSISI (facing page)
Refers to her presenting invaders with the Bleessed Sacrament (see p. 87). Gold ciborium on brown field.

11

ST CLARE OF ASSISI, *Foundress* (*c.* 1193-1253)

Clare, the foundress of the Poor Clares, or Minoresses, was born in Assisi about 1193 at a time of great economic change and even warfare that continued throughout her lifetime, as the cities grew ever wealthier and became centres of hitherto unknown migration. Hers was a largely aggressive world of people set on acquisition or concerned at least to protect and hand down what they already had. Clare's mother was Ortolana di Fiumi and her father Faverone Offreduccio. Her family is said to have been rich, but all we really know of her childhood and youth is that she had a younger sister, Agnes, and another, Beatrice. We may suppose that if Clare had no brothers, she and her sisters must have been desirable brides for second, third, and other sons of good families who had been unable to place them advantageously in prosperous religious houses. Since girls were usually married at fourteen or fifteen, Clare had probably contemplated a religious life for some time and had managed to resist family pressures. These must have been strong, for her sisters could not be married until she was.

Clare was eighteen when St Francis preached the Lenten sermons at the church of San Giorgio in Assisi. In a world very far from the simplicity and purity of the Christian gospel, she was inspired by his message of personal fulfillment and world transformation through total sacrifice. Her relatives (her father was probably dead) had proposed a husband whom she did not want to marry, but she entirely renounced the idea of marriage only when she heard Francis speak. She asked to see him privately and hear more about living as Jesus recommended. This does not mean that before she met Francis Clare was not a thinking person in her own right with well-formed religious sensibilities. The personal independence and authority which she showed later in her dealings with popes and others were already there at an early stage. They were nurtured by an unusually inspiring relationship, in which her contribution was necessarily more, though not exclusively, one of loyalty and support. She is said to have sent Francis money to buy food when he was rebuilding the Portiuncula chapel, where he lived with his little community. Clare and Francis met secretly, and he talked of contempt of the world, power, and glory; of loving God ardently; honouring poverty radically; and choosing absolutely to be "less." Clare was taken out of her everyday self and entered a new dimension of understanding. On Palm Sunday 1212 she attended Assisi Cathedral for the blessing of palms. The bishop saw that she was too shy to join the others at the altar-rails, so he went down to her and gave her the olive branch. In the evening of 18-19 March she ran away from home and went a mile out of town to the Portiuncula to forsake all her possessions and become a nun. Francis and the Brothers met her at the door of the Chapel of our Lady of the Angels with lighted tapers in their hands. She abandoned her fine clothes before the altar. Francis cut off her hair and gave her the penitential habit, a sackcloth tunic tied about her with a cord. He placed her temporarily in the Benedictine convent of St Paul near Bastia.

As soon as Clare's choice became public, her friends and relations came to take her home. She resisted them and tugged the cloths half from the altar when—sacrilegiously—they tried to drag her away. She showed them her shorn hair and said that Christ had called her to his service, that he was the only husband she wanted, and that if they carried on persecuting her God would give her all the more strength to withstand and overcome them. Soon after this incident Francis took her off to another nunnery, Sant'Angelo di Panzo on the slopes of Mount Subasio. Her sister Agnes (St Agnes of Assisi; 16 Nov.) joined her there. This renewed the campaign to persuade the sisters to go home. At last Agnes prevailed, and Francis gave her the habit too, though she was only fifteen.

The acceptance of such young women into an Order against their family's wishes must seem rather odd by modern standards (in the Western world, at least) and Francis' behaviour somewhat unconventional, but we must remember that the hazards of childbirth in the thirteenth century meant that most married women, even when rich, did not expect to live very long and that the sisters were not thought to be so very young as they would seem nowadays. Moreover, Francis and Clare, as narrative and tradition present them to us, are such delightfully exceptional individuals that we tend to think of them almost as characters in one of Shakespeare's more romantic comedies. They become acceptable on the small stage of our knowledge and enter into the timeless world of pastoral precisely because the conditions of their age are so remote. But this was a unique friendship between two real people, members of a revolutionary movement sharing the same ideals and very much concerned with the right way to live in a world of false aims that became harshly oppositional when challenged. Clearly, Clare was attracted by Francis ("in conversation, agreeable, ardent and penetrating, his voice firm, sweet-toned and clearly audible") and by what was inseparable from his personality: a message of joy and sorrow, peace and turbulence, love and suffering, and the transfiguration of all creation, and therefore of everyday life, by divine radiance.

Eventually Francis placed Clare and Agnes in a poor-house near the church of San Damiano, on the outskirts of Assisi, and appointed Clare superior. She was later joined by her mother and others, including three members of the illustrious Florentine Ubaldini family. Francis drew up a rudimentary Rule of life for them. Within a few years, monasteries of Clare's nuns were established at several places in Italy, France, and Germany. Bd Agnes (8 June), daughter of the king of Bohemia, founded a nunnery of the Order in Prague, where she took the habit; Clare called her "my half self."

Clare and her community practised austerities perhaps unknown until then among women of their station. Their way of life earned them insults and contempt. They wore no stockings, shoes, sandals, or any other covering on their feet. They slept on the ground, never ate meat, and never spoke unless necessity or charity demanded words. Clare recommended this silence in order to avoid sins of the tongue and concentrate on holy things. She was not content with fasts and other mortifications of the Rule but always wore a rough hair shirt next to her skin. This form of penance, so popular among saints in the past, was not only painful but encouraged another humiliation—vermin—and, of course, ill health. Clare fasted on vigils and all Lent on bread and water and on some days ate nothing at all. After a time Francis and the bishop of Assisi made her lie on a mattress and eat at least some bread every day. Discretion came with experience. Years later she wrote to Agnes of Bohemia: "Our bodies are not brass and we are not as strong as stone, but weak and subject to physical illness. I implore you most sincerely in the Lord to give up the excessively strict abstinence which I know you practise, so that, living and hoping in the Lord, you may offer him reasonable service and a sacrifice seasoned with the salt of prudence."

Perhaps Clare's frequent sicknesses and sometimes bedridden condition during the last twenty-seven years of her life were related to her severe penitential régime. Nowadays this behaviour may seem more neurotic than saintly, but in past centuries it would have been quite permissible, and we do not know enough about Clare to classify her conduct in accordance with the psychological categories of her own, let alone our, times. Possibly that degree of self-denial appeared necessary in a chaotic world: as an uncompromising expression of Francis' message of surrender to suffering and of reliance only on the bare earth as a symbol of reconciliation with one's self, with others, and with ultimate reality.

As part of their rejection of worldly values, Francis wished his Order never to own any rents or other property even in common but to rely on daily contributions in kind. Essentially, Clare thought the same way. This was an extraordinary—if not unprecedented—proposal at the time and eventually came to have socially critical implications for many friars and minoresses. One of the most revolutionary aspect of Clare's practice was that she was the first woman to write a Rule for other women. The divisions among the friars also gave her a unique function as the interpreter of Francis' ideals, for Clare was not and did not claim to be original. Her ideals were simply those of Francis—to be lived out as faithfully as the Church allowed. Nevertheless, she did not always agree with Francis, as in the matter of accepting gifts of money, which he totally rejected. She thought cash was acceptable if it was needed; if not, it could be given to the absolutely destitute. Gregory IX, however, wanted to modify the reliance on chance income implied by Clare's Rule and offered to give the Poor Ladies of San Damiano a yearly income. Clare persuaded him not to change the Rule. When the pope said that he was willing to offer them a dispensation from the vow of strict poverty, Clare replied, "I need absolution from my sins, but not from having to follow Jesus Christ." On 17 September 1228 Gregory granted the Damianites the *Privilegium paupertatis*, or privilege of poverty, and over the next years extended it to the Monticelli and Perugia houses. This allowed them to exist entirely by alms; no one could force them to accept possessions or to live by rents. Gregory said, "He who feeds the birds of the air, and who clothes and nourishes the lilies of the field, will not leave you without clothing or food until he comes himself to look after you for ever." Some convents thought it more prudent to accept a mitigation. This was the beginning of the two observances among the Poor Clares. The mitigated houses are called "Urbanist," from the modification of the Rule they received in 1263 from Pope Urban IV.

In the reigns of both Gregory IX and Innocent IV, Clare tried to obtain papal acceptance of an appropriate Rule rather than follow the Benedictine or Ugoline Rules. In 1247, after the death of Gregory IX (who as Cardinal Ugolino had drawn up the first written Rule for the Poor Ladies of San Damiano), Innocent IV published another version of the Rule. In some respects this made it closer to Franciscan than to Benedictine observance but allowed revenues to be received and property to be held in common. Innocent wrote that he did not wish to force this Rule on any community unwilling to accept it. Clare did not want it and drew up a Rule that she thought would truly express the spirit and tradition of Francis himself. It provided that the Sisters should own no property, either as individuals or as a community, and that all members of the community must share responsibility. It was not until two days before Clare's death that Innocent IV approved this formula for the convent of San Damiano. Only a few other nunneries adopted it in the thirteenth century. Clare's concern for the niceties of her Rule and the distinctiveness of her nuns may seem obsessive, but it is quite normal when we compare it with the known behaviour of most other founders of religious Orders. More importantly, however, it was part of the constant vigilance needed to stay detached from conflict, money, power, and control; to ward off domination; and thereby to find a form of self-negation that, paradoxically, would keep one's personality inviolate.

Francis had appointed Clare abbess in 1215, much against her will. She governed the convent for forty years and is said never to have left it. She always wanted to be the servant of servants, to wash and kiss the lay Sisters' feet when they returned from begging, to serve at table, and to look after the sick: "Do what you want with me. I am yours because my will is no longer my own. I have given it to God." When her Sisters were resting she stayed up to pray, and—quite the nicest of those few touches that bring Clare to life as a real person—she tucked the nuns up when their bed-clothes had come loose. Of course she was a contemplative in the tradition of Francis, and it is said that she had a similar love of the natural world: an appreciation of God's creation manifest in nature, of the ideal garden glimpsed in and behind the wilderness of this world. Though she led a relatively enclosed life she walked in the grounds, and from her roof garden she enjoyed individual features of what we would call a marvellous view of the surrounding countryside. But she did not compose them into a whole in any modern sense. (Clare's and Francis' enraptured perception of the extra-human world was unusual yet within the categories of their times; it had nothing to do with post-eighteenth-century notions of the vitality of nature, the picturesque landscape, and so on, which in various guises have been imported into accounts of their supposed view of plants and animals.) Her service was primarily conventual. She was first up in the morning, rang the choir bell, and lighted the candles. After prayer her face was so cheerful that it is said to have dazzled the eyes of anyone who saw her. Though she was often very ill, she made fine linen corporals and altar cloths, which she distributed among the churches of Assisi.

Clare prayed intently, and many anecdotes express the dedication and strength of her faith. Thomas of Celano contributes a typical legend, possibly a pious elaboration of an unsuccessful siege during the Frederician campaign. It has had immense staying power and is important in the artistic reception of Clare's life. In 1244 Frederick II (a difficult emperor in dispute with a difficult pope and widely regarded as the Antichrist), having imprisoned several bishops, proceeded to lay waste the valley of Spoleto, which formed part of the patrimony of the Holy See. The invading army included many Saracens who decided to plunder Assisi. San Damiano was outside the walls, and they attacked it first. Clare was sick but asked to be carried to the wall and for the Blessed Sacrament to be placed there in a pyx, in sight of the enemy. She prostrated herself before it and prayed, "God, do you really want the defenceless children whom I have fed with your love to fall into these beasts' hands? Good Lord, I beg you: defend those I cannot protect." She heard what seemed to be a little child's voice saying, "I shall always look after them." She prayed for Assisi and once again the voice reassured her. She turned to the trembling nuns and said, "Don't be afraid, little daughters. Trust in Jesus." The Saracens fled. Soon afterwards one of Frederick's generals besieged Assisi for several days. Clare told her nuns to do all they could for the city that supplied their needs. She ordered them to cover their heads with ashes and to ask Christ to save the town. They did so for a day and a night. The besieging forces melted away. The tale is more than a quaint miracle narrative. Its emphasis is thoroughly Franciscan: on the spirit of the poor infant Christ, who by total accessibility, vulnerability, and service brings peace and concord where there was strife and commotion. This aspect of Clare has much to do with the ethos of the Italian peace movement of the time known as the "Great Halleluja" and with the radical, critical spirit propagated by many Franciscans, very much by the Poor Clares, and to some extent by the Waldensians and largely urban Cathars. It stressed the spiritual interests of laypeople and women but above all the quest for perfection rather than complication, for primitive ideals, for absolute poverty, for the brotherhood and sisterhood of all living things, the church of the pure, and the spirit of apostolic self-denial.

Unfortunately, the Poor Clares and the Friars Minor disagreed about the relations of the two Orders even during the saint's life and at intervals long after her death. The observant Clares maintained that the friars were obliged to serve them in matters spiritual and temporal. Thomas of Celano says that in 1230, when Pope Gregory IX forbade the friars to visit the convents of nuns without his special licence, the rather inflexible Clare feared that this would mean a loss of the friars' spiritual help and a severing of the ties Francis had wished to exist between them. Therefore she dismissed all those who were attached to the convent with the words: "He has taken away our spiritual almoners. Now he can have those who serve our material needs."

Clare bore years of sickness patiently. Her final agony began in 1253. Twice during its course she was visited by Pope Innocent IV, who gave her absolution, saying, "Would to God *I* had so little need of it." For the last seventeen days she could eat nothing. Bishops and cardinals visited her, for there was a general conviction that the dying woman was a great saint. Her sister Agnes was there with three of Francis' companions, Leo, Angelo, and Juniper, who read aloud the Passion of Christ from John's Gospel as they had done at Francis' deathbed twenty-seven years before. When Brother Reginald advised Clare to be patient, she replied, "Dear Brother Reginald, ever since experiencing the grace of Jesus through his servant Francis, I have never in my whole life met with any pain or sickness that could really hurt me." She comforted her nuns and told them always to practise holy poverty faithfully. She blessed them, calling herself the "little plant" of her holy father Francis. She said of herself, "Go in peace; you have been on the right road. You can leave without fear; God who made you has blessed you, always looked after you, and loves you as a mother. I praise God for creating me." She died with her papally-approved Rule in her hands at the age of sixty, forty-two years after making her religious profession. She was buried the next day. Very soon, in 1255, Pope Alexander IV canonized her at Anagni. Within eight years of her death, Thomas of Celano had written her Life. Her relics were translated to Santa Chiara in 1260.

By the end of the fourteenth century there were more than four hundred nunneries under the control of the First Order: in Italy, Dalmatia, Syria and the East, Spain and Portugal, France, Germany, the Slav lands, and Britain. After many vicissitudes, suppressions, disputes, and renewals, by the late twentieth century the total number of enclosed Franciscan nuns of all observances was estimated at nearly 22,000 in 978 houses. They had spread to Asia, North and South America, Africa, and Oceania.

By a bizarre twist of allocation the reclusive Clare, for ever associated with voluntary poverty, is now the patron not only of embroiderers but of universally intrusive television. Pius XII chose her for the latter task (*cf.* apostolic letter, 14 Feb. 1958) because, he said, one Christmas Eve when sickness kept her in bed, she saw the crib and heard singing just as if she had been present in the church.

There are occasional references in *Speculum perfectionis* (Mirror of Perfection) (2d ed., British Society of Franciscan Studies, 1928), in the *Actus B. Francisci*, and in other early documents. We have five letters from Clare, her Rule, and her "Testament." See H. Roggen, *S. Claire d'Assise: Documents* (1983). The earliest Life is *The Life of S. Clare* ascribed to Thomas of Celano, trans. P. Robinson (with the Rule) (1910). An early Life of the saint in English was translated from a compilation by Francis Hendricq and published at Douai in 1635 as *The History of the Angelicall Virgin, glorious S. Clare*. There are many modern Lives. Among the more recent see R. M. Pierazzi, *Ste Claire* (1937); M. Fassbinder, *Die Heilige Klara von Assisi* (1934); N. de Robeck, *St Clare of Assisi* (1951); F. Casolini, *Santa Chiara d'Assisi* (1953); H. Roggen, *L'Esprit de sainte Claire* (1969); M. Bartoli, *Claire of Assisi* (1994), the best book on her in English. See also *Bibl.SS.*, 3, 1201-17; *H.S.S.C.*, 6, pp. 104-11. *Archivum Franciscanum Historicum* 6, 7, 11, and 13, contains useful articles, especially on the canonization in 13, pp. 403-507. See also L. Spätling, "Die geistige Gestalt der heiligen Klara von Assisi," in *Franziskanische Studien* 35 (1953), pp. 145-73; *Santa Chiara d'Assisi: Studi e cronaca del VII centenario 1253-1953* (1954). On the life of women and the Poor Clares see C. N. L. Brooke in D. Baker (ed.), *Medieval Women* (1978). On the origins and early expansion of the Order see L. Iriarte de Aspurz, O.F.M. Cap., *Historia Franciscana* (1979), trans. P. Smith, *Franciscan History* (1982), pp. 441-73. For the connections between Franciscan spirituality and reform movements, the Waldenses, Cathars, and so on, see M. D. Lambert, *Franciscan Poverty* (1961); D. Nimmo, *Reform and Division in the Franciscan Order 1226-1538* (1987), pp. 139-200, 240-79; M. Lambert, *Medieval Heresy* (2d ed., 1992), esp. pp. 189-214; D. Burr, *Olivi's Peaceable Kingdom* (1993). For the conventional view of Clare's "romantic" view of nature see, e.g., F. Cuthbert, *The Romanticism of St Francis* (1915), pp. 83-130, and, as a corrective, D. Pearsall and E. Salter, *Landscapes and Seasons of the Medieval World* (1975).

There are many paintings and other images of Clare. Her principal attribute is a pyx or a monstrance holding the Host (see the legend above). She may also appear with a lily (purity), a palm (victory), a cross, or a crozier (as foundress). She wears a grey habit, a black veil over a white coif, and a Franciscan cord. She is often shown with the Virgin and Child and with one or a selection of the following: Francis, Antony of Padua, Catherine of Alexandria, Mary Magdalen, and one or more donors. *Madonna and Child with SS Clare, Francis, William of Aquitaine, and Antony of Padua* (London, National Gallery) by Garofalo (1481-1559) is a typical example. In one of the most elaborate representations, the highly-stylized *The Death of St Clare* by the Master of Heiligenkreuz (Washington, National Gallery of Art), Our Lady holds Clare's head and she is attended by Bd Agnes, her sister, with a lamb, SS Margaret, Dorothy, Barbara, Catherine, and others. A very early, and moving, representation is a fresco of a group of Poor Clares by Ambrogio Lorenzetti (active 1319-79; London, National Gallery) from the chapter house of S. Francesco, Siena, where it was discovered under whitewash in the 1850s and probably formed part of a scene of *The Body of St Francis halted at S. Damiano, and wept over by St Clare and Her Companions.*

St Alexander "the Charcoal-Burner," *Bishop and Martyr* (*c.* 275)

Alexander's life consists of an exemplary triple reversal of fortunes, including a disclosure of high origins as found in folk literature worldwide, grafted on to credible history.

When the Christian community at Comana in Pontus had grown sufficiently large to need a bishop, St Gregory, bishop of Neocaesarea, went there to preside at the election. He rejected all the candidates suggested by the clergy and people, especially one favoured because of his high birth and wealth. Gregory reminded them that the apostles were poor and ordinary men. At this, someone is said to have exclaimed: "Well then, why not make Alexander—you know, the charcoal-burner—bishop?" Knowing that God moves in mysterious ways, Gregory sent for the charcoal-burner, who turned up dirty and blackened from his trade. Gregory's gaze pierced through rags and grime to the quality beneath them. He questioned Alexander in private and found that he was a man of good birth and education who had given away his possessions and become a charcoal-burner in order to follow Christ as the gospel recommended. Alexander agreed that Gregory should propose him for the vacant see, the people ratified the appointment, and the new bishop was consecrated. St Gregory of Nyssa (10 Jan.), who relates these events, speaks highly of Alexander as a bishop and teacher. He eventually gave his life for the Faith, being martyred (as symmetry demands) by fire, and duly became the patron of— charcoal-burners.

AA.SS., Aug, 2.

St Tibertius, *Martyr* (Third-Fourth Century)

The existence of Tibertius is known from an epitaph by Pope St Damasus (11 Dec.), which, however, contains no biographical information. The unreliable Acts of St Sebastian (20 June) say that he was a Roman subdeacon betrayed by an apostate during the persecution of Christians; that he was brought before the prefect Fabian and showed the power of his faith by walking unharmed over burning embers; that the authorities decided this was black rather than white magic; and that he was beheaded on the via Labicana, three miles from Rome. We know only that he was buried on the via Labicana at the place known as The Two Laurels, where a small church was built later.

See the texts quoted by Delehaye in *C.M.H.*, pp. 434–5; the article by J. P. Kirsch, "Die Martyrer der Katakombe 'ad duas Lauras,'" in *Ehrengabe deutscher Wissenschaft dargeboten von Katholischen Gelehrten* (1920), pp. 577–601; *Damasi epigrammata* (ed. Ihm), n. 30; and *AA.SS.*, Aug., 2, pp. 613–32.

The Baptism of Tiburtius is the subject of a superbly-composed painting of the four-teenth-century Florentine school in the Uffizi Gallery, Florence, Italy.

St Susanna, *Martyr* (Fourth Century)

All we know of Susanna is a brief notice in the Hieronymian martyrology (primitive and usually accepted as reliable): "In Rome, at the 'Two Houses' beside the baths of Diocletian, the birthday of St Susanna." This fragment became the nucleus of an interesting fiction which focusses on two houses belonging to two brothers, Gabinius and Caius, and rings an unusual set of quasi-historical changes on the familiar folk motif of the virgin who refuses a pagan suitor. The courtly intrigue and complications of the full tale are also reminiscent of non-Christian cycles such as the Arabian Nights, with a series of improbable conversions and property renunciations taking the place of other magical sequences. It is important as a clear example of very disparate elements and factors contributing to a hagiographical fiction.

We are told that Susanna was the beautiful and scholarly daughter of a learned priest, Gabinius, and niece of Pope St Caius (22 Apr.) about whose life and death nothing secure is known. The emperor Diocletian was looking for a wife for his son-in-law Maximian. He sent one of Susanna's uncles, Claudius, who held a post at court, to tell Gabinius that the emperor wanted Susanna to marry Maximian. Susanna, however, said she was the bride of Christ and would take no earthly husband. When Claudius arrived to discuss the matter and tried to kiss her, she drew back. He explained that it was only a natural sign of affection, but she said, "I don't mind your kissing me. It's your filthy mouth I can't stand. It's foul from idolatry." "How can I get it clean?" asked Claudius. "Repent and be baptized," was the reply.

Claudius found Susanna's refusal of such an advantageous marriage so impressive that he asked for instruction and was baptized together with his wife, Praepedigna, and his two sons. He then freed his slaves and gave his property to the poor. Not seeing Claudius at court again, Diocletian sent his brother Maximus, also in the royal household, to find out about Susanna and to inquire after Claudius, said to be sick. Maximus found his brother indeed very emaciated, but because of the penances he had undergone as a Christian. Claudius told him of Susanna's decision. They visited her and then talked matters over with Gabinius and the pope. All four brothers agreed that that it was wrong to force the girl to change her vocation. Maximus was baptized too and gave his possessions to the poor. When Diocletian heard of Susanna's obduracy and of the conversion of his two officers, he became very angry. He told one of his favourites, Julian, who had a grudge against the family, to arrest them and to do whatever he liked with them. Julian ordered Maximus and Claudius, with the latter's wife and sons, to be taken to Cumae, where they were burned alive and their bodies thrown into the water. Susanna was beheaded in her father's house, and her father was martyred too.

Duchesne skillfully traced the evolution of this story, in which the topographical basis is in a sense correct but the names have been taken from some blundering text of the first recension of the *Hieronymianum*. The extraordinary name Praepedigna, for instance, simply consists of the last part of a martyr's name, Euprepe, fused with the first part of the name of the place where she suffered—Dinogetia, miswritten Dignae Cotiae. Duchesne contends with reason that the *Passio Susannae* was fabricated around the year 500. See his article in *Mélanges d'archéologie et d'histoire* 36 (1916), pp. 27-42; P. Franchi de' Cavalieri, *Note agiografiche*, 7 (1928), pp. 184-202; Lanzoni, *I titoli presbiterali de Roma* (1925), pp. 34-50; and *C.M.H.*, p. 435.

St Equitius, *Abbot* (*c.* 560)

Equitius lived in the Abruzzi, Italy, at the time when St Benedict was establishing his Rule at Monte Cassino. As a young man Equitius is said to have suffered greatly from sexual temptations. He became a hermit in the province of Valeria and by prayer and discipline controlled his inclinations until he felt able to direct others. First he founded a monastery at Terni (Amiternum), then other houses for men and for women. St Gregory the Great (3 Sept.) describes Equitius from accounts he had received from Bishop Albinus of Rieti and others who knew him personally. Equitius diligently visited churches, towns, villages, and houses, where he preached effectively until his fame reached Rome. His clothes were poor and shabby and he carried his divinity books in leather bags hung on either side of a rather woebegone horse. Though eloquent, Equitius was something of a country bumpkin and, like many early abbots, not in Holy Orders. A patrician named Felix told him he had no right to preach without a licence, but Equitius retorted that a young man had carried out sacred surgery on his tongue in a vision and since then he had had to talk about God whether he would or no. Some fine Roman clergy also complained about his reputation, which they felt was undeserved, so the pope sent a priest named Julian to bring Equitius in for interrogation. He found the abbot in hobnailed boots mowing the grass and ready to set out at once. But Julian was tired, so they rested the night. The next day (so the story goes) a messenger arrived from the pope to say he had had a vision in which God had given him a perfectly satisfactory report about Equitius; he was a holy man and not to be disturbed. Equitius died on 7 March about the year 560, and on that day his body was translated to the church of St Laurence Aquila.

AA.SS., Mar., 1. There is a similar collection of fragmentary data in Mabillon, 1, pp. 655–8.

St Gaugericus, *Bishop* (*c.* 625)

St Gaugericus (in French, Géry) was a native of Yvoi, a small town in the Ardennes, now in Belgium. During an episcopal visitation there, St Magnericus (25 July), the successor of St Nicetius (5 Dec.) in the bishopric of Trier, approved of Gaugericus' sancity and talents and ordained him deacon (though his biographer says he had to learn all the psalms by heart first). Thereafter the future saint became even more zealous until his holiness and learning earned him the see of Cambrai. He is said to have devoted his episcopate to eradicating the remains of paganism in his diocese. At Cambrai he founded a monastery, which he named after St Médard (8 June). Popular tradition also attributes to him the foundation of the city of Brussels: he is said to have built a chapel on an island in the Senne (now Place Saint-Géry) around which a village grew up. He died about 625 after occupying his see for thirty-nine years. He was buried in St Médard's church, on a hill outside Cambrai.

For the oldest Life (in poor Latin, and possibly written fifty or sixty years after his death) see *Anal. Boll.* 7 (1888), pp. 388-98, re-ed. B. Krusch in *M.G.H., Scriptores Merov.*, 3, pp. 652-8. Cf. E. de Moreau, *Histoire de l'Eglise en Belgique*, 1 (1945), pp. 60-3.

Bd John Sandys, *Martyr* (1586)

John Sandys (or Sandes) was probably born in Lancashire (possibly in Cheshire). The records of the English College in Rome say that he was a poor scholar at Oriel College, Oxford, and later was appointed tutor to the children of Sir William Winter in Gloucestershire. He went to the English College at Reims on 4 June 1583, was ordained priest there on 31 March 1584, and was sent on the English mission on 2 October 1584. He visited old friends in Gloucestershire disguised as a layman, staying eventually at the house of the rural dean of Lydney. Some of the dean's enemies had recognized Sandys and betrayed him. In this way they hoped to incriminate the dean, who said that he knew nothing about Sandys' priesthood but only that he was honest and a gentleman. The dean was exonerated but Sandys was sentenced to death. The good clergyman's enemies are said to have visited the martyr in prison, asking for forgiveness, since they had only wanted to be revenged on the dean (which the source does not find strange). Challoner says that Sandys was hanged, drawn, and quartered at Gloucester on 11 August 1586, though some sources, including the English College in Rome, maintain that he died in 1587 with Bd Stephen Rowsham (12 Feb.). John Sandys was beatified by Pope John Paul II on 22 November 1987.

See *M.M.P.*, p. 116, but more specifically (citing the register of the Venerable English College, Rome, sc. 21, and T. F. Knox, *The First and Second Douai Diaries* [n.d.], pp. 196, 200, 203), Anstruther, 1 (1968), pp. 301-2.

R.M.

St Rufinus, supposedly first bishop of Assisi and martyr (? fourth century)

St Taurinus, bishop of Evreux (? fifth century.)

St Rusticola, abbess at Aix-en-Provence (632)

Bd Nicholas Appleine, canon of Nevers (1466).

12

St Euplus, *Martyr* (304)

Euplus (or Euplius), who is retained in the new draft Roman Martyrology, is said to have made a disturbance outside the governor's court at Catania in Sicily during the Diocletian persecution. He shouted, "I am a Christian and willing to die for it." Calvisian, the governor, ordered him to be brought inside, whereupon he appeared carrying a book of the Gospels. Someone remarked that they were forbidden by the emperor, so Calvisian interrogated the bearer. Euplus answered each question with a kind of saintly effrontery, and the dialogue reported in the *Acts of Euplus* (and possibly the individual himself) was clearly invented both to entertain and to instruct, for his initial daring makes nonsense of any evasive intention in his witty but impertinent answers.

When Calvisian asked if the book belonged to him, Euplus replied, "As you see." When the governor inquired who had taught him all he said, the answer came, "I learned it all from Our Lord Jesus Christ, the Son of God." Euplus was imprisoned and three months later interrogated again. Calvisian asked him if he still had the forbidden writings, and Euplus answered, "I do." The governor demanded to know where they were, and Euplus retorted, "Inside!" Calvisian continued, "If you still have them, bring them here," and Euplus explained again, "Inside!" pointing to his heart to show that that was how he knew them and thus possessed them still. The exasperated governor then ordered him to be tortured until he agreed to sacrifice to the gods but without success. Euplus was given another chance, on pain of death, but refused to abjure his faith, so he was sentenced to be beheaded.

The full interchange in the *Acts of Euplus*, and indeed the entire account, is the work of a skilled storyteller and quite captivating, though the wit evident in the Greek and Latin versions fades somewhat in existing German and English translations. For both ancient texts and for a discussion of the narrative by P. Franchi de' Cavaliere see *Studi e Testi* 49 (1928).

St Lelia (? Sixth Century)

The diocese of Limerick keeps the feast of St Lelia on this day, and she is commemorated in other Irish dioceses. She has been included in the new draft Roman Martyrology, though she was absent from the last edition. It is not known exactly when or where she lived, and it has been suggested that she presided over some religious foundation in the province of Munster. She has also been identified with the Dalcassian saint Liadhain great-grand-daughter of the prince Cairthenn, whom St Patrick baptized at Singland. She gives her name to Killeely (Cill Liadaini) within the borough boundary of Limerick.

See *L.I.S.*, 8, p.170; M. Moloney in the *North Munster Antiquarian Journal* (1936), p. 39.

St Porcarius and Companions, *Martyrs* (*c.* 732)

The tale of St Porcarius in his somewhat late Acts is rather quaint, but the summary account has not been expunged from the new draft Roman Martyrology.

At the beginning of the fifth century St Honoratus of Arles (6 Jan.) founded the abbey of Lérins on an island off the coast of Provence, opposite Cannes. By the eighth century the community numbered more than five hundred monks, novices, and so on. In about 732 an angel scout flew in with news of some Saracen (Moorish) marauders who had set sail for the island. Abbot Porcarius heeded the angelic warning, but the available boats could hold only the boys being educated in the monastery and thirty-six of the younger religious. They were packed off to safety while Porcarius exhorted the remaining five hundred to suffer bravely for the faith of Christ. The pirates killed all but four of them, whom they carried off as slaves.

Raids by Moorish corsairs from North Africa or Spain were not uncommon, and a presumably unarmed abbey would have offered rich pickings. Perhaps they were sighted by helpful fishermen, or a boat out from the island, too late to summon help from the mainland, but a massacre of this size seems improbable.

AA.SS., Aug., 2; B. Munke, "Die vita S. Honorati," in *Beihefte zur Zeitschrift für romanische Philologie* 32 (1911), pp. 23 ff.

Bd Charles Meehan, *Martyr* (1679)

Charles Meehan, O.F.M., was born in Ireland. He was about thirty-nine when he died at Ruthin, in north Wales, as one of the late Cromwellian martyrs, under Richard, son of Oliver. He was beatified on 22 November 1987.

Bd Innocent XI, *Pope* (1611-89)

Benedetto Odescalchi was born into a wealthy merchant's family in Como, Italy, in 1611. He was elected to the papacy on 21 September 1676 at the age of sixty-five, when he took the name Innocent. He was a man of great firmness and integrity and is the only pope to have been canonized or beatified between St Pius V in the sixteenth century and St Pius X in the twentieth.

Benedict was made a cardinal in 1645 and bishop of Novara in 1650. As a papal legate at Ferra he won a reputation as a pious, austere, though kind-hearted ecclesiastic with a special concern for the poor. He was a conscientious administrator of the Papal States, yet he was always ready even then to criticize nepotism and sinecures in Rome. As pope, he did not hesitate to act resolutely and, so it seems by modern standards, strictly and ungenerously, against thinking that he not only found personally distasteful but judged would upset due order. As so often, it is very difficult if not impossible to summarize justly the actions of such a complex and alert personality. He had an imperfect knowledge of human nature, an inadequate grounding in theology, and no acquaintance with another country; yet he was not only enmeshed in but able to affect political issues and currents of philosophical, spiritual, scientific, and cultural thought and practice with extraordinarily refined, if entangled and ultimately paradoxical, ramifications.

Innocent had been a candidate for the papacy in 1669, when the French king had opposed him fiercely, though he accepted Innocent's election in 1676. Innocent inherited a long-standing conflict with Louis XIV about the French king's right of appointment to church livings in vacant dioceses and to receive the revenues of bishoprics (the "right of regalia"). As pope he cancelled the faculty of asylum of embassies in Rome and their freedom from customs duty and police supervision. He excommunicated the French ambassador and condemned Louis XIV's absolutist interference in church affairs and revocation of the Edict of Nantes (which removed the existing minimal tolerance of all specifically Protestant activity, from publishing to worship) and the subsequent massacre and persecution of the Huguenots (which resulted in a vast emigration of people of all classes from France). "People must be led not dragged to the temple," Innocent remarked.

In general, where broad national movements were concerned, Innocent opposed persecution and the use of force in combatting heresy. Louis had also closed various convents, whereupon Innocent threatened him with penalties. This resulted in the publication by Bossuet, the great preacher and stylist, and other French ecclesiastics of the "Gallican articles" (drawn up by Bossuet himself), which held that the pope could not exert temporal power over monarchs, that an ecumenical council could overrule him, that if the Church did not consent to papal decrees they could be revoked, and that the pope had to submit to the decrees and privileges of the Gallican and other local churches. Innocent condemned Gallicanism by referring the articles to a Congregation and refused to approve two royal nominations of Gallican bishops. He chose an archbishop for Cologne who would not act in the political interests of France, thus causing Louis XIV to occupy the papal territory of Avignon and to imprison the papal nuncio. One of Innocent's great achievements, the maintenance of the Holy League against the Turks, was almost thwarted by French wars and Louis XIV's unhelpful attitude, though Innocent might be said to have encouraged this by a refusal to make concessions over matters of secondary importance.

Innocent also criticized James II/VII of England and Scotland when he tried to restore Catholicism there, especially the Declaration of Indulgence of 1687.

James was the sole supporter of Louis, who had recommended using force to make England Catholic.

Innocent condemned sixty-five lax propositions in moral theology in the Bull *Sanctissimus Dominus* (1687). He also condemned the supposed Quietism in the work of the Spanish priest Miguel de Molinos, whose immensely popular *Spiritual Guide* all but negated the efficacy of the will in human striving for perfection and recommended reliance on the divine presence in an act of pure faith, as well as the cultivation of a quasi-mystical state of quietude rather than the usual religious practices such as hearing Mass and all forms of mortification. Molinos' works were very influential, primarily in Italy, where they were first published. They are said to have had effects both beneficial, as on the thought of Mme Guyon and other contemporary mystics, and injurious to the discipline then thought necessary in religious houses, as among a growing number of rebellious nuns who shunned Confession and all forms of outward devotion. In 1685 Innocent had ordered the arrest of Molinos, who, though a Spaniard, had been resident in Rome since 1663 and was a much respected spiritual director. His arrest was accomplished largely through his immense correspondence: the officers of the Inquisition collected twelve thousand of his letters to compile their dossier of dangerous ideas. Molinos had a strong following, including such important ecclesiastics as Cardinal Petrucci. He had been a friend of Innocent's before the latter became pope; indeed Cardinal Odescalchi had been a member of his circle, but the pope had already shown that he was against nepotism and special favours.

Probably by means that would now be thought improper, Molinos was persuaded to recant. In 1687 he was brought to trial for his ideas and sentenced to life imprisonment on charges of immoral behaviour. Innocent also condemned thirty-four propositions from Petrucci's works, but the cardinal was persuaded to make an almost-private retraction and was not gaoled. He was allowed to retain his offices, but his works remained on the Index of prohibited books until the twentieth century. He is said to have been the only cardinal whose works were condemned in his lifetime. Innocent's final proscription of Quietism in the Bull *Coelistis Pastor* (1689) took the form of a rejection of Molinos' teaching and sixty-eight Quietist propositions. Unfortunately these actions and the general campaign against Quietism made meditation and mysticism seem dangerous activities for nearly a century and a half, so that the works of even St John of the Cross had to be published in severely cut versions. In spite of this show of papal firmness, Innocent's opponents accused him of Jansenism; yet he was a supporter of daily Communion and other scarcely Jansenist practices. He was not harsh to the Jansenists because he hoped to reconcile the more obdurate proponents of the tendency. The accusations had much to do with Innocent's continuous conflict with France but also with his abolition of various sinecures in Rome and with such over-scrupulous domestic measures as laws against gambling and immodest dress and his frequent prohibitions of carni-

97

vals. There was also local opposition to his severe economic measures. These enabled him to balance the budget and to contribute munificently to the Christian campaign against the Turks that culminated in Sobieski's victory at Vienna.

Throughout his term of office Innocent remained a man of simple habits and of generous nature but one firm in his dealing with error and with ecclesiastical ambition and extravagance. His autocratic yet also weak and gaunt features are well portrayed in the figure for his monumental tomb (a dark bronze sarcophagus) in St Peter's, Rome, by Pietro Monnot, after a design by Carlo Maratta (1625-1713). Innocent died on 12 April 1689 and was beatified in 1956. But for French opposition and for his suspected inclination to Jansenism he would probably have been beatified two hundred years earlier, for the Romans are said to have venerated him as a saint soon after his death. The cause was started in 1714 in the reign of Louis XIV, though it was dropped under Pope Benedict XIV. It was re-opened only in 1944, probably because of Innocent's reputation as a firm defender of the freedom of the Church (very much an issue during the Second World War) and his Holy League against the Turks. It is not certain whether the analogy was with the actual and supposed threats to Rome from both the Germans and the Allies, or with the need for a campaign against resurgent Communism in liberated Italy and France, and then the erosion of the Church's rights in the Soviet bloc. The new interest probably had very little to do with any revival within the Church of Quietist trends. In the end, the history of Innocent's beatification process raises in another form the same unresolved but fascinating and important questions that bedevil yet enrich any responsible discussion of his thought and actions and those of his contemporaries.

G. Papàsogli, *Innocenzo XI* (1956); Jedin-Dolan, 6, pp. 118-27; *A.A.S.* 48 (1956), pp. 754-9, 762-78; P. Gini in *Bibl.SS.*, 7, 848-56; E. Michaud, *Louis XIV et Innocent XI* (4 vols., 1882-3); L. O'Brian, *Innocent XI and the Revocation of the Edict of Nantes* (1930); J. Orcibal, *Louis XIV contre Innocent XI* (1949); E. Duffy, *Saints and Sinners: A History of the Popes* (1997), pp. 188-9. On Molinos see Orcibal, *op. cit.*; R. A. Knox, *Enthusiasm* (1951), pp. 295-318.

R.M.

SS Anicetus and Photius, martyrs of Nicomedia, ? 305

St Herculanus, bishop of Perugia, martyred by the Goths, *c.* 457

SS James Domai Nam, priest; Antony Nguyen Dich, peasant; and Michael Nguyen Huy Ay, catechist, martyrs in Vietnam (1838)—see "The Martyrs of Vietnam," 2 Feb.

13

SS PONTIAN, *Pope* (*c.* 236), **and HIPPOLYTUS** (*c.*170–*c.* 236), *Martyrs*

On this day the new draft Roman Martyrology associates Pontian and Hippolytus and, indeed, by commemorating the translation of their remains to the cemetery of Callistus, recalls their connection with Pope Callistus I, also a martyr. In certain respects they are connected historically, though some of the associations between them stressed in the past are dubious and others accidental. To deal with the relevant events and traditions adequately it is necessary to cover Callistus here, though it is possible that the revised Martyrology will retain his actual feast as 14 October.

When he became pope in 198 or 199, Zephyrinus made Callistus (or Calixtus) effectively his "chief minister" and eventually a deacon or archdeacon, with such major responsibilities as the Christian cemeteries and perhaps the organization of the Roman parish, or titular, churches. A rich widow, Cecilia, gave him the land on the Appian Way where he opened a cemetery eventually named after him and where the third-century popes were usually buried. Callistus' opponent, the priest (possibly a bishop) and theologian Hippolytus, tells us that Zephyrinus supported Cleomenes, a leading Roman supporter of the fashionable Monarchian heresy. Among other theories, mainline Monarchians held that the unity or "monarchy" of the Father did not imply the independence of the Son in what prevailed as, and therefore was held always to have been, the orthodox Christian sense. Sabellius, one of the main proponents of the Modalist, or Sabellian, version of Monarchism, held that the Godhead was differentiated only by successive modes or operations; that Jesus was God by derivation, that is, by an influence from the Father on his human person; and that the Father suffered as the Son. In a perhaps essentially accurate if biased philosophical and anti-heretical work, the *Philosopheumena*, once attributed to Origen, Hippolytus also tells us that Callistus had been a slave of an important Christian, Carpophorus, who put him in charge of a bank that failed. Accordingly, we are told, the creditors threatened to punish Callistus severely. He forced his way into a synagogue and tried to arrest some Jewish debtors to the bank. They promptly denounced him as a Christian. He was beaten and sent to the Sardinian mines. Marcia, the emperor Commodus' mistress, is said to have obtained his release, together with other Christians. Pope Victor I sent him—with a pension—to recover at Antium. According to Hippolytus, Callistus (probably while an archdeacon) also supported Sabellius and even publicly professed a version of the (Monarchian) heresy in which Jesus, as man, is certainly the Son, though, as God, he is the Father. It has been cogently suggested, however, that Callistus was trying to mediate between two rival groups. Now, of course, when such finely-modulated controversies and a mediator's somewhat delphic statements, composed to reconcile rival factions but misrepresented as heresy by one of them, are reduced (as here) to cryptic or ambiguous summary propositions—and they have long since given way to other notions of theological right and wrong with less dire implications—detection of the borderline between orthodoxy and heresy in this particular respect may seem a very nice procedure indeed. Eventually (probably when he became pope), Callistus condemned and excommunicated Sabellius, which some commentators interpret as exhausted patience but others—following, presumably, Hippolytus—as due recantation.

Hippolytus had been the president of a major school of theology for many years. He was widely respected. When Origen was in Rome (*c.* 212), he went to hear Hippolytus preach. He was a severe critic of intellectually inferior arguments and of middle-brow enthusiasts such as the apocalypticists, who expected an imminent end of the world and whom he reproved in his chronicle of world history to 234. Hippolytus had not accepted the teaching of Pope Zephyrinus and was not satisfied with Callistus' condemnation of Sabellius. Supported by a strong anti-Callistian party, he broke off communion with a pope he declared to be heretical. Presumably believing that he himself ought to have been elected after Zephyrinus, Hippolytus became a rival, or antipope. This parallel movement, or schism, extended for some years beyond the death of Callistus, whose successors, Urban and Pontian, Hippolytus continued to oppose. He issued a liturgical handbook for his followers, the *Apostolike Paradosis*, and his Canon of the Mass would seem to be the earliest surviving evidence for the Eucharistic Prayer of the Roman liturgy. One of the texts of the revised Roman Canon is based on writings ascribed to him. He was obviously held in great esteem, for among various testimonies certain Sacramentaries and the *Liber Pontificalis* acknowledge his cult, and a (by then headless) third-century statue in his honour showing him in philosopher's dress and bearing a list of his writings was found in the sixteenth century. It is now in the Lateran Museum.

Hippolytus also said that Callistus was morally suspect and claimed that he accepted sexual sinners as penitents and recognized marriages invalid in Roman law, such as those between freed-men and -women and slaves. It has been and remains a question of scholarly debate whether it was Callistus who issued a "lax" edict on penance adversely criticized by Tertullian. Hippolytus certainly refused to relax, as the Roman bishops did, the rules of penance to accommodate the large numbers of converts from paganism, including rich Christian women who might be forced into marriages with pagans or even Christians of an inappropriate class. For their part, both Zephyrinus and

Callistus accused Hippolytus of ditheism, and if the writings said to be his are his, then he would seem to have held that the Spirit is not a Person and that the Word has two aspects or states: the inward, eternal Logos and the outward, temporal Logos, who, so to speak, develops to the point of incarnation as the Son, so that the Son "was" not "for ever" in the same relation to the Father; and this would not accord with orthodox Christian doctrine. Here again, without very detailed explanation it is difficult to show just how that is so and even more difficult to demonstrate that what Hippolytus is said to have proposed differs essentially from what Callistus and Zephyrinus are said to have held. Another problem is that, as in the third century, when brilliant theologians such as Hippolytus tried (in his *Refutation of All Heresies*) to show that heresies were wrong by exposing the impropriety of—but thereby expounding—the Greek philosophical arguments on which they rested, these very expositions may, as then, be interpreted as a theologian's own theses.

Callistus built two churches with houses and offices on land donated by St Cecilia in the Trastevere area of Rome, where her family owned several blocks of flats. One became the "title" of St Cecilia; the other was named after Callistus but is now Santa Maria in Trastevere. The former non-Christian inhabitants of the district must have been evicted and would have seen the action not as slum clearance for God's own people, and thus for the greater good, but as partisan property development. They could not claim the emperor's support, for Alexander Severus was religiously inclined, liked to mix bits of different faiths, was sympathetic to Christians, and preferred the celebration of their rites to the taverns said to have been on the spot. It has been suggested that dispossessed artisans and shopkeepers were responsible for the martyrdom of Callistus, whom, his quite unreliable Passion tells us, a band of pagans threw into a well in the Trastevere, possibly on 14 October 222.

Pontian (or Pontianus) succeeded Urban I as bishop of Rome in about 230. He was said to have been a Roman by birth. The only known event of his pontificate is a synod held in Rome to confirm the condemnation of certain doctrines attributed to Origen. Origen had quarrelled with his bishop, Demetrius, apparently because Palestinian bishops had ordained him to the priesthood despite the fact that he was not thought suitable. This was because, when head of the catechetical school in Alexandria and a young and over-zealous ascetic, he had interpreted Matthew 19:12 literally and castrated himself. He was deposed in Alexandria and took refuge in Caesarea, where he established a school and wrote and preached. Controversy about his actual and supposed works (though supported by many famous persons, including saints) continued for centuries; Origenism was last formally condemned at the Second Council of Constantinople in 533.

The former guards officer Maximin (or Maximinus) became emperor in 235 and promptly intensified the persecution of church leaders. Pontian and Hippolytus (still a priest) were deported to Sardinia, which was reputed to be unhealthy. Pontian resigned his papacy and both he and Hippolytus died on the island in 235 or 236, from ill treatment rather than the insalubrious locality alone and are therefore venerated as martyrs. Traditionally, Pontian is said to have been beaten to death with sticks.

Some years later, when that particular persecution had stopped, Pope St Fabian, Pontian's next-but-one successor (236-50; 20 Jan.), had Pontian's and Hippolytus' remains moved to Rome, which would indicate that before his death Hippolytus was somehow reconciled to the rival party. Pontian was buried in the cemetery of Callistus. In 1909 his original epitaph was found there. It reads PONTIANUS EPISK MPT, but the last word is a later addition. He is commemorated on this day together with Hippolytus largely because their names were coupled in the fourth-century *Depositio Martyrum*: "Idus Aug. Ypoliti in Tiburtina et Pontiani in Callisti," for Hippolytus was interred on the Tiburtine Way on the same day as Pontian, 13 August. Nevertheless, for a long time the more illustrious Hippolytus was commemorated on his own, but gradually his fame was obscured. For many years he was confused with a fictitious Roman martyr, a soldier said to have been converted by St Laurence (10 Aug.) and condemned to be ripped in two by horses. Prudentius had already mistaken him for another martyr said to have been torn apart by wild horses; this also fitted his name, for Hippolytus means "loosed horse," and his mythical predecessor, the honourable but wrongly-accused Hippolytus, son of Theseus, had suffered the same fate when his grandfather, Poseidon, had sent a sea monster to frighten his horses. As a result of this confusion at least two churches in England were dedicated to Hippolytus, and ailing horses were brought through one of them to his shrine to be healed.

Florus restored Pontian to the Martyrology with 20 November as his date. The new draft Roman Martyrology may be said to have reunited all three saints, associated indeed not only by misadventure but by controversy, rivalry, and calumny. Thus through their martyrdom they may be said to have transcended the bitter divisions of those harsh times in the communion of saints.

For Callistus see L. Duchesne, *Le Liber Pontificalis*, 1, pp. 141-2; A. d'Alès, *L'Edit de Calliste* (1914); B. Altaner and C. B. Daly, "The Edict of Callistus," in *Studia Patristica* 3 (1961), pp. 176-82. See Hippolytus' *Philosopheumena* in the translation of F. Legge (2 vols., 1921); *The Apostolic Tradition*, ed. H. Chadwick (1968); J. M. Hanssens, *La Liturgie d'Hippolyte* (1965). On Hippolytus (and Callistus) see J. J. I. von Döllinger, *Hippolytus and Callistus* (Eng. trans., 1876); A. d'Alès, *La Théologie de Saint Hippolyte* (1906); G. Bovini, *Sant'Ippolito della Via Tiburtina* (1942); J. Quasten, *Patrology*, 2 (1953), pp. 165ff. On Pontian see *C. M.H.*, pp. 439-40; Marucchi in *Nuovo Bolletino* (1909), pp. 35-50.

The horrible sufferings of Hippolytus riven by horses, as in the legend, are shown graphically and elegantly in a panel painting by Dierik Bouts (Bruges cathedral). Callistus appears solemn and regal in Diamante's painting (Sistine Chapel, Rome).

St Cassian of Imola, *Martyr* (?)

A martyr named Cassian probably existed, and he is retained in the new draft Roman Martyrology, which also repeats the incident described below. His Passion, however, seems to be a prose version of a poem by Prudentius. According to this he was a Christian teacher who taught children to read and write at Imola, a town twenty-seven miles from Ravenna in Italy. There is no record of his becoming a patron of teachers in spite of his pre-eminent qualification for the role.

During a violent persecution of Christians Cassian was arrested and interrogated by the provincial governor. He refused to sacrifice to the gods, so the governor is said to have devised an appropriate punishment. He ordered Cassian's own pupils to stab him to death with their iron styli, or pens, which they used to form letters on their wax tablets. He was put naked in front of two hundred boys whose enmity he had incurred quite naturally in the course of instruction. Some threw tablets, pens, and knives at his face and head. Others cut his flesh or stabbed him with their knives. Yet others stuck their pens in him or cut letters out of him. Cassian, however, showed his readiness to die for Christ by urging them on. Christians buried him at Imola.

The Christian Latin poet Prudentius (348-*post* 405) says that he prayed before the martyr's tomb on his way to Rome and describes a picture over the altar depicting Cassian's sufferings, which provided part of his subject matter. This is clearly a literary device of the kind Prudentius favoured in his Christian ballads. More suspiciously, the stabbing incident recalls a similar occasion in a fragment by Apuleius (author of *The Golden Ass*, the second-century African Latin novel built on reversals of fortune and certainly known to Prudentius) or in one of the lost sources. The similar though more varied torture by schoolboys in the Acts of the remarkably contentious St Mark of Arethusa (28 Mar.) either has the same source or results from cross-fertilization by plagiarizing hagiographers.

See S. Lanzoni, *Le leggende di S. Cassiano d'Imola* (1913); *Didaskaleion*, 3 (1925), pp. 1-44; *C.M.H.*, pp. 440-1. For the sources see Prudentius, *Peristephanon*, 9, in *Works*, Latin and Eng. trans. H. J. Thomson (1949-53); P. Franchi de' Cavalieri, *Hagiographica*, p. 131.

St Radegund (518-87)

Radegund (or Radegunde) was the daughter of the Thuringian prince Berthaire, a pagan, who was murdered by his brother Hermenefrid. She was born in 518, probably at Erfurt. She was twelve and possibly already a Christian when she was captured by invading Franks, who destroyed the independence of Thuringia in about 531. The debauched Clothaire (Chlotar) I, king of the Neustrian Franks, was the youngest son of Clovis, the first Christian king of the Franks. Officially a Christian and a founder of monasteries, Clothaire is said to have had Radegund instructed in the Christian faith and baptized. She lived at first at Athies, near Péronne. She did not want to marry, but when she was about eighteen she agreed to become Clothaire's wife. He was violent and a womanizer. He was also very irritated by their childlessness, which he ascribed to Radegund. Their marriage was perhaps bigamous, for Clothaire is said to have been married at least five times.

Radegund comforted herself with pious practices and good works. She cared for the poor and founded a leper hospital where she looked after the inmates. She is said to have kissed their diseased bodies, but this is probably an exaggeration on the part of her over-enthusiastic biographers. Clothaire ignored her piety at first, but eventually he found it trying and remarked that he was married to a nun, not a queen, and that she was turning his court into a monastery. When he murdered her brother in about 550, she fled the court. She asked Bishop Médard of Noyon to let her become a nun. Wary of the notoriously brutal Clothaire, he refused. But Radegund turned up in church already veiled as a nun, and he decided to make her a deaconess. Soon after that she went to Tours, where she established a monastery for men, then to Candes, and on to her domain at Saix, in Poitou, where she lived a penitential life and looked after the poor for six months.

Eventually Radegund founded a monastery of nuns near Poitiers, which adopted the Rule of St Caesarius of Arles (27 Aug.) and where she withdrew in about 561. Radegund heard that Clothaire was very disturbed by this and was planning to carry her off again. She wrote to St Germanus of Paris (28 May) for help. He visited Clothaire and persuaded him to leave her alone. The king was so impressed, it seems, that he even went to Poitiers to ask Radegund's forgiveness and made gifts to the monastery. It was a double monastery, for men and women, and practised a strict and permanent enclosure. It was known first as St Mary's and later as the abbey of the Holy Cross.

Radegund made her friend Agnes abbess and spent the next thirty years of her life there in prayer, scholarship, and good works but also gathered round her a group of women who were not only devout but intelligent and cultivated. Some of them were from senatorial families, others of royal blood. The nuns had to study for two hours every day. The reference books say that they had a considerable influence on the Christian culture of Merovingian Gaul, but how far that went is difficult to gauge. There is as much evidence that Holy Cross was an extraordinary instance of a few oases of such refinement. Even the most celebrated abbeys, whether royal or private foundations, did not have a direct, widespread influence on the life of the Church in an already largely coarse and grim world, as the intellectual life of continental Europe went into decline. It was some time before the foundations following the example of Columban (23 Nov.) bore their full fruits of example. Radegund is also said to have had a great dislike of war and violence and to have sent letters advising peace to prospective combatants when there were rumours of conflict. This attitude did not extend to her own body, which she punished as was then common among enthusiastic religious. She is also said to have been keen on very hot baths—unusual at the time—which she recommended for the sick. She once made a very ill nun stay in one for two hours, by which time she was completely cured. This was said to be miraculous.

Eventually St Venantius Fortunatus (14 Dec.), Roman gentleman of fastidious taste, literary dandy, writer of exquisite poems, beautiful hymns, and pleasant occasional verse, ended his wanderings at Poitiers. Radegund's civilized abbey was the haven he had been looking for. He settled nearby and celebrated her as his "angel-watered lily" and her soul-mate and spiritual daughter Abbess Agnes and the other nuns of Holy Cross in similarly appropriate terms. Fortunatus' imagery and contemporary accounts make Holy Cross, its inhabitants, and their surroundings seem a tiny world out of time: like the loveliest of the gardens of Paradise in the best medieval illuminations: *"Hic ver purpureum viridantia gramina gignit, / Et Paradisiacas spargit odore rosas"* ("Here spring makes everything grow sparkling green and fresh, with heavenly-scented roses in between"), as one of his poems on a garden puts it.

Fortunatus became the lifelong friend, adviser, unofficial steward and later chaplain of the community, for he was ordained priest at Poitiers. To the abbey he brought the delights of secular as well as elegant religious culture. He exchanged highly-stylized verse letters with Radegund and Agnes, thanking them, say, for a gift of delicacies such as vegetables sprinkled with honey, accompanying a return gift of flowers or chestnuts ("I wove this basket with my own hands, dear mother and dear sister. It contains a rustic present for you: chestnuts from a tree in my own area"), or even describing a good meal but also inquiring about their health and commenting helpfully on their austerities. These lyrical notes could also combine playful and witty observations and effects with a kind of spiritual troubadour intensity. The inevitable rumours of an illicit relationship began to circulate, but Fortunatus scorned them in one of his *Carmina*.

At this time a scramble for relics began in France, hitherto an area with relatively few martyrs of its own and where such objects had received little attention. Radegund became a great collector of holy mementoes of the first class and enriched her church with those of a number of saints. She was very anxious to have incontestably the best of all relics. Between 560 and 570 she sent envoys to the East to find pieces of the true cross for the abbey. In 569 she received from Constantinople a fragment of the cross adorned with gold and precious stones, a gift of the emperor Justin II to her convent. It was accompanied by a book of the Gospels similarly decorated and was backed up with an array of major relics of important saints. Sigebert deputed (St) Euphronius, Archbishop of Tours, to depose the collection in Holy Cross on 19 November 569. All this inspired Fortunatus to write for the great occasion the famous processional hymn *Vexilla Regis prodeunt* (The royal banners forward go), in which the sonorous devices absolutely fit the profundity of the subject. It became the great hymn of the Crusaders. It was later sung in Passiontide, as were *Pange lingua gloriosi proelium certaminis* (Sing, my tongue, the glorious battle), in honour of the same relic, and some of the other hymns he wrote at Poitiers. He also composed a number of long epitaphs to console Radegund (and others among whom they were circulated) for the deaths of her friends and relations.

Radegund spent some of her last years in complete seclusion. She died peacefully on 13 August 587, and Agnes died about the same date. St Gregory of Tours (17 Nov.) describes Radegund's face as she lay in her coffin as "shining more beautifully than lilies or roses." By 589, Gregory also tells us, Holy Cross had become a centre of dissension when the community split into rival groups. But Fortunatus and the nun Baudenivia recalled the harmony of the era of Radegund in their Lives of the saint and disclosed the miracles which, they said, had been worked even in her lifetime. Baudenivia remembered the miraculous cure of a blind man during Radegund's funeral. Her body, deposited outside the walls of Poitiers some distance from the monastery, became an object of veneration; new miraculous cures were duly reported; and her memory and example were cited in the struggle against pagan idolators. It now appeared that she had led a somewhat more strenuous life in the service of the Church than had been supposed. On one occasion, the world learned, she had faced a multitude of pagan Franks armed with swords and clubs and had reduced them to docility by the sole power of the cross which she had with her. Her feast was first celebrated in the eighth or ninth century. A number of churches in France and several in England were named after her, and Jesus College, Cambridge, was formerly dedicated to her.

See *AA.SS.*, Aug., 3, pp. 66-92, and *M.G.H.*, *Scriptores Merov.*, 2, pp. 358-95, for the contemporary Lives by Venantius Fortunatus and the nun Baudenivia, the Life by Hildebert of Lavardin, and the anonymous Life by Henry Bradshaw, O.S.B. (d. 1513; attributed), ed. F. Brittain (1926); in French: E. Briand (1898) and R. Aigrain, 2d ed. (1952); in German: L. Schmidt, *St Radegundis in Gross-Höflein*, *Burgenländische Forschungen* 32 (1956); and English: F. Brittain, *St Radegund, Patroness of Jesus College, Cambridge* (1925). See also D. Tardi, *Fortunat* (1927); J. M. Wallace-Hadrill, *The Frankish Church* (1983).

Radegund became the patron of prisoners because she was a captive, of shoemakers because she cleaned and polished the other nuns' shoes, and of potters because she washed the convent dishes. She was invoked against wolves, to cure the plague, and to exorcise demons. She is shown as a queen with a crown, sceptre, and fleur-de-lys on her robe, or as a nun with an open book. She appears with Fortunatus and his disciple St Disciolus. There are eleventh-century miniatures of Radegund's life from a manuscript of Holy Cross (Poitiers Library); and stained-glass scenes after them (Chartres Cathedral). In a twelfth-century fresco she holds a chalice to her heart (church of St Pierre-de-la-Trimouille, Poitou). In the nineteenth century Ingres designed stained-glass images of her (former chapel of Louis Philippe, Freux), and Puvis de Chavannes painted a mural of her listening to Fortunatus' poems (town-hall staircase, Poitiers).

St Maximus the Confessor (*c.* 580–662)

John Scotus Erigena, himself a brilliant philosopher, called Maximus "the divine philosopher, the all-wise, the most distinguished of teachers." He is certainly a very interesting theologian, but his ideas have been obscured for the extra-scholarly world by his involvement in perplexing arguments and by his entrapment in Byzantine manoeuvres, nasty, brutish, but also labyrinthine. To appreciate the implications of known events in his career one must understand some of the political and ecclesiastical repercussions and theological and philosophical intricacies of basic controversies in the history of the Christian Church. Notions of "energy," "nature," "will," and so on, in seventh-century physics, psychology, and philosophy, and argument then about what Aristotle (for example) meant by them, are very different from their implications nowadays in contexts such as the present work, where their easy use disguises almost total disagreement about their meaning (if any) in even the foregoing areas. The present account is necessarily reductive.

Maximus was born into the Byzantine aristocracy in about 580 in, it is thought, Constantinople. The emperor Heraclius appointed him his main secretary. He resigned and became first (*c.* 614) a monk, then abbot of the monastery of Chrysopolis (Scutari), where he wrote some of his treatises. The Persians invaded in 626, and he fled to Alexandria, in Egypt, where he completed more of his writings. He was a resolute defender of Dyophysite (that is, Catholic Christian) orthodoxy against Monothelitism, a politico–religious heresy evoked by the Persian and later Muslim invasions and formulated to ally the Monophysites with their Chalcedonian fellow-Christians, who were Dyophysites. Very summarily, the original Monophysites held that there was a single, divine nature in the person of the incarnate Christ; Dyophysites that there was a double, divine and human, nature in him. Monothelites said that there were two natures in Christ but a single will and mode of activity. This compromise formula emerged from conferences of the emperor Heraclius with the leading Monophysites in 624. It seemed to have orthodox precedents, was supported by leading churchmen such as Patriarch Sergius of Constantinople, Bishop Theodore of Pharan, and Patriarch Cyrus of Alexandria, and proved immensely successful in reconciling Monophysites. It reached its best expression in nine propositions of a Pact (or "formula of union") proclaimed solemnly at Alexandria on 3 June 633: one and the same Christ operates divinely and humanly "with a single theandric energy."

St Sophronius (11 Mar.), patriarch of Jerusalem, fiercely rejected the formula and re-asserted the existence of two energies in Christ, for energy is derived from nature (*cf.* Aristotle). Sophronius and Sergius argued, agreed, disagreed. Not-so-subtle changes followed subtle ones in seemingly key terminology. When Sergius asked for his guidance in about 634, Pope Honorius (in two letters which referred to one will, *una voluntas,* in Christ) seemed to agree with the Pact and with a judgment of the patriarch which spoke of the "actual operating energy of the one operative Christ." Honorius is said to have meant by "one will" a specific act of Christ's human will determined only by the divine will, but of course different parties read their own position into his ambiguous phraseology, and even nowadays only like-minded people with the same philosophical background tend to agree on the meaning of what he wrote. In 638 Heraclius' *Ecthesis* declared that one will in Christ was the statement of faith. The *Ecthesis* is said to have referred to Christ's actual will rather than the faculty of willing, but again it was taken as meaning whatever its hearers wanted it to mean. The Eastern Church accepted the single will at two councils in Constantinople in 638-9. The emperors Heraclius and Constans II remained seeming proponents of Monothelitism.

Sophronius died in 638, and Maximus became the champion of orthodoxy in his place. He did not think that Honorius had actually held Monotheletic views and defended him as orthodox. He found this or that expression of the point at issue unsatisfactory and examined the whole question in a responsible and, it seems, far too intellectually sophisticated way.

After a dispute with Maximus at Carthage in 645, Pyrrhus (temporarily deposed as Monothelite), patriarch of Constantinople, had first abjured Monotheletism, then asserted the defeat of Maximus. In 648 Constans abrogated the *Ecthesis* and issued a decree, the *Typos*, intended as another compromise but seen by the exacting Maximus as still essentially Monotheletic. Maximus obtained rejections of surviving Monotheletism from a number of African synods, and in 649 he went to Rome and helped to ensure its condemnation by the pope and the Lateran Council. Eventually the emperor found all this independent enterprise tedious, politically inconvenient, and dangerous. In 653 Constans ("odious to himself and to mankind," says Gibbon) had Pope St Martin I (13 Apr.) arrested in Rome, banished to the Chersonese, and starved to death. Constans then summoned the far-too-learned divine to a conference in the capital. This, as so often, meant arrest by the imperial police, travel in custody, and trial for conspiracy, though with the opportunity to agree to the imperial formula as accepted by the church of Constantinople. Maximus refused. Unfortunately he had been a friend of the exarch Gregory of Carthage, who had had himself acclaimed as (anti)emperor. Therefore Maximus was guilty of high treason. He was exiled to Bizya, in Thrace, where he suffered from cold and hunger. After a few months Bishop Theodosius of Caesarea in Bithynia arrived with a commission to begin an accusatory theological debate. Maximus argued so eloquently for the two natures that, it seems, Theodosius was moved to conviction, to retraction of the imperial half-heresy—on, to make quite sure, the Gospels, the cross, and an image of Mary— and to pity. He gave the confessor money and clothes (which the local bishop promptly confiscated). Maximus was sent to a monastery at Rhegium. Soon Theodosius visited him with another deputation and an offer of imperial honours for the right answers. Maximus reminded him of his solemn change of mind and heart, and Theodosius replied: "Put yourself in my position. You try telling the emperor that!" Maximus stayed firm. He was thrashed, his few possessions were taken away, and the next day he was taken to Perberis, where his friends and supporters, Anastasius the Abbot and Anastasius the Apocrisiarius, were already captives. He remained there for six hard years.

In 661 he was again brought to Constantinople, with his two companions, and tortured. He was scourged, and the interrogators are said to have removed his tongue and cut off his right hand to make sure that he could neither utter nor write another inconvenient opinion. He was then pilloried in each of the city's twelve quarters. The others received the same punishment. This kind of treatment was not unusual in the reign of Constans, who made his brother a deacon to disqualify him for the throne, then murdered him, and in 668 was himself assassinated in his bath by a valet. Maximus was exiled again, this time to the Caucasus (to, it is said, Skhemaris, near Batum on the Black Sea). Not surprisingly, he died within a few weeks. Honorius' successors condemned Monothelitism. In 680 the Sixth Ecumenical Council at Constantinople un-equivocally proclaimed the existence of two wills, divine and human, in Christ, as the orthodox Catholic Christian belief. Pope Honorius was censured.

Maximus was not only a vigorous participant in open controversies but a writer of many works on liturgy (the *Mystagogia*, a mystical treatise on the "cosmic" nature of liturgy in a heavenly ritual-area); exegesis (the *Ambigua*, on Gregory of Nazianzus, and refuting Origen; *Quaestiones ad Thalassium*, on knotty points of scripture); and asceticism (the *Liber Asceticus* and *Capita de Caritate*); as well as theology (a number of doctrinal works against the Monophysites and Monothelites; paraphrases of Pseudo-Dionysius).

Maximus came to be called "the Confessor" because of his defence of what prevailed as orthodox Christian belief and his zealous support for the teaching authority of the Bishop of Rome. Yet his reputation has always been strong in the East. He is essentially an Eastern thinker. The background of Maximus' writings is as captivating as they are fascinating in themselves. Influences and sources range from Syrian and rabbinical visions and tales familiar to the Fathers of the Church to a Neoplatonist notion of eternal return to the Godhead. The principal complex of ideas in Maximus' dogmatico-ascetic thought may justly be characterized as mystical theology. He sees universal history as a process of cosmic illumination, obscuration, then redemptive enlightenment. Humans existed originally in a state of equilibrium. They were created as incorruptible beings with senses under the control of reason. In the culpable pursuit of pleasure they destroyed the supremacy of reason and made them-selves subject to passion. With this aboriginal collapse of order the light faded and evil entered the world. Jesus Christ the Word was born into the darkness of the human mind and existence to illuminate and divinize them and to restore the balance between reason and impulse. He now offers humanity the power to lead a virtuous and loving life, culminating in the full light of union with God.

An important aspect of Maximus' work which cannot be duly expanded here is its "dynamic" view of human development and a constantly re-created universe. This challenges not only the domineering State but also other forms of constraint, yet remains within an orthodox framework of support for hierarchy. Some commentators, to be sure, have said that Maximus is close to implying that knowledge and being are one; that to know God is, in a sense, to be God. But this "in a sense" is crucial; it was the very point, though in another context, of all that Byzantine heat, confusion, and brutality. Perhaps the best— indeed, the only—way in which we can appreciate what Maximus felt was so important is to explore his works and decide for ourselves what he means by "There is one energy of God and of the saints" and "We are made gods and sons and body and limbs and part of God."

See the English translations of *Liber Asceticus* and *Capita de Caritate* by P. Sherwood (1955); G. C. Berthold (trans.), *Maximus the Confessor: Selected Writings* (1985); the first translation of his theological treatises, with intro., in A. Louth, *Maximus the Confessor* (1996). See the early Life ed. R. Devreesse, "La Vie de saint Maxime le Confesseur et ses Recensions," in *Anal.Boll.* 56 (1928), pp. 5-49. See also *Anal.Boll.*, 53 (1935), pp. 49ff.; P. Sherwood, *Date-list of the Works of Maximus the Confessor* (1952); H. U. von Balthasar, *Kosmische Liturgie: Maximus Bekenner* (2d ed., 1961); L. Thunberg, *The Theological Anthropology of Maximus the Confessor* (1965); W. Völker, *Maximus Confessor als Meister des geistlichen Lebens* (1965); J.-C. Larchet, *La Divinisation de l'homme selon saint Maxime le Confesseur* (1996); Jedin-Dolan, 2, pp. 457-63. Les Editions du Cerf is undertaking a complete translation of all his major works into French, starting with the *Lettres*, intro. J.-C. Larchet, trans. E. Ponsoye (1996).

St Wigbert, *Abbot* (*c.* 745)

Wigbert was an Englishman who became a monk when young. Very little is known about him. St Boniface (5 June) invited him to take part in the conversion of the Germans and made him abbot of Fritzlar, a monastery three miles from Kassel, where St Sturmi (17 Dec.) was one of his disciples. Later he was transferred to Ohrdruf, in Thuringia. He successfully organized both these foundations. Eventually Boniface allowed him to return to Fritzlar to live quietly and prepare for death. He died in about 745. Some thirty years later St Lull (16 Oct.) translated his body to the monastery of Hersfeld, and he became its patron. This Wigbert is not to be confused with the other St Wigbert (Wictbert), a disciple of St Egbert (24 Apr.) who tried to evangelize the Frisians at the end of the seventh century.

See *M.G.H., Scriptores*, 15, pp. 37-43 for the many-miracled Life by Servatus Lupus written about a century after Wigbert's death; *B.T.A.*, 3, p. 322.

Bd Gertrude of Altenburg (1297)

Gertrude was the third daughter of St Elizabeth of Hungary (17 Nov.) married when she was fourteen, and her husband, Bd Louis of Thuringia (11 Sept.). She was born two weeks after her father's death in September 1227 at Otranto on his way to the Crusade in Palestine. Before leaving Louis had agreed with his wife that this child should be dedicated to the service of God in thanks for their years of happiness together. If a girl was born, she would join the Premonstratensian canonesses at Altenberg, near Wetzlar. Elizabeth had put herself under the direction of the severe and wholly insensitive Friar Conrad of Marburg. He insisted that the baby Gertrude should be taken to Altenberg when she was less than two years old. When she was old enough to choose for herself and her parents were both dead (her mother died at the age of twenty-four) Gertrude ratified their decision. She was formally received into the community. By the age of twenty-two she was abbess. She spent the inheritance she received from her uncle on building a new church for the monastery and an almshouse for the poor, which she ran herself. She is said to have taken little advantage of her station and, as far as pious works and mortifications were concerned, to have been indistinguishable from the other nuns.

During the Seventh Crusade Gertrude commemorated her father by solemnly binding herself and her community constantly to support, with prayers and penances, the efforts made to reclaim and protect the Holy Places. In 1270 she obtained permission for Corpus Christi to be celebrated in her monastery, and she was one of the first to introduce the feast into Germany. When Dietrich the Dominican was writing his Life of Elizabeth in 1289, he noted that Gertrude was still living. She died in her fiftieth year as abbess.

See *AA.SS.*, Aug., 3; *Stimmen aus Maria Laach* (1893), 2, pp. 415ff.

Bd William Freeman, *Martyr* (1595)

William Freeman (also known as William Mason) was a Yorkshireman. He was educated at Magdalen College, Oxford, where he took his B.A. in 1580. He was either much affected or converted by the martyrdom of Edward Stransham at Tyburn on 21 January 1586. On 4 May he arrived at Reims, where he was ordained priest on 19 September 1587. He was sent on the English mission on 3 January 1589 together with four other priests. The crew of the ship that took them up the Thames plotted to kill them all, but the priests drew their rapiers, kept the sailors below deck and forced them to allow a landing at Gravesend. William went to Warwickshire and Worcestershire, where he worked on the borders of the counties, and is said to have been in touch with several of Shakespeare's friends, but this suggestion may form part of the perennial speculation about the playwright's supposed latent Catholicism and even recusancy.

An old friend gave William the alias of Mason, for he was to be "a workman and layer of stones in the building of God's church." After six years of dangerous ministry and several escapes he was arrested on 5 January 1595 on the way to Dorothy Heath's house at Alchurch, Worcestershire, where he was engaged as tutor to her son. A breviary was revealed under his hat, but he concealed his priesthood. His hostess was also taken and they were imprisoned at Warwick. Since there was no evidence to show that he was a priest he was not sent up before the Lent assizes, but another prisoner betrayed him. He was sentenced at the assizes of 11 and 12 August. One tradition says that he was prosecuted at the instigation mainly of Archbishop Whitgift of Canterbury and that when he heard the sentence he sang the *Te Deum*. He was hanged, drawn, and quartered for his priesthood at Warwick on 13 August 1595. He asked to go up the ladder first, but the sheriff hoped that the others' deaths would frighten him into abjuring his faith. William said that if he had many lives he would willingly lay them down for the sake of Him who had been pleased to die on a cross for his redemption and clearly recited Psalm 41: "As the hart desires after the fountains of water, so does my soul after thee, my God. Oh, when shall I come and appear before thy face?" He was beatified in 1929.

See *M.M.P.*, pp. 227-8; *Publications of the Catholic Record Society*, 5, pp. 345-60; Anstruther, 1, pp. 124-5.

St John Berchmans (1599-1621)

At an early age John Berchmans is said to have provided the perfect, moderately Delphic quotation for that era of hagiography in which predictions of one's future sanctity were almost as important as the due quota of miracles: "If I do not become a saint when I am young," he remarked, "I shall never be one."

John was born in 1599, the eldest son of a master shoemaker, a burgher of Diest, in Brabant, Flanders. For the most part he was educated by Peter Emmerich, a Premonstratensian canon from Tongerloo abbey, who taught him how to write Latin verse and took him on visits to shrines and to other clergy. John preferred his own and adults' company but showed an interest in drama from an early age, and that meant associating with other boys. He was an enthusiastic actor in festival mystery plays and was especially praised for his rendition of Daniel defending Susanna's innocence after the lascivious elders accused her of adultery. When he was thirteen, John's father told him he had to leave school. Business was slack, so he would have to learn a trade and make his contribution to the household. He said he wanted to be a priest. His father compromised. He became a servant to a cathedral canon at Malines, where he could also attend classes at the seminary when he was not needed to wait at table. Canon Froymont had a broader range of interests than Emmerich. He took John duck shooting and taught him how to train dogs as retrievers.

John became one of the first students at the Jesuit college at Malines, which was opened in 1615, although the canon disagreed with this. He remained a keen player in sacred dramas (no others were allowed) and was notably pious. A year later, in spite of his father's opposition, he entered the novitiate. He kept detailed notes, wrote commentaries on his ascetical reading, and evolved a philosophy of the unpretentiously devout life said to have anticipated that of St

Thérèse of Lisieux (3 Oct.). He expressed it in his maxim "Prize little things most of all" and in such statements as "I like to let myself be ruled like a day-old baby." Soon after he became a novice, his mother died. Eighteen months later his father was ordained priest and made a canon of his native town. On 2 September 1682 John wrote to tell his father that he was about to take his first vows and asked for cloth and leather to make clothes. Unfortunately Canon Berchmans died the day before John's profession.

He went to Rome to study philosophy and arrived there on New Year's eve 1618 after walking with a companion from Antwerp in ten weeks. He was a diligent student at the Roman College, where the English martyr St Henry Morse (1 Feb.) was one of his fellows. Fr Massucci, who had been with Aloysius Gonzaga at the Roman College during the last year of his life, put John second only to his saintly predecessor.

John was successful at his examination in May 1621 and was chosen to defend a thesis in a public debate. But the strain of study throughout a hot Roman summer had been too much for him. His health began to fail. On 6 August he took a prominent part in a public disputation at the Greek College and had to be sent to the infirmary the next day. He showed exceptionally good humour: after a nasty dose of medicine he asked the attendant priest to say the grace after meals. When the doctor ordered his temples to be bathed with old wine, John said it was lucky such an expensive illness would not last long. He died peacefully on 13 August 1621. The sickness was never diagnosed.

He was soon cast in a saintly role. People behaved accordingly at his funeral, and numerous miracles were attributed to his intercession. His fame spread. Catholics in the Low Countries needed their own saints. Within a few years Fr Bauters, S.J., wrote from Flanders: "Though he died in Rome, and few of his countrymen know him by sight, ten of our best engravers have already published his portrait and at least 24,000 copies have been made. This does not include the work of lesser artists and several paintings." Nevertheless, although the cause was begun in the year of his death, John was not beatified until 1865. He was canonized in 1888. In the late nineteenth century there was a vogue for saintly though not notably intellectual religious who had died when young. But John's example never rivalled that of Aloysius or Stanislaus. His origins were dully bourgeois whereas they were aristocrats. Their excessive behaviour and abnormally scrupulous attention to what they thought of as purity made them much more useful figures for preachers and teachers and eclipsed their real virtues. John has faded into almost complete obscurity, thus exemplifying another of his statements about himself: "My penance is to live an ordinary life." Yet, as period exaggerations fade, he seems more human and worthy of record than the other members of the trio.

See *Anal.Boll.* 34 (1921), pp. 1-227. See also the translation of a French Life by H. Delehaye (1921); J. Daly, *John Berchmans, S.J.* (1921); C. C. Martindale, *Christ's Cadets* (1913). All these accounts must be faulted for sentimentality and overstatement.

He is shown with a crucifix, a rosary, and the Rule of his Order; he confronts death symbolized by a skull or bones. There is a fine seventeenth-century engraving of John by Anton Wierix.

St Benildus (1805-62)

Peter Romançon was the second son of his parents. He was born on 13 June 1805 at Thuret in Puy-de-Dôme in France. As a small boy he was impressed by the sight of a passing religious. He was told that this was one of the Brothers of the Christian Schools, a Congregation founded by St John Baptist De la Salle (7 Apr.) at Reims in 1684 for the free education of boys, especially the sons of poor parents, and the most up-to-date teaching Order in the Church. Though he was a priest himself De la Salle had been careful to ensure that his brothers were not ordained, took renewable vows, and were trained as teachers for different tasks and types of pupil. The image and idea remained with Peter, and he told his parents he wanted to be one of these Brothers. When the Order opened a school at Riom, he was sent there to complete his studies.

When Peter was fourteen he asked to be admitted to the Congregation. The unusual dedication of the Brothers and the exceptionally sympathetic and intelligent methods laid down by De La Salle suited his personality. He was a good student but was thought to be too small. He waited for two years until he had grown more. He was accepted into the novitiate at Clermont-Ferrand in 1820 and given the unusual name Benildus, presumably after Benildis, a woman martyr under the Moors at Córdoba, mentioned then in the Roman Martyrology on 15 June. At the end of his novitiate Benildus returned to the school at Riom to begin a teacher's training course. He was sent to various communities to gain experience, varying teaching with tasks such as cooking. Two years after his profession he was put in charge of the community and school at Billom. He was said to be strict but fair, to have encouraged the backward, and to have been especially interested in religious education.

Benildus proved so effective that in 1841, when he was thirty-six years old, he was sent to direct a community and open a school at Saugues, in the Haute-Loire. He spent the rest of his life there. The Brothers were popular in the town and were asked to start evening classes for adults. The government inspectors awarded Brother Benildus a silver medal for his work, and former pupils recorded their admiration of his work.

Benildus was a particularly good teacher of religion: "If through my fault these children don't grow in goodness, what is the use of my life? If I die teaching the catechism, then I die at my proper work." He worked hard to acquire an appropriate background of theological and other knowledge. Benildus was obviously a gifted teacher and had the rare ability to touch his pupils' hearts. A local curate remarked: "Brother Benildus did not worship like an angel only when in church or saying his prayers, but always and everywhere—even among his cabbages in the garden." Many of his former pupils became novices in the Congregation.

In 1855 Benildus began to suffer from ill health. Six years later he was seriously affected by painful arthritis. He struggled on and took the waters at Bagnols-les-Bains but died on 13 August 1862. The church was packed at his funeral, and from the moment of burial his grave became a place of pilgrimage. In 1896 the process was begun for his beatification, which took place in 1948. He was canonized in 1967.

See G. Rigault, Un *instituteur sur les autels* (1947). see also *B.T.A.*, 3, pp. 325-7; W. J. Battersby, *St John Baptist de la Salle* (1957).

BB Jakob Gapp (1897-1943) and Otto Neururer (1882-1940), *Martyrs*

Between 1933 and 1945 thousands of German and Austrian Catholic clergy and laypeople were sent to concentration camps and harsh prisons for supposed crimes of immorality, smuggling, and monetary corruption (largely before the war), but above all for their opposition to various aspects of Nazism (for the most part, after the German invasion of Poland). In Austria alone 724 priests were gaoled, and several died in the camps.

Jakob Gapp, S.M., and Otto Neururer were Catholic priests from the Austrian Tyrol. Both had formed their consciences in the light of the social encyclicals of the late nineteenth century and had firsthand experience of the suffering of the poor and underprivileged. Neither of them was an outstanding theologian like Dietrich Bonhoeffer, nor a thinker of the quality of Alfred Delp, S.J., both of whom also perished for their opposition to Nazism. So far as we know, unlike Bonhoeffer and Delp, Gapp was not associated with the organized, Christian-inspired resistance of the Kreisau Circle and the July 1944 bomb plot to assassinate Hitler. They were simply two members of an exceptional body of ordinary Christian people who just went on saying that what was obviously wrong should not be treated as right in order to avoid personal inconvenience, discomfort, torture or death, and persecution of the Church and its institutions.

Jakob Gapp was born the last of seven children of a poor working-class family in Watten, Tyrol, in the Innsbruck diocese, on 26 July 1897. He was well aware of the suffering and privations of workers and peasants. His social conscience was born out of his own experience and became a lifelong inspiration for his Christian practice. He attended the local primary school and, from September 1910, the Franciscan secondary school in Hall. On 24 May 1915 he volunteered for service in the Austrian forces. He was wounded on the southern (Italian) front on 4 April 1916 and was awarded a medal for bravery. He returned to the front line and was taken prisoner by the Italians on 4 November 1918. He returned to Austria on 18 August 1919, and on 13 August 1920 he became a postulant for entry to the Marianist Order at Greisinghof. He began his novitiate on 26 September. In 1921 he was sent to the Marian Institute in Graz to complete his philosophical studies and until 1925 worked as prefect of the boarding school there. He took final vows at Antony, France, in 1925 and from 1925 to 1930 studied at the international seminary of the Order in Fribourg, Switzerland. He was ordained priest on 5 April 1930 by the bishop of Lausanne, Geneva, and Fribourg. In autumn of the same year he was appointed prefect at the Marianist house in Freistadt. In autumn 1931 he became a catechist and spiritual adviser at the Order's school in Lanzenkirchen and from 1934 to 1938 taught at the Institute in Graz. He was especially concerned for the poor, visited their houses to recruit pupils, and often left his room unheated to provide fuel for needy families.

Jakob was opposed to extreme right-wing movements, especially National Socialism, in Austria. He followed the pre-unification recommendations of the bishops and Pius XI's anti-Nazi encyclical *Mit brennender Sorge* in this respect. He studied leading Nazi texts in order to confirm by his own intellect the inadequacy of their arguments and the evil consequences of their teaching. This confirmed, as he was to say at his trial, his empirical view of the "abhorrent nature of Nazism and its total irreconcilability with the Catholic faith." He considered it his duty to say this openly and to convince other people of it. His superiors, however, found his attitude dangerous. Under Cardinal Innitzer's enthusiastic leadership and in spite of their strong open criticism of German Nazism in 1937, the Austrian bishops issued a proclamation concluding with the words "Heil Hitler!" praising the "extraordinary accomplishments of National Socialism in the sphere of popular-national and economic reconstruction as well as social policy" and calling on the Austrian people to vote for union with Germany. On 10 April 1938 German troops marched into Austria, which ceased to exist as a country and was incorporated into Greater Germany.

Thereafter Austrians played a full part in the Nazi war of aggression and its numerous crimes, such as the extermination of the Jews. About fourteen hundred Catholic educational institutions were closed. Religious instruction was severely restricted to "purely religious matters." Catholic associations were dissolved. Funds and property were confiscated. The *Gauleiter* (regional administrator) of the Tyrol was especially keen on eradicating the Church and its influence. Hitler's portrait appeared in Marianist classrooms, as in other German schools; Marianist teachers were encouraged to tell their pupils about Nazi ideas; the Hitler salute was commonly accepted; and Jakob's headmaster asked him to use it in public and to wear a swastika badge. But Jakob refused. His views did not change and he continued to criticize Nazism in lessons and sermons. When some pupils asked if another teacher was right to say "Czechs and Jews should be hated and killed," Jakob said it was not.

A few days after the *Anschluss* (union of Germany and Austria) he was sent to the Freistadt community and was ordered not to speak to the pupils. He had to abandon teaching and the Marian Institute. In the summer he went to the Tyrol to stay with his family. On 1 September 1938 he became a catechist in primary and secondary schools at Breitenwang, near Reutte. He taught the

Christian duty of "love for everyone, irrespective of race or religion, and also for our enemies"; that one was commanded to "love French people, Jews and Communists alike," as they were all human beings; and that "God, not Adolf Hitler, is your God." After two months and a school inspection, the authorities forbade him to teach. On 4 November he was forced to leave Reutte. He lived with a relative in Wattens and continued to say what he thought was Christian truth. On 11 December 1939 he preached a sermon in Wattens in which he defended the congregation's contributions for the support of the Church and the papacy. This was adjudged provocative and the parish priest advised him to leave. He withdrew to other relatives in Terfens, Umlberg. He tried without success to obtain a passport in Innsbruck but was given one by the Vienna Neustadt authorities. On 21 January 1939 he left Austria with a French visa and went through Italy to Bordeaux. He studied French and worked in the library and as a confessor there. He preached an Easter sermon in which he asked the congregation to pray for German Catholics persecuted by the Nazi régime. On 23 May 1939 he travelled to Spain to teach in San Sebastián. There his Spanish colleagues, fresh from the civil war in which Franco's rebel forces, with German and Italian military help, had overthrown the legitimate (if effectively anticlerical) government, greeted him with the Fascist salute.

Jakob also taught in Cadiz and Lequetio and ended up in Valencia. He was appalled at the Spanish Marianists' enthusiasm for Fascism, their support for the Third Reich (which they equated with the forces of good in the "campaign against godless Bolshevism"), and their lack of social awareness, though he must soon have realized that openly-expressed sympathy for the working class was dangerously associated with the now-outlawed socialism, anarchism, and Communism. On 15 September 1941 he began to teach German, French, Latin, and religion at the Order's school in Valencia. For some time he had sought his superiors' permission to go to the U.S.A. but without success. Jakob described himself as a "friend of ordinary working people" and as an "unfailingly resolute defender of the rights of the proletariat." He was deeply shocked by the poverty, miserable diet and clothing, long working hours, and bad treatment of the people and found the "gulf between rich and poor worse in Spain than anywhere else." He considered the attitude of the Catholic middle and upper classes "pharisaical."

In summer 1942, even though he was a German citizen, Jakob took the first steps in applying for a visa to Britain at the consulate in Valencia, which he visited several times. He also sought information on the state of politics and the Church in Germany and Europe. British papers had a reputation for factual reporting and he collected some, including copies of the English Catholic weekly *The Tablet*, thereby—perhaps unwittingly—laying himself open to suspicions of intrigue. The paper provided Jakob with much information, including the text of the anti-Fascist bishop of Calahorra on the dangers of Nazism and the persecution of Catholics in Germany and the Netherlands, which Jakob passed on to others. *The Tablet* not only carried a large amount of war news and political commentaries on the war as well as the Church abroad but was said to contain coded messages to pro-British factions and resistance groups. Tom Burns, one of *The Tablet*'s owner-directors, was in Spain during the war, apparently in the diplomatic service but with other, clandestine functions. At least three German intelligence services were well aware of the paper's importance then and of certain British consular officials' functions: the *Abwehr*, or "official" German intelligence service under Admiral Canaris, an old friend of Franco's who nevertheless from 1938 onwards protected the "respectable"—non-Communist—German resistance at the highest possible level, which was party to efforts at the Vatican from 1939 to obtain approval for an alternative German regime and later played a dangerous double game by negotiating with the British; the rival *AO*, or Foreign Countries Organization, which had specialized in Austria and now in Spain; and the *Gestapo*, or Secret State Police, under Himmler. The *AO* and *Gestapo* had kept Jakob under surveillance since the *Anschluss*. In 1942 they intensified their interest in him.

Jakob had already given some instructions in Catholicism to two "Jewish" women (one a *Gestapo* agent named Irmgart detailed to watch Jakob) at the request of a German priest named Augustin Lange (exposed after the war as a particularly dangerous undercover *Gestapo* agent). That August Jakob was contacted by a German known as "Mendelssohn" (actually the Nazi agent Heger), who introduced himself as a Jewish refugee from Berlin requiring instruction before conversion. This was strange, for the few German Jews allowed into Spain either left the country speedily or kept a very low profile. On the other hand, some Catholic organizations across the free or neutral world helped converts, if not practising Jews, and some compassionate priests—such as the later Pope John XXIII—were liberal with baptismal certificates to provide funds and a safer country of refuge. For some months Jakob saw the Berliner regularly, sometimes with other supposed refugees. "Mendelssohn" even accompanied him to the British consulate on one occasion. Another pretended Jew, Hermann Treter (actually a Catholic and a *Gestapo* agent), joined the sessions. In November 1942 the Germans asked Jacob to join them on a picnic trip by car to the Pyrenees before he moved, as planned, to Tortosa. This now seems innocent; then it was dangerous exposure. They motored to Irún, where Jakob's companions somehow persuaded him (perhaps by force, though he had had to apply for a visa for France at Irún, where a Spanish policeman warned him of the danger) to make a short visit to Hendaye, in formerly Vichy-controlled, "unoccupied," but now fully German-occupied France. This was a very odd thing to do if they had been Jewish. Hendaye was a total no-go area for German Jews and for Jakob too. The *Gestapo* took Jakob from the car at Hendaye, arrested him, and sent him to Berlin.

After several interrogations about his attendance at the consulate and his collection of the "subversive" *Tablet* ("A good Catholic paper, with sound contents. I even intended to become a subscriber," he told the *Gestapo*), Jakob was imprisoned for further investigation. He was accused of treason and brought before the People's Court for trial under the notorious Nazi judge Roland Freisler, a sadistic bully who later sentenced countless patriots to death after the July 1944 plot against Hitler. Jakob told his interrogators and the court that it was his duty to act as a model opponent of a régime intent on destroying the Church. Himmler, unusually well-informed about the details of the interrogations, is said to have expressed his admiration for Jakob's commitment. Freisler sent the priest to the guillotine. On 13 August 1943 he was beheaded at Berlin-Plötzensee.

The most probable explanation of Jakob's hazardous conduct is that he had simply decided to be absolutely honest and trusting: to say what he thought and to take priests, would-be converts, and the like at face value. He probably never worked with or for the British, though such action cannot be ruled out. Of course, his apparent naivety and the strange events that took him to occupied France would be much more explicable if that were the case. His companions were perhaps political rather than "religious" *agents provocateurs*, and Jakob was supremely adroit under interrogation. (Canaris' assistant, who possibly knew the truth, left Germany for Spain on official business in time to escape the admiral's fate of arrest and execution by the SS. She became an enclosed nun, never re-entered Germany, and died in the late 1980s, having refused all spoken or written comment on the period.) Nevertheless, the later opinion of one of Jakob's main interrogators was that he was of unusual interest to the Nazis because he was so exceptional among Catholic priests. Hitler and Himmler especially paid great attention to invincible speakers of truth as psychological specimens, as it were, of the unconquerable human conscience.

Otto Neururer did not die in the same month as Jakob Gapp, but they were beatified together and were murdered for similar reasons, so an account of his life is given here. He was born on 25 March 1882 in Piller, in the Landeck district, and attended the Piller primary school. In 1895 he entered the junior seminary in Brixen.

In 1903 he began his theological studies and on 29 June 1907 was ordained priest by Prince Bishop Altenweisel. From 1907 he worked in various parishes and by 1919 was a catechist at several Innsbruck schools and spiritual adviser to a union of Catholic women workers. In 1932 he was appointed parish priest of Götzens, a strongly working-class area where he was particularly concerned with the care of young people and with social problems. He was noted for his help—often financial—to poor, backward, and disturbed children and poor students. He is described as reserved yet forthright, pious, and even mystical.

When Austria was incorporated into Germany in 1938, Otto was deeply shocked by the political changes. One innovation was secular marriage before a registrar, hitherto unknown in Austria. On 8 December Otto advised Elisabeth

Eigentler, a member of his congregation, not to marry Georg Weirather, by whom she was pregnant. Weirather was thirty years older and a divorced member of the *SA* (*Sturmabteilungen*, or storm battalions, a Nazi paramilitary organization of crude bullies devoted to street fighting and the torture and murder of political opponents, intellectuals, Jews, and anyone who expressed the least criticism of the régime). Otto helped Elisabeth to write a letter of rejection to her future husband, who told the *Gestapo*. Otto had already received a negative report from a schools inspector for asking children about their church attendance. He was arrested and imprisoned in Innsbruck.

The church authorities tried to obtain Otto's release, but on 3 March 1939 he was sent to Dachau concentration camp as an "enemy of the State." On 26 September he was transferred in a cattle waggon together with several other priests to Buchenwald concentration camp, one of the most cruel, constructed near Goethe's favourite oak outside Weimar, the home of German classical culture. In spite of particularly savage treatment and his failing health, at both camps Otto was noted for his spiritual aid to and comfort of other prisoners. In the course of 1940, after many appeals from the Church, it seemed that Otto would be released. But other prisoners reported that on 28 May he and a Fr Spanlang had been sent to the camp gatehouse, a grim torture block from which few people emerged alive. Apparently the two priests had discussed the possibility of a fellow-inmate's conversion with him. Any such activity was absolutely forbidden. Otto was hanged by his feet in a bunker by the gatehouse until his heart stopped. The same thing happened to Fr Spanlang. Otto's death was announced on 3 June. His body was reduced to ashes in the Weimar crematorium, and on 20 June the urn was sent to the Götzens cemetery where hundreds of people walked in silence behind the coffin.

Neururer was the first priest arrested by the Gestapo in Austria. He may be said to have defended the law of the Church by recommending obedience to it, as church authorities required. Nevertheless, the help he gave was more specific than many priests would have risked at the time. Both he and Gapp defied one of the cardinal principles of Nazism applied at the level of a country's (in this case, Austria's) existence; at that of independent institutions (the Church); and at that of the individual conscience: *Gleichschaltung*, or total reduction to conformity, and the penetration of Nazi ideology into every aspect of national life. Gapp's is a more complex case, for his refusal of *Gleichschaltung* was more uncompromising than that of most of his Catholic fellow-countrymen, his superiors, and bishops. He would certainly have agreed that "to the extent that the Church does accommodate itself to a secular régime, it becomes, in effect, an agent of that régime, supplementing the secular controls with those of the spiritual order" (Zahn, p. 325).

Neururer was murdered early in the war at a time of increasing confidence for the German war machine as one of a series of merciless warnings to all

Christian denominations that the totalitarian will invalidated institutional rules, the tenets of faith, and the individual conscience. His and similar cases were intended to show the German Church that by abandoning its political arm, the German Centre Party, in 1933 and by aligning itself with Hitler's war of ruthless military conquest as a "struggle against Bolshevism," it had not won freedom to operate "in its own sphere" but was subordinate to the régime. The year 1943, in which Jakob Gapp was executed, was one of severe military setbacks for Germany and its allies and one in the course of which Himmler and the *Gestapo* reached a state of near panic about the effect on public morale of influential and, especially, Christian critics of Nazism and decided to increase the number of exemplary deaths. They also knew that, after the armed forces and the Foreign Office, the churches offered frameworks for the consistent planning and contact with the Allies that any effective resistance demanded.

After the war the *Gestapo* priest Lange escaped from Allied imprisonment, was smuggled out to Bolivia, and returned later to a safe haven in an Order in Spain, where Tretter also found refuge. On 20 October 1946, Weirather was sentenced to ten years' hard labour for instigating the process that led to Otto's death. The two Austrian priests were beatified by Pope John Paul II in Rome on 24 November 1996 as martyrs for the defence of their faith. In spite of the enthusiastic, conciliatory, or reticent attitude to Nazism of most of their co-religionists and fellow-countrymen (German and Austrian), they had bravely and consistently refused to accept that this evil ideology was anything but wholly contrary to Christianity in theory and in practice. In different ways they called in question the Catholic Church's maintenance of formal relations with, and the German and Austrian Church's often highly-enthusiastic approval of citizens sacrificing their lives for, a régime determined to destroy the Church's values and ultimately (that is, when World War II was over) the Church itself.

See W. Kunzenmann et al./Diocese of Innsbruck, *P. Jakob Gapp SM: Ein Märtyrer des Glaubens: Dokumentation* (1996); *idem, Pfarrer Otto Neururer: Ein Seliger aus dem KZ: Dokumentation* (n.d.[1996]); C. Pongratz-Lippitt, "Faith before Fatherland," *The Tablet* (14.12.1996), p. 1647. See also J. Fried, *Nationalsozialismus und katholische Kirche in Österreich* (1947); G. C. Zahn, *German Catholics and Hitler's Wars* (1963); G. Lewy, *The Catholic Church and Nazi Germany* (1964); R. Schnabel, *Geistliche in Dachau* (1965); B. M. Kempner, *Priester vor Hitlers Tribunalen* (1966); K. D. Bracher, *The German Dictatorship: The origins, structure and consequences of National Socialism* (1971), pp. 469-83.

R.M.
St Antiochus, bishop of Lyons (*c.* 500)
St Ludolphus, abbot of Corbey in Westphalia (983)

14

SS Felix and Fortunatus, *Martyrs* (? Second-Third Century)

An ancient inscription was discovered at Vicetia (Vicenza) with the words: *Beati martyres Felix et Fortunatus* (the holy martyrs Felix and Fortunatus). According to their Acts they were brothers and natives of Vicenza, but they suffered at Aquileia. The Christians of Aquileia recovered their bodies and buried them, but those from Vicenza arrived to claim them. The dispute was settled by allowing the relics of Fortunatus to remain at Aquileia, whereas those of Felix were transferred to their native town. The new draft Roman Martyrology says merely that Felix of Vicetia and Fortunatus of Aquileia suffered martyrdom, that popular devotion associated them, and that they were joined in a common cult. Fortunatus is clearly located at Aquileia in the *Hieronymianum*. The poet St Venantius Fortunatus (14 Dec.) refers to both martyrs in one of his poems. The traditional, embroidered account said that they were racked in the persecution of Diocletian and Maximian. Lighted torches were applied to their sides but miraculously extinguished. Boiling oil was poured into them but they refused to renounce their faith. They were beheaded.

See *AA.SS.*, June, 1; H. Delehaye, *Origines du Culte des Martyrs*, pp. 331-2; *Notitiae* 27 (1991), nos 6-7, p. 326.

St Marcellus, *Bishop and Martyr* (*c.* 390)

The emperor Theodosius the Great continued Gratian's policy of establishing an orthodox Christian polity by trying to Christianize the Roman Empire thoroughly and forcibly. He was the effective founder of the first Christian police state in what was also the era of St Augustine (28 Aug.), the greatest Father of the Western Church. It was the emperor who decided who was a Catholic Christian, who was a heretic or a pagan, and how non-observance was to be punished.

In 380 Theodosius and his co-emperor, Gratian, issued a decree which said that all their subjects must profess the faith of the Bishops of Rome and Alexandria. Anyone who did not follow the faith defined by imperial edicts was "insane and mentally sick" (*Codex Theodosianus* 16, 2). Sacrifice was forbidden, and Arianism and other heresies were made legal offences. Illicit assemblies were forbidden even in private houses, which were subject to confiscation. In 384 the altar of Victory was removed from the Senate.

Eight years after the decree Theodosius sent an official to Egypt, Syria, and Asia Minor to enforce an edict that all pagan temples were to be destroyed. This violent policy was carried out ruthlessly and understandably aroused the anger of non-Christians. Monks began to tour the eastern provinces destroying temples and works of art, while less ideologically motivated bands of plunderers robbed not only the temples but villages and whole areas accused of impiety.

When the imperial prefect arrived at Apamaea in Syria, he ordered his soldiers to demolish the temple of Zeus. It was a large, well-built edifice. The inexpert soldiers made little progress. Bishop Marcellus of Apamaea told the prefect to take his men off to carry out their next assignment; he would see that the temple was efficiently destroyed in their absence. The next day a workman came to the bishop. He said that he would get the job done in return for double wages. Marcellus agreed. The man undermined some supporting columns, held up the foundations with timber and then burnt this away.

Marcellus dealt with other temples in the same way until he found one defended by its worshippers. The bishop "had to take up a position some way from the scene of conflict, out of reach of arrows, for he suffered from gout and could neither fight nor run away." While he was watching from this vantage point some of the worshippers crept up, captured him, and threw him into the flames. The bishop's sons wanted to take vengeance on his assassins, but the provincial council would not allow this, saying that instead they should rejoice at their father's death in a good cause.

This Marcellus should not be confused with another, born at Apamaea and an abbot in Constantinople, whose feast was traditionally observed on 29 December. One might think that the aggressive Marcellus commemorated today did not deserve the title of martyr when he so brutally interfered with others' practice of their religion in a way that Christians then would have found evil if directed against them. That, however, is an attitude born of a modern concept of toleration that has certainly had some, though few, supporters throughout the Christian centuries.

See *AA.SS.*, Aug. 3; Theodoret, *H.E.*, 5, 21; N. Q. King, *The Emperor Theodosius and the Establishment of Christianity* (1961). See also the translation by R. van Looy in *Byzantion* 8 (1933), pp. 7ff., of Libanius' oration *Pro templis.*

St Eusebius of Rome (Fourth-Fifth Century)

Eusebius lived in Rome in the latter part of the fourth and possibly in the early fifth century. His Acts are wholly spurious. They say that he was a priest who opposed the Arian emperor Constantius and celebrated Mass in his own house after he had been forbidden to use the churches. He was imprisoned in a tiny room in the same house and died there after seven months. He was buried, we are told, in the cemetery of Callistus on the Appian Way, with an inscription over his tomb: "To Eusebius, the Man of God." No trace of this tomb has been found, which of course does not erase the possibility of its existence at some time in the past.

Eusebius was a historical person who became the object of a cult, but the story told about him is untrustworthy. He certainly founded a church in Rome known as the *titulus Eusebii*, or "title of Eusebius." An annual commemorative Mass was offered for him as founder, and by 595 the parish was already referred to as the *titulus Sanctii Eusebii*, or "title of St Eusebius." That is the justification for his inclusion in the new draft Roman Martyrology.

See H. Delehaye, *Sanctus* (1927), p. 149; J. Wilpert in *Römische Quartalschrift* 22, pp. 80-2; J. P. Kirsch, *Die römischen Titelkirchen*, pp. 58-61; *C.M.H.*, pp. 443-4.

Eusebius is shown in full rococo glory, with a vast company of angels, in the ceiling (1758) by Raphael Mengs in the church of St Eusebius, Rome.

St Fachanan, *Bishop* (Sixth Century)

Fachanan (or Fachtna) was probably the first bishop of Ross in Ireland. He was born at Tulachteann, was one of the pupils of St Ita (15 Jan.), and founded the monastery of Molana on an island in the Blackwater, near Youghal. He established the monastic school of Ross at what is now Rosscarbery, in Co. Cork. This was one of Ireland's most famous schools. It flourished for three hundred years and survived in some form until the Normans arrived in Ireland. Fachanan was blind for some time but is said to have recovered at the intercession of Ita's sister, who was about to give birth to St Mochoemog (13 Mar.). Fachanan was remembered as a wise and upright man and a good preacher. St Cuimin of Connor said that he was "generous, steadfast, fond of preaching to the people, and said nothing base or displeasing to God." The St Fachanan who was commemorated as the patron of Kilfenora diocese on the same day may be a different person from this bishop.

Fachanan is mentioned in the *Félire* of Oengus and in the Latin Life of St Mochoemog. See *L.I.S.*, 8, pp. 191ff.

Bd Eberhard, *Abbot* (958)

Eberhard belonged to the ducal family of Swabia. He became provost of Strasbourg cathedral. In 934 he resigned this post and went to the hermitage of Einsiedeln in Switzerland to join his friend Benno, who had been bishop of Metz. Benno already had some followers there. Eberhard's reputation for spiritual wisdom and holiness brought many more in. He spent his fortune on building a monastery and a church for them. After Benno's death he was recognized as first abbot of the monastery of Our Lady of the Hermits.

In 942 there was a great famine in Alsace, Burgundy and upper Germany. Eberhard and his monks provided a large supply of corn to relieve the suffering of the people. St Conrad of Constance (26 Nov.) and St Ulric of Augsburg (4 July) probably consecrated the abbey church of Einsiedeln, incorporating the hermits' chapel, in 948, ten years before Eberhard's death. Einsiedeln remains a major pilgrimage centre.

See O. Ringholz, *Geschichte des fürstlichen Benediktinerstiftes Einsiedeln* (1904), 1, pp. 33-43; R. Henggeler, *Reliquien der Stiftskirche Einsiedeln* (1927), pp. 7ff.

The present buildings of Einsiedeln date from the eighteenth century, and the church is perhaps the most sumptuous baroque building in western Europe. See G. M. Grasselli and P. Tarallo, *Guia ai Monasteri d'Europa* (1995), pp. 179-80.

St Arnulf, *Bishop* (*c*. 1040-87)

Arnulf (or Arnoul) was born about 1040 in Flanders. When he was a young man he had a distinguished military career under Robert and Henry I of France. He became a monk in the monastery of Saint-Médard at Soissons. Eventually he chose to be a hermit within the community, leading a life of austere penance and prayer in a narrow cell, almost without any communication with others. In 1081 a special council elected him bishop at the request of the Soissons clergy and, it is said, people. When the deputies arrived to tell him of the choice he said: "Leave this sinner to offer up some fruits of penance to God. Don't force a fool like me to do something which needs as much wisdom as this does." He was compelled to accept the position and became a very zealous bishop. For reasons unknown a usurper drove him out, and he applied for permission to resign what he had already lost. Afterwards he founded a monastery at Aldenburg, also in Flanders, and died there in 1087. At a council at Beauvais in 1120 the then bishop of Soissons is said to have shown a Life of Arnulf to the assembly and demanded that his body should be enshrined in the church. He declared that if the body of his predecessor were in his diocese, it would have been brought in out of the churchyard long before. Accordingly, Arnulf's remains were translated to the abbey church of Aldenburg in the following year.

See *M.G.H.*, *Scriptores*, 15, 2, pp. 872-904, for the life by Hariulf. See also E. de Moreau, *Histoire de l'Eglise en Belgique*, 2 (1945), pp. 433-7.

Bd Antony Primaldi and Companions, *Martyrs* (1480)

In 1480 the Turks under Mohammed II took the city of Otranto in southern Italy. They massacred many of its inhabitants and defenders. Some of these victims have always been cited as martyrs, especially Bd Antony Primaldi (or Grimaldi) and the eight hundred people said to have suffered with him (the following are named in the Acts: Stella Tafuro, Peter Fascia, Nicholas de Coluccis, Andrew Faglio, Gabriel Caetano and his sons, Nicholas de Pasco, Alexander Longo, John Francis de Muro de Mazzapinta, N. de Luca, N. De Fascio, N. De Marco, Nicholas De Gaborti and N. De Foga).

He was a good workman, an old man, and a devout Christian. The Turks rounded up the men who had escaped the first massacre, sacked their houses, and carried off their wives. They took Antony and the others into a valley near the town and said they could have their freedom, wives, and goods back if they apostatized and became Muslims. Antony was spokesman for the whole company. He replied they all believed there was only one God, that Jesus Christ was his divine Son, and that they would never abandon that faith. The Turkish general said he would order them to be tortured vilely. Some people began to waver, but Antony is said to have shouted out: "We have fought for our city and for our lives. Now we have to fight for our souls and for Jesus. He died for us, now we must die for him." There was no more hesitation. Everyone was now quite resolute, so the order was given to behead them all. Antony was the first to die. His headless body was reported to have stayed upright until the last Christian was in the same condition. The Turks occupied the country for a year, and until they went the bodies remained unburied in what came to be know as the Valley of the Martyrs. The cult of these martyrs was confirmed in 1771, relying on testimonies deposed almost sixty years after the events described. There is no record of how witnesses came to be in the valley or how they survived.

See *AA.SS.*, Aug., 3, under "Martyres Hydruntini," for a description of the martyrs and the depositions. See also *D.H.G.E.*, 3, 805-6.

Bd Elizabeth Renzi (1786-1856)

Elizabeth was the daughter of John Baptist and Victoria Renzi and was born at Saludecio, in the diocese of Rimini in Italy, into a devout and wealthy family. She was educated first at home, then with the Claretians of St Bernard until 1807, when she entered an Augustinian convent. She was forced to return to her family in 1810 when the Napoleonic legislation dissolved religious Orders. Elizabeth nevertheless considered herself bound by her vows to resume the religious life as soon as the laws were changed. In 1824, on the recommendation of Fr Vitali Corbucci, she became a teacher at the school for poor girls founded in Coriani in 1818. From 1825 she discussed with St Magdalen of Canossa (Marchioness of Canossa; 10 Apr.), the merging of the Coriani Institute with the Canossian Daughters of Charity, the Congregation which Magdalen had founded for the care of poor children with some help from Napoleon himself. Magdalen recognized Elizabeth's aptitude as a teacher and her qualities of leadership. Eventually, in 1839, after many difficulties had been overcome, episcopal permission was obtained for a new Institute. In 1850 the bishop of Rimini approved final revised rules drawn up by Elizabeth for the Sisterhood for the education of girls from poor homes in Romagna. She dedicated her life to the care of the utterly poor and destitute. She was undaunted by the problems she faced to ensure their education, whether political, ecclesiastical, or material. She was beatified by Pope John Paul II on 18 June 1989.

D.N.H. 3, pp. 140-1.

St Maximilian Kolbe, *Martyr* (1894-1941)

The future St Maximilian was born Raimund Kolbe in Russian Poland at Zdunska-Wola near Lodz on 7 January 1894. He is one of the greatest saints of our own times, yet he was not a superlative thinker or theologian like Augustine or Thomas Aquinas, or the founder of a worldwide Order like Dominic or Francis. He stands for a form of sanctity appropriate to the incalculable hatreds and vast pointless inhumanities of the modern age: "If I give away all I have, and if I deliver my body to be burned, but have not love, I gain nothing."

Raimund's forebears came from Bohemia, and the name Kolbe seems to indicate Germanic rather than Slav origins. This was and remains common in Poland. His father was employed as a weaver and later as a factory worker. His parents struggled to feed and clothe their three children. His mother certainly and his father probably belonged to the Franciscan Third Order; they were associated ideologically with if not actual members of the twenty secret tertian Congregations established in Russian Poland by the Capuchin Honorat Kominiski (1829-1916) to teach and carry on the social apostolate among working people. They were deeply pious and deeply patriotic.

At the age of ten the character of the somewhat self-willed boy seemed to change. He told his mother that Our Lady had appeared to him. She had shown him, he said, two garlands and asked him to choose: "The white one means that you will remain pure; the red one that you will die a martyr. Which do you want?" He replied, "I'll take both." She smiled and disappeared. His mother opened a small general store to add to the minute family income, and Raimund helped behind the counter. But the takings were inadequate and Mrs Kolbe also had to work as a part-time midwife and sick-nurse. She sent the boy to collect some medicine from Kotowski, the chemist, who was astonished at his ability to rattle off the Latin names of drugs that he himself found difficult to recall. He soon discovered that Raimund was kept at home to work because the Kolbes could afford to send only his brother, Frank, intended for the priesthood, to the middle school. Kotowski gave Raimund Latin lessons so that he could take the examination at the same time as his brother. Raimund forged ahead and passed easily. His parents decided to keep him at school.

Four years later the Minorites held a mission in the local parish and deeply impressed the two brothers, who applied to enter the junior seminary at Lwow. They were accepted in 1907, when Raimund was thirteen. He was especially good at maths, physics, and what would now be called technology and design. He was never very interested in art, music, or even literature, and not at all in theology. By the time he was sixteen, in 1910, he decided that he probably had no vocation after all. He was about to see the provincial to explain this when his mother came to the seminary to tell him that the youngest son, Joseph, had also decided to enter a religious Order. This would allow both parents to fulfill their dream of becoming religious themselves. Mrs Kolbe wanted to be a Benedictine. Raimund immediately went to the provincial and asked to become a

Franciscan. For some months he was troubled by scruples, but these eventually disappeared. His mother did join the Benedictines, though she later became a lay Felician. His father was with the Franciscans until he left to run a religious bookshop at Czestochowa, near the shrine of Our Lady.

In autumn 1912 his superiors sent Maximilian Maria (his name in religion) to the international Seraphic College and to study at the Gregorian University in Rome. He became increasingly interested in the Church as a worldwide institution, in the ways by which its message was spread, and in what would now be called communications. He often showed an unusually independent spirit for the times. In 1917 the Freemasons celebrated their two-hundredth anniversary. One day Maximilian persuaded a fellow-student that it would be a good idea to interview the Grand Master of the Roman Freemasons (who were largely anticlerical) and convert him. Just before they set off Maximilian thought it best to explain the project to the rector; he was rather disconsolate when he was told that there was no objection to the plan, but for the moment it would be better just to pray for the Freemasons. On another occasion an abscess on his right thumb would not heal. The bone was infected and the doctors advised amputation. Maximilian made a special dressing with Lourdes water, and by the next morning the surgeon at the hospital declared that the thumb was mending and need not be removed. In a letter to his mother describing this event, Maximilian wrote for the first time of the *Niepokalana*, which was Polish for the *Immaculata*, or Our Lady of the Immaculate Conception (though the Conception was typically elided), to whom he attributed the cure of his thumb. Henceforth he was to be a knight of the *Immaculata*, his "Mamusia," to whom he developed a profound lifelong devotion, which shows clearly how the figure of Mary can serve as a means of access to the maternal aspects of God.

Outwardly, however, Maximilian became one of the main authors, advocates, and practitioners of a form of Marian piety difficult to reconcile with the New Testament, for it virtually ignored Mary's relation to Christ. It was extreme even in a national church one of whose distinguishing marks was its emphasis on Our Lady. His followers took it even further, referring to Christians as "slaves of Mary." This elaborately emotional phraseology seems extravagant, especially in most English-speaking countries, outside a context in which Our Lady had long been invoked as "Queen of Poland" and where she became the symbolic focus of very mixed aspirations. It does not translate easily into English, in which the nearest equivalent would be a rather stagy Pre-Raphaelitism. Maximilian took much of it from *The Golden Book* of Grignion de Montfort. It is at the opposite pole to an extreme Protestant underestimation of Mary. It has to be interpreted in an unfamiliar and very intricate framework of inherited sixteenth- and seventeenth-century baroque devotionalism; Polish nationalism in the face of Austrian, Russian, and German partitions and domination as well as the claims of other Baltic national interests and minorities in Poland; the Latinizing of the Uniate Ukrainian church there; and a centuries-long struggle against not only the Protestants and the Russian and Greek Orthodox, who were still a formidable presence in Poland, but Catholic schismatic movements between the world wars. The last-named—particularly the Old Catholic and Ancient Catholic Mariavites, or Imitators of Mary, and the Polish National Catholic Church founded in the U.S.A. and officially recognized in Poland in 1922—were scarcely austere and "low-church." They had their own often wildly excessive and highly-competitive devotions, publications, and religious artefacts. In addition, the effects of a then-considerable Jewish population with very different traditions and devotional emphases both profound and popular, apparent throughout Poland, should not be underestimated when trying to understand Maximilian's Mariology. Maximilian did not value Judaism and knew nothing whatsoever of its deep spirituality. He even edited a newspaper that can only be described as anti-Semitic. His attitude was no different, however, from that of most Polish Catholics, who, though it now seems hardly credible, totally ignored the fact that Jesus and his mother were pious Jews. In 1936, for instance, the primate of Poland, August Cardinal Hlond, issued a pastoral letter in which he solemnly declared: "There will be the Jewish problem as long as the Jews remain. It is a fact that the Jews are fighting against the Catholic Church, persisting in free thinking, and are the vanguard of godlessness, Bolshevism, and subversion. . . . It is a fact that the Jews deceive, levy interest, and are pimps. It is a fact that the religious and ethical influence of the Jewish people on Polish young people is a negative one." The quality of Maximilian's heart, however, is to be judged by his actions, which were contrary to what we might deduce from his writings.

In 1914, not long after the outbreak of World War I, Maximilian's father joined the Polish Legion under Marshal Pilsudski to fight on the side of the Central Powers (Germany, Austria, and Turkey) against the Russians with the ultimate aim of liberating Poland. He was captured and—as he was a Russian citizen—hanged as a traitor. In the same year Maximilian made his final vows and solemn profession in Rome, where he was ordained priest. On 17 October 1917 seven young seminarists, led by Maximilian, made their vows as Knights of the Queen of Heaven in the officially-approved *Militia Immaculatae*, or Militant Order of Mary the Immaculate. Maximilian was noted for his constant prayer in the college chapel, but he was also a diligent student. He received first-class doctorates in philosophy and theology before returning to Poland in July 1919 to teach church history in a seminary. Yet he can hardly be said to have developed these intellectual interests; his acute and agile mind was directed elsewhere. The pulmonary tuberculosis he suffered from all his life was diagnosed. At the end of the year he was sent to a sanatorium in Zakopane, where he organized lectures, distributed medals of the *Immaculata*, and made a number of converts among the despairing or religiously indifferent sick. He lost the use of one lung but within a year could return to Krakow. There he started a Marian militia, or sodality, which received papal approval as a religious association on 2 January 1922.

To Maximilian it seemed that Europe was turning away from God and that various media ancient and modern—"literature, art, drama, cinema, fashion, and so on"—were helping this process of alienation and indifference. In the language of his own Catholic context he acutely defined what would now be called the "psychic numbing" that blurred moral distinctions and within a few years led to mass acceptance not only of the loss of the basic human rights of millions of people but of unprecedented mass murder. Mary was the symbol of loving motherliness; of sinlessness; of non-contamination by numbness, hatred, and cruelty; and of unremitting, dedicated action against them.

A magazine was needed to spread the chivalric militia's ideas and "win the world for the *Immaculata*." Maximilian went from door to door begging from rich and poor. The first issue of *Knights of the Immaculata* appeared in January 1922. Somehow money turned up to keep it going. An American priest helped start a printing-press fund with a $100 contribution. But Maximilian's determination upset his Franciscan superiors. His colleagues then and later often found him at best unrealistically utopian and at worst irritatingly pushy. In October 1922 they transferred him with a few rather unenthusiastic Brothers to a half-ruined friary at Grodno, in north-western Poland. Maximilian took the press with him, and soon three rooms were devoted to publications on which the Brothers worked in the evening. Their pastoral duties were scarcely easy, for they covered—on foot—a number of villages several hours apart. Maximilian wrote nearly all the articles himself, and the print runs increased steadily. He was a popular priest and was praised especially for the simplicity and clarity of his sermons. He ensured that distinctions between Brothers and priests were largely ignored, as in the time of Francis. Soon there were too many candidates for the Order to accommodate in the friary.

The community was beginning to thrive when Maximilian's hard work brought on another attack of tuberculosis. This time he spent eighteen months in Zakopane. He ascribed his recovery to Our Lady: "She is trying to use an old scrubby brush to paint a masterpiece. I'm the brush; God's mother is the painter!" Now Maximilian entered into seemingly fruitless negotiations to buy a site forty kilometres to the west of Warsaw for his Niepokalanow, or "town of Mary the Immaculate." It was surely a miracle when Count Drucki-Lubecki, the owner, suddenly gave way and presented the ground to Maximilian, who, never doubting the outcome, had already erected a statue of Our Lady there. In spite of doctor's warnings, Maximilian joined his Brothers, who left Grodno on 27 November 1927, in the hard work of building a new friary. After several months it was ready.

The buildings were very simple barracks. Maximilian abhorred any kind of ostentation, especially in monasteries and churches, but he believed in technological progress to an extent that now seems both prescient and naive. The

Brothers lived frugally, but Maximilian made sure that they had state-of-the-art rotary presses for their publications—magazines and weekly papers for young and old, and in several languages, and in 1935 a Polish daily newspaper, *Maly Dziennik*. The contents of all these were based on a traditional religiosity. They were very simple and easily readable, designed not for intellectuals but for the poorly-educated masses, who, Maximilian thought, were the proper concern of Franciscans. The Brothers also produced devotional articles, such as statues of Our Lady—tawdry things indistinguishable from the plaster images of Lourdes and very distant from the fourteenth-century icon of Mary at Czestochowa. Maximilian's early interest in communications flourished. He had a broadcasting station before the outbreak of World War II, and by then his plans to build Catholic film studios and an airfield with four aeroplanes were well advanced and realizable.

One day he met some Japanese students and decided to go to Japan to start another *Niepokalanow*. Maximilian knew nothing about Japan except that many martyrs had died there. Early in 1930, with four Brothers, he set off for Nagasaki, where they arrived on 24 April. A month later they cabled the Polish house: "Posting first issue today. Have printing-press. Long live Mary the Immaculate!" They not only had to learn Japanese but how to set the two thousand characters of a new alphabet by hand and to work a manual press as in the first days in Poland. They suffered harsh weather and bad food in another ruinous building. Some gave up and went back to Europe. Two Brothers had to support the weak and feverish Maximilian at Mass. He spoke of spreading the message of the Knights of Mary to a billion readers as soon as possible, to half the human race, to the whole globe. After five years, severely ill, he was recalled to Lwow, but he was allowed to return to Japan and build the "Garden of the Immaculata," a settlement protected by a hill. It survived the terrible atom-bomb attack on Nagasaki in 1945; no one in the house died.

Soon the indefatigable Maximilian was off to India to found another *Niepokalanow*, made sure it was under way, then returned to erect a church in Japan. In 1936 he was recalled to Krakow, then made superior of the more than 760 friars at the original *Niepokalonow*. He started even more magazines and papers and regular broadcasts.

Poland had been an independent republic for only twenty years when the Germans and Russians invaded and partitioned the country in September 1939. The community found itself in the new German colonial territory known as the "General Government." Poles were to become serfs of the Greater Germany; education was reduced to almost nil, and they were forbidden anything approaching culture. Maximilian, a practitioner of non-violent resistance, advised his Brothers to return to their families and to report as helpers to the Polish Red Cross but not to join the armed resistance or underground. On their insistence, he kept only forty-eight of the hardiest Franciscans with him. On 19 September 1939 the authorities marched them off to Lamsdorf camp in

Germany; on 24 September Maximilian and twenty-four Brothers were transferred to the tents of Amtitz camp, which was harsh but tolerable, and Maximilian was able to preach to the others, encouraging them to be brave and accept suffering willingly. "Hitlerism will perish," he said. "Truth must prevail." One of his companions remembered Maximilian covering his feet in the night and giving his minute bread ration to another Brother for whom the pains of hunger were too acute. After two and half months they were again transferred, to Ostrezeszow. Maximilian remained calm, hopeful, and absolutely undaunted. Against all expectations the German military commandant suddenly released them and they were allowed to return to the plundered *Niepokalanow*. There, the same day, three thousand Polish refugees expelled by the Germans arrived from Poznan (now Posen, a purely German city) and had to be accommodated somehow. Soon fifteen hundred Jews also arrived. Maximilian welcomed them with the same immediate compassion he had shown to the Poles. They were given refuge in the buildings which the few Brothers were trying to restore.

A few days after the German invasion, the Nazi régime had begun a ruthless campaign against Poles, especially Jews. By the end of the war it had liquidated six million Poles, about half of them Jews. The Germans recognized the cultural and patriotic role of the Catholic Church, which they decided to destroy as a national entity. Although about fifty per cent of the occupiers were Catholics, they executed six Polish bishops, 2,030 diocesan and religious priests, 127 seminarians, 173 Brothers, 243 Sisters, and thousands of Catholic professors, lecturers, and teachers. Many more clergy and religious were imprisoned and punished by torture or inconceivably hard labour. Countless seminaries, libraries, monasteries, and churches were closed, taken over, emptied, or destroyed. In an encyclical of October 1939 appealing for peace, Pope Pius XII spoke of the "blood of innumerable human beings, even of non-combatants" which evoked "a poignant cry of sorrow, especially for the well-beloved nation Poland, whose services in the defence of Christian civilization . . . entitle it to the human and fraternal sympathy of the world." Thereafter, for reasons still unclear, he scarcely referred to the fate of Poland or its Church, and not at all to that of its own or any other Jews. Because of its traditional antagonism to Jews, the Nazis chose Poland as the centre for extermination of all the Jews in the countries they occupied or were allied with, most of which cooperated in their deportation to Poland. But Maximilian was not one of the many Poles indifferent to the fate of the Jews. At *Niepokalanow* in 1939-40 the reasons of the heart banished theory and tradition.

The community published articles critical of the occupiers but soon had to stop all publications. Because of his origins Maximilian was offered German nationality, which would have given him several privileges, including the superior ration card which allowed ethnic Germans almost double the inadequate Polish allocation (Jews got even less). He would have been compelled to aban-

don the Polish Order and any ministry to Poles. Maximilian refused. On 17
February 1941, as the drive to eradicate the Polish intelligentsia intensified, *SS*
men arrived to arrest him and four other priests. They were imprisoned in
Warsaw. Twenty Brothers offered themselves instead but were rejected.
Maximilian was brutally beaten and humiliated. On 28 May 1941, without trial
or sentence, he was transferred as No. 16670 to the Balice heavy labour section
of the German concentration camp near the town of Oswiecim; its German
name, Auschwitz, now stands for what even "hell" and "inferno" are too mild
to convey.

It was a place of unparalleled suffering and cruelty. From 1941 to 1945 it was
the location of mass murder on an industrial scale, mainly of Jews from all over
German-occupied Europe but also of Gypsies, Poles, and other "racially inferior" groups. Maximilian's part of the camp, centred on a former military
barracks, held 200,000 prisoners who suffered horribly and were often tortured
or killed for the guards' entertainment. In the extermination camp at Birkenau
nearby some prisoners, mostly Jews but also Gypsies and Poles, and various
other groups, were kept for a while until they were no longer fit to work in
associated factories. Over four million people were taken straight from death-
trains that arrived from as far away as Greece and Holland, systematically
robbed of everything from prayer shawls to toys and clothes, murdered with
poison gas, and deprived of gold teeth, hair to be made into matting, and even
their body fat to make soap. The remains were burned in ovens. Maximilian
was not one of these Jews, most of whom perished after him. He was not
directly associated with them; and it would be an insult to their memory to call
him "the" martyr of Auschwitz, before all else the place where those innocent
members of Christ's own nation were massacred. Maximilian's sanctity is in no
way reduced when we acknowledge that.

Though it was strictly forbidden and he was sick and weak, Maximilian
ministered heroically to his fellow-friars and others, encouraging them to hold
out in the conviction that God's justice would prevail. He accepted his fate as
God's mysterious choice for him. A doctor who survived the camp remembers
telling Maximilian that he could no longer believe in God in such a place.
Maximilian did everything he could to persuade him that even there God
watched over his children. He would always lead the food line to receive the
near-water from the top of the pot so that others could have the thicker soup
below. As a priest, Maximilian aroused the constant brutality of hardened
criminals in direct charge of the prisoners. His tasks included throwing bodies
on to carts and transporting them to the ovens as well as carrying impossibly
heavy loads. One day, when struggling with an especially huge log at the usual
running pace, he stumbled and was punished with fifty savage lashes. His
fellow-prisoners carried his bleeding body back to the camp. The next day he
was put among the very sick and half-dead, known as "Muslims" to the guards.
He chose the worst place, near the door, so that he could pray for the dead as

they were carried out. One day a guard secretly offered him a glass of tea but he refused to be an exception. Through the night he heard Confessions, though this was forbidden. "Children," he said, "look, our heavenly Mother is comforting us." After two weeks he was sent to the invalids' block, and then to labour block 14.

At the end of July someone escaped from the block. Every man there had to stand to attention for hours in the heat. In the evening ten men were chosen arbitrarily for slow execution in starvation bunker 11. As they removed their shoes, Maximilian did something absolutely forbidden. He took off his cap, stepped forward, and asked the deputy camp commandant, Fritsch, if he could take the place of one of them: "I am old and useless. My life isn't worth much now." Everyone expected the normal outcome: the SS-man would shoot the priest on the spot, but Fritsch asked him why. Maximilian pointed out Franz Gajowniczek, an infantry sergeant sent to Auschwitz for escaping from a prisoner-of-war camp. He had a wife and two children outside the camp. "What is your profession?" asked Fritsch. "Catholic priest," was the reply. There was a moment of terrible silence. To everyone's astonishment Fritsch merely said: "Right!" and No. 16670 was entered on the list instead. What Maximilian had meant by chivalry could not have been more unmistakably evident. Barefoot, he followed the others to their squalid death hole. They were stripped naked, the iron doors were closed on them, and they were left to die without food or water. Maximilian still comforted his fellow-inmates; soon, however weakly, the condemned men were singing. For the first time in Auschwitz the sound of hymns came from the bunker's mean air holes. The prisoner who carried out the bodies as the prisoners died said that he always found Maximilian standing or kneeling, and praying. After two weeks, on the eve of the Assumption, only four were still alive; only Maximilian was conscious. The bunker was needed for another cohort of sufferers, so the skeletal Maximilian was finally murdered by phenol injection on 14 August 1941. The prisoner who had to remove his body from the cell said that the dead Maximilian's eyes were still open and seemed calmly fixed on some point ahead. On 15 August his remains were thrown into an oven and his ashes joined those of millions of other victims already or soon to be scattered and blown over the wasteland of Auschwitz.

In 1971, five years after the millennium celebration of the conversion of Poland, Maximilian, a figure of exemplary selflessness who walked through the valley of the shadow of death fearing no evil, was beatified by Paul VI as a "typical Polish hero." The beatification was celebrated in Poland as an event of national significance. In Rome Cardinal Döpfner remarked that Maximilian's essential greatness would shine out for ever beyond the time-bound and uncritical aspects of his work. In 1982 he was canonized by John Paul II in the presence of the man whose life he had saved. Maximilian stands with the known and for the unnamed people of whatever faith whose love has challenged the darkness of our times. The *Niepokalanow* church in Poland and that in Japan are now places of pilgrimage, and the bunker in Auschwitz is always filled with flowers.

G. Bar, *The Death of Blessed Maximilian Kolbe in the Light of Canon Law* (1971); K. Wenzel O.F.M., *Pater Maximilian Kolbe, Ritter der Immaculata* (1971); W. Nigg, *Maximilian Kolbe* (1980); S. C. Lorit, *The Last Days of Maximilian Kolbe* (1981); D. Dewar, *Saint of Auschwitz* (1982); K. Górski, "L'histoire de la spiritualité polonaise," in *Millénaire du catholicisme en Pologne* (1969), pp. 281 ff.; *The New German Order in Poland* (1941); D. B. Barrett (ed.), "Poland," in *World Christian Encyclopedia* (1982), pp. 569-74.

Maximilian's main attribute is his striped and numbered convict's dress, which indicates his humiliation borne without reproach. He has inspired a great number of works of religious art—oils, cycles of woodcuts and other works on paper, and sculpture—mainly in Poland and Germany. There is a painting in Katowice Cathedral by an unknown hand showing him holding copies of journals in Japanese and in Polish, and clad both in his Franciscan habit and in his camp clothes. A statue over the Kolbe chapel altar in the church at *Niepokalanow* shows him as a communicator, holding the globe aloft. Among the most moving images of the martyr are simple painted wood-carvings in the inimitable Polish folk-art tradition. A poignant example is illustrated in Nigg, p. 60. In 1973 the West German Post Office issued a commemorative stamp bearing his image, name, date of death and the stark word "Auschwitz."

R.M.
St Ursicius, martyr in Illyria under Maximian (fourth century)
St Werenfried, priest and missionary in Guelderland (*c.* 760)
Bd Sanctus of Urbino, friar Minor in Ancona (1390)
BB Dominic Ibañez de Erquicia and Francis Shoyemon, martyrs in Japan (1633)—see "The Martyrs of Japan," 6 Feb.

THE BLESSED VIRGIN MARY (over page)
Ancient monogram incorporating the letters of "Maria."

15

THE ASSUMPTION OF THE BLESSED VIRGIN MARY

Apart from the infancy narratives in Matthew and Luke (see, in other volumes of this work: 25 March, The Annunciation; 31 May, The Visitation; 25 December, The Nativity) the New Testament does not tell us a great deal about Mary, the mother of Jesus. As today's feast corresponds to her *dies natalis* more closely than any other in the Calendar, a basic "biography" of Mary, constructed and to some extent deduced from the New Testament by conflating the authors' references to her, is given here. (This is consonant with the presentation of other Lives in this work and with the tradition of the Church, if not with strict scholarly practice, which would require each episode to be seen in the context of the relevant Gospel's possible chronology and literary design and with due attention to probable interpolations. Accordingly commentators offer various, sometimes conflicting, interpretations of the passages in question.) This narrative is followed by a historical account of the concept and dogma of the Assumption and of its implications in terms of Mary's "reception" in devotion and practice.

After Jesus' birth Mary is ritually purified in the Temple. This was the usual means of re-entry to society after childbirth. Joseph and Jesus are present and possibly have to be purified too because of contact with her. Unusually, however, Mary and Joseph are blessed by Simeon, who prophesies (enigmatically) that Mary's son "is destined for the falling and the rising of many in Israel" and that "a sword will pierce your own soul too" (see Luke 2:22-38). As so often, Mary does not fully understand the meaning of such pronouncements. The unfolding of the narrative and of its deeper meaning always requires Mary to show not only a natural sense of her son's capabilities but a tension between that and her incomprehension of his actual role, however enlightened she may be by her faith in God's ultimate justification of those who are truly his people. In the Temple she makes the customary offering of the poor: two turtle doves. This re-emphasizes God's vindication of the poor and humble personified in Mary and already expressed in the *Magnificat*, the song explaining her attitude to the Annunciation. The law also prescribed the payment of a temple tax to redeem a first-born male from temple duties; instead Jesus is "presented" to the Lord, to whom he belongs in a special way, a theme that recurs throughout Jesus' "conversations" with his mother. The theme of identification with the poor, marginalized and outcast continues as Mary becomes a refugee (the Flight into Egypt) and shares the fate of many before and after her. Herod's threats are explicitly linked to Jeremiah's prophecies, and Mary's suffering to that of Rachel. In Jerusalem she is already far from her home and family but she risks further flight to save her son from the massacre. A subsidiary topic here is her representation of the wandering, victimized people of God.

When she returns to Galilee, Mary leads the everyday life of a pious Jewish wife and mother. Every year the family celebrates the Passover feast in Jerusalem. When Jesus is twelve, he remains there without telling his parents. He cannot be found in the returning caravan, so Mary and Joseph go back to Jerusalem. On the third day they find him in the Temple sitting among the teachers, listening to them and asking questions. Mary is hurt and asks: "Child, why have you treated us like this? Look, your father and I have been searching for you in great anxiety." She does not understand Jesus' reply: "Why were you searching for me? Did you not know that I must be in my Father' house?"Nevertheless, Jesus returns to Nazareth with his parents and is "obedient to them"(see Luke 2:39-51). Jesus'reply to Mary shows her that, like any mother, she must now let him grow into adulthood and away from her. His readiness to seek information from the teachers and ability to answer their questions reflect not only his training in the Nazareth synagogue but the teaching and example of his mother, upright, pious, and humble. They also stress the differences between mother and son.

Mary is present at a wedding at Cana when Jesus performs the first of the "epiphanic actions," or signs, that mark his public life. By providing more wine he does answer the request implied in Mary's statement that it has run out, but he also affirms his concern with more important affairs, his "hour," by using water jars intended for ritual purification. The new spiritual wine is better than the old ritual wine. His words to her, "Woman, what concern is that to you and to me? My hour has not yet come," may be seen as indicating—beyond mere surprise—a new phase in Mary's release of her son into normal but also into his special maturity (see John 2:1-12). The formal "woman" was the correct term for the occasion, yet the statement has been interpreted as a rebuke and as showing that Mary is subordinate to her son. She, however, is still in a position of authority, and Jesus' words are possibly intended to remind her of her own sensitive if necessarily imprecise awareness that he has a special part to play yet is not quite ready for it. The occasion reveals the different degrees, and stages, of Mary's and Jesus' realization that this is a crucial time; it is also presented as his "birth" into public life. In that sense, it has been said, "Mary's faith begets and gives birth to the faith of the new messianic community" (Gebara and Bingemer). The Gospels do not make clear whether, after this episode, Mary returns to Nazareth and stays there, or whether she follows Jesus as one of his disciples.

In either case her role may be said to become that of a disciple. In one sense, this is shown when Jesus' family make the day's journey from Nazareth to "restrain" him, for the large crowds he attracts have given antagonistic observers an excuse to say he is out of his mind. When Jesus is told his family are looking for him, he asks the ambivalent question, "Who are my mother and my brothers?" and, looking at those sitting around him, supplies the plain answer, "Here are my mother and my brothers! Whoever does the will of God is my brother and sister and mother" (see Mark 3:31-5; Luke 8:19-21). We do not know what Mary and (probably) his cousins try to do, if anything, but clearly the physical bond between mother and son must now fade into the background. She has a new part to play as one of those involved in his ministry, and the Church has traditionally recognized this as making her eventually the mother of the infant Church. It also takes her to the foot of the cross, where John (unlike the other evangelists) places her first among those he lists as present: ". . . standing near the cross of Jesus were his mother, and his mother's sister, Mary the wife of Clopas, and Mary Magdalene" (19:25). It is to Mary that Jesus addresses the first of his words from the cross. He entrusts her to the care of John, the "beloved disciple": "Woman, here is your son." Mary's ordeal at the crucifixion has made her a lasting figure of suffering humanity, as well as motherhood, not only in popular devotion but in art and literature.

Mary reappears briefly (in the Acts of the Apostles) as a member of the first Christian community: "All these were constantly devoting themselves to prayer, together with certain women, including Mary the mother of Jesus . . ." (1:14). From this some writers have deduced the presence of women among those who directly receive the Spirit in the upper room at Pentecost.

This is all the New Testament says about Mary. We do not know where she was, or how old she was, when she passed on. From this point her story is largely the history of her reception; entirely so, as far as the present topic is concerned. It raises, according to one's inclination, none or all of the problems of apprehending any saint; any saint, that is, who existed in a historical time of which we have some knowledge from other sources, and which we can thus isolate and characterize, yet whose cult has persisted through a number of lifetimes and has undergone a vast number of influences and changes.

The Assumption is a feast commemorating the entrance into heaven of Mary because of the status she has by virtue of her Son. The actual sources of the story of Mary's miraculous preservation or rescue from death are lost to us. It seems to have been unknown in the earliest centuries of the Church. It is not mentioned by St Ambrose (7 Dec.; d. 397) or St Epiphanius (12 May; d. 403). It clearly arose by analogy with the resurrection or ascension of Christ but more with scriptural and popular narratives of the translation to heaven of the Old Testament saints Enoch, Moses, and Elijah. Any theological underpinning will have proceeded from the idea that people died because the body was corrupt as a result of sin, yet Mary was incorruptible: an aspect of what we know as the Immaculate Conception (see 8 Dec.). If Mary was preserved from sin to fulfill her role as *Theotokos*, or God-bearer (the title given her by the

Council of Ephesus in 431, as against Nestorius' *Christotokos*), in order to carry and yield the incorruptible Son, not only the soul that accepted but the body that did this must have been preserved from physical death and decay.

The cult of St Mary, the virgin mother of God, would seem to have begun in the second century. In ways unknown, forms of address and imagery from Hellenistic and Eastern goddess cults and, later, imperial and royal court practice affected ideas of Mary in popular devotion, visual and literary descriptions, and quasi-historical narratives. Over several centuries, whatever was most widespread, readily available, and impressive variously helped to form the unique combination of motherliness and majesty appropriate to an intercessor for human longings. Major figures in this process were clearly the Egyptian Isis (Io), queen of heaven, and the Horus-child, Semele, the mother of Dionysus, and Diana (or Vesta), goddess of the Ephesians. One need look no further than fourth-century Ephesus (which claimed to be the place where Mary died) to see similarities between the local cult of Mary of the Ephesians and the cult of Diana (whose feast was once celebrated on 13 August). In a very general sense, Semele's ascension into heaven, like all transitions of goddesses from wisdom into immortality, was an anticipation of the Assumption. One cannot, however, speak of direct adoptions; of, say, Cybele, the great mother of the gods, "becoming" the Virgin Mary. The whole process of influence is infinitely complex and includes many very different places, periods, and events. From the sixth century B.C. to the sixth century A.D. a divine mother-figure, or "mother of the gods," can be traced in various guises and manifestations, from polytheism to the cult of the *Meter ton theon* and the *Magna Mater*, in a vast network of associations between Phrygia and Asia Minor and Greece and Rome, including Gaul (Borgeaud). Yet scholars advance different, often contrary views on the nature of this evidence, let alone on any precise connections with the later and co-existent cult of the Virgin Mary. All we can say is that variously similar or analogous Christian tendencies, devotions, and practices existed and were authenticated and consolidated by late fourth- or early fifth-century pseudepigraphical writings, or apocrypha. Such non-canonical accounts were written to compensate for the New Testament's silence about the life of Jesus' mother. The most influential of these was the *Protevangelium* of James, available in Greek, Syriac, and Armenian, said to have been composed by James, Mary's step-son (and thought by some to have been composed in the second half of the second century; *cf.* Strycker). This contains an elaborate account of Mary's conception and birth, already graced with angelic visitations. Over the centuries this narrative, belonging to a literary genre very close indeed to that of the Greek novels circulating at the time, was variously rehandled, enhanced, and allegorized at different levels. These extended from mere superstition to the profound idea (as expressed by, say, the medieval German mystic Meister Eckhart) of Mary as the human soul in a state of purity so complete that in its innermost womb Christ must be born as pure awareness.

The earliest known legends of Mary's escape from death by divine intervention are found in fifth-century apocrypha in Greek, Latin, Coptic, Syriac, Ethiopic, and Arabic. They are thought to have an Egyptian origin and may be divided roughly into two groups: those that say that Mary's soul was taken straight to heaven, whereas her body was borne off by angels to be kept incorrupt until the general resurrection at the end of earthly time (Pseudo-John the Evangelist, *The Falling Asleep of the Holy Mother of God*); and those that assert that Mary died, but her body was resurrected three days after her death and then carried by angels to heaven (Pseudo-Melito [of Sardis], *The Translation of Mary*). (The dubious Syriac fragment known as *The Obsequies of the Holy Virgin*, possibly of the late fourth century, describes Mary's body as taken to heaven for insertion of her soul; and there is no agreement on the meaning of a fourth/fifth century homily ascribed to Timothy of Jerusalem, though a belief in a body-and-soul assumption of the living Mary has been deduced from it). The date given for the event varies from three to fifty years after the Ascension. Pope Gelasius (492-6) condemned these propositions as contrary to tradition in the *Decretum Gelasianum*, though some commentators claim that he anathematized not the belief itself but associated Gnostic ideas.

The two above-mentioned tendencies, with certain changes or new emphases, persisted in late sixth- to ninth-century legends. Mary was physically translated to heaven (St Gregory of Tours, d. 594, accepting Pseudo-Melito), a transition thought to have been observed by Dionysius (the Pseudo-Areopagite), the supposed disciple of St Paul (accepted as an eyewitness by Andrew of Crete, d. 740); she was physically incorrupt, though not translated directly to Heaven (John Damascene, d. *c.* 749, who described Bishop Juvenal of Jerusalem at Chalcedon relating the discovery of her empty tomb to the emperor Marcian); her body remained incorrupt but her soul was taken to heaven (*Epistle* of Pseudo-Jerome to Paula and Eustochium). In the ninth century we find accounts of her bodily assumption into heaven (Pseudo-Augustine, *On the Assumption of the Virgin*). These seemingly authentic narratives proved immensely and perennially attractive. Mary immaculately conceived, and so on, fulfilled the role of intercessor; Mary assumed into heaven, that of mediator for the aspirations of humanity. In either case this could be seen as a usurpation of Christ's unique role but also as a natural extension of its implications that satisfied human needs. Variations on these judgments have been recorded throughout the Christian centuries.

In the East Mary's death was commemorated possibly in fourth-century Antioch, certainly in fifth-century Palestine. It was assigned either to 18 January or to 15 August. After its proclamation in the East in around 600 by the emperor Maurice (582-603), the *Koimesis* or Dormition (Falling Asleep) of Our Lady was celebrated on 15 August (an indication of its part-function as a major harvest festival, or the chance result of the dedication of a church in Our Lady's honour). It was accepted gradually in the West and seems to have appeared first in Gaul in the early seventh century, though this may have been a general feast of Our Lady. It certainly existed in Rome under Pope Sergius I (687-701). By 813, in some calendars, it had been become an acknowledged Western feast as the Assumption of St Mary. The ninth-century popes Leo IV and Nicholas I elevated its official status. An account of a supposed vision of Mary's Assumption by the early-twelfth-century mystic Elizabeth of Schönau encouraged the reception of the feast and devotion.

Until the thirteenth century, however, some theologians argued against the bodily assumption of Mary. It remained a pious belief, though not an article of faith. Although SS Albert the Great (15 Nov.), Thomas Aquinas (28 Jan.), and Bonaventure (15 July) defended it, there were always scholars who regarded the Assumption with varying degrees of scepticism until the seventeenth and eighteenth centuries, when it became clear that the writings once taken as quasi-scriptural evidence for the Assumption were apocrypha. Before the Reformation, however, adverse criticism based on scriptural or theological legitimacy had little or no effect on what could be anything between a popular devotion integrated into the cycles of the seasons and the liturgical year and a highly-nuanced image in profound works of spirituality, literature, and art. In the *Divine Comedy*, for example, the vision of Beatrice draws Dante up through the heavens. He rises gradually through levels of ever-greater ecstasy and purification, leaving time for eternity, until he enters the presence of the Virgin Mary, already body and soul in heaven: "Maiden and Mother, daughter of thine own Son,/Beyond all creatures lowly and lifted high,/Of the Eternal Design the corner-stone! . . ./In thee is pity, in thee is tenderness,/In thee magnificence, in thee the sum/Of all that in creation most can bless." Dante's mind is transfigured through her mediation. He receives a vision of ultimate Truth: of the Trinity and thus of Christ in human form, reborn in his soul, and transforming all humankind.

Yet even throughout the Middle Ages and above all for many Renaissance thinkers but also for vast numbers of churchpeople of the Renaissance period who can hardly be described thus, the Assumption and other Marian beliefs were quite unproblematical for somewhat different reasons. Not only but especially in the multiple forms and echoes of art and poetry, architecture and astrology, questions of theological definition and doctrinal justification did not exist. The allegorical awareness was revitalized by the myths and figures of classical antiquity and of the East that had helped to form many figures and occasions of Christian devotion in the first place. The great works of Renaissance art, including depictions of the Assumption, drew on the new-found energy of the pagan gods and apotheoses of Greek heroes for their special mixtures of grandeur and pathos.

For most people in pre-Reformation western Europe, however, the Assumption was for centuries part of the pattern of Christian piety. In most countries and areas where the Reformation took hold, it was suppressed or faded away as

141

feast and devotion. Some reformers, such as Bullinger, accepted the Assumption, and Lutheranism was variously moderate in its presentation of Our Lady, but Calvinism was uniformly ruthless. In late-sixteenth-century Scotland, for example, the Assumption along with all Marian piety was expunged wherever Presbyterian discipline prevailed. The minimal acknowledgment of Mary in the earlier Episcopal tradition did not include the Assumption except for some cross-fertilization from the English Non-jurors in the seventeenth and eighteenth centuries and from the Tractarian movement in the nineteenth. In pre-Reformation England the celebration of the Assumption, or of "Our Lady in Harvest," was her most important feast. The 1549 Prayer Book eliminated the Assumption. Thereafter it disappeared from the official prayer of the Church of England and from the stained glass, paintings, and images destroyed or defaced by Iconoclasts. It survived, though, for some years as a popular devotion in many parts of the country in the works of the Caroline divines and then resurfaced a century later under Archbishop Laud, when an elaborate Life of the Blessed Virgin Mary could once again be published in London: "Concerning her death, some avouch that the Apostles, and the most eminent of the Primitive Church, were present at it. Damascene saith that Christ was also there in person. . . . As I will not justify all these their assertions for true; so, on the other side, I will not condemn them as erroneous . . . for ought I know, they may have passed by unwritten Tradition from man to man. . . . The same modesty I have shown in treating of her Death, I shall reserve in discoursing of her Assumption, which by many of the Fathers, all of the Romish Church, and some of the Reformed, is held for an undoubted truth" (Anthony Stafford, *The Femall Glory*, 1635).

The Assumption was one of the great devotional images of the Counter-Reformation. *In the Glorious Assumption of our Blessed Lady*, by the seventeenth-century English Catholic poet Richard Crashaw, gives some indication of the emotional intensity:

> Hark! she is called, the parting hour is come,
> Take thy farewell, poor world! heaven must go home.
> A piece of heavenly earth; purer and brighter
> Than the chaste stars, whose choice lamps come to light her
> While through the crystal orbs, clearer than they
> She climbs; and makes a far more milky way.

In baroque and rococo art, church decor, poetry, prayer, and liturgy the Assumption was raised to a new level of energy and flamboyance, and then, in the decadence of church art in the eighteenth and nineteenth centuries it was reduced to a cloying sentimentality, also found in portrayals of the Coronation of the Virgin, which imply a belief in the Assumption.

Through centuries of liturgical and popular practice cultic devotion to Our Lady had long been established, through the spread of ancient feasts, before the Catholic Church defined its two relatively recent dogmas. These were a response both to constant expressions "from below," among millions of ordinary people, especially the poor and children (or, rather, the thousands of cardinals and bishops who wrote on their behalf), of the fundamental need for a female figure in Christian devotion and to unmistakable evidence of the growing secularization of Western society and the dechristianization of its working masses. In 1854 the definition of the Immaculate Conception as a dogma (which Rome had declined to sanction when the Council of Basle declared it orthodox in 1439) opened up the way for similar treatment of the Assumption, which had long preceded the Immaculate Conception in liturgical expression. The early twentieth century was a period of intense Marian piety, especially in Latin countries, above all, those such as France (Lourdes), Portugal (Fatima), and Mexico (Guadalupe) where Mary was said to have appeared and where these manifestations were accepted by popular acclaim. Local churches pressed for a formal definition of the Assumption. The pressure reached a high point after the Spanish civil war and the start of the Second World War when right-wing authoritarian regimes held power in countries with large Catholic populations, such as Vichy France, Franco's Spain, Salazar's Portugal, Mussolini's Italy, and throughout most of South America. In 1940 more than eight million signatures in favour of a formal declaration were collected in Italy, Spain, and Latin America alone. A two-volume account of the "petitions" was published by the Vatican in the most crucial year of the war. By the late 1940s the war was over, the Soviets controlled eastern Europe, a relentless campaign against the Church there was in full swing, and elected Communist régimes with similar results seemed a real possibility in France and Italy. The consolidation of popular devotion to Our Lady was one of the more persuasive arguments for a public pronouncement, and offence to the Orthodox and Reformed traditions hardly a consideration in that pre-ecumenical era. In 1946-8 Pius XII was working toward a council of the Church, which eventually fell through. Documents had been prepared by theological groups, and there was a sense of expectation to be fulfilled in some way. There was a certain degree of episcopal consultation. For instance, Pius XII is said to have written to all Catholic bishops "in Dispersed-Council" (*i.e.*, not physically convoked) asking: Is it true? To be promulgated? Promulgated now/soon? The replies, it is said, came thus: ninety per cent Yes; eighty per cent Yes; seventy per cent Yes. On 1 November 1950, in the Bull *Munificentissimus Deus*, Pope Pius XII formally declared the Assumption an article of faith: "At the end of her earthly life, the immaculate mother of God, Mary ever-virgin, was taken up body and soul into the glory of heaven ('*ad caelestem gloriam*')."

Publication of the dogma in Poland was held up for some time by the then Communist government because they, or their Soviet masters, were convinced that the date of the feast was somehow associated with the defeat of the Russians after the First World War by the Polish patriot, Marshal Pilsudski, quasi-dictator of the country between the wars.

Promulgation of the definition in the mid-twentieth century, when the notion of a mechanical universe had eventually penetrated the popular mind (even though it had ceased to exist for the new physics), made it somewhat problematical. Objections raised in earlier centuries and various places about the Immaculate Conception, the resurrection, or the definitions of the Council of Chalcedon seemed newly apposite to this apparent addition to the matter of faith. If, for instance, one had to accept that Mary was taken up into the sky, at what speed did she rise? What would a passenger in a first-century airliner have seen above the clouds? What in the discernible universe, if not death, was (to use a later term) the interface between existence and mystery?

Such considerations were of no account to some serious commentators. One persistent line of commentary followed Newman's thinking on the "existence from the first, whether in individual minds or popular belief, of those doctrinal developments which afterwards became recognized portions of the Church's creed," and rehabilitated the function of tradition, suspect to the Enlightenment as the bearer of prejudice. Now tradition was seen dynamically. It did not baldly restate beliefs such as the Assumption but critically disclosed their origins and proposed them anew so as to "question the ways in which we are constrained by the plausible thinking of our own times, and to free the potential [of those beliefs] for the future" (Waldenfels, following the philosopher Gadamer). Tradition could even usefully undermine the same dominative political, social, and ecclesiastical structures that were used to support the status quo. Mary, the peasant girl who was described as saying, ". . . the arrogant of heart and mind he has put to rout, he has brought down monarchs from their thrones, but the humble have been lifted high. The hungry he has satisfied with good things, the rich sent empty away," is already enthroned above all others, a revolutionary in the courts of heaven.

In a superficially distinct but essentially related line of thought, Carl Jung, the father of analytical psychology, deeply interested in human aspirations, in striving for wholeness and completion, and in the archetypes, or ancestral memories said to appear not only in the individual consciousness and in dreams but in myths, was fascinated by the definition, "the latest development of the Christian symbol," standing for the total rebirth of the individual. Jung had long stressed the essential function of mother-archetypes in many myths and images, such as the Kingdom of God, representing the goal of human longing for redemption. He now spoke of the "quaternity of the One" as the "schema for all images of God, as depicted in the visions of Ezekiel, Daniel and Enoch" and saw the glorification of Mary as a necessary addition to the Trinity. It was an example of the "squaring of the circle": the "archetype of wholeness" and one of the most important of the "many archetypal motifs which form the basic patterns of our dreams and fantasies." More importantly, the definition came at a time when science and technology, a rationalistic and materialistic view of the world, threatened the human "spiritual and psychic heritage" with instant

144

annihilation: "Understood concretely, the Assumption is the absolute opposite of materialism. . . . Understood symbolically, however, the Assumption of the body is a recognition and acknowledgment of matter" that restores the symbolical unity of spirit and matter in the de-souled modern world in which human beings feel themselves uprooted and alienated. In his study of the assimilation of Greek mythology by Christianity, Hugo Rahner commented on Jung's penetration to that deep stratum of the human personality, "a territory which is common ground to all religious experience, the mysterious world of primitive human archetypes": "Catholic theology would here speak of our common human nature which is directed towards God. It would declare that it is this 'religiosity'—which always expresses itself in the same basic forms—that renders this human nature accessible to a possible revelation by the speaking God."

Certainly many difficulties disappear if we stop thinking of the Assumption in terms proper to eighteenth- or nineteenth-century physics and see it empathetically, in something like the same dimension of creative understanding as the artists, great and anonymous, who have interpreted it over the centuries, in that state "in which the mind liberated from the pressure of the will is unfolded in symbols" (W. B. Yeats). This is not so far from saying, "We must invoke the most wild and soaring sort of imagination; the imagination that can see what is there . . . the most incredible part of the story is that things which began thus should have developed thus" (Chesterton).

After the Second Vatican Council, Catholic interpretations of topics such as the Assumption (which survived the suppression of many Marian feasts in the 1969 Roman Calendar) became more open-ended, relying on the definition's silence about whether Mary died or not and its emphasis only on her passing, body and soul, into a "heavenly" state: "We may acknowledge that Mary is already glorified. It is true that her glory—like that of Christ himself—will only be perfect when the whole of [humankind] is gathered together. . . . The risen Christ and Mary assumed into heaven—the true Adam and Eve of mankind—are not to be sought far away from us, as though heaven were an immense theatre full of purely spiritual souls where only two places were bodily occupied, those of Christ and Mary. . . . Imagination in terms of space and time is powerless here. We can experience the presence of Christ and Mary by living on earth in the Spirit of Christ and by speaking to them in prayer" (*A New Catechism*). The first ecumenical (joint Catholic-Protestant) book of Christian faith referred to the dogma more specifically: "The formulation avoids any spatial conception in the sense of 'up there' and 'down here' and 'going up to heaven' and above all the images that are available to us from apocryphal writings and from many works of art. There is also no mention of how much 'time' has elapsed between the 'end of her life' and her assumption, nor is Mary's death once mentioned. All that is portrayed is Mary's glorification: nothing is said about 'how' this happened" (*The Common Catechism*). A disadvantage of such intellectually responsible commentaries, however, is that they reduce or cancel the very imaginative and devotional vitality of the Assumption that ensured its widespread acceptance and survival.

Nevertheless, from the 1970s not only Catholic but even Protestant and, more especially, feminist thinking began to re-evaluate all aspects of Marian devotion, including the Assumption, in the context of the human search for someone who as a human being "can be loved with the absoluteness of love for God. But it is not searching for [that someone] as an idea, because ideas cannot be loved, but rather as a reality, whether it is already present or is still to come" (Karl Rahner). Accordingly, as a symbolic representation the Assumption stands not only for divine acceptance of the fully-achieved life of Mary (of the role of the Church, of women, of humanity, and so on) but, more daringly, for the motherly nature, maternal aspects, feminine principle (and so on) of God. In the terms of one of the more modest of these statements: "The Assumption tells us that infinity is also a human world where we can be sure of the comfort and security of a mystery that is forever female and feminine. Where the world is as it ought to be, it becomes the cosmic womb of our mother in which we know that we are accepted body and soul" (Hasenhüttl). Apart from fashionable emphases there may be little difference between this approach, that of Jung, and indeed, the allegorical or Neoplatonizing tendencies of the Renaissance. Its eclectic vagueness similarly escapes (or expands) the strict formulas of Christian tradition and in that sense might be said to offend against (or elucidate) the prerogatives of Christ. Yet it also amounts to saying that our apprehension of, understanding of, devotion to, Mary remains part of our attempt, as we come to know more about ourselves, to communicate effectively with the inexhaustible mystery that we call God.

For the Christian understanding of tradition, the deposit of faith, and the Assumption see J. H. Newman, *An Essay on the Development of Christian Doctrine* (2d ed., 1846), esp. pp. 384-7, 437-45; G. K. Chesterton, *The Everlasting Man* (1925), pp. 15-9, 245-7; G. Hentrich and R. G. de Moos (eds.), *Petitiones de Assumptione Corporea B.V. Mariae in Caelum Definienda ad Sanctam Sedem Delatae* (1942); M. Jugie, *La Mort et l'Assomption de la Sainte Vierge: Etude historico-doctrinale* (1944); B. Capelle, "Théologie de l'Assomption d'après la bulle *Munificentissimus Deus*," *Nouvelle Revue Théologique* 72 (1950), pp. 1009-27; G. Miegge, *The Virgin Mary* (Eng. trans., 1955), pp. 83 ff.; E. de Strycker, *La Forme la plus ancienne du Protoévangile de Jacques* (1961); H. F. Davis, *Catholic Dictionary of Theology*, 1 (1962), pp. 170-9; E. Hennecke and W. Schneemelcher, *New Testament Apocrypha*, 1 (1963); *A New Catechism* (Eng. trans., 1967), pp. 475-6; *The Common Catechism* (Eng. trans., 1975), pp. 620-32; F. Rapp, *L'Eglise et la Vie Religieuse en Occident à la Fin du Moyen Age* (1971), pp. 149-52; R. R. Ruether, *Mary: The Feminine Face of the Church* (1977); V. and E. Turner, *Image and Pilgrimage in Christian Culture* (1978); K. Rahner, *Foundations of Christian Faith* (Eng. trans., 1978), pp. 387-8; G. Hasenhüttl, *Kritische Dogmatik* (1979), pp. 175-83; A. Stacpoole (ed.), *Mary's Place in Christian Dialogue* (1982); H. Waldenfels, "Tradition," in *Kontextuelle Fundamentaltheologie* (2d ed., 1988), pp. 437-88.

On the ancestry of Mary's attributes and on aesthetic, anthropological, psychological, and social aspects see R. Graves, *The White Goddess* (1948), pp. 245-58; J. Seznec, *The Survival of the Pagan Gods. The Mythological Tradition and Its Place in Renaissance Humanism and*

Art (Eng. trans., 1953), *passim*; C. J. Jung, *The Archetypes and the Collective Unconscious* (Eng. trans., 1959), pp. 75-110, 388-9; H. Rahner, *Greek Myths and Christian Mystery* (Eng. trans., 1963), esp. pp. 6-45, 89-176; M. Warner, *Alone of All her Sex: The Myth and Cult of the Virgin Mary* (1976), pp. 81-102; P. Brown, *The Body and Society: Men, Women and Sexual Renunciation in Early Christianity* (1988); I. Kalavrezou, "Images of the Mother: When the Virgin Mary becomes *Méter Theou*," in *Dumbarton Oaks Papers* 44 (1990), pp. 165-72; S. Benko, *The Virgin Goddess: Studies in the Pagan and Christian Roots of Mariology* (1993); S. Elm, *The Virgins of God: The Making of Asceticism in Late Antiquity* (1994); V. Limberis, *Divine Heiress: The Virgin Mary and the Creation of Christian Constantinople* (1994); P. Borgeaud, *La Mère des Dieux: De Cybèle à la Vierge Marie* (1996). The summary of the New Testament account at the start of the above is indebted to T. Beattie, *Rediscovering Mary: Insights from the Gospels* (1995); on Mary as identified with the poor, see I. Gebara and M. C. Bingemer, *Mary, Mother of God, Mother of the Poor* (1989).

There are countless images of Mary. The following covers only some examples of the main ways of representing her passing on—whether Dormition or Assumption—in the great ages of Christian art.

In some of the most moving icons and other paintings of Mary's death in the Orthodox tradition accepted for centuries in the West, she lies on her death-bed while Christ behind carries her miniature self, or soul, in his hands: *e.g.*, the tenth-century ivory from Constantinople on the cover of the German emperor Otto III's Gospels (Munich State Library); the *Novgorod Dormition* (*c.* 1230); that by Theophanes the Greek (*c.* 1380; both Tretyakov Gallery, Moscow); and that by Prochor of Gorodez (1405; Annunciation Cathedral, Moscow), in which she and Christ appear in a mandala. Jesus is shown bearing Mary's soul in the luminous mosaic *Dormition* in the twelfth-century La Martorana church in Palermo, Italy. The tympanum of Senlis cathedral (*c.* 1150) shows one of the earliest Dormition scenes among those sculpted on French churches. The *Winchester Psalter* (British Library), illuminated for Bishop Henry of Blois at Winchester *c.* 1140-60, contains among its northern Romanesque miniatures a "Byzantine" diptych of the death of the Virgin and the Virgin in glory, presumably copied by an English painter from icons from the Latin kingdom of Jerusalem; there is a curious variation in the English version: the footstool found at the foot of the bed in the archetype has become an open tomb. A fascinating Dormition of the fifteenth-century Tyrolese school shows St Peter censing the dead Virgin (there are thirteen apostles; National Gallery, London). The early tradition that combines the death and Assumption of Mary appears in Gerolamo da Vicenza's panel painting (1480; National Gallery, London).

The death of Mary is still an acceptable subject in the early sixteenth century, as is shown by countless examples (see that by an imitator of Campin; National Gallery, London). Yet Francesco Botticini's altarpiece (*c.* 1470, from a Benedictine convent, Florence; National Gallery, London) shows the heavens open to reveal a magnificent array of nine orders of angels and Our Lady kneeling before Christ; it is impressively heretical for, after Palmieri's poem, *The City of Life*, it includes a great number of saints in seven of the hierarchies. Orcagna's sculpture (1357; S. Michele, Florence) shows the disciples and others mourning at her death-bed below while angels bear her through space and time, seated in serene glory in a shell-like capsule above. The same construction, though with SS Jerome and Francis as mourners at an empty coffin, is used in Andrea di Giusto's *Assumption of the Virgin* (Philbrook Art Centre, Tulsa, Oklahoma). Paolo di Giovanni Fei's version (1372-1410; National Gallery of Art, Washington) shows the disciples at an empty tomb, while she is borne aloft on clouds. Filippino Lippi's (d. 1504) *Madonna della Cintola* (Alinari, Milan) shows the doubting St Thomas convinced of the Assumption by Our Lady's sash, which she dropped from heaven for the purpose.

Titian's *Assumption* (1516-8; church of the Frari, Venice) is one of the pre-eminent

Renaissance portrayals of the topic, in which Mary rises between the amazed crowd below and the welcoming Father above. Tintoretto's extraordinarily vital *Assumption* (1583-7; Scuola di San Rocco, Venice) shows Mary as it were bursting out of the tomb in an explosion of clouds. His version in the Duomo of Verona (*c*. 1543) is altogether calmer. Examples of the Assumption conceived and expressed with full Counter-Reformation intensity, so that Mary is shown ascended, fulfilled, and in a scarcely less than divine glory emphasized by the ecstatic contemplation of a company of saints and angels, are Peter Paul Rubens' panel (*c*. 1620-5; Mauritshuis, The Hague), Guido Reni's canvas (*c*. 1614; St Ambrogio, Genoa), Anthony van Dyck's resplendently coloured sketch on panel (*c*. 1630-2; Vienna Academy), and Pietro da Cortona's ceiling-painting (1655-6; apse of S. Maria in Vallicella, Rome). The tendency reached its height (or became decadent, depending on one's viewpoint) in the Assumptions of Murillo (1618-82).

The firm continuation of the Dormition tradition in the East is exemplified by a Greek *Entombment of the Virgin* (*c*.1800; National Gallery, London).

St Simplician, *Bishop* (401)

St Augustine (28 Aug.) consulted Simplician as a devout, learned, and shrewd Milanese priest well acquainted with the Christian Platonism in which he was interested. Simplician had directed the theological studies of Bishop St Ambrose (7 Dec.), for whom Plato's followers were the "aristocrats of thought." Augustine gave Simplician an account of his spiritual and intellectual odyssey to date. He mentioned that he had read some works of Marius Victorinus, an eminent African professor of rhetoric in Rome, who had taught most of the senators yet died a Christian, and had translated Plotinus and other Neoplatonists into Latin. Simplician said that he had known the famous teacher. He mentioned a conversation with Victorinus that he knew would appeal to Augustine because it was very much in line with his own attitude: "He used to say to Simplicianus—not publicly but privately, as between friends—'I want you to know that I am a Christian now.' Simplician would reply: 'I shall never believe it or count you as a Christian until I see you in the Church of Christ.' Victorinus laughed at that and said: 'Is it the walls of a church, then, that make people Christians?'" Simplician described how he had persuaded Victorinus to profess his private convictions publicly and become a Christian. When Julian the Apostate forbade Christians to teach rhetoric or literature, he abandoned his school. Augustine was deeply moved by the example of Victorinus, and the influence of Simplician took him closer to his own conversion.

On several occasions Ambrose praises Simplician's learning, judgment, and faith. When he was dying, it is said, he overheard someone suggest the priest as his successor and called out, "Simplician is old but he is a good man." Simplician succeeded to the see of Milan but governed it for only three years. When he was troubled by some difficulties in the Letter to the Hebrews, he referred them to Augustine. Among other things, he asked: "Why did God say: 'I hated Esau?'—Why do people experience their particular fates?" *Ad Simplicianum de diversis quaestionibus* (To Simplician on Various Problems), one of Augustine's most profoundly revealing works, was written in reply. It is not the freedom of the human will but the grace of God that is supreme: "Undoubtedly God's choice is concealed from us. . . . Even if some people can see it, I have to admit that in this case I just do not know the answer. I simply cannot decide what criterion to use when deciding which people should be chosen to be saved by grace. If I were to think what this choice might be based on, I myself would instinctively choose those with a superior intellect or fewer sins, or both. Then, I think, I would add a sound and thorough education—But as soon as I decide that, He will simply laugh me to scorn." Paul, indeed, has the (still enigmatic) answer: "You must work out your own salvation in fear and trembling; for it is God who works in you, inspiring both the will and the deed, for his own chosen purpose" (Phil. 2:12-3).

One practice of Simplician (and of Augustine) was wearing a black leather belt on account (it was said) of a vision of St Monica's (27 Aug.) in which Our Lady told her to wear one in her honour. The Augustinian friars adopted this belt as part of their habit. Simplician died in May, but his feast has long been celebrated in August.

See *AA.SS.*, Aug., 3; *D.C.B.*, 4, pp. 688-9; St Augustine, *The Confessions* (any good modern translation), bk 8, ch. 1, 2; P. Brown, *Augustine of Hippo* (1967); *Ad Simplicianum de diversis quaestionibus*, French trans. by G. Bardy in *Bibliothèque augustinnienne, sér. I*, 10 (1952), pp. 383-578. See also under St Augustine in the present work (28 Aug.)

St Alipius, *Bishop* (*c*. 360-430)

Nearly everything we know about Alipius (or Alypius) comes from the writings of that great psychologist St Augustine (28 Aug.). For this reason he emerges as a real human being from the general obscurity of hagiographical rhetoric. No incident in the *Confessions* is described for its own sake. What Augustine has to say about someone he knows well throws light on their two psyches in a subtle reciprocity that gathers momentum throughout the book as, we are made to feel, it did throughout their lives.

Alipius was born in about 360 at Tagaste in North Africa. He was a relative of a local grandee, Romanianus, who was the young Augustine's patron. He was a boyhood friend of Augustine's. He studied grammar at Tagaste and rhetoric at Carthage, both under Augustine, until his father and Augustine quarrelled. Alipius and his master remained friends. The charismatic Augustine interested both Alipius and Romanianus in his version of the illegal and exotic Manicheism, in its local form a non-doctrinaire religion for the cultivated few. It assured the complex, guilt-ridden, and ambitious Augustine of an irreducible core of perfection within himself, and its anti-authoritarianism connected with his feelings about his father and the Christian Church. It had a different attraction for Alipius; he had experimented with sex when quite young—"by stealth and by snatches"—but something distressing had happened which had always repelled him afterwards. As Augustine remarks, he just wasn't interested any longer. He found the extreme chastity recommended by the Manichees congenial and admired their austerity. But he still had a problem. He resolved this temporarily by finding another release for his strong impulses.

Romanianus liked to put on wild beast shows in Tagaste to demonstrate his power and wealth, and the otherwise solemn Alipius became dangerously addicted to the sight of slaughter and to what Augustine called the "madness of the circus." He was so obsessed with the noise and sight of bloodletting that Augustine had given up any hope of curing him. When he was in Carthage, Alipius slipped into one of Augustine's lectures—absolutely forbidden him— and happened to hear a chance comparison with the events in the arena and the master's rebuke for anyone obsessed with them. Alipius took this as a direct personal reproof and immediately gave up his interest. Augustine was afraid that this would somehow turn Alipius against him, but in the way of their relationship it made Augustine seem all the more attractive. Alipius never did anything by halves, and he now managed to persuade his father to let him become a student at Augustine's school.

Alipius had decided to follow the career chosen by his parents and to become an administrative lawyer. Accordingly, he went to Rome to complete his studies. Unfortunately, his new friends and fellow-students, as is the way of things, sensed his compulsion and "with a kind of friendly violence" took him off to the amphitheatre one day after dinner. Alipius fatally claimed that he was so changed that he could sit through the spectacle without opening his eyes or mind to it. But the wild excitement and deafening shouts were too much for him. When he heard one especially terrible scream from a wounded combatant, he became more addicted than ever to the gladiatorial shows and "drunk with delight in blood. He wasn't the Alipius who had come there. Now he was one of the common herd he joined there. . . . He gazed, he shouted, he burned with the desire of it. He went home so crazed with the excitement of blood-lust that he just had to go back, and not only with the companions who had made him go that day, or with people who had debauched him by introducing him to it in the first place. He became even more enthusiastic than them and went one better by seducing other innocents into going with him." It was a long time before Alipius came to terms with his weakness. In the end, he did so only by following a more powerful compulsion that channelled into achievement his drive to be and to express whatever nature had made him.

In the meantime he followed his studies in the law, though not without useful lessons in the ways of the world—which for Augustine meant knowing oneself. As Augustine perceived, Alipius' obduracy and enthusiasm went with a kind of fatal openness to what could seem mere misfortune. One day he was arrested on suspicion of theft. A young scholar had been cutting away the valuable leaden gratings over the silversmiths' booths but made too much noise and fled, dropping his hatchet. Alipius, who had been strolling along carrying his lecture notes and half-sunk in scholarly reverie, picked it up out of curiosity. He was accused of the crime and was rescued from imprisonment only by a chance meeting with an architect who knew him and after a difficult process of identification and tracing of the culprit that might have come out of a modern crime thriller. In spite of numerous local temptations he remained chaste (largely for the reasons already given), worked hard, and was appointed to a judicial office, that of assessor, which he exercised responsibly and fairly. Courteous, calm, and quite authoritarian (as he would remain), he resisted bribes and particular pressure from a corrupt senator to take one in return for a wrong judgment. The judge himself, a Mr Facing-both-ways, did not directly refuse the senator but satisfied man and morality by pretending that Alipius was inconveniently naive and about to blow the whole thing open by a public resignation from the court.

When Augustine came to Rome they were inseparable. Alipius accompanied him to Milan in 384 and later to a country retreat. When Augustine's mother decided that her son should be married and found him a suitable bride, she persuaded him to separate from the woman he had lived with for so long. Augustine was deeply upset. His companion was so close to him that when she left for Africa, she swore she would never have anything to do with another man: "My heart longed for her. It was broken and wounded until it bled." Nevertheless he quite liked the new girl, although she was two years under a marriageable age and he would have to wait for her. Accordingly, while planning with Alipius a life apart from worldly pursuits, he found a temporary concubine. Throughout all this, Alipius tried to persuade him not to marry. To enhance his own confused excitement and knowing his power over Alipius, Augustine devised "certain sweet snares to entangle" his friend's "honest and still free feet." Knowing that for Alipius it was "all in the head," he summoned his powers of language and emotional conviction and set about reawakening Alipius' interest in sex. He compared his friend's immature experiences with his own "everyday delights," and pointed out that if Alipius were married, those pleasures could be enjoyed quite honourably and he could pursue the search for divine Wisdom without any qualms. He was successful in making Alipius want to marry, but only out of "curiosity." In spite of his friend's cajoling, Alipius went no further than that, it seems, before Augustine experienced his great change of heart as well as mind and persuaded Alipius to share it.

Alipius was not "miserably racked by inquiry," by Augustine's intellectual uncertainty. He was "speechless and astonished" when Augustine in his torment asked (with regard to the monks of Egypt): "What is the matter with us? . . . These men have none of our education yet they stand up and storm the gates of heaven while we, in spite of all our learning, lie here grovelling in this world of flesh and blood!" Alipius "silently awaited the outcome of all this agitation," then straightforwardly and resolutely accepted his new life of dedication to God. In a telling image Augustine described him as "so assured and in control of himself that he would walk on the frozen Italian soil with bare feet." Their names were inscribed together among the *competentes* at the beginning of Lent 387. Alipius followed the exercises catechumens had to make before Baptism and, together with Augustine, received the sacrament from St Ambrose (7 Dec.) on Easter eve.

Some time after that they returned to Africa and lived together at Tagaste, in a small community of like-minded people, for three years. This provided the kind of framework of order yet understanding and support that Alipius needed. When Augustine was ordained priest they all went to Hippo and continued the same way of life. Alipius, now a priest, made a pilgrimage to Palestine, where he met St Jerome (30 Sept.). When he went back to Africa he was consecrated bishop of Tagaste, about the year 393. He preached zealously. He was Augustine's main assistant in all his public work, often helping him on juridical and technical points. He was socially and professionally adept, able to communicate effectively with eminent and cultivated persons in high places, and well acquainted with the ways of the imperial bureaucracy. He was also, as a firm, legalistic churchman, often ready for direct action when not only Augustine's sense of paradox and ability to see many different factors but his psychological acuity made him less exacting than his pupil. Alipius took a leading part in the arguments against and in the repression of the Donatists. From Rome he sent Augustine work after work of Julian, bishop of Eclanum and supporter of Pelagius, so that the master could deal with the latest attacks from his controversial opponent. He had to engage in protracted negotiations in Rome on behalf of the African bishops until the end of Augustine's life. In a letter he wrote to Alipius in 429, Augustine calls Alipius old, and he probably did not live long beyond Augustine's own death on 28 August 430.

See *AA.SS*, Aug., 3; St Augustine, *The Confessions* (in any modern translation); J. O'Meara, *The Young Augustine* (1954); P. Brown, *Augustine of Hippo* (1967). See also under St Augustine (28 Aug.).

St Athanasia (Ninth Century)

Athanasia appears in some texts of the synaxaries on 4 April. She is retained by the new draft Roman Martyrology as "a widow, famous for her observance of the monastic life and for the gift of miracles," but there is no evidence of a strong early cult. She may be fictitious. The traditional narratives are interesting and deserve a summary account.

Athanasia was born on the island of Aegina in unsettled times, when the area was subject to constant attacks from Muslims or Bulgarians, there were continual movements of population, the village communes were showing the first signs of failure, and the consolidation of property in large estates was a major concern. It was possible for peasants to become magnates by careful manipulation of land and by strategic alliances, especially through marriage. A well-organized police state enforced its decrees rigorously. Athanasia had long been attracted to the religious life but married an army officer who was killed sixteen days later while repelling an Arab incursion on the Grecian coast. Encouraged by a dream-vision of the transience of worldly things, she was now very anxious to become a nun, but her parents persuaded her to remarry. In their eyes it was necessary to choose quickly, as an imperial edict ordered all widows or unbetrothed girls to marry barbarians settling in the area in order to assimilate them proficiently.

Fortunately Athanasia's second husband was a good choice. He had a religious disposition and even shared her good works. She gave alms liberally, helped the sick, strangers, prisoners, and people in need. She interpreted the Bible for her neighbours after Mass. After a time, however, her husband expressed a wish to enter a monastery. Athanasia agreed. Now she could be a nun after all. She turned her house into a convent and appointed herself abbess. However, in her determination to make up for all the lost years she became over-enthusiastic. She and the Sisters she gathered round her practised excessive austerity until they were so weak that they could hardly walk.

They came under the direction of a sensible abbot named Matthias. He was horrified by their condition and insisted that they tone down their mortifications. He arranged for the nuns to move from their noisy town house to a quiet one at Timia. The community grew and the buildings had to be enlarged.

Unfortunately, Athanasia was an exceptionally gifted thaumaturge. She became famous and received an offer she could not refuse. She was summoned to Constantinople as an adviser to Empress Theodora. This was a dubious honour. The court was always interested in religion, theology, and ecclesiastical politics, which as often as not involved intrigue, depositions, banishments, torture, and assassinations. A call to the capital generally meant trouble for any cleric. Theodora's husband had had the Sicilian monk Methodius, an iconodule, flogged and imprisoned, then released him and found him a secluded room in his palace because his scholarship was entertaining. There was usually a company of fashionable men of God and interesting schismatics or heretics tucked into various houses and palaces about the city. Athanasia was a novelty. The empress found her a cell rather like that she had occupied in her own monastery and kept her there. Eventually—seven years later—the empress grew tired of Athanasia and sent her back to Timia. She had not been there long when she fell ill. For twelve days she tried to carry on as usual, but at last she had to send her nuns to sing their office in church without her. When they returned, Athanasia was dying and survived only long enough to bless them. She is said to have died in about 860.

See *AA.SS.*, Aug., 3, for the unsatisfactory Greek Life, whose author claims—improbably—to have been a contemporary of Athanasia. It rings true with regard to the marriage problem in the late ninth century. The behaviour of the empress seems very like that of the ghastly ex-actress Theodora, wife to Justinian. But the date is wrong, and this must be the empress-dowager and regent Theodora, mother of Michael III, "the Drunkard" (842-67). She re-established orthodox veneration of images when her husband, Theophilos the Iconoclast, died in 842. Perhaps Athanasia had to return when Theodora's brother Bardas tried to force the empress into a convent in 856-8, perhaps when Michael was murdered and replaced by his favourite, the ex-groom Basil.

St Hyacinth (1185-1257)

Hyacinth (or Jacek) was born into the Silesian nobility in the district of Oppeln between Wroclaw (formerly Breslau) and Cracow. He is venerated as an apostle of Poland. That is all we can say of him with some certainty. The achievements attributed to him depend on biographies of dubious historical value.

Hyacinth is said to have been educated in Bohemia and Italy and to have become a Dominican, possibly in Rome, where he met St Dominic (8 Aug.), between 1217 and 1220. He accompanied other Dominicans to Cracow, where Bishop Ivo Odrowaz gave them the church of the Holy Trinity. Hyacinth is said to have been at this priory again in 1228 and ten years later preached a Crusade again the non-Christian Prussians. His missionary endeavours were all but superhuman. He is reported as going north-east into Lithuania, east to Kiev, south-east to the Black Sea, south to the Danube, and north-west to Scandinavia, leaving Silesia, Pomerania, and Bohemia to his fellow-Dominican, Bd Ceslaus (17 July), said to have been his actual brother. We know that during Hyacinth's supposed lifetime the Friars Preachers did penetrate down the Vistula to Gdansk (formerly Danzig) and toward Russia and the Balkans, and some priories were founded, but their missions suffered after the Mongols crossed the Volga in 1238. He died on 15 August 1257, after exhorting his Brothers to persist in holy poverty, and was possibly buried in the Dominican church in Cracow. He was canonized in 1594, when the consolidation of Polish Catholicism and the campaign against Protestantism had reached a high point.

See the earliest but extravagant Life by Stanislaus of Cracow, written a century after the saint's death, in *Monumenta Poloniae Historica*, 4, pp. 841-94. See also *Anal. Boll.* 65 (1927), pp. 202-3; *Archiv. Fratrum Praedicatorum*, 27 (1957), pp. 5-38; B. Altaner, *Die Dominikanermissionen des 13. Jahrhunderts* (1924), pp. 196-214; *B.T.A*, 3, pp. 338-9.

Zuccheri's (1529-66) painting (St Sabina, Rome) shows Hyacinth being robed as a Dominican; three tapestries within the picture are vignette-like representations of some of his evangelical achievements.

St Stanislaus Kostka (1550-68)

He was born Stanislaw Kostka, the second son of Jan, a senator or member of the upper house of Parliament, and his wife, Margaret Kryska, in the family castle at Rostkow, in the then very large kingdom of Poland, which incorporated Lithuania and fragments of what had been or later became other countries. The king was Catholic, but his powers were restricted by the nobles' defence of their unusual privileges. The Polish nobility—including the landed gentry of the lower house—made up less then ten per cent of the population and were determined to restrict the powers not only of the monarch and towns but also of the clergy. In 1562, for example, the Church lost its disciplinary powers over heresy.

Poland at that time could scarcely be called a Catholic country. Half the population was Greek or Russian Orthodox; many Jews had sought refuge there from frequent persecutions in the Middle Ages; and Hussites, Lutherans, Bohemian Brethren, Unitarians, and others were spreading their ideas, with considerable success, in an atmosphere of—for the times—extraordinary religious liberty. For the most part the nobles defended this situation. Half of the members of Parliament were Protestant (though more Calvinist than Lutheran), and many Catholic nobles were sympathetic or considered toleration to be in their interests. The Church, however, considered Protestants, above all the Lutherans, to be its most redoutable and dangerous opponents. After entering the country in 1565 in Stanislaus' lifetime, but mainly after it, the Jesuits helped to make Poland a predominantly Catholic nation. They did this slowly but methodically, largely as a result of their control over education granted by the king. The process continued until the start of the eighteenth century.

As a child Stanislaus was shy, very religious, but also very determined. Recent studies reveal that he also had a passionate nature, which he soon learned to control. As he grew up he found his parents' sophisticated worldliness as unsympathetic as they no doubt found him puzzling. "Don't tell that story in front of Stanislaus," his father would say. "He would faint!"

At first he was educated privately by a Dr Jan Bilinsky. When Stanislaus was fourteen, Bilinsky accompanied him and his sixteen-year-old brother, Paul, to Vienna, where they were to attend the Jesuit college. Initially they lived in a student hostel—a house on loan to the Jesuits from Ferdinand I, German (*i.e.*, Holy Roman) emperor (1556-64). Stanislaus felt at home there, and everyone was struck by his hard work, wide reading in classic and secular authors, and intense inwardness. Unfortunately Ferdinand died soon after their arrival and his son, Maximilian II (1564-76), reclaimed the house. Paul, who was less introspective and sensitive than his brother, saw this as an opportunity to enjoy himself. He persuaded Bilinsky to rent rooms for them in a Lutheran's home. Stanislaus objected to living in a heretic's, especially a Lutheran's, establishment. Paul answered this scruple with amused derision. One day Stanislaus rounded on him: "If you go on like this I shall run away and you'll have to explain things to Father and Mother." But Paul was insistent, and Bilinsky ignored the younger brother's complaints.

Stanislaus was so single-minded and his behaviour so unusually pious for a boy of his age that he was treated with the contempt schoolboys reserve for someone they consider an insufferable prig. He received Communion as often as the custom of the time allowed and fasted the day before; when not in church or attending college he could be found praying or studying in his room. He dressed unobtrusively, especially resented going to dancing classes, and practised physical mortifications. Paul turned from teasing to bullying, which Bilinsky, not unreasonable but no more understanding of Stanislaus than anyone else, did little to restrain.

After two years of suffering, Stanislaus had what was probably a breakdown of some kind. He felt so sick that he asked for the Last Sacraments. The landlord refused to have the Blessed Sacrament in his house. Stanislaus prayed to St Barbara, to whose confraternity he belonged, and claimed that by her intercession two angels had brought him the Sacrament. He also said that Our Lady had appeared to him, saying that he would not die on this occasion and that he ought to become a Jesuit. Since he had already thought of joining the Society, when he recovered he went to the provincial in Vienna and asked to be admitted. The provincial was reluctant to anger Stanislaus' father and refused. The boy decided to go to Rome and speak to the father general in person.

On 10 August 1567, Stanislaus began his 350-mile journey on foot. Paul and Bilinsky rode in pursuit but either failed to recognize him or could not overtake him. In Dillingen he was kindly received by the German Jesuit provincial, St Peter Canisius (21 Dec.), who had himself covered thousands of miles on foot as well as on horseback. Peter was one of the great educators of the Counter-Reformation, who at an early age helped to vanquish Protestantism in Cologne and by gaining control of education in Austria largely subdued it there as well as in Bavaria and Bohemia. He clearly saw the virtues and future value of this youth's faith and determination, probably with a view to the Jesuit campaign in Poland. He encouraged Stanislaus' vocation but tested it before sending him on to Rome. Stanislaus spent the next three weeks waiting on the students at table and cleaning their rooms. When he arrived in Rome on 25 October, the general, St Francis Borgia (10 Oct.), admitted him to the Society. He was not yet eighteen.

Jan Kostka had planned a career as a diplomat for his son. He wrote angrily to Stanislaus to accuse him of choosing a profession unworthy of his station. He threatened to have the Jesuits driven out of Poland. The boy replied politely but stood his ground and devoted himself to the demands of what proved to be the last nine months of his life. His observance of the Rule was irreproachable; his spirit of prayer was generally acknowledged; he was said often to be in a kind of ecstasy at Mass; but the Roman summer of 1568 was too much for him. He fainted often and realized that he did not have long to live. He became seriously ill on 10 August. In the early morning of the 15th, the feast of the Assumption, he claimed to have seen Our Lady in the midst of a vast company of angels and died peacefully just after three o'clock.

Shortly afterwards, Paul arrived in Rome with instructions from his father to take Stanislaus back to Poland at all costs. He was shocked by his brother's death. He reconsidered his own behaviour and—together with Dr Bilinsky— was one of the main witnesses for the cause during the beatification process. Bilinsky said: "The blessed boy never had a good word from Paul. And we both knew all the time the holiness and devotion of all he did." Paul is said to have bitterly regretted treating his brother with disdain. At the age of sixty he became a Jesuit. In 1726, Stanislaus was canonized together with another Jesuit novice, St Aloysius Gonzaga (21 June). He is the second patron of Poland.

At an early stage, Stanislaus was proposed as a model of angelic purity and innocence, which he has remained, though since the 1960s and postconciliar shifts in Jesuit education to more psychologically acceptable and socially effective emphases awareness of him outside Poland and Polish immigrant groups elsewhere has dwindled almost to zero. Not long after his death he began to be used by the Jesuits as an important model in the long-drawn-out campaign against Protestantism in Poland. This started in earnest in 1565 when they were granted control of higher education there and had reached a satisfactory conclusion by the time of Stanislaus' canonization.

There are many portraits of Stanislaus, though he seems never to have elicited any of artistic merit from a painter of real note. Not a few were produced in the century after his death, but his real influence on devotional art was in the second half of the nineteenth and the first half of the twentieth centuries, when the combined effects of Jesuit instruction and Polish national sentiment created an almost universal market for a vast flood of tawdry oleographs, lithographs, and cards bearing his supposed image. These matched the now scarcely credible sentimentality of printed sermons, pamphlets, and other writings on the saint (and on Aloysius, with whom he was often paired), intended for young people and boys in particular. It is very difficult to disentangle truth from pious fiction and exaggeration in contemporary accounts of Stanislaus. When a serious attempt is made to do so, as in the most recent biography in English, a more stalwart and interestingly complex character begins to emerge. Nevertheless, his image will always be obscured by the religious, and to some extent by the political, campaigns of his time and place, if not so much now by the suasions of nineteenth-century sexual morality.

See *AA.SS.*, Aug., 3, pp. 146, 200; U. Ubaldini (ed. Arndt), "Vita S. Stanislai Kostkae," in *Anal. Boll.* 9 (1890), pp. 360-78; 11 (1892), pp. 412-67; 13 (1894), pp. 122-56, 14 (1895), pp. 295-318; 15 (1896), pp. 285-315; 16 (1897), pp. 253-96; C. C. Martindale, *Christ's Cadets* (1913); M. Monahan, *On the King's Highway* (1927); J. Brodrick, S.J., *Life of St Peter Canisius* (1935), pp. 674-6; J. E. Kerns, *Portrait of a Champion* (1957); J. N. Tylenda, *Jesuit Saints and Martyrs* (1985). See also H. F. Broadway, *Cambridge History of Poland*, vol. 1 (1950), *passim.*; K. Górski, "L'histoire de la spiritualité polonaise," in *Millénaire du catholicisme en Pologne* (1969), pp. 281 ff.

Stanislaus' emblem is a lily, symbol of purity. He is shown on his knees adoring the Blessed Sacrament, receiving Communion, or with the Infant Jesus in his arms. Typical eighteenth-century images are Carlo Maratta's oil of him on his knees receiving the Infant Jesus from Mary and an engraving after Nicolas Dorigny. There is a polychrome marble funerary effigy of the saint by Pierre Legros the Younger (novitiate of St Andrew of the Quirinal, Rome).

Bd Isidore Bakanja, *Martyr (c. 1885-1909)*

Isidore presents the remarkable if not unique case of a native-born African killed by a European and declared a martyr. He was born to pagan parents at Ikengo in what was then the Belgian Congo (subsequently Zaïre and now the Democratic Republic of Congo). He worked as an assistant bricklayer for a Belgian State enterprise in Coquihatville (now Mbandaka). There he came into contact with Catholicism, which he embraced with great enthusiasm. He was baptized on 6 May 1906, taking the name Isidore.

When his work contract expired he returned to his native region and then moved to Busira, staying as a guest of his cousin Cammillo Boya, an employee of the Belgian mining company S.A.B., through whom he became a servant of one of the directors, named Ruijders. He took Isisdore with him to Itiki in the Buch-Bloc region in 1909. There he came up against an atmosphere of extreme hostility to Catholicism engendered by the local S.A.E. manager Van Canter, who saw Catholicism as destroying European authority over "natives."

Isidore's refusal to abandon his practices, and in particular to remove a scapular of the Virgin he wore round his neck, so infuriated Van Canter that he had Isidore beaten until he streamed with blood; he then placed him in solitary confinement with chains on his ankles. This came to the notice of the director, who rescued him and took him to Busira, where, having been reduced to total exhaustion by the torture he had undergone, he lived for only another six months, dying on 15 August 1909. He expressed forgiveness for Van Canter, who was nevertheless dismissed from his post, tried, and condemned by a court in Coquihatville.

Convinced that Isidore's death was brought about by his adherence to his faith, the local church authorities immediately began collecting the necessary evidence to start the process of his beatification, which was eventually pronounced by Pope John Paul II on 24 April 1994.

A.A.S. 37 (1995), p. 340; *Bibl.SS.*, Suppl. 1, 114; G. Dabrulle, "B. Isidore martelaar," in *Archief Missieclub M.S.C.* (n.d.).

R.M.

SS Strato, Philip, and Euthychianus, martyrs at Nicomedia (second-third century)

St Altfridus, bishop of Hildesheim (874)

St Arduin, priest at Rimini (1009)

Bd Rupert, abbot of Ottobeuren (1145)

Bd Aimon Taparelli, O.P., at Savigliano (1495)

Bd Juliana Puricelli, Augustinian nun of Novara (1501)

16

ST STEPHEN OF HUNGARY (1038)

Vaik was the son of the third Magyar duke of Hungary. He was baptized Istvan, or Stephen, at about the age of ten, when his father became a Christian. In 995, when he was about twenty, he married Gisela, sister of Henry, duke of Bavaria (the emperor St Henry II; 13 July). Two years later he succeeded his father as Magyar leader.

Stephen consolidated his dominions by wars with tribal leaders and others. He then sent St Astrik (12 Nov.), his intended first archbishop, to Rome to ask Pope Silvester II to approve an ecclesiastical organization for the country. He also requested the title of king. Silvester agreed, confirmed Stephen's religious foundations and episcopal elections, and is said to have had a crown made, which he sent to Hungary with his blessing. The diadem may be preserved in a crown kept in Budapest (there has been much tedious debate about this). Stephen treated the papal ambassador with great honours and was crowned king by him in 1001.

Stephen's religious and ecclesiastical changes were considerable, even though the uniformity of practice he aimed at was eroded in the next few reigns. He founded bishoprics gradually, as Magyar clergy became available. Vesprem is the first recorded. Esztergom was established within a few years and became the primatial see. At Szekesfehervar he built a church in honour of Mary, where the kings of Hungary were afterwards crowned and buried. He made the city his usual residence and called it Alba Regalis to distinguish it from Alba Julia in Transylvania. He completed the foundation of the great monastery of St Martin, or Martinsberg, begun by his father, which still exists as the motherhouse of the Hungarian Benedictines. Stephen ordered tithes to be collected to support churches and priests and to relieve the poor. Every tenth town had to build a church and support a priest. The king equipped the churches. He ruthlessly abolished pagan customs and set severe punishments for blasphemy, murder, theft, adultery, and other crimes. He ordered all people except religious and churchmen to marry and prohibited marriages between Christians and pagans. He was very concerned to establish a national church, though always with papal approval, just as he was a fierce defender of his country's borders. There were years of difficult relations with the German emperor, including such assertions of sovereignty touching on matters ecclesiastical as denying Bishop Werner of Strasbourg, the imperial ambassador to Constantinople, a passage through Hungary in 1027. He went to war with the emperor Conrad in 1030 after various incursions by the Bavarian nobles but mainly because Conrad refused Stephen's request that Conrad's son Henry (nephew of the emperor whose sister had married Stephen) should be granted the dukedom of Bavaria. The invading Germans were ousted and Stephen took Vienna, which he did not restore until 1031.

Stephen is said to have been willing to listen to the complaints of people of all ranks, especially the poor. One account says that he liked to distribute alms in disguise. One day when he was doing this, a group of beggars knocked him down and took his purse, but he bore this indignity humbly and with good humour. His nobles asked him to stop the practice, but he became all the more determined never to refuse alms to any poor person who asked him.

Stephen had a code of laws promulgated throughout his dominions. They were not to the taste of the many people who still opposed the new religion. Some of the wars he fought were religious as well as political. After putting down a Bulgarian rising, he organized his subjects politically. He abolished tribal divisions and separated the country into "lands," ruled by governors and magistrates. He made the nobles vassals of the crown and kept direct control of the masses to prevent the lords accumulating excessive power. In this way he founded an independent but feudal Hungary. Its continuance, however, depended on monarchs of equal determination, gifts, and ideals.

Eventually Stephen decided to give his son, Bd Emeric (4 Nov.), a greater share of the government, but his heir was killed while hunting. During the last years of Stephen's life he suffered from a painful sickness, and there were many disputes about the succession. One of the four or five claimants was the son of his ambitious sister (named, like his wife, Gisela, who had lived at the court since her husband's death. She took advantage of Stephen's ill health to advance her son's claims. Stephen died, aged sixty-three, on 15 August 1038. He was buried beside Emeric at Szekesfehervar. Miracles were duly reported at his tomb. Forty-five years after his death, at King Ladislaus' request, Pope St Gregory VII (25 May) ordered his relics to be enshrined in a chapel of Our Lady at Buda; Stephen was canonized and his son beatified. In 1686 Innocent XI made 2 September his festival, as the emperor Leopold had taken back Buda from the Turks on that day. Stephen was succeeded by his nephew Peter, who had promised his uncle to maintain his widow, Gisela, but soon broke his promise. She became impoverished. Peter began raids on Germany, set the country in turmoil, and was driven from his throne. The new king, Obo, was elected by the Magyar chiefs, and the new government favoured paganism. His successor, Arpad, also promoted the revived paganism, though under a superficial Christianity. Little remained of Stephen's achievements.

For two apparently eleventh-century Lives, see *M.G.H., Scriptores*, 11; for Bishop Hartwig's twelfth-century compilation from these, see *AA.SS.*, Sept., 2; and consult the Life of Emeric in *AA.SS.*, Nov., 2, pp. 477-87; and J. Szalay in *D.H.G.E.*, 15 (1963), 1235-7. The pope may have given Stephen powers similar to those of a legate; see L. L. Kropf in *English Historical Review* (1898), pp. 290-5. See also W. Fraknói, *Monumenta Vaticana historiam Hungariae illustrantia*, vols. 1-6 (1884-91); F. Banfi, *Re Stefano il Santo* (1938); B. Hóman, *Der heilige Stefan* (German trans., 1941); P. J. Kelleher, *The Holy Crown of Hungary* (1951); C. A. Macartney, *The Medieval Hungarian Historians* (1953); D. Sinor, *History of Hungary* (1959).

Two contemporary works reproduce his image: on an eleventh-century crucifix (1008; Reichskapelle Munich) he is one of two figures kneeling at the foot; the other is his wife, Gisela; on the coronation cope (1031; Budapest Palace) Stephen, Gisela, and Emeric appear in border medallions. There is a twelfth-century head of a marble statue from Kolocsa in the Budapest Museum. A thirteenth-century statue by an unknown sculptor on the Adamspforte of Bamberg cathedral, Germany, is an image of a curly-headed and suitably benign Stephen. There are numerous imaginary portraits.

St Armel (Sixth Century)

Armel (Ermel, Erme, Arzel, Arkel, Arthmael, or Ermyn) is the saint of Ploërmel and other places in Brittany. There is no trace of him before the twelfth century, and the recorded events of his life are presumably wholly legendary. He is retained in the new draft Roman Martyrology, though as a hermit and not as an abbot.

He is said to have been a pious Welshman who spent his youth under the abbot Carentmael. He decided to follow a life dedicated to God, became a monk, and went to Armorica together with his master and other companions. They lived an evangelical life together at Plouarzel but were disturbed by the usurper Conmor, who had killed Jonah, the local chieftain. They went to Paris to ask King Childebert for help. After Jonah's son defeated and killed Conmor in 555, Armel was given some land near Rennes, where he re-established his community at St Armel-des-Bochaux or Plouarmel. He founded another monastery at Ploërmel in Morbihan and died there peacefully. There are many legends of St Armel. One says that he got rid of a troublesome dragon by taking it up to Mont-Saint-Armel and ordering it to jump into the river. His assistance was asked for a wide range of diseases and complaints. Henry VII of England was convinced that Armel's protection had saved him from shipwreck off the Breton coast. Armel's feast was noted in the Sarum calendar of 1498.

See *L.B.S.*, 1, pp. 170ff; F. Duine, *Saints de Brocéliande: S. Armel* (1905); J. Macé, *Histoire merveilleuse de S. Armel* (1909).

St Armel is shown wearing armour and a chasuble and leading a dragon. There is a sixteenth-century sequence of scenes from the saint's life in the windows of the church at Ploërmel. A statue of him appears in the chapel of Henry VII at Westminster Abbey and an effigy on the tomb of Cardinal Morton in Canterbury Cathedral. There are images of the saint on the reredos of Romsey Abbey and in the church of St Mary Brookfield, London.

Bd Laurence Loricatus (1243)

He was born at Fanello, near Siponto in Apulia. He accidentally killed another young man and made a pilgrimage of penance and expiation to Compostela. On his return in 1209 he went to Subiaco. There he joined a community but was soon allowed to become a solitary. He lived in a mountain cave near the Sacro Speco of St Benedict (11 July) for thirty-three years, practising mortifications of the body that were extreme even in an age when self-inflicted pain was a normal religious practice and many aspects of everyday life were hideously unconfortable by modern standards: he attacked himself by wearing next to his skin a coat of mail studded with sharp points. Hence the name *Loricetus* "the cuirassier." We know little else about him and nothing to his credit except pious generalizations. In his case we certainly lack the evidence of a richly complex personality that enables us if not completely to understand, then usefully to place mortification of times past in some kind of individual and approximate social context (as, say, with St Teresa of Avila; 15 Oct.). We do know, however, that many sick people, including young persons suffering for various reasons from feelings of intolerable though usually unjustifiable guilt, inadequacy, loneliness and so on, injure themselves and need help. We also know that compulsive sado-masochistic behaviour practised for the sake of the increments of sexual satisfaction it purports to repress can be masked by religious idealism. These insights were scarcely available when the cult of Bd Laurence Loricatus was approved in 1778, and he was proposed as the model he cannot be.

See *AA.SS*, Aug., 3; E. Menninger, *Man against Himself* (1953).

St Rock (1378)

There is no authentic history of the life of Rock (or Roch). He was venerated in France and Italy in the early fifteenth century and became a popular saint and a very important figure in folk religion. He was possibly born at Montpellier, in southern France, and nursed the sick during a plague in Italy. His Lives consist of legends with no ascertainable basis in fact. He is cited here as an example of the way in which certain incidents in saints' lives, actual or fictitious, caught the general imagination, became associated with major aspects of life and culture, and assumed an ever-burgeoning power of their own.

According to the biography written by a Venetian, Francis Diedo, in 1478, Rock was the son of the governor of Montpellier. He was left an orphan at the age of twenty and went on a pilgrimage to Rome. The plague was raging in Italy, and he cared for the sick in Acquapendente, Cesena, Rome, Rimini, and Novara. He was said to have cured large numbers of victims simply by making the sign of the cross on them. At Piacenza he was infected himself. He did not want to burden any hospital so he dragged himself out into the woods to die. He was miraculously fed by a dog, which brought him bread every day. Its master soon found Rock and looked after him. When he was convalescent he returned to Piacenza, where he miraculously cured more people and their sick cattle. He returned eventually to Montpellier. His surviving uncle did not recognize him. He was imprisoned for five years until his death. When his body was examined, a cross-shaped birthmark on his breast showed that he was the former governor's son. He was given a public funeral and performed as many miracles when dead as when alive.

Another Life says that he was arrested as a spy and died in captivity at Angera in Lombardy, which claimed his tomb and attendant miracles. Relics of the saint were also reserved at Venice and at Arles. There is no evidence that he was a Franciscan tertiary, though the Franciscans venerated him as one.

Mainly in Italy, France, and Germany but also in England and elsewhere, Rock became the pre-eminent saint for invocation in time of plague, for centuries regarded as the most effective form of protection after flight, isolation, and cleanliness—precautions open to very few people. Survival through natural immunity or hardiness was ascribed to Rock. His popularity in France did not diminish with the disappearance of the bubonic plague from western Europe, for his power was transferred to other diseases such as cholera and to threats such as fire and lightning. In several areas of France until quite recently it was the custom to bless a bunch of "St Rock's grass" and hang it from doorposts for protection. He was also associated with concern for animals. At Vézinnes, in the Yonne, there is a chapel of St Rock. Each year on his feast, within living memory, the farmers would take their cattle there to be blessed, together with the large loaves used to feed them. The chapel had been erected in the seventeenth century when a rabid dog caused the destruction of cattle. Similar customs are reported in the Morvan and elsewhere. In Provence blessed fragments of bread were distributed in churches on his feast-day in return for an offering and kept as a protection against rabies.

A particular rich wheat was known as "St Rock's wheat." In one of the many legends of the saint, a man blasphemously doubted the divine origin of this fine wheat, so God destroyed the entire harvest with a fierce storm. There was nothing to make flour with. St Rock turned to God and prayed, "Dear God, let me have a little wheat, just enough to grind for my dog." This became a favourite prayer. Again in living memory, mothers would invoke St Rock's help in the chapel of Montbois, near Château-Chinon, to ensure that their infants learned to walk at an early age. There is evidence that in England St Rock was asked for protection against the pestilence even after the Reformation. The examples across Europe are many and various. More than one book could be devoted to the reception of St Rock.

See *AA.SS.*, Aug., 3; *Anal.Boll.* 68 (1950), pp. 343-61; 55 (1937), p. 193; G. Ceroni, *San Rocco* (1927); M. Bessodes, *San Rocco, storia e leggende* (1931); A. Maurino, *San Rocco, confronti storici* (1936); G. Bidault de l'Isle, *Vieux Dictons de nos Campagnes*, 2 (1952), pp. 585-6; C. Seignolle, *Le Folklore de Provence* (1980), pp. 280-1.

Rock's attributes are his pilgrim's cockleshell, wallet, and staff. He also wears a pilgrim's garment and is often shown with his dog. He sometimes raises his robe to show the mark of the plague on his thigh, as in Giorgione's beautifully flowing painting (*c.* 1508; Prado, Madrid) of him with Anthony before the Virgin and Child, or in Lorenzo Costa's (1460-1535) portrayal of him as an equally elegant youth (Art Association Galleries, Atlanta, Georgia). Tintoretto shows him in fine robes, with other saints before the Virgin and Child (1566; Academy, Venice) and, in a series on his life (1549; 1567; St Rock, Venice), appearing before the pope, visiting plague victims, healing animals, and in prison; a ceiling-painting (Scuola di San Rocco, Venice) portrays him in glory; another in passionate emotion. Pre-Reformation screen-paintings with the traditional attributes but of no particular merit survive in churches in Norfolk and Devon. The present St Roche's Hill in Sussex was St Rokeshill in 1579. The former Glasgow parliamentary division of St Rollox is said to have derived its name from St Rock. The once-traditional celebration of "Rock-Monday," sometimes associated with the saint in works of reference, has nothing to do with him.

Bd Angelo Augustine of Florence (1377-1431)

Angelo Agostino Mazzinghi was born into an important family in Florence in 1377. He became a Carmelite and was successively prior of the Carmels of Le Selve, Frascati, and Florence, then provincial of Tuscany. He was noted for religious devotion as well as efficient administration but above all for preaching: images of the saint show him with garlands of flowers emerging from his mouth and entwined among his audience. At the end of his term as provincial he returned to Le Selve. He spent the rest of his life continuing the reform of the Order begun by James Albert in 1413. He abolished the use of all private property and would allow no friar to accept or keep a post that compelled him to live outside the monastery. He died at Florence on 16 August 1438. His early cult was confirmed in 1761.

See R. A. Faci, *Noticia breve de la vida de S. Angelo Augustini* (1761); *D.H.G.E.*, 3, 40.

St Beatrice da Silva, *Foundress* (1424-90)

Brites da Silva Menses was born at Ceuta in Portugal in 1424. Her brother was Bd Amadeus, who started the Franciscan "reform of Marignano." She was brought up in the court of Princess Isabel, daughter of Prince John of Portugal, and soon after her twentieth birthday went to Spain with Isabel when the latter married King John II of Castile. The queen is said to have grown jealous of Beatrice's beauty or to have listened to jealous gossip that suggested she was a dangerous rival, and she ordered Beatrice to be imprisoned without food for three days. Understandably, this experience made her leave the court, and she was allowed to retire to the protection of the Dominican convent of St Dominic at Toledo, Spain, where she spent thirty years.

Beatrice reported a personal vision of Our Lady, and it seems that she had long thought of founding a new women's Order in honour of and for continual glorification of the mystery of the Immaculate Conception. In 1477 a Mass and Office for the feast of the Immaculate Conception devised by a Franciscan were approved by Pope Sixtus IV for the diocese of Rome. In 1484, together with other women of rank, Beatrice established what was to become the Congregation of the Immaculate Conception of the Blessed Virgin Mary (the Conceptionists) at Toledo. Queen Isabella the Catholic donated the castle of Galliana as the community's first house. The Sisters followed an adaptation of the Cistercian Rule and wore a white habit with a blue mantle (in accordance with Our Lady's dress as she appeared to the foundress). On 30 April 1489, at the request of Beatrice and Queen Isabella, Pope Innocent VIII authorized the foundation of the new convent and approved the new Rule as submitted to him.

Beatrice died at Toledo on 1 September 1490, before the Sisters were able to lead a conventual life under the Rule with full pontifical approval. Soon after her death the Order came under the influence of the Franciscan cardinal Ximénez de Cisneros, archbishop of Toledo (the Franciscans had long defended the cult of the Immaculate Conception), and it was finally approved in 1511 with a modification of the Rule of the Poor Clares. The Institute expanded rapidly in various countries in Europe and in the New World. The first foundation of the Order in Mexico was in 1540. It still exists in Spain, Italy, and elsewhere and numbers almost three thousand nuns in 150 convents, with an emphasis on the penitential and contemplative way of religious life. Historically, the Institute testifies to the importance in the Counter-Reformation Church of devotion to Our Lady's conception as immaculate (except— strange to say, given the present context—among the Dominicans and Cistercians) long before the proclamation of the dogma by Pope Pius IX on 8 December 1854. A decree confirming Beatrice's cult and her status as beatified was issued in 1926; she was canonized on 3 October 1976.

See *A.A.S.* 18 (1926), pp. 496-9, for the decree of equivalent beatification and an account of her life. See also Jeronymo de Belem, *Chronica Serafica da santa Provincia dos Algarves*, 2, pp. 736-48, for a full account of Bd Amadeus. On the Conceptionist Order see Heimbucher, *Die Orden und Kongregationen der Katholischen Kirche*, 2, pp. 488ff.

R.M.

St Theodore, at Sion, first bishop of the Valais (fourth century)

St Phambaldus, monk near le Mans (sixth century)

Bd Ralph of Fusteia, founder of the monastery of St Sulpice, near Rennes (1289)

Bd John of St Martha, Franciscan martyr at Meako, Japan (1618)—see "The Martyrs of Japan," 6 Feb.

BB Simon Bocusai Kiota; Magdalena, his wife; Thomas Ghengoro and his wife and son, James, martyred by crucifixion upside-down at Cocura, Japan (1620)—see "The Martyrs of Japan," 6 Feb.

Bd Rose Wang-Hoei, martyr under the Boxer Rebellion in China (1900)—see "The Martyrs of China," 17 Feb.

17

St Mamas, *Martyr* (273-4)

St Basil (2 Jan.) and St Gregory Nazianzen (2 Jan.) tell us that Mamas was a pious shepherd at Caesarea in Cappadocia, where he was martyred. That is all we know of him. According to Eastern tradition, he was still a boy when he was stoned to death under Aurelian.

The cult of Mamas was very popular. The stories told of him belong essentially to the world of Graeco-Roman romance. Many pleasing fables collected around him, including some that derive from the legends of Orpheus, commonly represented in Roman art as charming the beasts. Mamas is said to have left the "wolves" of the city to live among the peaceful animals of the countryside, feeding on milk and honey. When he was exposed to wild beasts in the arena, the animals treated him as if he were their shepherd and they his sheep: "They lay at his feet, and showed their respect by moving their tails affectionately." Later, a "huge lion," seeing how heavy his chains were, kindly licked his limbs to give him some comfort. When soldiers were sent to fetch Mamas, the lion picked them up and dropped them at his feet. Mamas, however, told his friend to go to his lair. The lion "wept and sobbed," but did as he was told.

See H. Delehaye, *Origines du culte des martyrs*, p. 174; *idem, Passions des Martyrs et les genres littéraires*, pp. 198-200; *Anal. Boll.* 58 (1940), pp. 126-41. A. Hadjimiolaon-Marava, *O agios Mamas* (1953).

His attributes are a lion, a trident, and a doe. The earliest known image is an eleventh-century miniature from the Menologion of Basil (Vatican Library). In the fifteenth century Michael Gambone shows him seated on a lion (Verona Museum). In a seventeenth-century oval painting by Jean Tasset (Langres Cathedral) he holds his entrails in his right hand.

St Eusebius, *Pope* (310)

Eusebius was born a Greek, the son of a physician. He was elected in succession to Pope St Marcellus (16 Jan.), whom he survived by only a few months. During his predecessor's episcopate great dissension had been caused in the Roman church about how to treat apostates during the Diocletian persecution who asked to be reconciled. A party led by Heraclius, who probably wanted immediate reconcilation without further penance, opposed the pope, who upheld the canons which demanded it. The apostates went so far as to propose Heraclius as an antipope. An inscription placed by Pope St Damasus (11 Dec.) over Eusebius' tomb in the cemetery of Callistus shows that this dispute was prolonged into his pontificate. The strife in Eusebius' time was so great that the emperor Maxentius banished both Eusebius and Heraclius from the city. Eusebius went to Sicily, where he died almost at once. Accordingly, for a time he was venerated as a martyr, a title which Damasus accords him. Yet Maxentius probably sent both him and his predecessor, Marcellus I, into exile to avoid granting them the honour of martyrdom.

See *AA.SS.*, Sept., 7; *Liber Pontificalis*, 1, p. 167; J. Carini, *I lapsi e le deportazione in Sicilia del Papa S. Eusebio* (1886). There is a (clearly imaginary) medallion-portrait of Eusebius in the elegant series attributed to Giovanni Battista Pozzi (*c.* 1570; *e.g.*, British Museum).

St Clare of Montefalco, *Abbess* (1308)

At one time there were disputes between Franciscans and Augustinians about which Order this Clare—an important acquisition for one or the other—belonged to. The answer is both. For fifteen years she was a member of a community of pious young women living penitentially as secular tertiaries of St Francis in hermitages under the direction of her sister Joan. When they decided to adopt a regular conventual life, the bishop of Spoleto gave them the Augustinian Rule. Their convent, of the Holy Cross, was built in 1290.

In 1291, when her sister died, the reluctant Clare was elected abbess. She was already noted for her austerity. This she increased to an extent that was uncommon then and now seems childish if not perverse. When she breached the rule of silence, she stood barefoot in the snow and said the Lord's Prayer a hundred times. It is difficult to reconstruct the atmosphere of quite recent times in which this famous example of her conduct was cited as admirable, let alone the setting of a fourteenth-century convent in which it was so. Clare's nuns certainly held her in great respect as a model of perfect conventual behaviour, intense meditation, and devotion to Christ's passion. She was said to experience frequent holy ecstasies. She also had a reputation as a miracle-worker. She once said to a Sister: "If you are looking for Christ's cross, take my heart. You will find the suffering Lord there." These words were interpreted literally. After her death in 1308 her heart was examined and reported to have an image of the cross imprinted on it. Her cult was already spreading. Pope Urban VIII (1623-44) gave permission for a special office and Mass for her commemoration.

Clare is alleged to have been honoured by three divine favours: her remains stayed incorrupt; an image of the cross and instruments of the passion appeared in the fibrous tissue of her heart; her blood liquefied. These supposed phenomena have excited the usual interest and tediously pseudo-scientific literature. She was canonized by Pope Leo XIII in 1881.

For Berengarius' Life (said to have been compiled in 1309), see F. Pulignani, *Vita di Santa Chiara da Montefalco* (1885). See also A. N. Merlin, *Sainte Claire de la Croix* (1930); E. A. Foran, *St Clare of the Cross* (1935); A. Semenza, *Vita S. Clarae de Cruce* (1944); *Bibl.SS.*, 3, 1217-24.

St Joan of the Cross, *Foundress* (1666-1736)

The narrative of Joan's progress to sainthood is very odd in some ways: both she and her main spiritual benefactor might be inventions from a collaboration between the imaginative Perrault (author of fairy stories) and the more sober Marmontel (writer of moral tales) devised to illustrate the maxim: "God moves in a mysterious way his wonders to perform." Yet their characters and the events that followed from their bizarre relationship are well attested.

She was born Jeanne Delanoue, the last of a family of twelve children, on 18 June 1666 at Saumur, Anjou, France, where her parents had a small draper's shop near the shrine of Notre Dame des Ardilliers. However good the local trade, it was hard to provide for twelve children, so the shop also dealt in crockery and various other goods, but the main sideline was the sale of religious perquisites—holy pictures, rosaries, and so on—to pilgrims to the shrine. Joan's father died when she was six. Though still very young, she had to help her mother run the shop to provide a living for the whole family.

Mme Delanoue was known to be kind and generous to beggars, but when she died in 1691, Joan, who had always been devout but almost over-scrupulous, showed herself to be not only intelligent and a good worker but avaricious. All her efforts went into building up the shop, which she had inherited together with the house and which she kept open even on Sundays and feast-days. This hardly fitted the shop's quasi-sacred function as a repository and was unfair to other, less grasping shopkeepers. Joan also began to offer pilgrims lodgings for payment, but at the back of the house in unsavoury holes quarried in the cliff years before. She made her seventeen-year-old and equally mercenary niece a partner and was said to retain enough scrupulosity to send her to buy food just before meals so that she would tell no lie when rejecting beggars with the assurance that there was no food in the house. Joan had before her the prospect of becoming, by hard work, a successful businesswoman, if always on a small scale. She is said to have resolutely pursued that goal as the worst type of money-grubbing small shopkeeper.

In 1693, on the eve of the Epiphany, a shabby old woman turned up in Saumur as a pilgrim. She was a widow, Frances Souchet from Rennes, and seemed at first to be a tedious though harmless religious eccentric who spent her time travelling between shrines. She claimed to be on intimate terms with the deity, but his communications as she reported them usually turned out to be more nonsensical than profoundly cryptic. She nevertheless approached the borders of meaning with "God sent me this first time to learn the way," when the shopkeeper acted out of character and let her stay in the house for next to nothing. Joan is said to have been very disturbed by the visit.

Next Lent she began listening to sermons as she made her own little tour round various churches. Eventually she asked the advice of Fr Geneteau, a priest with a reputation as a spiritual counsellor who was chaplain to the town hospital. She soon closed her shop on Sundays and started fasting three days a week; otherwise she seemed as mean as before. But at Whitsun Mme Souchet was back with some more divine pronouncements, which the people of Saumur now found so confused that they declared her to be quite insane. But Joan interpreted these oracular sayings as straightforward instructions to give and give unstintingly. She took her best dress from the wardrobe and handed it to Mme Souchet. "I know she doesn't need it," she said, "but Jesus says I've got to give it to her." Joan went into a peculiar trance for three days and nights and announced her conversion to a life of dedication to the poor, yet seemed uncertain of their whereabouts.

Mme Souchet passed on an unexpectedly circumstantial message from God, who wanted Joan to care for six poor children in a stable at Saint-Florent. Joan took a cart of food and clothing to them and their equally cold and hungry parents and for the next two months devoted nearly half the week to their relief. Mme Souchet claimed to have seen the children in a vision, but this unusual woman was obviously a brilliant and empathetic counsellor with great understanding of Joan's nature and how her abilities could be turned to good ends. Soon Joan was caring for other unfortunate cases, and in 1698 she closed the shop. The poor were coming to her instead of waiting for her visits. From about this time she practised mortifications to atone for her previous avarice: she slept sitting in a chair or on a chest with a stone for a pillow.

In 1700 Joan took a poor child into the house, followed by the sick, old people, and the destitute. She lodged a dozen orphans and others in the house and the caves behind. It was soon known as Providence House. In 1702 the cliff collapsed. It destroyed the house and killed a child. Joan moved her beneficiaries to the stables of an Oratorian house, but the priests could not stand the constant stream of beggars and expelled her. Nevertheless, it is hard to know if the Oratorians were quite as unwelcoming and grasping as the narrative paints them, for they were often accused of a residual Jansenism, whereas Joan (and her hagiographers) represented a somewhat different tendency in the Church. Anyway, together with her niece she moved into another house with three rooms and with a cave attached, where they could not lodge all those who came to them. In 1704, after four years of battling in this way, she found two other young women ready to help her and even become religious if that could be managed, for Jesus had told Joan that she would found a Congregation. On the feast of St Anne in 1704 they were clothed with the religious habit as Sisters of St Anne. This was the start of the Congregation of St Anne of Providence. In 1706 the Oratorians leased Joan a big house but are said to have raised the rent by 150 per cent because of the noisy, unclean people she wanted to look after. The bishop of Angers approved the Order's Rule in 1709, and Joan took the name in religion of Joan of the Cross. The Oratorians, said to disapprove of Joan's over-enthusiastic practices such as daily Communion, tried to control the Sisterhood and its charitable work. Joan evaded this attempted takeover, though in the famine year of 1709 there were more than a hundred people in the Providence. Eventually Joan founded the first hospice at Saumur, in 1715, even though Louis XIV had requested its establishment as early as 1672. Henry de Vallière, governor of Annecy, and other benefactors had bought the large Three Angels House and other buildings for her and provided for their repair. In 1717 Providence House became Great Providence House. About this time Joan's spiritual director had to persuade her to lessen her mortifications, which had become extreme, though her charitable work extended beyond Saumur and the diocese. She soon had forty helpers ready to follow her example of devotion to the poor and prayer.

For many years Joan suffered from severe toothache and earache and from rheumatism, and in September 1735 a violent fever announced her final illness. At her death on 17 August 1736, Joan had founded twelve communities, hospices, and schools. She was already referred to as a saint for her unstinting work for orphans, old people, the poor, and the destitute. There are now some four hundred Sisters of St Anne of the Providence of Saumur (that is, of Joan of the Cross, for they must be distinguished from the Congregation of the same name, but of Turin) in France, Madagascar, and Sumatra.

Joan was beatified in 1947 and canonized on 31 October 1982.

The standard biography remains that by F. Trochu (1938), which is based largely on the memoirs of Sister Mary Laigle, a member of the Saumur Providence from the early years of the eighteenth century.

R.M.

St Myro, at Achaia, priest and martyr under Decius, at Cyzicus (third century)

St Caroloman, at Vienne, France (755)

St Elias the Less, at Thessalonica, monk of the Order of St Basil (903)

SS Benedicta and Cecilia, Benedictine abbesses of Susteren and daughters of King Zwentibold (tenth century)

St John, bishop of Monte Marano, Campania (eleventh-twelfth century)

Bd Nicholas Politi, hermit at Monte Calanna, Sicily (1107)

St Donatus, monk in Lucania (1198)

BB Francis of St Mary, Franciscan priest; Caius Jiyemon; Magdalena Kijota; Bartholomew Laurel, Franciscan physician; Gaspar Vaz and his wife, Maria; Antony of St Francis, catechist; Francis Culioye; Aloysius (Matzuu) Shomeyon; Martin Gómez; Francis Kurobioye, catechist; Francis (Kiota) Pinzokera; Thomas Wo Jinyemon; Luke Kiyemon. Michael Kizayemon, matrys at Nagasaki, Japan (1627)—see "The Martyrs of Japan," 6 Feb.

SS James Hyushei Gorobioye Tomonaga, Japanese Dominican; and Michael Kurobioye, Japanese lay catechist, martyred at Nagasaki, Japan, under the shogun Ieyasu Tokugawa, on 17 August 1633—see "The Martyrs of Japan," 6 Feb.

18

St Agapitus, *Martyr* (274)

All we know of Agapitus is that he was a martyr buried at Palestrina. His early cult is well attested. He is mentioned in sacramentaries, and there are traces of the ruins of his basilica a mile out of Palestrina and of an epitaph bearing his name. Several other churches were dedicated to him in the eighth and ninth centuries.

His spurious Acts say that he was a Christian boy of fifteen who was brought before the governor Antiochus at Praeneste in Palestrina under the emperor Aurelian. He refused to abjure his faith and was scourged, imprisoned, and beheaded. His sufferings are described with gory details once thought to be both entertaining and edifying. The story is a model of its kind; the improbabilities include condign punishment (Antiochus has a stroke and dies before his victim) and signs of divine election (the wild beasts in the arena refuse to touch the boy) and intervention (the tribune Anastasius is so impressed by this that he is converted on the spot).

See *AA.SS.*, Aug., 3, pp. 524-9; *C.M.H.*, pp. 448-9; A. Kellner, "Der heilige Agapitus von Praeneste," in *Studien und Mitteilungen* (1930), pp. 404-32.

The Martyrs of Utica (Third or Fourth Century)

The story of these martyrs, known also as the "White Mass" (*Massa Candida*), was popularized by Prudentius in one of his Christian ballads, in which he spun a fanciful allusion out of a colourful place-name. It is recorded in the new draft Roman Martyrology in these words: The passion "at Utica in Africa of the army of the Blessed of the White Mass [or, of the White Farm] who, loyal to their own bishop Quadratus, and more numerous than the fishes caught by the Apostles in their net, all with one voice confessing Christ to be the Son of God, gladly sacrificed their lives." The Latin of the new version is vague and carefully ambiguous regarding the "Mass" or "Farm." (The word *mas* still denotes a farm in southern France.)

The traditional account reproduced in the former Roman Martyrology was more specific. They were said to be three hundred martyrs in the time of Valerian and Gallienus. The governor, among other torments, ordered a lime kiln to be heated as a furnace and charcoal and incense to be made ready in his presence. He said to them, "Choose one of these two things: either offer incense to Jupiter on these coals or be thrown into that oven." With a rapid movement they all threw themselves into the fire and were reduced to white powder in the white smoke of the furnace. "Accordingly this white-robed company of Saints earned for itself the name of the White Mass." Yet Massa Candida is really the name of a place, the White Farm. A number of martyrs were buried there, but there is nothing to show that they suffered under Valerian. An early sermon, once attributed to Augustine, mentions the bloodshed and the readiness of the martyrs to submit to the sword. There is no evidence that they numbered 300 or 153 (the latter figure perhaps suggested to the unknown author of the sermon by a reference he had just made to the draught of fishes in John 21:11).

See Prudentius, *Peristephanon*, 13, lines 76-87; P. Franchi de' Cavalieri, in *Studi e Testi*, 9 (1902), pp. 37-512; G. Morin in *Miscellanea augustiniana*, 1 (1930), p. 647; *C.M.H.*, pp. 449-50; *idem, Origines du culte des martyrs* (1933), pp. 384-5.

St Helen (*c.* 329)

Helen (Helena or Ellen) was the mother of the emperor Constantine. The most memorable thing about her is presumably apocryphal: her discovery of the true cross, which has excited the imagination since the fourth century when reputed relics of the true cross spread throughout the known world: "The Empress Dowager was an old woman, almost of an age with Pope Sylvester, but he regarded her fondly as though she were a child, an impetuous young princess who went well to hounds, and he said with the gentlest irony: 'You'll tell me, won't you?—if you are successful.' 'I'll tell the world,' said Helena" (Evelyn Waugh). She is honoured because she was the mother of an important Christian monarch but also on account of her objective virtue, which, if the "finding" were ignored, would somewhat reduce her status to that of a devout and influential patron of church-building, the indigent, and ecclesiastics.

She was probably born at Drepanum (later Helenopolis) in Bithynia. Her father was possibly an inn-keeper. She became the wife of Constantius Chlorus. He was a general close to the then emperor and later became emperor himself. Their son Constantine was born at Nish (Serbia) in 274. Her husband divorced her in about 270 and for political advantage married Theodora, the step-daughter of the emperor Maximian, in 292. Constantine was proclaimed emperor by his troops at York in 306. After his victory at the Battle of the Milvian Bridge on 28 October 312, Constantine entered Rome. Helen was elevated to a position of honour and given the title "*Nobilissima Femina*" (most noble woman); the name of her birthplace was changed. She became an enthusiastic Christian in 312. Constantine remained a catechumen until his death-bed. Helen was extremely devout and charitable, using the treasures of the empire to provide alms; she was most generous to churches.

By the Edict of Milan in 313 Christianity was tolerated throughout the empire. After his victory over Licinius in 324 Constantine became master of the

East and stressed the importance of Palestine as a centre to give cohesion and a sense of community to his disparate and newly-Christian empire. In a tradition packed with implausible because anachronistic yet lastingly impressive details, Constantine is said to have had a vision before his victory at the Milvian Bridge (312). According to the tractate *De inventione crucis dominicae* (On the finding of the Lord's cross, *c.* 550), described as doubtful in the pseudo-Gelasian decree *De recipiendis et non recipiendis libris* (On acceptable and non-acceptable books), Constantine was faced with hordes of barbarians on the Danube and was in danger of defeat. A vision of a brilliant cross appeared in the sky with the legend "In this sign you will conquer." He was victorious and was instructed and baptized by Pope Eusebius in Rome. The vision inspired his mother.

In 326, when relatively old, Helen almost certainly visited the Holy Land, established a basilica at Bethlehem, and planned another on the Mount of Olives, the Eleona, which Constantine built as a memorial to her. This encouraged an increase in pilgrimages from all over the East to Palestine. Helen spent much of her time in the Holy Land liberating prisoners, helping orphans and the needy, endowing convents, making gifts to all sort of individuals and towns, overseeing the erection of shrines, and collecting relics. She is said to have lived humbly in a convent where she did the housework. She died in Palestine in 329 or 330.

Later authors (*c.* 395-400) such as Sulpicius Severus, Ambrose, and Rufinus cite the tradition that she found the true cross on which Jesus was crucified, and the new draft, unlike the old, Roman Martyrology explicitly says not only that she went to investigate the places where Christ was born, suffered, and rose again but that "she discovered Our Lord's manger and cross" ("*praesaepe et crucem Domini invenit . . .*"). Yet St Ambrose's sermon of 385 is the first ascription of the finding of the cross to Helen. St Jerome (30 Sept.), who lived nearby at Bethlehem, does not mention her part in the recovery of the cross. Eusebius does not say that she visited the Holy Land to look for the cross, though St Paulinus of Nola (22 June) tells us that she went to search for the Holy Places. Constantine wrote to St Macarius, bishop of Jerusalem (10 Mar.), commissioning him to look for the cross on Mount Calvary. The supposed sites of Golgotha and the holy sepulchre were laid bare, it seems, by removing the terrace and temple of Venus built there by the emperor Hadrian. Constantine ordered a basilica to be built, which, he told Macarius, must be "worthy of the most marvellous place in the world." Helen went with the primary aim of overseeing this work and to pray and thank God for mercies to her family.

In the apocryphal account three crosses and four nails were discovered in a rock cistern just to the east of Calvary; the difficulty of deciding which was Christ's and which were the thieves' had to be resolved. Various legends and traditions record different solutions. One says that a "title" was attached to one cross, which was recognized as Our Lord's; another that there was no way of telling to which cross the detached inscription belonged and that it was identified by seeing which one healed a dying woman; yet another that one upright bore the notice but that the separated cross beams had to be sorted by the same test on a dying man. One tradition says that Helen took a large fragment of the cross to Nicomedia in 328 and that part of it was put in the basilica of S. Croce in Gerusalemme, which had been Helen's Sesorian Palace in Rome. Constantine was also said to have placed a fragment inside his statue in Constantinople. A late-fourth-century account (discovered in 1884) of a pilgrimage by the nun or abbess Egeria (Etheria) describes the veneration of a relic of the cross in Jerusalem on Good Friday. There is an elaborate account of the quest for the cross in *Elene*, a fervent Old English near-epic in fourteen cantos by Cynewulf, composed (possibly *c.* 750) during a period of resistance to the Iconoclastic movement against reverence for images and based on the account which appears in the *Acta Sanctorum*. The Old English Church celebrated two feasts of the cross, its Invention (or discovery; 3 May) and Exaltation (or veneration, also known as Holy Cross Day; 14 September).

Until the 1969 reform of the Calendar, when the Exaltation was removed, the Church retained the two feasts. It would appear certain that 14 September was the original date of the commemoration of the finding even at Rome but that the exaltation under Heraclius took its place and the finding was fixed for 3 May in accordance with a Gallican usage. The old Roman Martyrology and the Breviary explicitly stated that the Exaltation commemorated the recovery in 629 by the Emperor Heraclius of the relics of the cross taken from Jerusalem in 614 by Chosroes II, king of Persia. Some commentators suggested, however, that the "Exaltation of the Cross" actually referred to the physical act of lifting of the sacred relic when it was exhibited for veneration and that the title was used in this acceptation before the time of Heraclius. The suppression of the feast would seem to indicate that this opinion is now approved. In the past the Invention would seem to have taken precedence, yet evidence suggests that the Exaltation was the more primitive celebration.

Another story, in the Syrian *Doctrine of Addai*, says that less than ten years after Jesus' ascension Protonike, wife of the emperor Claudius Caesar, went to the Holy Land, forced the Jews to reveal the hiding place of the crosses, and identified that of Jesus by a miracle worked on her own daughter. Some commentators who think that *The Doctrine of Addai* was earlier in date that the *De inventione crucis dominicae* (*e.g.,* Duchesne) contend that the Protonike legend prompted the story of Helen and the discovery of the cross in the time of Constantine.

In catechetical lectures (*c.* 345) St Cyril of Jerusalem (18 Mar.) refers to the wood of the cross. "It has been distributed," he says, "fragment by fragment, from this spot and has already nearly filled the world." Of the proliferation of pieces of the true cross, Waugh remarks: "It used to be believed by the vulgar that there were enough pieces of this 'true cross' to build a battleship. In the last century, a French savant, Charles Rohault de Fleury, went to the great trouble of measuring them all. He found a total of 4,000,000 cubic millimetres, whereas the cross on which Our Lord suffered, would probably comprise some 178,000,000. As far as volume goes, therefore, there is no strain on the credulity of the faithful."

In the Middle Ages the legend arose that Helen was born in England. Historians would seem to have confused her with another Helen, Helen Luyddog (or Luicdauc, *i.e.*, "Helen of the hosts," a description later transferred to the authentic St Helen). She was the wife of Magnus Clemens Maximus, emperor in Britain, Spain, and Gaul (383-88); they had a number of sons, one of whom was named Constantine (Custennin). Geoffrey of Monmouth and others said later that Helen was the daughter of the legendary tribal leader Coel of Caercolvin, or Colchester ("Old King Cole"). Another tradition said that she was born at Trier, in another part of Maximus' realm.

Helen's tomb was attached to the church of SS Peter and Marcellinus in Rome, the first church built as a memorial to martyrs. From the ninth century the abbey of Hautvillers, near Reims, claimed to have her body.

Helen's feast-day was 21 May (with St Constantine) in the East and 18 August in the West. It was kept in a number of English monasteries at an early date, and many churches were dedicated to her, especially in north-east England. Those in Wales, Cornwall, and Devon may have been named after the pseudo-Helen, Helen Luyddog. Like other towns, St Helens in Lancashire grew around one of her churches. St Helena, now a British island in the Atlantic, where Napoleon died in exile, was discovered by Spaniards on her feast-day.

For early lives see Eusebius, *Vita Constantinii*; Zosimus, *Historia*, 2, p. 8; Eutropius, *Breviarum*, 10, p. 2; for main passages of these and later Life by Almannus of Hautvillers see *AA.SS.*, Aug., 3 (1737), pp. 580-99; H. Thurston in *The Month* (May 1892), pp. 88-100); *C.M.H.*, p. 450; R. Couzard, Sainte *Hélène d'après l'histoire et la tradition* (1911); H. Leclercq in *D.A.C.L.*, 6, 2 (1925), 2126-45. On her churches, cult, and legend, and the cross, see F. Nau, "Les constructions Palestiennes dues à Sainte Hélène," in *Revue de l'Orient chrétien* 10 (1905), pp. 1622-88; A. Heisenberg, *Grabeskirche und Apostelkirche. Zwei Basiliken Konstantins*, vol. 2 (1908); *B.H.L.*, 1 (1899), nos. 3772-90; A. M. Rouillon, *Sainte Hélène* (1908); J. Maurice, *Sainte Hélène* (1929); A. Halusa, *Das Kreuzesholz in Geschichte und Legende* (1926); H. Thurston in *The Month* (May 1930), pp. 420-9; P. Grosjean, "Codicis Gothani Appendix," *Anal.Boll.* 58 (1940), pp. 199-203; F. Frolov, *Le Culte de la Sainte Croix à Byzance* (1956). Quite the best book written about Helen is the novel by E. Waugh, *Helena* (1950), though he followed the "Old King Cole" story and, of course, as he said: "The story is just something to be read; in fact, a legend."

Helen was a popular subject in art. She usually wears a royal crown and an imperial cloak and carries a cross, and perhaps a hammer and nails. The cross may be borne by angels who are showing it to her in a vision. She sometimes carries a model of the Holy Sepulchre; this may appear elsewhere in the picture. She may be accompanied by St Constantius.

Coins were produced in Helen's honour and bore her name, Flavia Julia Helena; the last were minted in 330. A tenth-century representation exists in a Byzantine triptych in the

Bibliothèque Nationale, Paris. There is a twelfth-century statue of Helen in the church of St Just de Valcabrère in the Pyrenees, and Helen is shown venerating the cross in the chapel of the monastery of Camp near Elne, Roussillon, France. There is a thirteenth-century statue on the façade of Reims cathedral. Among famous fourteenth-century images are Agnolo Gaddi's frescoes (S. Croce, Florence) and those by Piero della Francesca (choir of S. Francis of Arezzo). There are eighteen stained-glass panels illustrating events in Helen's life in Ashton-under-Lyne church, Lancashire (reproduced in E. Tasker, *Encyclopedia of Medieval Church Art* [1993], pp. 137-41). Sixteenth-century paintings include Veronese's *Vision of St Helen* (National Gallery, London) and *St Helen before the Pope* by Bernard van Orley (Brussels Museum). In Tintoretto's *Helen with Other Saints* (1560-70; Brera, Milan, Italy), she stands embracing a full-sized cross implanted in the ground. The painting of her by Rubens ordered by Archduke Albert for S. Croce, Rome, is now in the chapel of Grasse hospital, France.

St Firminus, *Bishop* (? Fourth Century)

Firminus, or Firmin, is a classic case of probable total invention, accretion of superstition and its local acceptance, and multiple nominal confusion. His worthless Acts say that Firminus I (formerly 25 Sept.) was a native of Pamplona in Navarre introduced to the Christian faith by St Honestus, a disciple of St Saturninus of Toulouse (29 Nov.), and consecrated bishop of Toulouse by St Honoratus (16 Jan.) to preach the gospel in remote parts of Gaul. He decided to settle in Amiens. He was martyred there, and Bishop St Firminus II (formerly 1 Sept.) built a church over his tomb, dedicated to Our Lady but now known as St Acheul's. Two early English churches were dedicated to the supposed martyr Firminus I.

If they/he existed at all, Firminus I and Firminus II were probably only one man. They are both unheard of before the ninth century. The first known bishop of Amiens was Eulogius in the mid-fourth century. Perhaps there was a Firminus who was a missionary bishop in Gaul. Yet another, equally supposititious fourth-century bishop, Firminus III, is ascribed to Metz and commemorated today, as in the new draft Roman Martyrology. We possess, however, a ninth-century discussion of Bishop St Firminus in one of his manifestations.

Agobard, archbishop of Lyons from 816 to his death in 860, was an unusually cautious authority on superstitions and extraordinarily sceptical for the period. He was the author of a surviving treatise, "Mistaken Popular Opinions concerning the Origin of Hailstorms and Thunder," and probably preached many sermons on credulity. He castigates the "blind idiocy" of all ranks of society and admirably identifies and delineates varieties of "crowd effect": the ways in which beliefs spread by contagion and any number of witnesses produced who will swear that the non-existent exists and that phenomena contrary to nature not only are possible but that they themselves have seen and experienced them.

Bishop Barthélemy of Uzès consulted the redoutable Agobard on a phenomenon of collective hysteria in his diocese. A certain church (perhaps the cathedral) claiming to possess the body of "a certain St Firmin" was plagued by crowds of men and women behaving like epileptics who filled the church with embarrassing gifts of silver, cattle, and so on, invoked St Firmin's help, suffered a terrible burning sensation, were never cured of anything, yet kept on coming merely, it seemed, for the experience. The bishop and Agobard refer to Firmin as *quidam* ("a certain"), putting his existence in doubt. Agobard remarks that an interior pilgrimage is better than such supersition and that it would be better to give these things to the poor. Agobard's correspondence on the subject and his prudent judgment have come down to us. Later records say the body was then removed in spite of the destruction or sacking and emptying of the cathedral on several occasions over the centuries (by the Cathars, the Protestants, and during the French Revolution), the supposedly rediscovered relics of this Firmin, the local patron, have been displayed there since 1873.

See *AA.SS.*, Sept., 7, pp. 24-57; Sept., 1, pp. 175-99; C. Salmon, *Histoire de S. Firmin* (1861); J. Corblet, *Hagiographie du diocèse d'Amiens* (1870), 2, pp. 311-216; B. Egon, *Erzbischof Agobard von Lyon. Leben und Werk* (1969); G. Chauvet, *Uzès* (1991), pp. 136-9.

As San Fermín he is celebrated in Pamplona by the famous running of the bulls through the streets to the bullring on 7 July.

St Macarius the Wonder Worker (*c.* 850)

He was baptized Christopher and was a native of Constantinople. He was well educated and an enthusiastic student of the Bible who later went to the monastery of Pelekete where he took the name Macarius. He was a model monk and chosen to be abbot. Miracles of healing were reported and crowds flocked to Pelekete to be cured. St Tarasius, patriarch of Constantinople (and a firm opponent of Iconoclasm), heard of Macarius' sanctity and miracles and sent Paul, a patrician, to escort him to the city. Paul had been cured by the abbot, who had also recently restored his wife's health even though the physicians had said nothing could be done for her. Tarasius gave Macarius his blessing and, before he returned to Pelekete, ordained him priest.

The cloister did not remain peaceful for long. Emperor Leo the Armenian, a fierce Iconoclast, attacked prominent supporters of the cult of holy images one by one. Macarius was tortured in various ways and imprisoned until the emperor's death. His successor, Michael the Stammerer, released Macarius and used promises and threats to try to win him over to the Iconoclast position. Macarius remained inflexible. He was banished to the island of Aphusia off the Bithynian coast and died in exile there on 18 August; the year of his death is unknown.

See *Anal.Boll.*, 16 (1897), pp. 140-63, 32 (1913), pp. 270-3.

Bd Mannes (*c.* 1230)

Mannes was one of the three sons of Felix de Guzmán and Bd Joan of Aza (2 Aug.). Antony was the eldest and St Dominic (8 Aug.) the youngest. Mannes was born at Calaruega in the province of Burgos in the mid-twelfth century. He is said to have dedicated himself to God before Dominic was born in 1170. We know nothing of most of his life.

He was among Dominic's first followers and one of the sixteen who adopted the Rule of St Augustine in 1216 and made their profession at Prouille in the following year. Mannes had already helped his brother on his anti-Cathar preaching campaign in the Languedoc. Dominic sent Mannes with six others to Paris to make the first French Dominican foundation, under Brother Matthew of France, near the university. He is next heard of as chaplain to the nuns at Prouille, established by Dominic in 1207. Later he was put in charge of their new convent at Madrid. The founder refers to him in a letter to the Sisters: "Our very dear brother, Brother Mannes, who has spared no pains to bring you to this high state, will take whatever steps he thinks necessary to ensure that it continues. He has our authority to visit the convent, to correct whatever he finds wrong and, if he thinks it necessary, to change the prioress, as long as most of the Sisters agree."

Dominic evidently had a high opinion of his brother's qualities, and he remained director of the Madrid nuns for twelve years. He outlived Dominic, but the year of his death is not certain. Though it is generally given as 1230, there is a story that he visited Calaruega after Dominic's canonization in 1234 and urged the people there to build a chapel in his brother's honour: "Be satisfied with a small one for the present: my brother will know how to enlarge it when he wants to." Thirty years later, King Alfonso X did extend the chapel. Mannes was buried at the Cistercian church of St Peter at Gamiel d'Izan. His cult was approved in 1834.

See A. Mortier, *Maîtres Généraux O.P.*, 1, pp. 2, 29, 90; Procter, pp. 213-5; *Année Dominicaine*, 7, p. 819.

R.M.

St Eonius, bishop of Arles (502)

St Rusticus, bishop and martyr at Cahors (630)

Bd Leonard, abbot in Campania (1255)

Bd Rainaldus, bishop of Ravenna (1514)

Bd Paula of Montaldo, Poor Clare abbess at Mantua and mystic (1514)

19

ST JOHN EUDES, *Founder* (1601-80)

On 14 November 1601 in Ri, a very small Norman village near Argentan, Jean Eudes was born into a France which had suffered the terrible carnage and dissension of the wars of religion between Catholics and Protestants. It was a country of Catholics largely uneducated in the articles and practice of their faith. They were much in need of the spiritual and catechetical renewal brought about by such great preachers and educators of the Counter-Reformation as St François de Sales (24 Jan.), Pierre de Bérulle (1575-1629), and St Vincent de Paul (27 Sept.). St John Eudes was to follow their example.

John's parents, Isaac Eudes and Marthe Corbin, had prayed for a child for three years. They vowed, should one be born to them, to make a pilgrimage to a chapel of Our Lady over thirty miles away. They did so as soon as Marthe was pregnant and offered the boy to Our Lord and to his mother. They had six other children after John. In the spiritual journal he kept toward the end of his life, John recorded the total inadequacy of the religious instruction in his child-hood parish. He made a direct connection between that and the scant religious practice of the village, far from atypical in France. Very few people, for instance, received Communion other than at Easter. John showed early signs of religious awareness. From about the age of twelve he began to communicate every month, after a general Confession. Not long afterwards he made a vow of chastity, though we cannot know if he realized its full implications. He went to a neighbouring village for his first catechism and grammar lessons, from Fr Jacques Blanette. On 9 October 1615 his father sent him to a Jesuit college in Caen, fifty kilometres away. He was very impressed by the sincerity and piety of his teachers, and especially Fr Robin, the rector. In 1618 he joined the pupils' sodality of Our Lady. On 19 September 1620 he received the tonsure and minor orders, but he was reluctant to join the ranks of the diocesan clergy, who seemed discouragingly mediocre. Nevertheless, the religious life did not attract him at the time.

Bérulle had founded the Oratory of Jesus in Paris eleven years before, on the model of the Oratory of St Philip Neri (26 May). In 1622 the Oratorians opened a house at Caen. It was not a religious Order but a society of priests living in community. They were determined to set an example that would prompt the spiritual and pastoral renewal of the French clergy. Bérulle had established a tradition of spirituality so influential that it became known as "the French school." His christocentric approach was eclectic: it drew on the Greek

Fathers of the Church, the Flemish mystics, and contemporary Jesuit practice. For him, the aim of Christian devotion was effective imitation. The individual should model his or her own piety on the true adoration offered by Christ to the Father: meditation on and reproduction of his different "states" (his hidden and public life, and so on) on earth and, in perfection, in heaven. The believer was to focus on Christ as Word but also on Christ as human being. By self-renunciation, Communion, and due contemplation the individual's life could participate in the life of the head of the Mystical Body. The ideal Christian way comprised adoration, elevation, self-oblation, and servitude.

This highly-nuanced, mature spirituality, coupled with a mission to make the hierarchical priesthood spiritually and pastorally worthy of respect, deeply impressed John, as it did very many Oratorians and Sulpicians. Nevertheless, not a few of them proved somewhat obdurate when Bérulle tried to insist that Carmelites and Oratorians make a vow of perpetual servitude to Jesus and Mary. John, however, was a model Bérullian, which meant that he followed the master's recommendations in ways proper to his own life and environment. On 25 March 1623 he was admitted to the Oratory in Paris. After a year he was sent to Aubervilliers to study under Charles de Condren. He was ordained priest on 20 December 1625.

He was suddenly struck down by an unexplained sickness. It made him so physically weak that he could not carry out any duties but spent two years in retreat, praying and reading. When he recovered he heard that the plague was ravaging an area near his village. He asked permission to go there. For two months he cared for the sick and brought them the sacraments. The plague disappeared in November 1627, and he went to the Caen community as preacher, confessor, and spiritual director. In 1630 the plague attacked Caen. Once again John risked his life to tend the victims, deserted by most people out of fear of infection. To protect his fellow-priests he lived in a vast wine cask which Madame de Budos, the Benedictine abbess who had been appointed at the age of thirteen and now came under his spiritual direction, put at his disposal in the Caen abbey fields. He was fed from the convent. In April 1631 he left his quaint retreat to look after the other Oratorians, two of whom had just died. He became seriously ill himself but soon recovered.

From 1631 onward John preached more than a hundred missions in Normandy, and others elsewhere, each lasting six to eight weeks. He thought this was the minimum necessary, given the appalling ignorance of most parishioners. The chief end of these missions, directed primarily to adult Catholics (and sometimes, unsuccessfully, to Protestants who had not fled the country), was conversion, which meant a total change of life. It is difficult now to realize how original and impressive this method was in the existing state of laxity and neglect. But there was often friction between missioners and parish clergy. The people often complained of the inefficiency and cupidity of their regular pastors. They were reluctant to help finance the missions, as state taxes were already high; support had to be sought from rich patrons. John's journal shows that he relied on about fifty people of good will—merchants or individuals with inherited wealth. All sorts of devices were used to draw in as many people as possible. Processions, devotions to the cross, plays, mime, brought people to the core of the effort: instruction in the principles of the faith. This meant the creed, the sacraments, examination of conscience, and the right dispositions for a good Communion. A general Confession rounded off the weeks of hard work ("Preachers beat the bushes. Confessors catch the birds!" said John).

By the end of the seventeenth century these missions began to concentrate not on inculcating the rudiments of belief in the totally ignorant but on renewing the already aroused spirit of faith. By the end of the eighteenth century the efforts of the Eudists and others had produced a strong body of more knowledgeable, motivated, and zealous parish clergy whose own catechizing and sermons could do the essential work.

In 1637 John published *The Life and Kingdom of Jesus in Christian Souls*, which summarizes the essence of his devotional thinking. It went into sixteen editions in his own lifetime. This is mysticism and theology adapted to the results of popular preaching and therefore a practical manual of the Christian life. The structure is twofold. It offers thoughts and exercises for different aspects of everyday experience, but it also follows the "states and mysteries of Jesus' life" through the liturgical year as sources of grace. It is open-ended and developmental, yet patristic: "The mysteries of Jesus are still on the way to fullness and perfection. They may be perfect and complete in the actual person who is Jesus Christ, but they are by no means finished and absolute either in our own selves, who are members of Christ, or in his Church, which is his mystical Body. The Son of God had a plan. The mystery of his becoming human is an unfinished process extended and continued in us and in his Church as a whole."

To the ideas which he took from Bérulle, Condren, and others John added his own developing understanding of the generosity of Jesus, of the "emotions and sympathies of his heart." This allowed him to present such difficult concepts as that of the Trinity in ways unusually direct for his times: "The union of Father and Son is the model for our union with God through baptism. The Holy Spirit is the link uniting One with the Other and you and me with God, and enabling us to be with Jesus and relate to him perfectly as long as we live." John followed his key work with other successful texts, above all his *Meditations*, in which he emphasized the Christian life as a vital and varied relationship with Jesus in all the aspects of his humanity.

In 1641 he met someone very different from Bérulle. Marie des Vallées (1590-1656), the "saint of Coutances," was a very unusual young woman of humble origin. As sometimes happens, her beneficial influence on John's piety outweighed any discernible originality of thought if not of behaviour. She reported intriguing and possibly genuine mystical experiences, largely inspired by her enthusiastic reading of the somewhat abstract works of the English Capuchin mystic Benet Canfield (d. 1611) and other out-of-the-way writers. She also suffered from epileptic fits and undoubtedly neurotic yet quite fascinating syndromes. These prevented her from receiving Communion, and she and her acolytes interpreted them as phases of diabolical possession. John, passionately interested in all the phenomena she recorded, became her spiritual director and wrote three unpublished works on her life

In 1641 John was inspired by Madeleine Lamy, who had taken charge of some former prostitutes. He founded the unofficial Order of Our Lady of Charity, under the direction of Madame Morin, a convert from Protestantism, to look after such women and girls. In 1644 he entrusted it to the Visitandines of Caen. In 1643 he left the Oratory and opened a seminary at Caen. In spite of Oratorian opposition, he established a new Congregation to educate priests in seminaries, the Congregation of Jesus and Mary (the Eudists), with foundations later at Coutances, Lisieux, and Rouen and a fifth, less happily, at Evreux. The sixth, at Rennes, took two years to establish, in 1670-2. He tried to set one up in Paris in 1672, but his enemies persuaded the Paris Parliament to reject the project.

John never intended his priests to take religious vows that would distinguish them too greatly from diocesan priests. This often made things more difficult. For years he had to combat enormous resistance in the dioceses, in Paris, and at Rome to put his seminaries and the refuge on a sound, officially-sanctioned footing. It was not until 2 December 1657, for example, that John was appointed superior of Caen as a diocesan seminary with full episcopal, royal, and local parliamentary approval. In 1657, too, he helped the Caen Sisters to found the Sisters of our Lady of Charity of the Refuge, who opened numerous refuges to care for fallen women.

These efforts also opened up years of resistance and bureaucratic delay in obtaining due recognition. Financial problems were always present. Pontifical approval for Our Lady of Charity was obtained only on 2 January 1666 with a Bull of Alexander VII. Moreover, the continuing near-enmity of the Oratorians was supplemented by opposition from Jansenists and the many priests influenced by their thinking. Invitations to conduct missions to the court, in 1671 and 1673, nevertheless showed that the Eudists had friends in high places. The queen was immensely impressed by John's fervour. In 1673, however, when royal support seemed about to secure final papal approval for the Eudists, John's enemies showed the king a copy of a document of 1662 which, unknown to John, had promised irrevocably that the Congregation would always support the authority of the Roman Pontiff, even in uncertain cases. Given the always fluid lines of demarcation between royal and Roman authority, the king found this disloyal. In 1674 he withdrew his promised protection. John was ordered to leave Paris for Caen and to remain within its confines. Paradoxically, the king's disapproval had an equivalent effect in Rome. A terrible period of rumours, accusations, and libels ensued. A Cistercian abbot circulated a 127-page pamphlet against John. Notes taken by a former secretary of John's and some of his private writings on Marie des Vallées and her odd behaviour were re-worked and exaggerated to show that Fr Eudes was a dangerously wild heretic, guilty of thirteen heresies, including Arianism, Nestorianism, Monothelitism, and Jansenism. Some of his thinking on the heart of Mary was sufficiently unorthodox, the Cistercian concluded, to have him executed in any country where the Inquisition held due sway. The author made it clear that he devoutly hoped John would suffer this fate as soon as possible. John was also accused of burning an anti-heretical book by a Eudist, twice superior of the Rouen seminary, which said that Mary deserved no more honour than any other saint and should be called not mother of God but mother of Jesus. The confusion of the whole episode is shown by the fact that the book was actually quasi-Jansenist and that John's thinking on Mary and devotion to the hearts of Jesus and Mary was measured and reticent compared with other tendencies of the period. John's supporters published a refutation of the false accusations, but they persisted and were repeated in many works, including dictionaries, in the eighteenth century and later.

John helped to spread devotion to the Sacred Heart, but his notion of it was more theocentric than the popular, physical version propagated by St Margaret Mary Alacoque (17 Oct.), who claimed special revelations (in 1673-5) with promises of divine rewards for particular observances. John's more sophisticated devotion was in line with the tradition that had begun in the twelfth century and emphasized Jesus as sharing our human nature and suffering. It stressed the heart of Jesus as the image of his "inwardness" and made it an emblem of devotion to his person as the everlasting heart of the world: "This humanly divine and divinely human heart is the Father of all the hearts of the children of God." Margaret Mary's approach focussed on the directly assimilable imagery of anatomical rupture, bleeding, and localized pain, whose attractiveness is shown by the rapid spread until the present day of cheap, crude, hand-coloured engravings, then oleographs, lithographs, and line-block reproductions based on her supposed visions and hung in a multitude of Catholic homes. Its appeal also relied on a calculable outcome resulting from measurable activity. In 1643 John made the first efforts to recommend an actual feast-day for the Sacred Heart and received a degree of support from a few bishops who appreciated this more generally amenable expression of Bérullian mysticism. In 1646 John instituted the feast of the Holy Heart of Mary, and in 1672 that of the Sacred Heart of Jesus, but the response was lukewarm. He wrote several offices for the feasts and, in 1670, *The Admirable Heart of the Mother of God* (published in 1681, after his death). The feast of the Sacred Heart of Jesus was not approved until 1765, by Clement XIII.

Attempts in 1676 to persuade the archbishop to intercede with the king and direct appeals to Louis XIV did not succeed. This posed a very real threat to the future of the Eudists. John became weaker after the efforts demanded by the missions he still insisted on preaching. In 1678 he wrote a movingly desperate appeal to the king's conscience in which he protested that he would "give a thousand lives rather than do the least thing contrary to the king's interests." We do not know if this actually reached Louis, though later, especially during the canonization process, it was cited as evidence of John's antipapal "Gallicanism." Eventually episcopal pleas elicited an invitation to an audience on 16 June 1679. Louis did not refer to the past but said he knew that John's work was praiseworthy and that he could be sure of royal protection. This was tantamount to an assurance that the Congregation would survive. The Constitutions of the Order called for a general assembly every three years. John had ignored this but now summoned the first in June 1680. A new superior was appointed. John died peacefully at Caen on 19 August 1680. He was beatified by Pope St Pius X in 1909 and canonized by Pius XI in 1925 as "Father, doctor and apostle of the liturgical cult of the Sacred Hearts of Jesus and Mary."

The Eudists almost disappeared during the French Revolution. The Order was reconstituted in 1826. For the most part it is now devoted to secondary education and has been very active in North and South America and in the West Indies, as well as in Europe. In 1835 the Sisters of Our Lady of Charity of the Good Shepherd were established as an Order to run reform schools.

All existing English translations of the works irremediably befog their style and meaning. See *Oeuvres complètes*, vols. 1-12 (1905-9). There is an early Life by P. Hérambourg (2d ed., 1869; best Eng. trans. 1960). The main modern Lives are by D. Boulay (4 vols., 1905-8); H. Joly (1907; Eng. trans., 1932); E. Georges (1925); D. Sargent, *Their Hearts be Praised* (1949). C. Guillon, *En tout la volonté de Dieu: St Jean Eudes à travers ses lettres* (1981) is an excellent selection of the letters with an up-to-date account of the life. On his spiritual tradition and practice see E. Dermenghem, *La Vie admirable et les révélations de Marie des Vallées* (1926); C. Lebrun, *La spiritualité de St Jean Eudes* (1933); P. Cochois, *Bérulle et l'école française* (1963); L. Cognet, *Le Coeur du Seigneur* (1955), esp. pp. 180-91; idem., *Histoire de la Spiritualité chrétienne*, vol. 3, 1: *La spiritualité moderne* (1966), pp. 360-404, 406-10; F. G. Preckler, *Bérulle aujourd'hui 1575-1975. Pour une spiritualité de l'humanité du Christ* (1978). On the missions see M. Venard, "Les missions des oratoriens d'Avignon aux XVIIe et XVIIIe siècles," special no. of *Revue d'Histoire de l'Eglise de France* (1962); C. B. du Chesnay, *Les Missions de S. Jean Eudes* (1967); R. Chartier, M. M. Compère, and D. Julia, *L'éducation en France du XVIe au XVIIIe siècle* (1976). On the Order see E. Georges, *La Congrégation de Jésus et Marie, dite les Eudistes* (1933).

John's emblems are the flaming heart and the crucifix, both of which he holds, or the hearts of Jesus and Mary, mystically one. There is an appealing anonymous engraved portrait (*c.* 1645) in the Bibliothèque nationale, Paris. The best image is a fine copperplate engraving by P. Drevet, after a painting by Jean Leblond of John in 1673, aged seventy-two; it brings out the saint's nobility and dedication more effectively than the rather conventional oil on which it is based.

St Andrew the Tribune, *Martyr* (*c.* 300)

There is no early evidence for the cult of this St Andrew. He is retained by the new draft Roman Martyrology. The fictitious story of his martyrdom was popular at a later date, and he is the object of great devotion in the East. There is an Andrew in the *Hieronymianum*, but there is nothing to connect him with this date or with the story in his alleged Acts.

Andrew was a captain under Antiochus in the army of Galerius, which Diocletian sent against the Persians. During a battle Andrew called on the name of Christ (having heard that he was a powerful protector) and told his men to do the same. They were victorious and decided their prayers must have been effective. Andrew and some others decided to become Christians. They were denounced to Antiochus, who wrote to Galerius to ask what to do about this breach of discipline. The general thought that executions would be bad for morale at a time of victory, so he ordered Antiochus to discharge the offenders and to punish them later when an opportunity arose. Andrew and the other converts went to Bishop Peter of Caesarea in Cappadocia, and he baptized them. Seleucus, military governor of Cilicia, heard of this and sent a detachment to arrest the new Christians. They fled into the Taurus mountains but were tracked down, surrounded, and put to death.

AA.SS., Aug., 3.

St Sixtus III, *Pope* (440)

Sixtus (Xystus) was a prominent Roman cleric before his pontificate. He warmly defended the African bishops against the Pelagians. When he succeeded Pope St Celestine I (6 Apr.) on 31 July 432, St Prosper of Aquitaine (25 June) wrote: "We trust in God's protection. We hope that what he did for us in Innocent, Zosimus, Boniface and Celestine he will also do in Sixtus. Just as they guarded the flock against declared and openly professed wolves, may he drive off the hidden ones [that is, heretics]." The reference was to the teachers of the Semi-Pelagian heresy (who held that even though grace is necessary to do good works, it is not needed to initiate them; that it is obtained by merit; and that merit can enable us to persevere in good works).

Sixtus did not disappoint Prosper. He sent the bishops of Gaul a recapitulation of recent papal decisions on grace. Nevertheless, he was peace-loving and conciliatory and never defined the exact meaning of the doctrine of predestination. This attitude invited accusations of Pelagian and Nestorian leanings. He supported the decision of Ephesus but refused to uphold Cyril's condemnation of the Antiochene bishops and tried to reconcile Alexandria and Antioch. In 433, on the anniversary of his consecration, John of Antioch and Cyril were reconciled by a joint profession of faith.

Sixtus restored several buildings in Rome, including the basilicas of St Paul and St Laurence, the catacomb of Callistus, and the Liberian basilica, now called St Mary Major. He had this inscription set up there: "O Virgin Mary, I Sixtus have dedicated a new temple to you, an offering worthy of the womb that brought us salvation. You, a maiden who knew not man, bore and brought forth our Salvation. Behold! These martyrs, witnesses to the fruit of your womb, carry their crowns of victory to you. Beneath their feet lie the instruments of their passion: sword, flame, wild beast, water, and cruel poison. One and the same crown awaits these various deaths." Over the arch of the apse these words can still be read in mosaic: "Sixtus the bishop for the people of God." Sixtus also consecrated a number of churches He died on 19 August 440. Ado inscribed his name in his martyrology in the ninth century.

See *Liber Pontificalis*, 1, pp. 232-7.

Portraits are late; a particularly fine medallion head of him (*e.g.*, British Museum, London) is attributed to Giovanni Battista Pozzi.

St Mochta, *Abbot* (? Fifth Century)

Some Lives of St Patrick (17 Mar.) mention Mochta (Mochteus, Mochuta), and there is a late Latin and moderately entertaining because highly fabulous Life of him. It was clearly one of the texts that inspired the brilliant twentieth-century Irish novelist Flann O'Brien. Mochta is retained in the new draft Roman Martyrology.

He was born in Britain and was taken to Ireland by his Christian parents while still a child. A pagan bard, Hoa, travelled with them. During a bad storm Hoa wanted to throw Mochta overboard as a sacrifice but the tempest immediately calmed down, and later on Mochta converted Hoa. Mochta became a disciple of St Patrick. Being, like all the heavenly host, specially kind to saints of the country of the Gael, an angel taught him how to write on a tablet. Mochta questioned the accuracy of the ages of the patriarchs in the Old Testament, so St Patrick rewarded his cheek by sentencing him to a suitably long life. To complete his education he was sent to Rome, where Pope St Leo I (d. 461) made him a bishop and the grateful Mochta presented the pope with the angelic tablet. He collected twelve young men as missionaries and returned to Ireland. One young missionary was left behind on the way, but he put to sea on the bough of a tree and got there first.

Mochta stayed first in Meath, but the people there did not like his style, so he settled eventually at Louth, where a large community, including two hundred bishops, gathered round him. He made an agreement with Patrick that one of the two of them would care for the community of whoever died first. He never spoke a false word or a foolish one. He liked fat but out of austerity never touched even a morsel of it. In accordance with Patrick's sentence, he lived till he was three hundred years old, though another account says ninety.

See *AA.SS.*, Aug., 3; *B.T.A.*, 3, p. 356; W. W. Heist, *Vitae Sanctorum Hiberniae* (1965), pp. 394-400.

St Bertulf, *Abbot* (640)

Bertulf was one of the many relatives of St Arnulf of Metz (18 July) venerated as saints. He was brought up as a pagan but was impressed by Arnulf's teaching and example and became a Christian. In 620 he was professed as a monk at Luxeuil. He stayed there for some years, learning the discipline of St Columban (23 Nov.) from his successor, St Eustace. Then he attracted the interest of St Attalas (10 Mar.), who had succeeded Columban as abbot of Bobbio. Bertulf was given permission to go to that monastery. In 627 he became its abbot on the death of Attalas. He proved a holy and learned superior, maintaining Columban's austere Rule. Outside the monastery Bertulf resolutely opposed the Arianism then prevalent in northern Italy.

The year after Bertulf's election Bishop Probus of Tortona claimed a wide jurisdiction over the monastery. Bertulf appealed to Ariovald, the Lombard king, who said the matter should be taken to Rome and paid for the abbot to go there to state his case. Bertulf took the monk Jonah with him as a secretary (he later wrote a Life of Bertulf). Pope Honorius I knew of the monastery's good reputation and declared it exempt from episcopal control and immediately subject to the Holy See. This, the first recorded exemption of the kind, is said to have started a new era in the relationship of the regular clergy to the bishops. Jonah says that on his way home Bertulf was struck down by a fever. He seemed likely to die, but on the vigil of SS Peter and Paul he fell into a deep sleep, during which he had a vision of St Peter. On waking, he was quite well again.

M.G.H., Scriptores Merov., 4, pp. 280ff.

St Sebald (? Eighth Century)

Very little is known about him. He was said to have been a solitary near Vicenza for a time and to have been in Rome during the pontificate of Gregory II and when SS Willibald (7 June) and Winebald (18 Dec.) were there. When St Gregory II sent Willbald to Germany, Sebald went with him. He lived as a hermit in the Reichswald, preaching to his neighbours. Even in 1072, he was recognized as the patron of Nuremberg. One of the reliefs on the base of his shrine at Nuremberg, the best-known work of Peter Vischer, on which he worked from 1505 to 1519, represents the miracle of the icicles attributed to Sebald: one snowy night he took refuge in a peasant's cottage. The fire was small and low, which made it almost as cold inside as outside. Sebald suggested that more fuel might be put on the fire, but the peasant said he was too poor to have a roaring blaze. Sebald turned to the housewife and asked her to bring in a bundle of the long icicles hanging from the eaves. When she did so and Sebald threw them on the fire, it burned merrily. Other miracles are recorded on the shrine: giving sight to a blind man, filling a jug with wine from nowhere, and causing the earth to part and swallow a scoffer.

AA.SS., Aug., 3; *Kirchenlexikon,* 11, 24-6.

St Louis of Anjou, *Bishop* (1274-97)

Louis had the misfortune to be born with a rank and status almost always contrary to his inclinations throughout a relatively short life. He was born Louis d'Angio at Brignoles in Provence, the second son of Charles II (Charles the Lame), king of Naples and Sicily, and Mary, daughter of Stephen V, king of Hungary. He was a grand-nephew of St Louis of France (25 Aug.) and connected with the family of St Elizabeth of Hungary (17 Nov.).

In 1284 the king of Aragon captured Louis' father, Charles, then prince of Salerno, in a sea battle. Though his father died in a few months and he thus became king of Sicily, Charles was kept in prison for four years and released only on hard conditions: one of these was that he had to send three of his sons, including Louis, to Aragon as hostages. Louis remained in captivity at Barcelona for seven years. Nevertheless, he is said to have been cheerful and to have taken part in sports and other activities with which the prisoners whiled away their time. Louis kept their entertainment in strict bounds: chess, for instance, was encouraged; gambling was forbidden. Louis was noted for his unusual modesty; one biographer (Surius) says, "He refused to embrace even his sisters and his own mother. He shunned any kind of conversation with, and even the sight of women." Though the circumstances of his life partly dictated his evasion of women, Louis' strategies for avoiding what he thought of as impurity were so extreme that he was taken as a patron and model by the very odd St Aloysius Gonzaga (21 June), who would not allow even his valet to see his foot uncovered.

Louis studied enthusiastically and was influenced by the Friars Minor. When he became seriously ill at the castle of Sciurana, he vowed to join that Order if he recovered. He obtained permission for two Franciscan friars to look after him in his own apartments. He got up at the appropriate times to pray with them during the night and followed their instructions in philosophy and theology. Richard Middleton (de Media Villa), an English Franciscan and theologian, was one of his tutors.

Louis was freed in 1295 when his father concluded a treaty with James II, king of Aragon. The new alliance had to be cemented in the usual way, and it was decided that Louis should marry James' sister. But he was inflexibly set on a religious life. He resigned his right to the crown of Naples, and his brother Robert became heir to the throne. "Jesus Christ," Louis said, "is my kingdom. If he is all I have, I shall have everything. If I don't have him, I lose everything." His family opposition was so resolute, however, that the superiors of the Friars Minor prudently refused to admit him for some time. He withdrew to a castle near Naples. There he became a close friend of a poor scholar from a well-to-do middle-class family of Cahors, James d'Euèse, who was elevated to the papacy as Pope John XXII and eventually canonized his benefactor.

Yet Louis was too important a person to escape the responsibilities of his station. If he chose religion, it would certainly not be on his own terms. Bishops were usually appointed with tactical and geopolitical considerations in mind. The extremely autocratic Pope Boniface VIII spent much of his time extending the property and power of his own family and placing his own men in positions that would ensure him and his faction within the Church superiority in domestic and international affairs. At this time he was involved in one especially tricky conflict with Philip the Fair of France over the general reservation of bishoprics and major benefices to the papacy, the taxation of clergy, and the transit to Spain of a considerable sum of money belonging to the Holy See in connection with the war against Aragon, and in another conflict with a group of churchmen led by the powerful Colonna cardinals. Moreover, he was not sympathetic to self-effacing men of God. After all, he had prevented his predecessor Peter Celestine (19 May) from becoming a simple hermit and had kept him under close guard until his recent death, in May 1296. Boniface gave Louis a dispensation to be ordained priest when he was twenty-three and to be consecrated bishop with an appointment to the see of Toulouse. It was made plain to the reluctant Louis that this was a matter of obedience. For Boniface he was merely one of many potentially useful pawns in a very intricate game of survival. Louis obeyed but first fulfilled his earlier vow by going to Rome and making his profession on Christmas Eve, 1296, with the Friars Minor in the Ara Coeli convent. He was consecrated in St Peter's a mere five days later.

Louis travelled to his see as a poor religious, but he was received at Toulouse with the pomp and ceremony appropriate to a prince. Nevertheless, he remained modest and humble. He stopped the use of plate and jewelled vessels in his episcopal house and replaced them with pewter and wooden bowls. He wore an old darned habit as an example to his clergy, who seemed too interested in the quality of their clothes. He celebrated Mass every day and preached frequently. But after a few months he found his episcopal duties too exhausting and asked permission to resign: "The world can call me mad. If I can get rid of a burden that is too heavy for me, I am satisfied. Surely it's better for me to throw it off than to sink under it?" He was not allowed to leave, but he was taken ill at Brignoles when returning from a visit to his sister in Catalonia. He said, "After a dangerous voyage, at last I am in sight of the port I have been trying to get to for so long. I shall now be able to enjoy my God whom the world wants to rob me of, and I shall be freed from a heavy load which I just can't bear." He died on 19 August 1297, when he was only twenty-three and a half years old. He had asked to be buried in the convent of the Franciscan friars at Marseilles, and his wish was granted (though his relics were later translated to Valencia). Pope John XXII (in only the second year of his unexpectedly long and troubled papacy) canonized him at Avignon in 1317 and sent a special Brief on the subject to Louis' mother, who was still alive.

AA.SS., Aug., 3, pp. 775-822; *Anal.Boll.* 9 (1890), pp. 278-353; 46, pp. 344-54 ; *Bibl. SS.*, 8, 300-7. See M. R. Toynbee, *St Louis of Toulouse and the Process of Canonization in the Fourteenth Century* (1929); L. Chancerel, *Saint-Louis de Toulouse* (1943).

Renaissance painters show Louis as a beardless young man and usually as a bishop, with golden fleurs-de-lys embroidered on his cope or elsewhere to show his relation to the French throne. The crown and sceptre which he renounced are at his feet. His brother Robert may kneel before him, and he may appear together with St Francis of Assisi, St Bonaventure, St Elizabeth of Hungary, and with other Franciscans, sometimes in pictures in which Our Lady is the main figure. He is a prominent figure, for instance, in *The Adoration of the Child with Saints and Donors* by Biagio d'Antonio da Firenze (Philbrook Art Center, Tulsa, Oklahoma). Simone Martini (*c.* 1284-1344) completed a sequence of elegantly-portrayed scenes from his life (National Museum, Naples).

Bd Jordan of Pisa (1311)

We know nothing about his parents, birth, or early youth. A reference in a sermon may show that he was studying in Paris in the late 1270s. He became a Dominican at Pisa in 1280 and afterwards was sent to Paris to complete his studies. At the Dominican provincial chapter at Rieti in 1305 he was appointed lector in Florence. He held the post for three years, during which the house of Santa Maria Novella became celebrated as a centre of excellence. The chronicle of the Dominican convent at Pisa says that Jordan had learned by heart "the Breviary, the Missal, most of the Bible and the marginal notes, the second part of St Thomas Aquinas' *Summa* and many other things."

He not only taught but preached eloquently. He is said to have preached as often as five times a day in Florence, in churches and in the open air, with people following him from site to site as he developed a subject. Many hearers took notes, and some of these have survived. His preaching was simple, yet so powerful that it was said to have helped to change the tone of Florentine public morality, for he both emphasized major aspects of Christian life and doctrine and offered practical advice on perseverance. Sometimes his friend and disciple Bd Silvester of Valdiseve (9 June) would wait at the foot of the pulpit with wine to refresh the exhausted Jordan. Several other of his penitents became well known for their sanctity. Jordan founded several confraternities in Pisa, one of which survives with its primitive Constitution.

Jordan is also known to historians of language and literature as one of the first Italians to use the vernacular—that is, the Tuscan dialect—instead of Latin in his addresses and sermons and to do so at a high level of competence and versatility.

In 1311 he was appointed professor of theology in the friary of St James in Paris but was taken ill on the way there and died in Piacenza. His cult was confirmed in 1833.

See S. Razzi, *Historia degli Uomini illustri O.P.*, 1, pp. 66ff.; A. Galletti, "Fra Jiordano da Pisa, predicatore del secolo XIV," in *Archivio istorico italiano* 33 (1899); Fr Taurisiano, *Catalogus Hagiographicus O.P.* (1918), p. 25.

Bd Hugh Green, *Martyr* (*c.* 1564-1642)

Hugh Green (also known as Ferdinand Brooks or Ferdinand Brown) was born to Protestant parents in London in around 1584. His father was a goldsmith. He was educated at Peterhouse College, Cambridge. He became a tutor, then travelled on the Continent. Impressed by the zeal of Catholics there, he was received into the Church. He went to the English College at Douai and was ordained priest on 14 June 1612. Ill health prevented him from joining the Capuchins, and he went on the English mission. He remained in England for nearly thirty years and was eventually appointed chaplain to Lady Arundell's household at Chideock Castle, Dorset.

In 1642 Charles I issued a proclamation requiring all priests to leave the country by a certain date. Lady Arundell tried to persuade Hugh to stay at Chideock, as the time allowed for departure had elapsed. He had not seen the proclamation, thought he still had some days left to make a legal journey, and decided to go to Lyme, the nearest seaport. As he was boarding a ship for France, a customs officer interrogated him. Hugh said he was a priest and was leaving in obedience to the king's order. The officer said the time was up, arrested him, and brought him before a justice of the peace, who committed him to Dorchester gaol. On 17 August 1642, after five months in prison, he was sentenced to death as a priest.

In prison he had converted two of three women criminals now waiting at the gibbet to be executed before him. They confessed their sins from the scaffold and he absolved them. A Jesuit in disguise and on horseback was there and gave Hugh absolution. He gave his handkerchief to the chief gaoler and his rosary, breviary, girdle, spectacles, and other items to various Catholics looking on. He then addressed the crowd in a long discourse, occasionally interrupted by some ministers of religion anxious for a learned disputation. Hugh pointed out that he died for his religion and his priesthood.

He stayed hanging for a time but was still alive, if stunned, for a time when he was cut down. He regained his senses while being dismembered, felt his disclosed bowels with his left hand, and made the sign of the cross with the right, crying three times: "Jesu, Jesu, Jesu, mercy!" Mrs Willoughby, a Catholic who visited priests in prison, kept her hand on his forehead, for Hugh lived for half an hour throughout the barbarous procedure of quartering. Eventually another woman went to the sheriff, her uncle's steward, to plead for mercy. The sheriff ordered the martyr's throat to be cut and his head struck off. His heart was put on a lance, shown to the crowd, then flung into the flames. It is said to have rolled out of the fire and to have been carried off by a bystander. The fanatical Puritans present (Dorchester was a stronghold of the faction) danced around the priest's mangled remains. Later the two Catholic ladies asked a sympathetic Protestant woman to wrap the quarters in a shroud; she did so and and buried them near the gallows. The mob played football with the martyr's head and then buried it near the body with sticks in the apertures.

Hugh died when fifty-seven, on 10 August 1642. He was beatified in 1929.

See De Marsys, *De la Mort Glorieuse de Plusieurs Prestres* (1645), pp. 86–93; Elizabeth Willoughby, in *Palmae Cleri Anglicani* (1645); *M.M.P.*, pp. 421–8; Gillow, 3, pp. 118–24. Mrs Willoughby's lengthy account of Hugh's speech and of the martyrdom, from which most of the above details are taken, is gory but an important contemporary source for knowledge of how martyrs, crowds, and especially attendant Catholics behaved during the Parliament.

Bd Ezekiel Moreno Diaz, *Bishop* (1848–1906)

Ezequiel Moreno Diaz was born at Alafaro (Logroño) in Spain on 9 April 1848. In 1868 he became an Augustinian and a missionary in the Philippines, where he was ordained priest in 1871. He was a zealous and indefatigable worker wherever he exercised his ministry: at Manila, on Palawan Island, and at Imus, then at the novitiate of Monteagudo (Navarre). He reorganized the order at Candelaria, Colombia, where he became first vicar apostolic of Casanare and later bishop of Pasto. He was noted not only for his spiritual counsel and as a confessor but for his readiness to help the sick at any hour of day or night. After much suffering he died in Madrid on 19 August 1906. He was beatified on 1 November 1975 and is proposed as an example of episcopal holiness, of pastoral love and of readiness to devote his life entirely to the service of his diocese.

N.S.B. 2, p. 131.

R.M.

St Magnus of Fabrateria, martyr at S. Giovanni in Carico (third century)
St Maginus, martyr in Tarragon (? third-fourth century)
St Timothy, martyr at Gaza (*c.* 305)
St Elaphius, bishop of Châlons (*c.* 580)
St Credan, abbot of Evesham (after 780)
St Bartholomew, abbot, at Grottaferrata in Calabria (1130)
Bd Guerricus, abbot of Igny (1151 or 1157)
Bd Leo, abbot in Campania (1295)
Bd Angelus the Hermit, in Ancona (1373)
BB Fifteen Martyrs of Nagasaki (1622; beatified 1967): Ludovic Frarjin or Flores, Dominican priest; Peter de Zúñiga, O.E.S.A, priest; Joachim Firaiana; Leo Sukemenion; John Foiamon; Michael Díaz; Mark Takenascika Xineiemon; Thomas Coianaghi; Antony Yamanda; James Matsuwo Densci; Laurence Rocuceman; Paul Sanchiki; John Yengo; Bartholomew Mafioie; and John Matasaki Nangata. Three of them were burned alive; the others were beheaded. See "The Martyrs of Japan," 6 Feb.

20

ST BERNARD, *Abbot and Doctor* (1090-1153)

Bernard, the "last of the Fathers," is one of the great figures of Western Christianity. He is also one of the few saints—Augustine (28 Aug.) is another—who has left such detailed and revealing, even if enhanced and rehandled, records of his personality and actions that several lifetimes could be—indeed are—spent discussing yet never exhausting them and trying to separate possible fact from certain exaggeration. There are, indeed, several Bernards and pseudo-Bernards, which makes him misty and even mysterious in some respects. From these accounts or, rather, interpretations there emerges a person of considerable intellect, unremitting conviction, profound devotion, wide human sympathies, and, it seems, great irritability. He could be very pushy, dominative, and angry; but as often tender-hearted or contrite. He was a very popular thaumaturge: a star with real charisma. He had an unusual ability to move others and to persuade them to act. He expressed himself in a versatile prose style ranging, at one extreme, from gentle to barbed irony and, at another, from lucid to lyrical piety. He identified himself with the vitality of the Cistercian Order, which spread rapidly under his influence in the twelfth century, yet did so by maintaining Bernard's insistence on compassion and self-denial, on preaching and worship, and on *oratio ignata*—prayer fired by love. He prized above all "a pure heart and unfeigned faith which leads us to love our neighbours' good as well as our own.... Charity alone can turn the heart from love of self and the world and direct it to God alone. Neither fear nor love of self can turn the soul to God; they may sometimes change the aspect or influence the actions of a person, but they will never change his or her heart" (*Letters*, p. 43).

Bernard was born to aristocratic parents at Fontaines, a castle near Dijon in France, in 1090. The world he entered was rapidly changing in ideas, systems of rule, and economy, and throughout Europe the nobles were testing the limits of their sovereigns' power. The Church was developing too, and the Gregorian reforms were beginning to take effect, yet there was a persistent spread of popular movements that opposed a centralized authority and rigorous church laws and concepts and were therefore technically or actually heretical. Bernard's father was Tescelin Sorrel, one of the ancient Chevaliers de Châtillon, with feudal lordships in Burgundy and Champagne. Aleth, his mother, was related to the dukes of Burgundy. Bernard was one of seven children whom she dedicated to God at birth: Bd Guy, Bd Gerard (13 June), Bernard, Bd Humbeline (21 Aug.), Andrew, Bartholomew, and Bd Nivard.

Bernard studied under secular canons at Châtillon on the Seine. His mother died when he was seventeen, and for some time he suffered from depression as a result.

In 1112 he was received into the monastery of Cîteaux—the first of the strict Benedictine observance therefore known as "Cistercian." It was relatively poor and austere, yet not so unimportant and moribund as Bernard's biographers would have us believe. He was accompanied by thirty-one other young Burgundian noblemen, including some of his brothers and an uncle. The house had been established by Robert of Molesme to follow the Rule of St Benedict (11 July) in its full simplicity. In 1115 St Stephen Harding (17 Apr.), the abbot, asked Bernard to find a site for a new monastery. Together with twelve monks, he founded a house at Clairvaux, which became one of the main Cistercian centres. William of Champeaux, bishop of Châlons-sur-Marne, installed Bernard as abbot and became a close friend. Bernard ran the house on severely reformed lines, though before long his monks became discouraged and he had to relax his initially strict régime, especially the harsh diet of coarse barley and even boiled beech leaves. In 1117 his aged father and his youngest brother, Nivard, joined the others. Many foundations were made from Clairvaux, including some as far away as Rievaulx in Yorkshire (1132) and Mellifont in Co. Louth, Ireland (1142).

Bernard was soon a great influence on monasticism and Christianity throughout Europe, not only ideologically, in ethics and monastic discipline, but in areas such as architecture. He opposed the cult of images, which by then were often odd and complex, and fulminated against "that beauty rooted in deformity and that deformity which aspires to beauty." He banned the variegated patterns of the Romanesque baroque and Cluniac refinements. He recommended manuscripts with an austere iconography and the building of ascetic churches without stone towers or externally projecting chapels but with plain glass, restrained foliage on the capitals, and a simple 2:1 ratio of the nave to the aisles.

As his reputation grew he became an adviser to bishops and other leading ecclesiastics, a role which he obviously enjoyed. He was very often on the road but sufficiently confident to refuse even papal invitations if he thought them unnecessary. He was a superb letter writer, one of the best of all time. He conducted an immense and directive correspondence with people of various ranks, including the pope and the king of France, but also with quite unimportant persons. Bernard's letters might be said to play the same part in our understanding of him as the *Confessions* in our picture of Augustine. In them he speaks directly to us through all the darkness and noise of the centuries in between. They sometimes seem too long and over burdened with scriptural citations and tricks of style, such as inversion, paradox, and alliteration, and too mannered for modern taste, even in Latin and certainly in English. But Bernard is a master of metaphor. The point of each letter is always clear, and the sometimes subtle emphases accompanying it depend on the stylistic devices. He asks his nephew, enticed to Cluny: "If warm and comfortable furs, if fine and precious cloth, if long sleeves and ample hoods, if dainty coverlets and soft woollen shirts make a saint, why do I delay and not follow you at once?" (*Letters*, p. 8). He reminds the new bishop of Geneva: "The bishop's throne for which you, my dear friend, were lately chosen, demands many virtues, none of which, I grieve to say, could be discerned in you, at any rate in any strength, before your consecration" (p. 62). When he hears he has been criticized in Rome, he tells the chancellor of the Holy See to "bid the noisy and importunate frogs to keep to their holes and remain contented with their ponds" (p. 81). He advises a nun who wants to leave her convent: "If you are one of the foolish virgins, the convent is necessary for you. If you are one of the wise, you are necessary for the convent" (p. 180). He censures the gluttony of the Cluniacs with a list of their little treats that seems too long—until we realize that he is suggesting that the monks have turned themselves into tasty dishes: "Who can count in how many ways eggs alone are prepared and dressed, how diligently they are broken, beaten to froth, hard-boiled, minced; they come to table now fried, now roasted, now stuffed, now mixed with other things, now alone" (*P.L.*, 182, 209). He asks the archbishop of Sens if he thinks everyone is as lacking in any sense of justice as he is. He lashes, consoles, admires, inspires, asks forgiveness. Bernard said that he never left a letter unanswered, whoever the correspondent was. He dictated more than one letter at a time and needed more than one secretary for what was something like the work of a prominent secretary of state busy on the international scene. He was not afraid to expose wickedness and condemn stupidity in even the great and powerful—in cardinals, abbots, the members of the Curia—and meanness and narrow-mindedness in anyone. Though people often heeded his rebukes, some resented them.

In 1128 Bernard was secretary to the synod of Troyes and supported the recognition there of the Rules (which he possibly composed) of the Order of Knights Templar, founded as ecclesiastical Crusader knights and to look after pilgrims and the sick. After the death of Pope Honorius II in 1130, he became prominent in public, indeed, world affairs. He was concerned with a number of disputes abroad, especially that about the succession to the see of York (see St William of York; 8 June). He was firmly on the side of Innocent II against the antipope Anacletus (Peter Leonis). He travelled throughout Europe encouraging and threatening anyone important who vacillated in this time of crisis for the Church. As accuser and arbitrator, he was at the diet of Bamberg in 1135, then at Milan. He alone stood up to the emperor Lothair, who wanted the right of investiture from Innocent in return for his support. Bernard publicly criticized Lothair in front of his bishops and defeated any opposition. Soon the Church as a whole was on the pope's side. Grateful for his triumph over Anacletus, the pope granted the Cistercian Order unusual privileges. In 1145 one of Bernard's pupils, a Cistercian monk, became pope as Eugenius III, and Bernard's influence was even stronger.

Throughout all this Bernard was not only directing his own community but overseeing many other establishments. During the schism period twenty foundations were made from Clairvaux alone. He suffered constantly from ill health, from digestive trouble, and from what may have been a gastric ulcer.

Bernard was also a fierce critic of what he thought was dangerous error. He fiercely pursued, engaged in written and oral controversy with, and condemned Abelard at the Council of Sens in 1140. He produced the short work *Against some Errors of Abelard*, which unfairly attacks what Bernard saw as the substitution of mere dialectics and judgment for the due fusion of reason and faith. Yet many modern scholars have assessed Abelard's dialectics as the foundation of the Scholastic method. He was certainly no heretic. The truth is that Bernard, who thought there was "much more to be found in the book of nature than in dry tomes" ("*Aliquid amplies invenies in silvis quam in libris*"), was a very different person from his opponent. He had a mystical sensibility and an allegorical understanding almost totally removed from what he saw as the "hydra-headed" Abelard's "running riot with a whole crop of sacrileges and errors." The trouble with Abelard was that he was not Bernard, for whom the "sweetness" of God was to be "tasted" and "felt" and who saw his opponent as a rationalist—discursive, scientific, and essentially secular, neither inwardly enlightened nor fired by mystery: he lacked vision. Abelard summed it up when he told Héloïse, somewhat ruefully: "The world hates me for my logic." Bernard was similarly fierce in his pursuit of the interestingly speculative theologian Gilbert de la Porrée, bishop of Poitiers, whom he attacked at the Council of Reims in 1148. The general opinion, on this occasion, was that Bernard had abused his prestige.

Bernard's help was also enlisted against heretics. Everwin of Steinfeld called him to Cologne to preach against a group of near-Albigensians. In 1145, in response to a request from the papal legate, Cardinal Alberic, Bernard strongly opposed the heretical doctrines of the monk Henry of Lausanne in the Languedoc, who rejected ecclesiastical authority and dreamed of a "purely spiritual" Church. He preached an exhausting campaign against the Cathars (see St Dominic, 8 Aug.), meeting with considerable resistance, especially in Toulouse and Albi. Nevertheless, he was easily satisfied that he had restored the whole country to orthodoxy. This was a total illusion. Twenty-five years later, as Dominic discovered, Catharism was stronger there than ever.

On Christmas Day 1444 the Turks captured Edessa, one of the four principalities of the Latin kingdom of Jerusalem, which appealed to Europe for help. Pope Eugenius persuaded Bernard to preach the Second Crusade. He started at Vézelay on Palm Sunday 1146, and the response was immensely enthusiastic. He wrote to the rulers of western and central Europe and went in person to Germany to preach there. First he had to deal with an ill-educated and fanatical but successfully rabble-rousing monk named Raoul (or Rudolf), who was wandering about the Rhineland. He quoted Bernard's name in an anti-Semitic campaign that included inciting people to massacre Jews before setting off on the Crusade itself. Bernard abhorred the Christian persecution of the Jews, which had become murderous on several occasions since the First Crusade. He condemned Raoul, did all he could to protect the Jews who were threatened, and wrote to influential people such as Archbishop Henry of Mainz with his judgment of the situation: "I find three things most reprehensible in [Raoul]: unauthorized preaching, contempt for episcopal authority, and incitation to murder. . . . Is it not a far better triumph for the Church to convince and convert the Jews than to put them all to the sword? . . . Otherwise where does that saying come in, 'Not for their destruction I pray,' and 'When the fullness of the Gentiles shall have come in, then all Israel will be saved'? . . . Who is this man that he should render void the treasures of Christ's love and pity? . . . What horrid learning, what hellish wisdom is his! A learning contrary to the prophets, hostile to the apostles, and subversive of piety and grace. It is a foul heresy." He wrote in similar vein to the English nation and to the archbishops, bishops, and all the clergy of eastern France and Bavaria: "The Jews are not to be persecuted, killed or even put to flight. . . . The Jews are for us the living words of Scripture. . . . We are told by the Apostle that when the time is ripe all Israel shall be saved. . . . It is an act of Christian piety both to 'vanquish the proud' and also to 'spare the subjected,' especially those for whom we have a law and a promise, and whose flesh was shared by Christ whose name be for ever blessed" (*Letters*, pp. 460-6).

The emperor Conrad III took the cross from Bernard and set out in May 1147, followed by Louis of France. But Conrad's forces were defeated in Asia Minor, and Louis did not get beyond laying siege to Damascus. The Crusaders themselves were partly responsible for this. Many of them thought only of plunder, were lawless, and committed crimes of disorder and destruction on the march. Bernard was deeply disappointed. The Crusade failed completely. He was not responsible for this, but those who disliked and were jealous of him blamed him for the disaster.

Bernard was a good theologian, a sharp controversialist, and an eloquent yet controlled preacher—though for the most part only in written form. He was well acquainted with Augustine, Ambrose (7 Dec.), Gregory the Great (3 Sept.), Origen, and some of the Eastern Fathers and other writers of the mystical tradition, probably even Pseudo-Dionysius. He had an exceptionally detailed knowledge and acute understanding of the Bible. Works such as *The Degrees of Humility and Pride* (*c*. 1124), *Apologia to William of St Thierry* (*c*. 1124), *On the Commandment and the Dispensation* (*c*. 1143), and the five volumes of *De Consideratione*, which he wrote for Pope Eugenius' guidance, are essentially biblical in inspiration and in their message of the threefold way of love, humility, and freedom:

What is God? He is length, breadth, height, depth. . . . Length is eternity, which is so long that it knows no limits in time or space. Breadth is love, and God's love knows no bounds, for he hates nothing that he has created. . . .

197

Height is the power of God and depth is his wisdom. They are exactly balanced, since God's elevation is as inaccessible as his profundity cannot be plumbed. . . . Is it possible to burn with greater fervour than in meditating on his love? Can we show more patience and perseverance in love than in whole-hearted longing for this everlasting love? Yes, our perseverance is a kind of prefiguration of this eternity. It is the sole virtue that will be granted eternity, or rather that will allow human beings that state of eternity which they have lost" (15, 27-31).

Bernard was also a profound mystic, but in the tradition of affective or intuitive allegory and deductive meditation. For him, contemplation leads to action and thus nourishes the Church. His *De Diligendo Deo* (On Loving God; 1126-41) concentrates on the thesis that God is to be loved simply because he is God, a theme that runs through his works: "There are those who praise the Lord because he is powerful, and these are slaves and fearful for themselves; there are those who praise him because he is good to them, and these are hirelings seeking themselves; and there are those who praise him because he is Goodness itself, and these are sons doing homage to their father" (*Letters*, p. 43). His *De gratia et libero arbitrio* (On Grace and Free Will) is one of the most convincing reconciliations of divine grace and human free will in the context of love. His eighty-six sermons on the Song of Songs—wonderfully resonant and rhythmical—are an original commentary stressing the joint contributions of reason and faith to love in action, and the expression of the eternal word and wisdom reflected in each individual, who is responsible for knowing, assessing, defining, and reducing his or her own particular distance from that ideal image. In this sense, like Augustine, Bernard emphasizes the importance of self-knowledge, which should prompt the aware person to emulate Jesus' own humility, selflessness, and compassion toward others until he or she understands more and more about the loving will of God "Divinization" means, then, our return to our true human nature: our remaking as the images of God that we were intended to be. Self-awareness and charity lead us ever closer to perfect harmony: to a state analogous to Christ's eternal nature, to the accordance of what we are with what we ought to be. Though his terminology is somewhat different and less confusing, Bernard's descriptions of this process have much in common with similar expositions by Eastern writers such as Maximus the Confessor (13 Aug.).

Bernard was also noted for his devotion to Mary, who, he said, was an aqueduct for the rivers of heaven flowing down to us. He called himself "*Beatae Mariae capellanus*" (Our Lady's faithful chaplain), and he was known as "*citharista Mariae*" (Mary's harper). A measure of Bernard's (or of pseudo-Bernard's) importance in this respect is Dante's choice of him as his final guide and patron in his journey through the extra-mundane dimension to eternity. Bernard's prayer to Mary obtains for Dante the divine vision with which the *Paradiso* ends, and Bernard is chosen as the culmination of all the poets and sages of antiquity when he utters the fundamental paradox and the key to disclosure of ultimate truth: the daughter has conceived the Father and borne Him as her son: "*Vergine madre, figlia del tuo figlio*" (Virgin mother, daughter of your son). Bernard's conception of Mary is in the tradition of the Song of Songs. For him, woman in the figure of Mary remains the dispenser of joyous love, but now it is love wholly spiritualized; love, that is, which does not reject or spurn but takes up into itself all human joy. Mary is womanhood fully realized: that element in the divine dispensation which softens and restrains judgment and makes it amenable to us. She prevents her Son from judging us duly by showing him her maternal breasts. Ultimately, Bernard's Mary may be seen as feminine power invading and suffusing not only the cosmos but our conceptualization of the deity, in something like the sense of the unconscious, or *anima*, as described by Jung (see The Assumption; 15 Aug.). On the other hand, Bernard, it is often said, did not accept the Immaculate Conception (8 Dec.) but celebrated Mary's "maternal virginity." There has been much argument about exactly what he accepted and rejected in this respect. Some commentators think he would not have agreed with the nineteenth-century definition; others believe he was essentially of the same mind. On the whole, the "Marian Bernard" has been much exaggerated, largely on the basis of works falsely attributed to him and of unusually fanciful (if iconographically intriguing) legends.

It might be thought that the writings, ecclesiastical and political statesmanship, monastic foundations, and similar activities of Bernard were a sufficient basis for his great reputation in his lifetime and afterwards. Nevertheless, it depended to a great exent not only on the miracles ascribed to him but on the cures expected from him. Bernard's work as a faith healer is one of the most fascinating aspects of his life (or of his life as reported to us, which is equally important in this respect). Many detailed descriptions of these phenomena have survived and constitute one of the main sources for the study of their function in twelfth-century religious and general culture and in the later reception of the saint, in which they play a very important part. In spite of the obviously partisan credulity of the authors of the *Vita Secunda* (by Alain d'Auxerre, *c*. 1170); the *Vita Tertia* (by Jean l'Ermite, *c*. 1180); the *Book of the Miracles of St Bernard* (by Herbert, a monk of Clairvaux, *c*. 1178); the *Great Exordium* of the Order of Cîteaux (by Conrad of Eberbach); and the *Dialogues* (by Caesar of Heisterbach), a reductive scrutiny of the accounts reveals Bernard not as a quaint magician but as *philanthropos*—a truly loving person.

As with many saints, Bernard's miracles occurred *in via*, when he was on the road. It is difficult to grasp just how popular he was—to many people he was something like Mahatma Gandhi, the Dalai Lama, and Mother Teresa rolled into one. Once this reputation was established, he could not escape it. It was often an immense embarrassment, which he at first bore patiently, then came to welcome. When he was travelling in Germany, for instance, in 1146-7, the sick and maimed lined the roads in many places. They blocked the entrances and exits to built-up areas and begged pitifully for his help. Outside and inside churches where he prayed or celebrated Mass, similar crowds confronted him before and after worship. At places where he lodged, "consultation times" had to be organized so that those seeking a cure could be admitted in an orderly fashion. When he began his German tour, they filled several fields outside Binche. At Schaffhausen he had to stop blessing the sick and flee, as there was almost a riot. The crowd besieged and threatened the episcopal palace in Cologne when he was staying there. All traffic was stopped. Eventually a compromise was reached: he had to stand at a window, and selected petitioners were allowed up a ladder one by one for a blessing. In desperation, after supper he went out to bless the crowd as a whole but could scarcely get back inside; that he stayed alive was, Philip the archdeacon remarks wryly, the greatest miracle of all. At Maastricht he had to bless the crowd from a hill outside the town. They lay in wait for him everywhere, and different techniques had to be adopted. Sometimes he would confine himself to those recommended to him by others, or he would pick out those who caught his eye and bless them individually. Sometimes he would lay his hands on them. If several organs were affected, he would bless each part separately. Occasionally he anointed people. At Clairvaux and elsewhere there was also a constant demand for Bernard to bless loaves and wine brought by the sick or their friends and relatives; they were then considered to be prime medicines for fever, mental illness, and other maladies. Bernard modelled his curative practice on Christ's and insisted on the role of the patient's faith in any cure effected (he reproved Bishop Anselm of Havelberg in this respect when asked to heal his sore throat in 1147). This, as his biographers record, distinguished him from most other saintly thaumaturges of the period whose personal virtue was seen as the source of the cure. If we are to believe his biographers, Bernard also had the disconcerting habit of declaring exactly who would be cured.

Bernard's last illness began early in 1153. He improved a little in the spring. The inhabitants of Metz had been attacked by the duke of Lorraine and were seeking revenge. The archbishop of Trier went to Clairvaux to beg Bernard to go to Metz to reconcile the warring parties. He travelled to Lorraine and made both sides lay down their arms. They had to accept a treaty he had drawn up. He then returned to Clairvaux, where his illness attacked him again. There were about four hundred Cistercian houses throughout Europe and seven hundred monks at Clairvaux when Bernard died there on 20 August 1153. He was canonized in 1174. In 1830 he was formally declared a Doctor of the Church, although he had been recognized as such for centuries.

For the original works see the edition by J. Leclercq, C. H. Talbot, and H. M. Rochais (1957-75); Eng. trans. in Cistercian Fathers series (1970ff.); *On the Love of God*, Eng. trans., T. L. Connolly (1937); *Of Conversion*, Eng. trans., W. Williams (1938); *The Twelve Degrees*, Eng. trans., B. R. V. Mills (1929); *Concerning Grace and Freewill*, Eng. trans., W.

Williams (1920); *The Letters of St Bernard of Clairvaux*, Eng. trans., B. Scott James (1953); *On the Song of Songs*, Eng. trans., K. Walsh (1979). There is a selection of his letters in J. Cumming (ed.), *Letters from Saints to Sinners* (1995). See the contemporary Lives in the edition of works by J. Mabillon, 2 vols. (1667); *A.A.SS.*, Aug., 4, pp. 101-368; *Vita Prima*, Eng. trans., G. Webb and A. Walker (1960). At least three people—William of St Thierry, Arnaud de Bonneval, and Geoffroy d'Auxerre—worked on this prime source, making it very much an interpretation of Bernard. See also *D.T.C.*, 2 (1905), 761-84; *D.H.G.E.*, 8 (1935), 610-44; E. Vacandard, *Saint Bernard*, 2 vols. (1895). Modern Lives by W. W. Williams (1935); B. Scott James (1957); H. Daniel-Rops (1962); I. Vallery-Radot (1963); J. Leclercq (2d ed., 1966); P. Riché (1989); J. Berlioz (1990); and B. P. Maguire's usefully sceptical *The Difficult Saint* (1991). On aspects of his life and works see W. W. Williams, *Studies in St Bernard of Clairvaux* (1927); E. Gilson, *The Mystical Theology of St Bernard* (1940); J. Leclercq, *Etudes sur Saint Bernard et ses écrits* (1953); *idem*, *Recueil d'etudes sur St Bernard et ses écrits* (1962); *Saint Bernard théologien* (the Dijon Congress papers; 1953); Commission d'histoire de l'ordre de Cîteaux, pref. T. Merton, *Bernard de Clairvaux*, 3 (1953); A. H. Bredero, *Bernard of Clairvaux between Cult and History* (1996); B. Ward (ed.), *The Influence of Saint Bernard* (1976); G. R. Evans, *The Mind of St Bernard of Clairvaux* (1983); P.-A. Sigal, *L'homme et le miracle dans la France médiévale* (1985), pp. 18-35 and *passim*. On the iconography see J. Marillier, *Iconographie de Saint Bernard* (1949); P. Quarré, *L'iconographie de Saint Bernard de Clairvaux et l'enigme et l'origine de la Vera Effigies* (1953).

Bernard has several attributes which symbolize his many virtues and actual and legendary achievements. The words *"Sustine et abstine"* ("Bear and forbear," from the Stoic Epictetus) may appear as his motto. He is often shown as a beardless young man but also with red hair and a red beard. He appears as a mitred abbot in the white Cistercian habit (*alba cuculla*) and with an abbatial cross. His main attributes are a beehive or honeycomb (which stands for his eloquence as *"Doctor mellifluus"*), the Host (which he offered to the duke of Aquitaine), a cross with the instruments of the passion on his heart (referring to his writings), a chained dragon or demon (to indicate his defeat of heresy), a wheel (which he compelled a demon to repair), and one to three mitres at his feet (to represent his humility in refusing an archbishopric or three bishoprics). He usually carries a book or a pen, or both (to indicate that he is worthy to be a Doctor of the Church). There are many legends of St Bernard. Among the most important are those which involve appearances of Christ or Mary, and many encounters with demons or the devil. Perhaps the most bizarre is the occasion when he forced the devil to reveal the nine verses of the psalms which, when recited every day, would guarantee entry to Paradise.

Bernard promoted an architecture which allied ethics and asceticism and whose space and bare stones expressed the Cistercian ethos of *"sobria ebrietas"*: fervent sobriety and detachment, poverty, and simplicity. He was an enemy of art in the conventional sense, of fun, elaboration and imagination, and especially of sculpture and ornamentation, pernicious luxuries forbidden in Cistercian churches, yet he is one of the saints most often portrayed by artists. There is no portrait from the life. Among the earliest images are twelfth-century miniatures from Cistercian monasteries, *e.g.*, Mount St Bernard in England, Heiligenkreuz and Zwettl in Austria; a thirteenth-century mosaic from St Petronilla's chapel (now in the Vatican); a fourteenth-century retable from a Templar chapel (Museo Arqueológico, Palma de Mallorca); a fourteenth-century frontal showing Bernard avidly responding to the "miracle of lactation" when our Lady is said to have fed him with a stream of milk from her breast (Museo Luliana, Mallorca). One of the most elaborate representations is *St Bernard's Vision of the Virgin* by Filippino Lippi (1457-1504) (1486; Badia church, Florence, Italy), which shows the saint at a writing slope in a rocky landscape; he is contemplating a visitation of Our Lady with angels. Another fifteenth-century version of the same appearance is Orcagna's (Academia, Florence). Pietro Perugino's (1445-1523) *Vision of St Bernard* portrays him as reverentially contemplative at his desk. Bernard's devotion to Mary made him especially popular among Counter-Reformation artists. Zurbarán shows him as straightforwardly serene, in his habit, and with book and crozier (1641-58; Monastery of St Camillus de Lellis, Lima, Peru). A typically exaggerated seventeenth-century painting by Murillo shows the Virgin pressing her nipple to feed the saint (Prado, Madrid). Only photographs and part-copies survive of a splendid ceiling by Tiepolo of the apotheosis of Bernard (sacristy of S. Ambrosio, Milan, destroyed in 1944).

St Oswin, *Martyr* (651)

When his father, Osric, king of Deira, was killed by the British pagan king Cadwallon in 633, the young Oswin was taken to Wessex for safety. He was baptized and educated there. St Oswald (9 Aug.) ruled Deira and Bernicia as one kingdom. After Oswald's death in battle in 642 Oswin returned (*c.* 644) to take possession of Deira, whereas Bernicia, the northern part of Northumbria, was ruled by Oswald's brother, Oswy. Oswin is said to have been a courteous and humble man and a prudent and much-loved ruler: "He was generous to high and low alike and soon won the affection of everyone by his regal qualities of mind and body, so that nobles came from every province to serve him. But among his other special endowments of virtue and moderation, the greatest was what one may describe as the singular blessing of humility" (Bede). We are told that he criticized St Aidan (31 Aug.) for letting a beggar have a horse which the king had given him. Aidan said: "Is this foal of a mare more valuable to you than the Son of God?" Oswin later knelt at Aidan's feet and apologized. The bishop was so moved that he wept and told his attendants in Irish (incomprehensible to the king and courtiers) that a king as humble and good as that would not live long because the nation was not worthy of him.

Oswy declared a state of open warfare out of, it is said, jealousy of Oswin, who, finding his own forces outnumbered, eventually dismissed them at Wilfaresdon, near Catterick. The motive was perhaps a mixture of prudence and fear of too great a loss of life. Oswin and a loyal thegn withdrew to Gilling, near Richmond in Yorkshire, an estate which he had given to his good friend Hunswald not long before. Oswy ordered his reeve, Ethelwin, to find Oswin and kill him. Hunwald betrayed his guest; Oswin and his thegn were killed together; they were buried at Gilling. To expiate his crime, Oswy and his wife, Queen Eanfleda, daughter of St Edwin (12 Oct.), founded a monastery at Gilling, where prayers were to be offered for both kings in perpetuity. It was later destroyed by the Danes. Before that, Oswin's body was translated to Tynemouth but lost sight of until it was rediscovered in 1065 by a monk (who, he said, had learned of its whereabouts in a vision). It was re-enshrined in 1100. Oswin was traditionally venerated as a martyr for the cause of justice.

See Bede, *H.E.*, 3, 14; Stanton, *Menology*, pp. 401-3; *B.T.A.*, 3, pp. 366-7.

St Philibert, *Abbot* (*c.* 608-85)

Philibert was born in Gascony, France. His father, Philibaud, received Holy Orders and was made bishop of Aire. He was educated under his father's supervision and then sent to the court of Dagobert I. He was impressed by the chancellor, St Audoenus (24 Aug.), founder of the abbey of Rebais, which Philibert entered at the age of twenty. He was appointed abbot after St Aile but was too inexperienced to deal with the uncooperative monks. He made a tour of monasteries to study various observances and eventually withdrew to Neustria. Clovis II gave him some land there in the forest of Jumièges, where he founded a monastery in 654. The community increased rapidly, and he also built a nunnery at Pavilly.

When visiting the court, Philibert criticized Ebroin, mayor of the palace, for injustice. The reward was a slanderous report to Audoenus, which resulted in Philibert's imprisonment at Rouen and his expulsion from Jumièges afterwards. He retired to Poitiers and then to the island of Her (or Heriou) on the Poitou coast, where he founded a monastery later called Hermonasterium (now Noirmoutier). He also founded the priory of Quinçay, near Poitiers, which he put in the charge of St Aichardus (15 Sept.), whom he later made abbot of Jumièges. His responsibilities increased when Bishop Ansoald of Poitiers put a monastery he had founded at Luçon under Philibert's supervision. He was buried at Her, and his relics eventually reached Tournus.

The main source is the monk Ermentarius' ninth-century Life; Alcuin also mentions him. See *AA.SS.*, Aug., 4, pp 75-95; *M.G.H., Script. Rer. Meroving.*, 5 (1910), pp. 568-604; R. Poupardin, *Monuments de l'histoire des abbayes de Saint-Philibert* (1905); L. Jaud, *Saint-Philibert* (1910).

Bd Bernard Tolomei, *Abbot and Founder* (1272-1348)

Giovanni Tolomei was born at Siena in Italy in 1272. He was educated by his uncle, a Dominican, and at the local university. He was awarded a doctorate in law and became a local official in Siena. He was said always to have been devout but underwent some unusual religious experience. In 1312 he replaced a promised lecture on philosophy with a sermon on contempt of the world, resigned his position, withdrew to a place ten miles from the city, and lived there as a solitary. Two other Sienese, Ambrose Piccolomini and Patrick Patrizi, joined him, and they lived together in the desolate, grey countryside between Siena and the woods of Mont' Amiata. They were rumoured to be insane or subversive (which at that time usually meant they were thought to be Waldenses or Cathars), so they were ordered to appear before Pope John XXII, This involved a long and hazardous journey to the papal court at Avignon in France. The pope decided that their doctrine was orthodox but told them to follow an approved monastic Rule. When they returned to Italy, Bishop Guy of Arezzo gave them the Rule of St Benedict (11 July) and asked a Camaldolese monk to clothe them in the monastic habit, but white instead of the usual black.

Giovanni took the name Bernard and became abbot; their hermitage at Chiusuri was called Monte Oliveto, and the Benedictine Congregation of Our Lady of Monte Oliveto came into existence in 1319. The observance was "primitive," and certain austerities (including, at first, total abstinence from wine) were added to the original Rule. The Order was extraordinarily successful. Within a few years Bernard had founded a second monastery at Siena and others followed elsewhere. The penitential life attracted even more disciples, and in 1344 the Congregation was confirmed by Clement VI. Later a bad epidemic of plague broke out around Siena. The Olivetan monks devoted themselves to caring for the victims and burying the dead. They seemed miraculously preserved from contagion, but in August 1348 the first monk, Bernard himself, succumbed to the disease. He died at Monte Oliveto on 20 August.

In 1644 the cult of Bernard Tolomei was confirmed, and the Roman Martyrology records him as *beatus*. Nevertheless, the Olivetans, still a small independent Congregation of Benedictines, have always venerated him as "Saint."

AA.SS., Aug., 4; P. Lugano, *Origine e primordi dell' Ordine di Monteoliveto* (1903).

Bd Mary de Mattias, *Foundress* (1805-66)

Mary was born in 1805 at Vallecorsa, on the borders of Lazio and Campania in Italy. She was the eldest of four children of a lawyer.

In 1834 Mary was asked by Bishop Lais, administrator of Anagni, to take charge of a school at Acuto in the diocese. She decided not only to teach but to found a religious house. She welcomed her first recruit, Anna Farrotti, in 1835, and they committed themselves to the establishment of a Congregation on the model of del Bufalo's missioners.

Mary had a gift of straightforward and convincing speech. This she used to advantage in religious instruction and in the girls' and women's societies she organized. She also conducted spiritual exercises for mothers of families.

In 1840 a second school was taken over, under the auspices of the Missioners of the Precious Blood, in Mary's old home at Vallecorsa. Other foundations followed, and the work for adult women and girls was expanded. She died at Rome on 20 August 1866 in her sixty-first year, and she was beatified in 1950.

See the official Life by M. E. Pietromarchi (1850).

R.M.

St Maximus, in the fortress of Chinon, France (fifth century)

SS Leovigild and Christopher, martyrs at Córdoba, Spain (852)

SS John Yi and his Seven Companions, martyred at Seoul, Korea: John Yi, Rosa Kim, Martha Kim, Anna Kim, Teresa Kim (a widow), Magdalen Kim, Lucy Kim and Maria Wan (1839; canonized 6 May 1984)—see "The Martyrs of Korea," 21 Sept.

21

ST PIUS X, *Pope* (1835-1914)

Pius X is a controversial figure. His papacy would seem to have been divided between repressive and philistine measures that did vast and lasting harm to the intellectual life of the Church and encouraged much persecution and cruelty, and forward-looking internal reforms. As an individual he impressed many people with his kindness and simplicity, as expressed in his will: "I was born poor, I have lived poor, and I wish to die poor." He inspired great popular devotion.

Pius was born Giuseppe Melchior Sarto into a poor and eventually large family at Riese in upper Venetia, Italy, in 1835. He was the second of ten children. His father was the local postman, his mother a seamstress. Giuseppe entered the Padua seminary in 1850. His cultural and intellectual background was restricted, though not so minimal as suggested in the past. He lacked a university education. He was ordained priest at the age of twenty-three and became a hard-working chaplain at Tombolo in 1858. In 1867 he was appointed archpriest of Salzano. In 1875 he was made a canon of Treviso, the bishop's chancellor, and spiritual director of the episcopal seminary. In 1884 he was consecrated bishop of Mantua; he went there in 1885 and successfully revived a moribund diocese. In 1893 he was made cardinal and patriarch of Venice and won a reputation for simplicity, sincerity, and forthrightness. He refused to allow anyone but his sisters to cook for him. He called liberal Catholics "wolves in sheepskin" in his pastoral letters. He was never a Vatican diplomatist; his experience was almost entirely pastoral.

Sarto pleaded to be excused from the office when elected pope in 1903 after an attempt by the Austrian emperor to veto the strong votes in the first two scrutinies for Cardinal Rampolla, the previous pope's secretary of state, who was thought to be pro-Russian and to favour democratic ideas. In the next scrutiny Rampolla's vote increased further, but it decreased thereafter. The cardinal eventually withdrew his candidature, though under protest. In the seventh ballot Sarto received an overwhelming majority. He adopted the motto *"Instaurare omnia in Christo"* (To restore all things in Christ; Eph. 1:10). He told the Sacred College that he had chosen the name Pius in memory of the popes who had defended the Church's interests and "fought against sects and rampant errors." He made clear his intention to be a pope concerned more with religion than with politics. In November 1903 he appointed the English-educated Raffaele Merry del Val, an experienced Vatican diplomatist, his secretary of state, and made him a cardinal. In many respects, Pius remained as self-deprecating as before. He refused to follow the usual practice in conferring titles of nobility on his relatives. He disliked Vatican pomp. "Look how they have dressed me up," he said to an old friend, and burst into tears. To another he said: "It is certainly a penance to be forced to accept all these practices. They lead me about surrounded by soldiers like Jesus when he was seized in Gethsemane." In his inaugural encyclical, however, he demanded "for God's sake omnipotent power over man and beast." He was convinced that "the one hope, the one remedy" for a sick society was the pope, speaking of whom, "we must not quibble, but obey."

Those who had known Pius X before his election noted the decline in his previous serene and even jovial nature as supposed crises became actual ones. He was a reluctant actor in the political arena, but when he thought it necessary to enter it he spoke autocratically. In Italy he made no real change in the situation in which Catholics stood apart from political life as a result of the occupation of Rome in 1870, though in practice he relaxed the ruling of the Holy See that it was inexpedient for faithful Catholics to associate themselves publicly with the despoilers of the Papal States by voting in parliamentary elections; he allowed local bishops to recommend moderate liberal candidates if a socialist victory seemed possible. Pius repeatedly insisted that the laity had to follow the Church's instructions in politics.

In 1904 the French president returned a visit by the king of Italy, which had already evoked a church protest at what it considered formal recognition of Italian sovereignty over the city of Rome. Merry del Val sent a letter of protest, which was published in the French press. In July 1904 the French government withdrew its embassy staff from the Vatican and broke off diplomatic relations. In July 1905 France separated the Church from the State, thereby unilaterally denouncing the 1801 Concordat, and planned to set up *associations cultuelles*, or religious associations, responsible to the civil authority and in control of any remaining but now effectively confiscated church property and funds. In theory, these bodies would have allowed churches supervision of part of their possessions, paid the clergy, and provided for public worship; in fact, they prevented the ecclesiastical authorities from exercising any control over the associations. Though the French bishops were willing to accept this, especially since the separation allowed direct appointment of bishops by the Holy See without nomination by the civil power, Pius rejected any kind of compromise or even negotiation. In 1906 he issued two encyclicals, *Vehementer nos* and *Gravissimum*, which condemned the new organizations and protested against the abrogation of the Concordat as a violation of international law. Some French bishops offered to resign as a result of this intransigence. Twenty years later, however, the French government agreed to another arrangement for administering church property. Before then, in 1911, the Portuguese government introduced anti-ecclesiastical measures similar to those implemented in France. With regard to Portugal and Spain, Pius also risked a break in relations.

In his encyclical *Il fermo proposito* Pius established the principles of Catholic Action, which included social action, principles for solving the labour problem, and an emphasis on Christ in the home, schools, and society. For the most part, however, he was consistently anti-liberal in his pronouncements on political questions. He even opposed the political programme of an Italian youth movement led by Romolo Murri, which was trying to become a Catholic political party under the title Christian Democracy, and similar efforts on the part of Luigi Sturzo. In 1910 he condemned a French social movement of young Catholics founded by Marc Sangnier and known as the *Sillon,* which tried to identify Catholicism with political democracy; the pope affirmed that it was intent on spreading ideas derived from those of the French Revolution. Nevertheless, Pius X's encyclical *Singulari quidam* (1912), largely concerned to promote only denominational trade unions, allowed interdenominational trade unions under special local conditions. He later tried to condemn these too but was dissuaded by influential church people who told him that this would cause havoc in Germany, where both kinds were common. After complaints, Pius also toyed with the idea of condemning some aspects of the royalist, anti-Semitic, and right-extremist *Action Française* (which he approved of because "It advocates the principle of authority, it defends order"), such as the books of its agnostic leader, Charles Maurras, but this passing intention was not made public until after his death. He decided against any action because Maurras was a strong opponent of the Modernists, democrats, and anticlericals. The movement was eventually condemned by a decree of Pius XI in 1926. Pius X also risked relations with other countries by incidents such as those in 1910 when he insulted Luther and Protestantism in an encyclical commemorating St Charles Borromeo, which was released in Germany, and refused to grant the American president an audience unless he abandoned a visit to the Methodist congregation in Rome.

Pius X instigated the publication of new frameworks of study and conduct in seminaries and guidelines for the training of priests. In certain places, above all in southern Italy, regional seminaries were set up to help dioceses incapable of providing adequate facilities from their own resources. Rome reserved the right to appoint directors of studies and teachers to these foundations. This was both to ensure a supply of good instructors and to control the type of instruction.

Pius distrusted scholarship and science. He did not understand the reasons and need for biblical and theological research, which was a concept utterly beyond his comprehension. He had specialized in elementary catechesis and had written a very simple catechism for children (revised later and published throughout the world as *The Catechism of Pius X*); he conceived of theological studies along similarly direct and simple lines. Though he was unassuming himself and, for example, preached publicly on the day's Gospel in one of the Vatican courtyards every Sunday, he believed in the complete subordination of the clergy, as well as the laity, to ecclesiastical authority. Anything else was dangerous. In this respect he remained intransigent.

In the late nineteenth and early twentieth centuries the groundwork of liberal Protestant and unaffiliated—particularly German—scholars in papyrology, ancient history, history of religions, mythology, the study of biblical sources and manuscripts and of Christian sources and origins, comparative theology, church history and order, philosophy, and so on, was welcomed by a number of responsible and sometimes ingenious and imaginative Catholic experts and theologians. In some ways they advanced beyond critical Protestantism, for they were interested not so much in the origins as in the historical development of Christianity. For the most part liberal and anti-Scholastic, well aware of the critiques of Kant, Hume, and others that had undermined essentialist philosophy, apologetics, and fundamental theology, they rejected an infinite repetition of obfuscating or dead formulas in language both stale and sentimental and began to produce their own research and critical or speculative commentaries. The doyen of the school was the French layman Maurice Blondel (1861-1949), the author of *L'Action* (1893), who favoured not the "extrinsicism" of neo-Scholasticism but an experientially-based "immanentism" (phenomena and events in the world are explicable in terms of other phenomena and events in the world, but all human activity exhibits a longing for supernatural fulfillment). To superficial readers he also seemed to suggest that God is wholly or more apprehensible as immanent in the world, or more so as such than as transcendent to it. Blondel had a considerable influence on the seminarian who later became pope as John XXIII. The French exegete Alfred Loisy (1857-1940) has been seen as following Blondel, largely because his major work, *L'Evangile et l'Eglise* (The Gospel and the Church), was published in 1902. He was actually an independent thinker whose notion of the shifting nature of truth as dependent on context, and his adventurous application of the principles of German higher criticism to dogma in an attempt to define its symbolic and emblematic constituents, evoked the puzzlement of literally-minded seminarians and the uncomprehending fury of Pius X and the Roman Curia.

Other Modernists (the tendency was known at first as "New Catholicism") stressed the experiential nature of revelation, the meaning of history as lying in its issue rather than its origins, the symbolism of subsequent dogma and the need to live it in order to understand it, the ways in which the biblical authors were subject to the usual limitations of historians, and the Gospels not as historical documents but as expressing the developing beliefs of the first Christian generations. Not all the new theologians were gifted communicators; they expressed these ideas in language that was sometimes obscure and ambiguous, as happens when concepts are being developed. The new trends were especially evident in the newly-founded Catholic Institutes and faculties of theology in France. A vast amount of valuable scholarship was produced by people of the calibre of Père Lagrange at the School of Bible Studies in Jerusalem and the Abbés Duchesne and Loisy at the *Institut Catholique* in Paris. In Italy there was a strong connection between some theological innovators and attempts to develop forms of Christian democracy, either wholly apart from or in conjunction with secular liberalism. There was no concerted movement but a number of variously inspiring and, indeed, often conflicting discoveries and ideas, a sensitive probing which, to the uninformed, seemed offensive and willfully designed to upset the "simple faithful" by undermining the historical bases of scripture and doctrine.

Pius called these writers, lay and clerical, "thoroughly imbued with the poisonous doctrines taught by the enemies of the Church, and lost to all sense of modesty." He lumped all these tendencies together as what he called a "synthesis of all the heresies" under the pejorative collective term "Modernism," first used by him or his curial advisers in this acceptation and previously met with in English in such contexts as that of the conflict between medievalists and modernists in architecture (cf. *O.E.D*). This was an unknowingly perceptive identification of innovation in matters religious and ecclesiastical with not only the philosophical but the scientific, technological, philosophical, artistic, architectural, and to some extent political revolution then taking place, which is now also known as "modernism." Here, too, there was no definable alliance but a number of similarly tending, often overlapping trends, or "modernisms."

In so many areas people and society were moving from autocracy to democracy. The world was investigated no longer from a static but now from a moving point of reference. Two years after Pius was elected pope Einstein proposed simultaneity as the new point of view in science to replace Newton's restricted system. His and Max Planck's theory of the nature and behaviour of matter and energy stressed uncertainty as the characteristic principle of the operation of atoms and molecules; quanta are a feature of all radiation, and its spectral distribution is independent of all source material (quantum mechanics and quantum field theory). The notion of cause and effect in classical mechanics was too crude and inaccurate a principle of analysis for a universe that demanded a highly differentiated and sensitive system of exploration. A simultaneity of many different viewpoints was the equivalent mark of modernity in art, literature, music, and so on. Artists no longer studied space in relation to one viewpoint but examined it more thoroughly and variously. In music the diatonic system gave way to one in which each note enjoyed equal status. The nineteenth-century imitations of subordination to a dominant central feature or aspect that was the mark of the fixed baroque order gave way to an equivalence of subdivisions and elements, just as individuals rejected centralism, absolutism, manipulation, and unchanging authority. Fixed space became variable space-time.

The theologians castigated as "Modernists" can scarcely be said to have carried out a revolution in the most profound structures, the actual formal devices, of their specialisms as far-reaching as that of, say, the cubists, futurists, or constructivists, but they were on the way there. The foundations, in Tillich's words, were beginning to shake.

A few months after his election Pius, through the Holy Office, condemned five works of Loisy, whose students from the St Sulpice seminary had already been forbidden to attend his lectures and who had been dismissed. In subsequent years the Frenchmen Lucien Laberthonnière (1860-1932), Edouard Le Roy (1870-1954), and E. L. Mignot (1842-1918); the Anglo-Irish George Tyrrell, S.J., (1861-1909); the Italians Ernesto Buonaiuti (1881-1946), Antonio Fogazzaro (1842-1911), Romolo Murri (1870-1944), Salvatore Minocchi (1869-1943), and Giovanni Semeria (1867-1931); and many other less illustrious authors of equal good faith were affected. On 3 July 1907 Pius issued the encyclical *Lamentabili sane exitu*, which contained a syllabus of sixty-five Modernist errors that he unequivocally anathematized, and on 8 September 1907 another encyclical, *Pascendi dominici gregis*, condemning supposedly organized tendencies and ideas known as "Modernism." They were described as a system of thought designedly agnostic and immanentist and wholly opposed to Christian teaching. Disparate exegetical and theological ideas were represented as the programme of a conspiracy of which there was no evidence whatsoever in any of the writings concerned or anywhere else. Pius suggested that the contradictory nature of the opinions pilloried was an especially wicked device of the Modernists to hide the actual lines of their plot to destroy the Church. A direct connection was made between philosophical, theological, and biblical ideas and political standpoints deemed pernicious, such as the political independence of Catholics with regard to ecclesiastical authority.

Disciplinary measures followed. Teachers thought to promote the new heresy were dismissed from seminaries and universities. The leading clerical "conspirators" were excommunicated, but in general laymen such as Blondel and Friedrich von Hügel (1852-1925) were not. Many people submitted. Some joined other churches or became "independents." The lives of many were ruined. Central and local censorship was enforced. Modernist periodicals were compelled to cease publication. Many books, such as Duchesne's much-respected *Ancient Church History*, were put on the Index of Prohibited Books. Most of Lagrange's and many other suspect works were taken out of seminary and monastery libraries or placed in the closed-off *"enfer"* (hell) section for consultation only by the privileged few specifically commissioned to criticize them adversely (Lagrange himself was minimally rehabilitated later). Pressure groups were set up throughout the Church and official vigilance committees were established in every diocese to pursue suspected heretics. "Delation," or observing and reporting on suspect priests and religious, was encouraged. An unscrupulous ecclesiastical spy organization, the *Sodalicium pianum* (in memory of the inquisitor pope, St Pius V [30 Apr.], who excommunicated Elizabeth I of England), also known as SP, or *La Sapinière,* was established under the direction of Mgr Umberto Benigni. A wave of persecution and fear led eventually to a debilitating self-censorship. This took Catholic writing and preaching into a new dark ages in which persistent scholars had to engage in double-think and devise an equivocal language decipherable only by the similarly initiated. A *motu proprio, Sacrorum antistitum,* on 1 September 1910, introduced the anti-Modernist oath to be taken by all priests teaching theology and the ecclesiastical sciences and by all engaged in the pastoral ministry. After a time, under pressure from the German Church, it was not applied in the theological faculties of some German universities. The decree also prescribed the study of Thomist Scholasticism, which came to be thought of as the sole permissible method. It is not clear whether Pius himself, as opposed to the Holy Roman and Universal Inquisition, was aware of all the excesses and calumnies that his encyclicals provoked. Historians are divided on the subject. Some suggest that he became increasingly isolated from reality and the victim of higher ecclesiastics as well as of his own mentality. However, though he reprimanded some militant integralists, it has been shown (cf. Poulat) that he supported and encouraged Benigni, who sent daily reports to Pius and received orders to "make inquiries."

Pius X's attitude was certainly so contrary to the fundamentally innovatory tendencies of his time, so out of true with reality, as to prompt the supremely modernist French poet Apollinaire to declare him the first post-modernist (*avant la lettre*) in the ironic verses of *Zone* (1913), which became the main poem of his famous collection *Alcools*: "*L'Européen le plus moderne c'est vous Pape Pie X*" (You, Pope Pius X, are the most modern European). This summed up the views of all progressive circles. Ruefully, Raymond Queneau, the brilliant French novelist, poet, and mathematician, later recorded these words of Pius X in his journal: "Freedom of worship is a monstrous error, an insanity, a freedom of damnation, an error than which none can be more damaging to the Catholic Church and the salvation of souls. A disastrous and always deplorable heresy, a horrible system. Denominational freedom corrupts both mind and manners, protects the plague of indifference, and amounts to a real social crime."

Pius' actions, however, were far from exclusively negative. He abolished the right of Catholic sovereigns to veto the election to the papacy of any cardinal they did not approve of. With the help of the future Cardinal Gasparri, and after consulting the universal episcopate and the future Pius XII, Pius also codified the new canon law eventually issued under Benedict XV in 1917. He set up a commission to promote biblical studies primarily concerned with the revision and correction of the Vulgate text (or Latin translation) of the Bible, which was entrusted to the Benedictines, and encouraged daily reading of scripture. In 1909 he founded the Biblical Institute for scriptural studies in charge of the Jesuits. He made administrative changes in the Roman tribunals, offices, and congregations with the *motu proprio Arduum sane munus* of March 1904. With the constitution *Divino afflatu* of 1911 he introduced a reform of the Breviary that simplified and reduced its complexity and the demands it made on priests. He issued decrees on sacred music, most importantly the *motu proprio* of 1903 that restored Gregorian chant and sixteenth and seventeenth-century polyphony to predominance in the liturgy and almost eradicated the use of secular music during the Church's offices. His decree of 1905, *Acerbo nimis*, laid down guidelines for teaching Christian doctrine. His encyclical *Communium Rerum* of 1909 defined the standards of practice required of bishops. In 1905 he recommended frequent and even daily Communion, and a year later children's Communion. He made fasting less onerous for sick people. With the decree *Quam singulari*, on 8 August 1911, he lowered the age for first Communion to seven. All these reforms were considered revolutionary in his time, for previously the laity had received Communion scarcely more often than the stipulated minimum, defined in the Catechism as "once a year, and that at Easter or thereabouts."

Joseph Sarto had been noted for his charitable work as canon of Treviso and as bishop and patriarch. As Pius X his general charities in Rome and throughout the world were also exemplary. He denounced the ill treatment of indigenous workers on Peruvian rubber plantations and encouraged missions among native Peruvians. He sent a commission of relief after the Messina earthquake and sheltered victims at his own expense in the hospice of Santa Marta near St Peter's.

He is said to have made some efforts to stop the coming First World War. Some witnesses stated that he wrote to the Austrian emperor imploring him to prevent the declaration of war; others that when asked to bless the Austrian cause, he refused and threatened to excommunicate the emperor; yet others that, when asked to intervene on behalf of peace, he said: "The only monarch on whose behalf I would intervene is the Emperor and King Franz Josef, because he was always loyal to the Holy See." There is no primary written evidence for any of these incompatible statements, though Cardinal Merry del Val admitted telling the Austrian legate that "Austria had to stand firm." On 2 August 1914 Pius X issued an appeal to the Catholics of the world that expressed his personal sorrow at the rush toward conflict but it was ineffectual. This is said to have hastened his final illness. He developed bronchitis on 19 August 1914 and died the next day.

Pius X was venerated as a saint in his lifetime. Miracles were reported. A typical example was that of a man at a public audience who pointed to his paralyzed arm and said: "Cure me, Holy Father." The pope smiled, stroked his arm, and said, "Yes, yes." He is said to have been healed. Pius X was much respected, and his actions were supported by very many Catholics. Yet his successor, Benedict XV, who as Cardinal della Chiesa had been placed on the list of suspect Modernists, appreciated the harm done during Pius X's pontificate and soon tried to mitigate it by declaring that where there was no danger to faith or morals, and the Holy See had not yet formally decided a particular question, entirely free discussion was lawful and necessary. Yet the oath was still enforced, and "Modernism" remained a term of abuse for officially distasteful tendencies, which were attacked as such until the 1960s.

In 1923 the cardinals in Curia decreed the introduction of Pius X's cause. He was beatified in 1951 and canonized in 1954 by the centralizing Pope Pius XII, who admired his predecessor's unflinching insistence on the Church's prerogatives, defence of uniform thinking, and exaltation of the papal office. For his own part, Pius XII issued the encyclical *Humani generis* in 1950. This contained an intellectually ludicrous assertion of the truth of "monogenism" and the historical existence of Adam, and a condemnation of evolutionary theory and of leading (mainly French) theologians practising a mistily defined "new theology." All this accorded with the practice of Pius X. This approach was seriously modified only during the papacy of Pope John XXIII and the Second Vatican Council.

Acta Sanctae Sedis (1903-8); *A.A.S.* 2-7 (1909-14); *Letters*, ed. N. Vian (1955). See *D.T.C.*, 13 (pt. 2; 1935), 1716-40; R. Merry del Val, *Memories of Pope Pius X* (1939); Lives by R. Bazin (Eng. trans., 1928); K. Burton, *The Great Mantle* (1951); C. Ledré (1952); P. Fernessole, 2 vols. (1952-3); C. Maurras (1953); E. A. Forbes (2d ed., 1954); I. Giordani, *Pius X, A Country Priest* (1954); G. Dal Gal, *St Pius X* (Eng. trans., 1954); G. Papini, *The Popes in the Twentieth Century* (1967); J. D. Holmes, *The Papacy in the Modern World* (1981); D. Agasso, *L'ultimo papa santo—Pio X* (1985); *idem, Sulle orme di Pio X* (1986); G. Romanato, *Pio X. La vita di papa Sarto* (1992); E. Duffy, *Saints and Sinners: A History of the Papacy* (1997), pp. 245-54. See also G. Rivière, *Le Modernisme dans l'Église* (1929); A. Loisy, *Mémoires*, 3 vols. (1930-1); *Disquisitio circa quasdam obiectiones modum agendi servi Dei respicientes in modernismi debellatione* (1950); E. Poulat, *Intégrisme et catholicisme intégral. Un réseau secret international antimoderniste: la "Sapinière," 1909-21* (1969); P. Scoppola, *Crisi modernista et rinnovamento cattolico in Italia* (1969); P. Droulers, *Politique sociale et christianisme. Le père Desbuquois et l'Action populaire* (1969); A. R. Vidler, *A Variety of Catholic Modernists* (1970); R. Marlé (ed.), *Roman Catholic Modernists* (Eng. trans., 1970); T. M. Loome, *Liberal Catholicism, Reform Catholicism, Modernism* (1979); E. Poulat, *Histoire, dogme et politique dans la crise moderniste* (1979); G. Daly, *Transcendence and Immanence: A study in Catholic modernism and integralism* (1980); J.-M. Mayeur, *La Séparation des Eglises et de l'Etat* (1991). See also G. Tyrrell, *Medievalism: A Reply to Cardinal Mercier* (1908, rp. 1994); Jedin-Dolan, 9, pp. 381-523.

There are several portraits, other than photographs, of Pius X. None is of any artistic merit.

St Luxorius, *Martyr* (Fourth Century)

The unreliable Acts of Luxorius sound suspiciously like a fiction used to make a catechetical homily more amenable, yet he is retained in the new draft Roman Martyrology. His erstwhile boy companions in martyrdom, Cisellus and Camerinus, have been expunged from the entry.

Luxorius was a literate Roman soldier who was very impressed by the contents of a psalter he had read. He borrowed more books of scripture and learned the psalms and words of the prophets by heart. Eventually he was allowed to read the Gospels themselves. He was converted immediately, believed in Jesus Christ, and was baptized.

The Diocletian persecution began just then. Delphius the prefect enforced the imperial decrees in Sardinia, where Luxorius was stationed. The soldier was one of the first Christians to be brought before him at Forum Trajanum (now Fordingiano). Delphius ordered Luxorius to deny Christ, but he refused. He was tied to a post and scourged but sang psalms while he suffered, so the prefect had him put to the sword.

AA.SS., Aug., 4; *C.M.H.*, pp. 454-5.

St Sidonius Apollinaris, *Bishop* (*c*. 423-80)

Gaius Sollius Apollinaris Sidonius was a Gallo-Roman born into a noble family at Lyons in about 430. His father and grandfather had been prefects of the praetorium.

He managed not only to maintain but to raise his standing in spite of all the vicissitudes of the time, which he survived successfully and, a remarkable achievement in itself, honourably. As a result, we know much more about him than about many other saints of the period. He was not only politically and socially astute but a highly competent writer of occasional verse, that is, poems for the right person on the right occasion. This was scarcely a minor if not the major factor in ensuring his survival. He received a classical education at Arles and studied under Claudianus Mamertus of Vienne.

He married and had a son and three daughters by Papianilla, daughter of Avitus, who brought him the estate of Avitacum in the Auvergne. Avitus, chosen by the aristocracy of Gaul, became emperor in July 455. Sidonius went to Rome with the emperor and on 1 January 456 recited a verse panegyric in his honour (in the manner of Claudian, which he kept to thereafter). A statue of Sidonius was erected among the poets in the Forum of Trajan as a reward for this service. Sidonius was the kind of person who attracted recognition of this type during and after his lifetime.

Not long afterwards Avitus was deposed, and Sidonius took part in a revolt on behalf of his father-in-law, which was centred on Lyons. This was a bad choice, for the insurrection failed, and, in the way of things, we would expect Sidonius to have disappeared from history as a result. Eventually, however, he gained the favour of the new emperor, Majorian, and in 458, at Lyons, recited a panegyric in his praise. This won him a post in the civil service at Rome, which he took up in 459 or 460. In 461 Majorian was killed by Ricimer the Goth, who made Severus emperor. Sidonius retired to France for a few years. In 465 Ricimer poisoned Severus, and in 467 Anthemius was chosen in his place. In the same year Sidonius went to Rome at the head of a Gallo-Roman deputation to the new emperor, and on 1 January 468 he recited a panegyric in his honour. As a reward he was made *praefectus urbi*, prefect of Rome.

In 469 Sidonius returned to Gaul again and reluctantly—for he had no ecclesiastical experience whatsoever—accepted his appointment as bishop of the Auvergne, with Clermont-Ferrand as the centre of his see. It was important to have the right relations, and many bishops belonged in some way to senatorial families. They often needed this background and authority to resist powerful interests. Sidonius is said to have been a serious and efficient bishop who devoted to his priests and diocese the same concern he had formerly shown for the moral welfare of his slaves. He renounced light verse, such as his neat little piece on night fishing and another in which he declines to go fishing because his daughter has a bad cold; fasted every second day; gave much of what he owned to monasteries and charities; helped to maintain more than four thousand Burgundian refugees in time of famine; organized rogation processions in time of war; and defended his people courageously, especially against the Visigoths when they besieged Clermont. His statesmanship and patriotism were probably decisive elements in choosing someone who, like him, would keep the interests of the central power in mind in the face of an enemy. The city nevertheless fell in 474. Sidonius was appalled by the Arian heresy but even more shocked when the Roman authorities formally surrendered the Auvergne to Euric the Goth in 475. He was exiled to the fortress of Liviana, near Carcassonne, but was treated well, released in 476, and allowed to act as bishop again until his death, possibly in 479-80, perhaps later, in 489-90. He devoted much of his time in his last years to collecting and editing his letters.

A certain amount of Sidonius' verse survives: essentially three long panegyrics and some possibly youthful poems to friends. We also have nine books of his *Epistolae*, or letters to friends and relations, seven books of which belong to his period as bishop. The letters are literary products modelled on the style of the younger Pliny, and if any were written at the supposed dates of composition they must have been carefully reworked for the collection. We owe to them numerous insights into the Christian life of the period: the local aristocrats gathered round the tomb of the consul Syagrius on the feast of St Just, shaded by a trellis on a warm autumn day; the multi-coloured interior of the new cathedral at Lyons, with one of Sidonius' poems in the mosaic decoration of the basilica wall; Claudianus Mamertus, philosopher, architect, orator, exegete, poet, and musician meticulously rehearsing choirs in his own settings of the psalms ("... *instructas docuit sonare classes*").

Sidonius' writings show him as a strong Gallo-Roman patriot and as an aristocrat very conscious of his station yet aware of the duties of friendship. He was a very mannered stylist, ready to display his knowledge of rhetorical devices and to embellish statements with as many flourishes as the sense could reasonably bear. But there are very few original writers; and his poems, like his letters, are often pleasant and creditable performances that repay investigation; they certainly do not deserve the inherited condemnations of standard reference works. The spiritual content of his work is minimal, though there are many edifying references to classical mythology. The fauns, dryads, satyrs, and Bacchantes of his metaphors are more lively than his Christian sentiments, and when with seigneurial disdain he describes the *plebs furibunda*—the raging mob—throwing St Saturninus of Toulouse (29 Nov.) from the Capitol's highest step and tying him to a bull for denying Jove and Minerva, those very deities are essential decorative elements of his line. In the centuries during which compendia of Latin authors, sacred and secular, were issued for the instruction of Christian youth, a typical *Chorus Poetarum* (such as that issued by Louis Muget at Sidonius' own Lyons in 1615) classified Sidonius' works, along with those of Claudian and Ausonius, as "profane" yet seemly, whereas Prudentius, Venantius, Lactantius, and others were "religious." For a long time, therefore, Sidonius was (and in one sense remains) the last representative of classical culture at the end of a line including Lucretius, Horace, Catullus, Propertius, and Martial. St Gregory of Tours (17 Nov.) made a—now lost—collection of his Eucharistic Prayers, the *Contestatiuncula*. Sidonius was venerated throughout Gaul, probably, it has been said, because like so many other saints he was a bishop who left no unhappy memory behind.

Works, ed. with Eng. trans. W. B. Anderson, 2 vols. (1936-65); Letters, 2 vols., Eng trans., O. M. Dalton (1915).See *D. C. B.*, 4, pp. 649-61; C. E. Stevens, *Sidonius Apollinaris and his Age* (1933); *Sidoine Apollinaire et l'esprit précieux en Gaule aux derniers jours de l'Empire* (1943); W. H. Semple, "Apollinaris Sidonius, a Gallo-Roman Seigneur," in *Bulletin of the John Rylands Library* 1 (1968), pp. 136-58.

Bd Victoria Rasoamanarivo (1848-94)

Victoria Rasoamanarivo was born at Tananarive in Madagascar in 1848 into a powerful leading family of the Hova or Merina tribe (or, more properly, ethnolinguistic group). The country had been subject to a monarchy since the sixteenth century. Her mother, Rambohinoro, was the daughter of Queen Ranavalona's chief minister (who held office from 1837 to 1852) and the sister of chief minister Rainilaiarivony (from 1864 to 1895). Victoria was adopted by her father's elder brother, General Rainimmharavo. Until she was thirteen she was raised in a traditional non-Christian religion with a belief in Zahahary—God as creator—but based on an ancestral cult.

The Catholic Church had tried but failed to set up missions in Madagascar during the nineteenth century. The Reformed Churches were more succesful. The London Missionary Society established a mission in the country in 1819. By 1836 there were some two thousand Christians, thirty thousand had learned to read through the mission, and a translation of the Bible was available. Nevertheless, under an anti-Christian queen, all missionaries were forced to leave the country in that year. They were not allowed to return until she died in 1861, when the missionaries found that about five thousand followers had retained their Christian beliefs. There were some 13,000 Protestants by 1867, 230,000 by 1870, and 455,000 among the Hove by 1885. The new queen and her husband were baptized in 1869, and this made conversion less difficult. Reformed—essentially Anglican—Christianity became firmly based in the north and among the various élites. It was encouraged and protected by the crown.

Jesuit missionaries arrived in 1861 and were followed by Sisters of the Congregation of St Joseph of Cluny. They concentrated on the southern and coastal area and on the peasantry, but they also reached some members of the educated and ruling classes through their schools. There were about fifteen thousand Catholics by 1875. Victoria was one of the first pupils at the Sisters' mission school. She soon asked to be baptized, and her wish was granted on 1 November 1863, when she took the name Victoria. Even in the new reign it was not easy to remain a Catholic in Victoria's circle. Nevertheless, she persisted. Catholicism was identified with French imperialism; King Radama II had close ties with the French, and when he was deposed a persecution of Catholic missionaries broke out. Madagascar did not become a full French colony till 1896, after Victoria's death. Then, initially at least, Catholicism obtained certain advantages, and the Jesuits took over most of the Protestant schools, but there was considerable tension between Catholic and Anglican missionaries. Soon, however, Catholics had to cope with enmity from a new source—an anticlerical French government. By 1900, however, there were 112,000 baptized Catholics and 275,000 catechumens.

In the meantime, when the Catholic missionaries were expelled, Victoria's adoptive father tried to persuade her to join the Church of England to escape persecution. She refused and even expressed her desire to become a nun, although she was betrothed to Rainilaiarivony's son, a high-ranking officer. The missionaries themselves dissuaded her from a dangerous attempt to join a Catholic Order and advised her to work for Catholicism at court. On 13 May 1864 she was married to the chief minister's son and somehow managed to ensure that a Catholic priest was present at the ceremony. Her husband was a very trying man: he drank heavily and had relationships with other women. His own father and the queen advised Victoria to leave him, but she thought this would contradict her marriage vows and set a bad example to her fellow-Christians. She stayed with him until his death in 1887 and even persuaded him to accept Baptism before he died.

At court and among the peasantry Victoria earned a reputation as an exceptionally resolute Christian. A new persecution of Catholicism broke out on 25 May 1883; the French missionaries left, and Catholics looked to Victoria for protection. She was courageous and indefatigable. She visited and corresponded with Catholics in outlying districts and defended them and Catholic schools and churches at court. When the missionaries returned in 1886, institutions had been ravaged, but they found a living Catholicism. Victoria was one those primarily responsible for its survival. She was not only exceedingly devout but actively helped the poor, prisoners, and other disadvantaged people.

She suffered from various illnesses and died aged forty-six on 21 August

1894. On 24 August she was buried—against her expressed wishes—in her ancestral tomb. She was beatified by Pope John Paul II in Anatananarivo, the capital of Madagascar, on 30 April 1989.

See *D.N.H.*, 3, pp. 120-7; D. B. Barrett (ed.), *World Christian Encyclopedia* (1982), pp. 465-9.

R.M.

St Privatus, bishop and martyr at Gevaudan (*c.* 257)

SS Agathonicus, Zoticus and their companions, martyrs at Nicomedia under the emperor Maximian (third century)

St Cyriaca, at Rome in the Campo Verano, under Valerian (third/fourth century)

St Quadratus, bishop and martyr at Utica in Africa (third/fourth century)

St Euprepius, first bishop of Verona (third/fourth century)

SS Bassa, martyr on the island of Halona, and her sons Theognius, Agapius and Pistius, martyrs at Edessa in Syria (fourth century)

St Leontius, first bishop of Bordeaux (*c.* 541)

St Albericus, bishop of Utrecht (784)

SS Bernard (Ahmed) Cistercian monk and martyr, and his sisters Mary (Zaida) and Grace (Zoraida), martyrs in Valencia (*c.* 1180)

St Joseph Dang Dinh (Niên) Viên, Vietnamese secular priest, martyred Hung-An (1838; canonized on 19 June 1988)—see "The Martyrs of Vietnam," 2 Feb.

22

St Symphorian, *Martyr* (Third Century)

Symphorian was martyred at Autun in France. At that time Cybele, Apollo, and Diana were among the favourite deities in Autun. The statue of Cybele was borne through the streets in a chariot on one day in the year. Symphorian is said to have been disrespectful to the statue and so was seized by the crowd and taken to Heraclius, governor of the province. Heraclius asked him why he refused to honour the statue of the mother of the gods. Symphorian said he was a Christian and worshipped the true God. If he had a hammer he would destroy their idol. The judge thought this sounded seditious as well as impious and asked the officers whether Symphorian was a citizen of the place. They said he was and that he came from a noble family.

The judge asked him if he was too proud to obey or had not heard of the emperor's orders. He had the imperial edict read out. Symphorian remained obdurate, so he was beaten and imprisoned. He was brought before the tribunal once again but stayed firm. Heraclius condemned him to be beheaded for treason. As he was being led out of the town, his mother, standing on the wall of the city, cried out: "My son, my son Symphorian, remember the living God and be brave. Don't be afraid. You are facing a death that will lead to certain life." His head was struck off and his body was buried in a cave near a fountain. In the mid-fifth century (St) Euphronius, bishop of Autun, built a church over it in honour of Symphorian. The village and church of Veryan in Cornwall are named after the martyr (Simphoriani in 1278; Severian in 1545).

B.T.A., 3, pp. 380-1; G. H. Doble, *St Symphorian* (1931).

St Sigfrid, *Abbot* (690)

While St Benedict Biscop (12 Jan.) was away on his fifth visit to Rome, St Esterwine (7 Mar.), his kinsman and coadjutor abbot at Wearmouth, died. The monks elected the deacon Sigfrid in his place. Bede says that he was "well versed in Holy Scripture, of admirable conduct and perfectly chaste, but his vigour of mind was rather depressed by physical weakness and his innocence of heart was accompanied by a distressing and incurable disease of the lungs." About three years after Sigfrid's promotion and Benedict's return, both saints became seriously ill. They knew that they were about to die. Sigfrid was carried on a stretcher to Benedict's cell and laid on his bed but they were too weak to embrace one another unaided. After consulting Sigfrid, Benedict sent for St

Ceolfrid (25 Sept.) and, with general approval, made him abbot of both monasteries to ensure peace and unity. Sigfrid died two months later. He was buried in the abbey church of St Peter beside Benedict and his predecessor, Esterwine.

See Bede's *Historia Abbatum* and the anonymous history covering the same ground in *Baedae Opera Historica*, ed. C. Plummer (1956), 1, pp. 364-404; 2, pp. 355-77. There is no trace of any liturgical commemoration, not even an entry in a church calendar.

St Philip Benizi (1233-85)

Philip Benizi was born in Florence on 15 August 1233 to parents who had been childless for some time. He came from two noble families: the Benizi and the Frescobaldi. When he was thirteen, he was sent to study medicine in Paris. He then went to Padua where, aged only nineteen, he received his doctorate in medicine and philosophy. He practised medicine in Florence for a year and studied the Bible and the Fathers in his spare time.

At this time the Servites had been established as an Order for fourteen years. The seven gentlemen-founders lived at their main house on Monte Senario six miles from the city. They led an austere life in little cells. living mostly on alms. On the Thursday in Easter Week 1254 Philip was praying at Fiesole when the figure on the crucifix seemed to tell him to go up the hill to see his mother's servants. Philip attended Mass at the chapel at Carfaggio and took to heart the epistle of the day, in which the Holy Spirit told the deacon Philip to "Join yourself to this chariot." Philip thought he saw Our Lady approaching him in a chariot in a world full of dangers. He went to Monte Senario and was admitted to the Order as a lay brother by St Buonfiglio Monaldi. "I wish," he said, "to be the servant of the Servants of Mary." He was made a gardener and questor for alms and given hard manual work. He lived cheerfully in a little cave behind the church. In 1258 he was sent to the Servite house at Siena. On the way there he astonished two Dominicans and his companion, Br Victor, with his ability in controversy. As a result, the prior general promoted Philip to Holy Orders.

Philip had wanted to lead an obscure life, but in 1262 he was made novice-master at the Siena monastery and one of four vicars assisting the prior general. Soon after, he became the chief assistant to the prior general. In 1267 he was unanimously elected general of the Order. During his first year of office he made a visitation of the northern provinces, then suffering from the conflict between the Guelfs and Ghibellines. He was said to have miraculously supplied the almost starving Servites of Arezzo with food. Philip codified the Rules and Constitutions of the Order.

When Pope Clement IV died it was rumoured that Cardinal Ottobuoni, protector of the Servites, had suggested that Philip should succeed him. Philip hid in a cave in the mountains near Radicofani, where Br Victor looked after him for three months. When the danger was over he set out on a visitation of the Order in France and Germany. In 1274 he was present at the Second

General Council of Lyons, where he made a profound impression, even being credited with the gift of tongues.

Philip was renowned for his good effect on sinners and for his ability to reconcile warring factions. In 1279 Pope Nicholas III asked Philip to pacify the Guelfs and Ghibellines, and he succeeded in this difficult task. He also managed to attract a number of excellent men into the Order, some of whom were later canonized. He was the effective founder of the Servite nuns. He sent the first Servite missionaries to the East, where some even reached Tartary, where they were martyred.

In 1285 Philip felt that his life was drawing to a close. He set out to visit the newly-elected Pope Honorius IV at Perugia. At Florence he convened a general chapter and announced his departure. "Love one another!" he told the friars. He went to the smallest and poorest house of the Order, at Todi, where the citizens welcomed him. He went straight to Our Lady's altar and fell prostrate on the ground, declaring, "This is my place of rest for ever." He was taken ill at 3 P.M. that day. He sent for the community and said, "Love one another, respect one another, bear with one another." He died seven days later, contemplating the crucifix. He was canonized in 1671, and his feast was extended to the whole Western Church in 1694.

AA.SS., Aug., 4 (1739), pp. 655-719; P. Soulier, *Life of St Philip Benizi* (Eng. trans., 1886); *B.T.A.*, 3, pp. 385-8.

A somewhat primitive but fascinating etching of the Florentine school, *c.* 1460, in the British Museum, has as its central figure Philip receiving the triple crown from Jesus, surrounded by twelve engaging scenes from the saint's life.

Bd Thomas Percy, *Martyr* (1528-72)

Thomas Percy was the seventh earl of Northumberland. He was the elder son of Sir Thomas Percy, a younger son of the fifth earl, and brother and earl-presumptive to the sixth earl. Sir Thomas, together with his younger brother, Sir Ingelram Percy, played an important part in the Pilgrimage of Grace in 1536, a protest against, among other things, King Henry VIII's claim to be supreme governor of the church in England and the prescriptions and proscriptions that derived from that title. The two brothers were taken prisoner. Sir Thomas was executed at Tyburn on 2 June 1537. The sixth earl voluntarily surrendered his estates to the crown. In 1537, on his death, the title fell into abeyance. His widow, Eleanor, had inherited a large estate, to which she retired with her two sons, Thomas and Henry, after her husband's execution. Later the two boys were taken from their "treasonable" mother and entrusted to the care of Sir Thomas Tempest; in 1549 they were restored "in blood" when the attainder they had suffered under because of their father's behaviour was lifted to a certain extent.

Thomas Percy was restored to full royal favour after the accession of Queen Mary. He was made governor of Prudhoe Castle, and in 1557 he was promoted to the earldom of Northumberland and nominated high marshal of the army in the north. In 1558 he married Anne Somerset, daughter of the Earl of Worcester. On Elizabeth's accession he was so harshly criticized that he resigned his office. Nevertheless, in 1563 he was made a Knight of the Garter, yet in 1565 Burghley's agents reported that he was "dangerously obstinate in religion." When Mary, Queen of Scots, tried to flee from Scotland and was captured on Elizabeth's orders and brought to Carlisle, Thomas interviewed her and expressed his sympathy. He was thought to favour the suggested match between her and the duke of Norfolk, who indeed planned to marry her, contracted himself to her, sent her a diamond ring in token of this, begged Elizabeth's forgiveness, but was imprisoned in the Tower when she read his letters to Mary. Thomas was ordered to leave Carlisle.

For some time there had been great discontent and anti-government plotting among a number of nobles, Protestant, nominally Catholic, and resolutely Catholic. An alteration of religion seemed a real possibility. Thomas welcomed a suggestion of Thomas Markenfield, who had lived abroad for some time and together with the Earl of Westmorland planned the uprising of 1569, based in the still largely Catholic area north of the Humber and east of the Pennines where the Pilgrimage of Grace had originated thirty years before. The government got wind of the rebellion when a report reached it on 7 November that Westmorland was apparently assembling his retainers and tenants at Brancepeth Castle, south-east of Durham, and that Northumberland and the Sheriff of Yorkshire, Richard Norton, were there too. Only eight days before that, the two earls had by excusing themselves refused a summons from the queen to attend Court, which was repeated on 4 November.

The wavering leaders were forced into premature action by the Nortons, Tempests, Markenfields, and others but above all by the thought that, like Norfolk, they were bound for the Tower and probable execution anyway. When Burghley questioned Thomas later about the purpose of the rebellion, he said: "The intent and meaning of us upon our first conferences and assemblies was only and specifically for the Reformation of Religion, and the preservation of the second person, the Queen of Scots whom we accounted by God's law and man's law to be right heir if want should be of issue of the Queen's Majesty's body, which two causes I made with full account, was greatly favoured by the most part of Noblemen within this Realm, and especially for God's true religion." The two earls overestimated the depth and spread of Catholic feeling and sympathy at this late stage. Nevertheless, they were advised by Mary not to move and probably would not have done so if the government had not taken the reports far too seriously in demanding that the two earls come unarmed to London and thus put themselves at their enemies' mercy. In the second week of November young Westmorland began earnestly to muster his men. Even then, Northumberland was only seeking safe refuge in his own county but was persuaded to join what quickly became an actual uprising.

They marched a force of men through Durham and occupied the city. The Protestant Bible and Book of Common Prayer were ceremoniously destroyed with other works in a bonfire on the bridge. The traditional Mass was sung in the cathedral for the last time. Their banners displayed the Five Wounds; sermons were preached against the Protestant heresy; great crowds were absolved of excommunication; and similar scenes occurred in towns throughout the county, with priests confessing to their congregations that they had deceived them for ten years. The earls issued a proclamation saying that they were determined to free the queen from "divers new set-up nobles, who not only go about to overthrow and put down the ancient nobility of the realm, but also have misused the queen's majesty's own person" and "also have by the space of twelve years now past, set up and maintained a new found religion and heresy contrary to God's word." The Catholic forces marched on to Ripon with 5,000 foot accompanied by 1,200 horse, but avoided York and, on 24 November, stopped and then turned back at Bramham Moor, where government reports assessed their strength at 3,800 foot and 1,700 horse. Mary had been moved from Tutbury, fifty miles further south, to Coventry. The royal armies started to move up country. On 16 December the earls held a council of war in Durham, where their lack of any overall plan or strategy became quite clear when they discussed and argued about the real purpose of the rebellion. Their forces were dispersed or melted away, and the earls made for the supposed safety of the Scottish border country.

There were eight hundred executions in Durham and Yorkshire, mostly of "the meanest of the people." Only nine of the really well-to-do were executed; most of them were attainted, and the queen received their lands and goods. Fines were levied on more than a thousand victims, and in January and February 1570 the southern soldiers ruthlessly plundered the north from Doncaster to Newcastle until starvation threatened. Pardons were issued only if Catholicism was renounced and the Oath of Supremacy was taken.

Thomas lived as a fugitive for some time. Finally he took refuge in Scotland; his wife stayed on the borders to try to help him and to raise money as a ransom. She went to Antwerp with their newly-born daughter Mary in August 1570 to raise funds and plan her husband's release and escape to Flanders, but her efforts failed. In August 1572 Thomas was arrested, and the Scottish regent, the Calvinist earl of Mar, sold him to Elizabeth's officers for £2000. He was taken to York and offered his life if he abjured his religion. He refused and, aged forty-four, was beheaded on 22 August 1572. He was beatified in 1895.

Thomas' wife remained in the Spanish Netherlands but in 1576 was temporarily expelled at Elizabeth's request. In 1596 she died of smallpox in a convent at Namur. They had a son, who died young in 1560. The title passed to Thomas' brother Henry, the eighth earl. They also had four daughters. Three of them married, and the fourth, Lady Mary Percy, founded the English Benedictine abbey at Brussels.

See C. Sharpe (ed.), *Memorials of the Rebellion of 1569* (1841); Gillow, 5, pp. 265-7; P. Hughes, *The Reformation in England*, 3 (1954), pp. 265-72.

At Petworth, in Sussex, there is a portrait of Sir Thomas by an unknown hand dated 1566 and stating his age as thirty-eight; an engraving was made after it by R. Easton for Sharpe's *Memorials*; a copy by Philips of a portrait showing him in the Garter robes was recorded at Alnwick Castle in Northumberland.

BB William Lacey and Richard Kirkman, *Martyrs* (*c.* 1531-82)

William Lacey (or Lacy) was born about 1531 at Horton near Settle, in the West Riding of Yorkshire. He was the son of Robert and Elizabeth Lacey. He was a lawyer with an official position and was married to the mother of Joseph Cresswell, S.J., who was the widow of a member of a county family of some standing. William was suspected of being a Catholic at heart. After the visit of Dr William (later Cardinal) Allen to the north of England in 1565, the suspicion became a certainty, and he was dismissed from office. For fourteen years he was bitterly persecuted, undergoing the usual sequence of fines, visits, interrogations, and imprisonment. Eventually he fled with his family and was hunted from place to place. Mrs Lacey finally broke down under the strain. In spite of her serious illness, the archbishop of York would have had her arrested as a recusant if she had not died first.

On 22 June in the next year, 1580, although he was fairly elderly, Lacey became a student at Reims. On 23 September he went to Pont-à-Mousson and then to Rome, where he was ordained in the English College on 5 March 1581, though he was not a student there. Having been married to a widow, he had to receive a dispensation from the pope. He was sent on the English mission in 1581 but ministered in Yorkshire for only twelve months. Together with other priests, he made regular visits to the Catholic prisoners in York Castle goal. One of the priests, Fr Thomas Bell, had been imprisoned and tortured there before his ordination and now dreamed up the foolhardy project of bribing the turnkeys and singing a High Mass there as an act of thanksgiving. On Sunday, 22 July 1582, the Mass was sung in one of the prisoners' cells, with William Lacey as deacon and a Fr Hart as subdeacon. The Mass was over when an alarm was given and the authorities began to search the building. Frs Hart and Bell escaped, but William was captured coming out of the castle. He was examined first by the mayor and then by Archbishop Sandys of York, who sentenced him to solitary confinement in irons. After three weeks he was brought up for trial. The letters of Orders he carried with him were shown in evidence, and he admitted his priesthood, for it was not high treason at that point for a priest to enter the country. When he was asked if he acknowledged the queen as head of the Church he said, "In this matter, as well as in all other things, I believe as the Catholic Church of God and all good Christians believe." His dispensation from the pope was the only charge brought against him: he was convicted and sentenced "for obtaining of a bull and popish orders from Gregory

XIII pope, contrary to the statute of 13 year of the queen, who had also taken upon him many other indulgences, writings, instruments, relics, beads, books, laces and trifles brought from Rome." On 22 August he was hanged, drawn, and quartered at the Knavesmire, outside the city of York.

Richard Kirkman (alias Jennings) was executed at the same time and place. He and William were drawn on the same hurdle and confessed to each other on the way to the scaffold. Richard was born at Addingham, near Skipton, in the West Riding of Yorkshire. He went to Reims in 1577 and was ordained priest there on 18 April 1579. He was sent to England on 3 August 1579 and is said to have entered the household of Robert Dymoke, hereditary Champion of England, at Scrivelsby, Lancashire, where he became tutor to Dymoke's three younger sons and ministered to Catholics in the neighbourhood. After eleven months, Dymoke (who died in prison) and his wife were indicted for not attending the state church. Kirkman had to leave Scrivelsby. He worked in Yorkshire and Northumberland until, on 8 August 1582, he was stopped near Wakefield by Justice Wortley and arrested merely on suspicion; but his "mass-books, chalice, wafer-cakes, wine and all things ready to say Mass" were found on him, and he admitted his priesthood. On 11 August, found guilty of "persuading and withdrawing traitorously her majesty's poor simple subjects from their natural allegiance to H.M. to the obedience of the pope and Romish religion contrary to the last statute made in 17 year of H.M. reign," he was sentenced to death at the York assizes. He shared William's cell for four days, but after a private examination by the sheriff and two ministers he was confined on his own in a dungeon without light, food, or bed, until he was taken out for execution.

William Lacey and Richard Kirkman were beatified in 1886.

See (Cardinal) W. Allen, *A True, Sincere, and Modest Defence of English Catholics that suffer for their faith both at home and abroad* (1584); *M.M.P.*, pp. 66-70; Gillow, 4, pp. 53-6, 88-93; *L.E.M.*, 2, pp. 564-88; Anstruther, 1, pp. 199, 202-3.

St John Wall, *Martyr* (1620-79)

John Wall (also known under the aliases Francis Johnson, Webb, Marsh, and Dorner) was born (possibly at Chingle Hall, near Preston) in Lancashire in 1620. In 1633, when a boy, he was sent to Douai. He entered the Roman College in 1641, was ordained priest in 1645, and in 1648 was sent on the English mission for a few years. In 1651 he became a Franciscan as Joachim-of-St-Anne at St Bonaventure's friary in Douai and served there until 1656, when he returned to England. He spent over twenty-two years as a priest in Worcestershire, with his base at Harvington Hall, the property of the Talbot family. He was arrested in December 1678 at Rushock Court, near Bromsgrove, by a sheriff's officer actually in search of a debtor. He was imprisoned in Worcester Castle for five months and is said to have reconciled a number of former Catholics there. He was sentenced, probably on 17 August 1679, as a priest who had entered the country unlawfully. He blessed God, the king, the judge, and the bench, whereupon the judge commended him and said he did not intend that John should die, at least for the present.

John was interrogated several times in London and was publicly declared to be free of any complicity in the Titus Oates conspiracy, the ramifications of which among Catholics were both thought and made out to be more widespread than could ever have been the case. In spite of this and the judge's good will, after a month John was sent back to Worcester for execution, mainly because he refused to renounce his religion. The day before he died, Fr William Leveson, a fellow-Franciscan, visited him in prison to hear his Confession and give him Communion. The next day John was hanged and quartered at Redhill, and Fr Leveson stood by the scaffold to give him the final absolution. He was the only one of the acknowledged English martyrs to be executed at Worcester.

He was beatified in 1929 and canonized by Pope Paul VI in 1970.

See *M.M.P.*, pp. 550-5; B. Camm, *Forgotten Shrines* (1910), pp. 253-80; *idem.*, *Bd John Wall* (1932); F. Davey, *Blessed John Wall* (1961).

St John Kemble, *Martyr* (1599-1679)

He was the son of John Kemble, a gentleman from a family originally from Wiltshire, and Anne, one of the Morgans of Skenfrith. He was born in 1599, possibly at Rhydicar Farm, St Weonards, Herefordshire, or at Pembridge Castle nearby. They were a Catholic family, and there were said to be four other related Kemble priests at that time. Eventually John was smuggled to Douai, where he was ordained priest on 23 February 1625. On 4 June he was sent on the English mission to work in and around his birthplace. He ministered there for fifty-three years, though one archive entry suggests that he was in London for a time in or around 1649. The Westminster archives show that in 1643 he was recommended as a suitable candidate for the archdeaconry of South Wales. He had a considerable reputation as a good priest in Monmouthshire, and with the help of the Jesuits at the Cwm in Llanorthal he founded mission centres at the Llwyn, the Graig, Hilston, Codanghred, and elsewhere, which lingered on into the nineteenth century; they are testified to by the remains of a graveyard and a ruined chapel at Coed Anghred, on a hill above Skenfrith. His base for most of this period was at Pembridge Castle, the home of his brother.

In 1678 the persecution resulting from the Gunpowder Plot and the supposed vast Titus Oates conspiracy began. It reached Herefordshire in the autumn. The Cwm was sacked, and John's friend St David Lewis, S.J. (27 Aug.), was arrested. John, who was almost eighty, was warned that he would be taken but refused to escape, saying that it would be an advantage to suffer for his religion.

In November Captain Scudamore of Kentchurch (whose wife and children were Catholics and ministered to by John) arrested the priest at Pembridge Castle and dragged him through the snow to Hereford gaol. He remained there for four months until he was brought up at the March assizes and sentenced to be hanged, drawn, and quartered for "being a seminary priest." On 23 April he and Fr Lewis were sent to London for interrogation by the Privy Council. John could only ride sideways and suffered considerably on the journey, but a few weeks later he was allowed to walk most of the way back. After his return, Scudamore's children visited him in gaol. He is said to have remarked that their father was the best friend he had in the world, which was interpreted as meaning that the captain had opened up his way to the privilege of martyrdom. John was not sentenced on any charge relating to conspiracy: "I die only for professing the old Roman Catholic religion, which was the religion that first made this kingdom Christian." At the summer assizes his execution was fixed for 22 August.

It is said that when Digges, the under-sheriff, arrived at the gaol, John asked for time to finish his prayers, then smoke a pipe and have a drink. The governor and under-sheriff joined him, and Digges delayed in his turn to finish his own pipe. (This incident is said to have originated the Herefordshire custom, still recorded in the nineteenth century but lost with the disappearance of communal pipe smoking and snuff taking in favour of cigarettes, of calling the last pipe of a sitting "the Kemble pipe.") Toward evening John was dragged on a hurdle to Widemarsh Common. He denied all knowledge of the plot before a huge crowd. He was allowed to hang until he was dead before being hacked about; nevertheless, the hanging was botched and he lived for half-an-hour after the cart was withdrawn. His nephew, Captain Richard Kemble, put the headless body in a coffin and buried it in Welsh Newton churchyard, and his hand is enshrined in the Catholic church at Hereford. He was beatified in 1929 and canonized by Pope Paul VI in 1970.

See *M.M.P.*, pp. 555-7; Gillow, 3 (1880), pp. 685-8; T. P. Ellis, *Catholic Martyrs of Wales* (1932), pp. 126-9; B. Camm, *Forgotten Shrines* (1910), pp. 333-42; M. V. Lovejoy, *Blessed John Kemble* (1960).

R.M.
St Anthusa, at Tarsus in Cilicia (third century)
St Timothy, martyr at Rome on the Via Ostia (303)
St Aldoaldus, bishop of Bagnorea in Tuscany (*c.* 873)
Bd James Bianconi, O.P., founder of a monastery at Bevagna in Umbria (1301)
Bd Timothy of Montecchio, Franciscan friar at Ocra in the Abruzzi (1504)
Bd Bernard Peroni, Capuchin friar of Ancona (1694)

23

ST ROSE OF LIMA (1586-1617)

Rosa was born in Lima, capital of Peru, on 20 April 1586 to Gaspar de Flores, who had come to Peru from Puerto Rico in 1548, and his young wife, Maria del Oliva. She was christened Isabel de Flores on 25 May, which was the feast of Pentecost that year. An Indian maid, struck by the beauty of the infant, declared, in a phrase still common in Spanish, that she was *"como una rosa"* (like a rose), and her mother agreed that this was how she was to be known. She was confirmed by the archbishop of Lima, St Turibius de Mogrovejo (23 Mar.), when she was fourteen, and later she added "de Santa María" to her name.

As an adolescent she took St Catherine of Siena (29 Apr.), whom she would have known through the Life by Raymond of Capua, as her model. She was impressed not only by the mystical ecstasies but by the stigmata and pains which Catherine specifically referred to as outward signs of inward suffering. Whether in imitation or from the circumstances of her own life she developed the self-induced vomiting after frugal meals (now known as bulimia) and the self-inflicted violence (reported, probably with exaggeration, in the Life as a total of four hours of flagellation a day) that Catherine, even as a child, practised both to make plain her dedication to God and to ward off the threat of betrothal and the attentions of young men in her father's workshop. This made Rose an object of ridicule to parents and friends, but that, in the way of things, only confirmed her inclinations. One day, for instance, her mother put a garland of flowers on her daughter's head to make her look nice for the visitors. Rose promptly stuck a pin through it and into her head, so deeply that it was difficult to remove the garland.

Her parents were very proud of her good looks and people would often praise her for her beauty. She was being prepared in the normal way for the marriage market, and she was absolutely determined not to be given in marriage, having vowed herself to God. Unable simply to refuse, Rose would discourage potential suitors by rubbing her face with pepper to make sure she was constantly disfigured with blotches and blisters. This was insufficient, for one day a woman admired the fine skin of her hands and her well-shaped fingers. Rose rubbed them with lime. The results were so painful that she could not dress herself for a month. She worked hard to subdue what she called her own will and to obey her parents, unless their will seemed contrary to what she took to be the will of God. She wished to enter a cloister, but her parents refused to allow her to.

Her parents lost money by speculating in an unsuccessful mining venture. Rose worked in the garden by day, selling the flowers she grew, and as a seamstress till late into the night to help the family keep alive rather than to restore their income. They tried to persuade her to accept a husband, but she refused to marry, took a vow of perpetual virginity, and, like Catherine, became a Dominican tertiary. The marriage arguments went on for ten years. She lived in her own home, but (like Catherine in her cell) as a near-recluse in a hermitage she had built in the garden as a child, where she slept on a bed of broken tiles. When she was discouraged by the prospect of yet another night of torture, a voice strengthened her resolution: "My cross was even more painful." On her head she wore a "crown of thorns"—a silver circlet studded with small spikes on the inside with a garland of roses on the outside to please her mother. Ecstatic moods were reported when she talked about God or received the Eucharist. Among her more appealing habits was that of joining in the humming of birds and insects and performing duets with them. She was continually criticized by relations, friends, and others and suffered from constantly recurrent states depressive and desolate as well as ecstatic, attributing the former to demonic interventions. Nevertheless, her attentions were not all focussed on herself: in one room of the family house she set up a little infirmary where she cared for destitute children and sick elderly people. It was probably quite considerable in scope and has been described as "the beginning of social service in Peru" (*N.C.E.*). Possibly this rather than her mortifications accounts for her extraordinary popularity in Lima by the time of her death.

She spent the last years of her life in the home of Don Gonzalo de Massa, a government official, and his wife, who was fond of Rose. She died in their house on 24 August 1617, aged thirty-one. Ordinary people in her life and after her death described some events as miraculous, but they aroused the suspicions of the religious authorities. During her lifetime a commission of priests and physicians had examined her and declared that her experiences were the result of "impulses of grace." After her death the chapter, senate, and honourable corporations of the city carried her body by turns to the grave, through crowds so great that it was impossible to hold the funeral for several days. She was buried privately in the cloister of St Dominic's Church, as she had requested, but her body was later translated into the church itself and is now interred under an altar in the crypt. She was beatified by Clement IX in 1668 and canonized by Pope Clement X on 12 April 1671, in the same ceremony in which he beatified John of the Cross (14 Dec.). She is the first canonized saint of the New World and was proclaimed patron of Peru, of all of (South) America, of the Indies, and of the Philippines.

She may be thought of as resisting undue pressures on the disadvantaged, and above all on women, though this is not how she has been recommended in the past. It is sometimes assumed that because, for mixed reasons, "the Church" has beatified or canonized historical persons, their declared sanctity defies criticism. That is not the case. Canonization is time-bound: Clement X was engaged in struggles with Louis XIV of France and looked to Spain for support. Iberian Catholicism, with its extravagant penitential practices and processions, was making a deep impression in Rome. Canonization also often ignores mundane causes of supposedly religious phenomena or ascribes them to worthy intentions that later research shows, or leads us to suspect, are very mixed motives or symptoms of known illness.

Of course Rose could not examine her social, family, and personal predicament in the terms of the enlightened discourse of her own, let alone of our day. Since the subject herself cannot be tested, interviewed, or examined, even judgments in accordance with modern psychology and psychiatric medicine are impossible. We can try to place her with other, similar saints (such as Catherine of Siena) in a general context. Then, while being wary of descriptions that have been handed on to us by hagiographers, we may say that she exhibits a need for extreme physical expressions of a certain mental state; and that in her reported behaviour the body becomes an extended metaphor for personal, familial, and social comment and argument. So far we remain within the area of description rather than judgment. Rose attacked herself in ways only too familiar among the insecure, anxious, deprived, self-deprecating, and self-hating in our own times, whom we class as sick. As always, repetition reinforced the behaviour once acquired. But we cannot say exactly how psychotic she was and whether her flight into religion was entirely a mixture of personal sickness and justifiable escape from social constraints or partly a turning of that experience through mature judgment to religious ends. As records present her to us, she is certainly no model for young women in the way she was presented as such in the past, but if the psychotic elements and the probable exaggerations of them are ignored, she remains a determined witness to commitment to God in a confusing and violent society.

AA.SS., Aug., 5 (1741), pp. 892-1029, has the original Latin Life by L. Hansen, O.P. and the Bull of canonization. The following are largely uncritical if amenable biographies: F. M. Capes, *The Flower of the New World* (1899); R. Vargas Ugarte, *Vida de Santa Rosa de Santa Maria* (1951); S. Kaye-Smith, *Quartet in Heaven* (1952); F. P. Keyes, *The Rose and the Lily* (1962). Works such as the following prompt more refined speculation: E. Fromm, *Fear of Freedom* (1942), pp. 121-59; J.-N. Vuarnet, *Extases féminines* (1980); C. Walker Bynum, *Holy Feast and Holy Fast: The Religious Significance of Food to Medieval Women* (1987); C. Optiz, *Evatöchter und Bräute Christi* (1990); R. M. Bell, *Holy Anorexia* (1994).

Rose's attributes are a crown or a rosary of thorns.

Angelino Medoro's portrait painting (1617), presumably from the death-mask, survives in the sanctuary of St Rose, Lima. A number of major artists painted scenes from her life. Sassoferrato, Carlo Dolci, Murillo, and Valdés Leal are among her seventeenth-century portraitists. The eighteenth-century altarpiece by Tiepolo (church of Gesuati, Venice) is the best; she appears with Catherine of Siena and Agnes of Montepulciano and holds the Infant Jesus.

SS Claudius, Asterius, and Neon, *Martyrs* (*c.* 303)

According to Greek tradition Claudius, Asterius, and Neon were brothers who were crucified in Isauria, whereas the Latin Acts say Cilicia. The brothers are said to have been denounced as Christians by their stepmother at Aegea during the Diocletian persecution. They refused to sacrifice to the gods. They were tortured but remarked that fire and other torments were great benefits, for they suffered for God's sake and were happy to die for Jesus Christ. Eventually they were crucified well outside the city to allow the birds to pick them clean and to discourage urban Christians from hunting for relics; for the same reason one of the women's bodies was thrown into the sea. This aspect of the story rings true, for at a point in the period when the original of this narrative was perhaps composed, the emperor Julian campaigned against the cult of martyrs and "turning from the gods to worship corpses and relics." His friend the Sophist Eunapius (*c.* 345-420) said: "Pickled heads and mouldy bones have become the new gods of the Roman people."

AA.SS., Aug., 4.

St Eugene, *Bishop* (Sixth Century)

Eugene (Eoghan, or Owen) is said to have been the first bishop at Ardstraw in Tyrone, predecessor of the see of Derry in Ireland. He is mentioned in the *Félire* of Oengus on this day. His untrustworthy Latin Life says that his father was from Leinster and his mother from Co. Down, and that he was related to St Kevin of Glendalough (3 June). While a child he was carried off with two other boys, Tigernach and Coirpre, first to Britain and then to Brittany. They were sold as slaves and had to grind corn. One day, so we are told, the chieftain found the boys reading, but since some angels were obligingly working the corn mill in their place, he ordered the redundant captives to be released. Somehow they returned to Ireland, where Coirpre became a bishop at Coleraine. Eugene was a monk for fifteen years with St Kevin at Kilnamanach in Co. Wicklow. He went to the north of the country, helped St Tigernach (4 Apr.) to found the monastery of Clones, settled in the valley of Mourne, and was made a bishop.

AA.SS., Aug., 4.

R.M.

SS Abundius and Irenaeus, martyrs at Rome under Diocletian (third century)

SS Cyriac and Archelaus, martyrs at Ostia (third century)

St Luppus, martyr in Moesia in the Balkans (third-fourth century)

St Justinian, hermit in Wales (sixth century)

24

ST BARTHOLOMEW, *Apostle and Martyr* (First Century)

He was one of the twelve apostles. Only the Synoptic Gospels (Mark 3:18, Luke 6:14, Matt. 10:3) and Acts (1:13) mention him. Bartholomew was probably not his proper name but a patronymic, for it means "the son of Tolmai." We know nothing more of him. Some commentators identify him with Nathanael (John 1:45-51, 21:2), a native of Cana in Galilee, of whom Jesus said: "Behold! an Israelite indeed, in whom there is no guile." The argument for this is roughly that, as John never mentions Bartholomew among the apostles, so the other evangelists do not notice the name Nathanael. They continually put together Philip and Bartholomew, just as John says Philip and Nathanael came together to Christ. Only the number of the Twelve is constant.

Popular traditions and legends say that Bartholomew preached the gospel in India, then went to Greater Armenia. After converting a number of people there he was flayed alive by the barbarians, whereupon King Astyages ordered him to be beheaded at Albanopolis (Derbend, on the west coast of the Caspian Sea). The story of the flaying was almost certainly taken from that of the flaying of Marsyas by the jealous Apollo.

Bartholomew is also said to have preached in Mesopotamia, Persia, Egypt, and elsewhere. Eusebius in the early fourth century gives the earliest reference to India. He says that when St Pantaenus (7 July) went to India about a century before, he found some people there who still knew about Christ. They showed him a copy of St Matthew's Gospel in Hebrew, which they said Bartholomew had brought with him. Nevertheless, "India" was used indiscriminately by Greek and Latin writers for Arabia, Ethiopia, Libya, Parthia, and the lands of the Medes; and Pantaeus probably went to Ethiopia or Arabia Felix. Another Eastern legend says that Bartholomew met St Philip (3 May) at Hierapolis in Phyrgia and travelled to Lycaonia, and St John Chrysostom (13 Sept.) tells us that the apostle instructed people there in Christianity.

The travels attributed to Bartholomew's alleged relics seem even more bewildering than those ascribed to him while alive. The main itinerary was, so it seems, Lipara, then Benevento, and finally Rome. On the other hand, when other regions, but especially areas of Italy, were ravaged by invasions, local relics were often sent to Rome for safekeeping. This policy reached its height in the mid-sixth century. Among churches now claiming relics of the apostle are Benevento and St Bartholomew-in-the-Tiber, Rome. Queen Emma presented an arm to Canterbury in the eleventh century. The number of churches dedicated to the apostle in England has been estimated at 165. His legendary loss of his skin made him the patron saint of tanners.

Fragments survive of an apocryphal *Gospel of Bartholomew* and a Coptic *Acts of Andrew and Bartholomew*. See *AA.SS.*, Aug., 5, pp. 7-108; *Anal. Boll.* 14 (1895), pp. 353-66; *B.T.A.*, 3, pp. 391-2; A. Romeo, in *Enciclopedia Cattolica*, 2 (1949), 916-8; E. Mâle, *Rome et ses vieilles Eglises* (1942).

Bartholomew's attribute is the strangely-shaped knife with which he is said to have been martyred. He is often shown wearing, sometimes gruesomely, sometimes elegantly, his own flayed skin over one arm, as in Michelangelo's *Last Judgment* in the Sistine Chapel, Rome. His inscription is "*Credo in Spiritum Sanctum*," from the Apostles' Creed. He is usually middle-aged, has dark hair, and is bearded.

As one of the apostles, Bartholomew has appeared many times in Christian art and is shown preaching, exorcizing, baptizing, and being arraigned for refusing to apostatize. His flaying is the preferred subject in the Renaissance, and above all in the baroque period; classical models of the flaying of the innocent Marsyas by Apollo (such as the sculpture from Pergamum in the Capitoline Museum, Rome) were sometimes closely followed. His minimal characterization in scripture is one reason for the lack of powerful individual images, though the *Last Judgment* Bartholomew is said to be a portrait of the painter himself. In typically stylized portraits, by Norde di Cione (S. Croce, Florence, Italy), Pietro Perugino (*c.* 1445-1523) (Museum of Art, Birmingham, Alabama), or Cola dell'Amatrice (*c.* 1517; part of a polyptychon, Pinacoteca Civica, Ascoli Piceno, Italy), he holds the gospel he preached and the sword he was slain with. In Zurbarán's compelling portrayal (1633; National Museum of Art, Lisbon) he is mysterious and deeply contemplative; in a later portrait by the same artist (1641-58; Monastery of St Francis of Jesus, Lima, Peru), Bartholomew is a figure of simple faith and commitment.

St Audoenus, *Bishop* (*c.* 600-84)

Audoenus was born Ouen (or Dado) into a Frankish family at Sancy, near Soissons in France, in about 600. His father was St Authairius (Authaire). He and his brother Ado (Adon) were still children when their father entertained St Columban (23 Nov.), exiled by King Thierry II, and his grandmother Brunehaut, in his house at Ussy-sur-Marne. The brothers received a good education. Eventually they were sent to the court of King Clotaire II. Audoenus became a member of a group of talented and pious young men that included St Eligius (Eloi; 1 Dec.), St Wandregisilus (Wandrille; 22 July), and St Desiderius of Cahors (Didier; 15 Nov.). Audoenus was in favour with the king and his son and successor, Dagobert I, who made him his chancellor. The king granted him some land in the forest of Brie, and there in 636 Audoenus erected a monastery, now known as Rebais. St Faro (28 Nov.), bishop of Meaux, advised him to send for Aile, a disciple of Columban's from Luxeuil. He did so and appointed him first abbot. Audoenus wanted to retire to Rebais, but Dagobert and his nobles would not allow this. Though a layman, Audoenus was said to be as learned and pious as any bishop.

Dagobert died in 639. His son, Clovis II, kept Audoenus on as chancellor. At length he allowed him to be ordained. Shortly afterwards he was elected bishop of Rouen at a time when bishops exercised a quasi-political power. His friend Eligius was chosen bishop of Noyon. They spent a long time preparing for this by retreat, fasting, and prayer. They were consecrated together at Reims in 641.

Audoenus was noted for his episcopal humility, austerity, and charity. He founded monasteries, encouraged learning, and repressed simony. He was a resolute extirpator of vestiges of idolatry in the lower Seine region and sent missionaries to still-pagan parts of his diocese. He was a trusted adviser to King Thierry III and is said to have upheld the policy of Ebroin, the mayor of the palace, so assiduously, that he was, perhaps inculpably, involved in Ebroin's ill treatment of St Leger (2 Oct.) and St Philibert (20 Aug.), who withdrew to the island of Noirmoutier). On returning from a political mission to Cologne Audoenus went to Clichy-la-Garenne (later Saint-Ouen), where he fell ill and died on 24 August 684.

Rouen, where there is still a church named after him, was said to have his relics, and forty churches in the diocese were dedicated to him. Boursies claimed to have his head and Clichy his finger. Evreux had twenty-nine churches named in his honour. Canterbury maintained a counter-claim to hold his body. Eadmer says that under King Edgar four clerics brought Audoenus' bones to the court and that their origin was demonstrated by their healing powers. St Odo of Canterbury (4 July) approved these miracles. The clerics took the bones to Canterbury and were professed as monks there.

For the earliest, eighth-century, Life, see *M.G.H., Scriptores Merov.*, 5, pp. 536-67. For ninth-century Lives, see *AA.SS.*, Aug., 4, and *Anal.Boll.* 5 (1887), pp. 76-146. See also E. Vacandart, *Vie de Saint Ouen* (1902); *Anal. Boll.* 52 (1933), pp. 285-92; 64 (1946), pp. 50-3; Eadmer, "Vita S. Odonis," in H. Wharton, *Anglia Sacra* (1691), 2, pp. 78-87.

St Joan Antide-Thouret, *Foundress* (1765-1825)

Jeanne Antide-Thouret was born on 7 November 1765 at Sancey-le-Long, near Besançon in France. Her father was a tanner, and she was the fifth child of a large family. Her mother died when she was sixteen. She managed the household for six years until her sense of vocation became so compelling that she applied to and was accepted by the Sisters of Charity of St Vincent de Paul in Paris, where she suffered two serious illnesses. When the Revolution began the Sisters continued to work only on sufferance; when the religious Orders were dispersed in 1793, Joan had not yet made her profession. She escaped from Paris and eventually reached Sancey on foot. Her father was dead and one of her brothers was a revolutionary. She went to live with her godmother and opened a free school, where she taught the village children in the morning. She spent much of the rest of the day and night visiting the sick and needy.

In 1796 Joan took refuge in Switzerland with the Sisters of the Christian Retreat and accompanied them to Germany but then returned to Switzerland and begged her way on foot to Landeron, in the canton of Neuchâtel. There she met the vicar general of Besançon, who invited her to return to run a school, as conditions had improved. Her lack of training made her reluctant, but the school was opened in April 1799. In October, with four other Sisters, she moved it to a larger house with a soup-kitchen and a dispensary. In 1800 the community numbered twelve, and a regular novitiate started. She was criticized for not returning to her own Congregation in Paris, but the community was not yet re-established, she had taken no vows, and the existing Institute had been founded in obedience to her superiors. The prefect of the city asked her to run the municipal female asylum at Belleveaux, which sheltered orphans, beggars, and criminals as well as the mentally ill. She was also criticized and even persecuted for this work. In 1807, however, the archbishop approved the Sisters' Rule. They had spread into Switzerland and Savoy by 1810, when the king of Naples invited Joan to occupy the Regina Coeli convent and to administer a hospital in his capital. She went there with seven Sisters and remained until 1821.

In 1818 Pope Pius VII approved the Institute. In 1819 he confirmed it with a Brief. This made some minor alterations in the Rule and decreed that for the future all convents of the Congregation of the Daughters of Charity under the protection of St Vincent de Paul (as they were to be called) must be subject to their local bishop and not to the archbishop of Besançon. In the Gallican tradition the then archbishop, Mgr Cortois de Pressigny, refused to accept these Roman amendments. He separated all the convents in his diocese from the rest of the Congregation and forbade them to receive their foundress and mother general. This virtual schism troubled Joan for the rest of her life. In 1821 she went to France and spent eighteen months in Paris trying to resolve the problem. She even went to the motherhouse, but the Sisters, duly obedient to their archbishop, would not admit her. Eventually Joan returned to Naples. After three years founding new convents in Italy she died on 24 August 1826. She was canonized in 1934.

There are Lives in French by F. Trochu (1936) and in English by B. Anderdon (1938).

St Emily de Vialar, *Foundress* (1797-1856)

Anne Marguerite Adelaide Emilie de Vialar was the eldest child and only daughter of Baron Jacques Augustine de Vialar and his wife, Antoinette, daughter of Baron de Portal, physician to Louis XVIII and Charles X of France. She was born at Gaillac in the Languedoc in 1797. She left school in Paris when fifteen to be companion to her father, now a widower, in Gaillac. She refused to consider a suitable marriage, whereupon her father demoted her in the household. Without a sympathetic priest or friend to advise her she became rather closed-in on herself and spent much time in private conversations with God, which she interpreted as visions.

In 1818, when she was twenty-one, a young curate named Fr Mercier came to Gaillac and said he would help her find out if she really had a religious vocation. She started a fifteen-year period of caring for the poor and for neglected children. Her father objected to this and especially to his terrace being used for the sick, destitute, and depressed.

In 1832 Emily inherited a considerable fortune from her maternal grandfather, Baron de Portal. She bought a large house at Gaillac for herself and three companions, Victoria Teyssonnière, Rose Mongis, and Pauline Gineste. They were joined by others. Three months later the archbishop of Albi authorized Fr Mercier to clothe twelve postulants with the religious habit. They called themselves the Congregation of Sisters of St Joseph of the Apparition (an unfortunate term in English, but meaning the appearance of the angel to St Joseph). They were concerned with educating children and looking after the poor and sick. The Sisterhood became a primarily missionary Congregation. In 1835 the archbishop formally received the profession of Emily and seventeen other Sisters and approved the Rule of the Congregation.

In 1834 they had founded a second house in Algier in North Africa, where Emily's brother Augustine, a city councillor, invited them to take charge of a hospital. They established another house at Bône, then convents in Tunis and Constantine. The Tunis house had a filiation in Malta, and that gave rise to houses in the Balkans and the Near East. The Sisters of St Joseph were the first Catholic nuns in modern times to be established in Jerusalem.

Emily was a shrewd, lively, but strong-willed woman, and a long dispute about jurisdiction arose between her and Bishop Dupuch of Algiers. She was particularly immovable when the constitutional integrity of her Congregation seemed threatened. Rome decided in her favour, but the bishop was supported by the French colonial authorities. The Sisters had to give up their Algerian establishments. Emily turned her attention to Tunisia and then to Malta.

Fr Mercier died in 1845. When Emily returned to Gaillac in 1846, she found that a rash trustee had left the Congregation's headquarters in a bad state financially. After inconclusive lawsuits the motherhouse was moved to Toulouse, but several senior nuns left the Congregation. Emily's solution was to set out for Greece, where she founded a convent on the island of Syra. This was her last long journey, but foundations were made elsewhere during her lifetime. Six Sisters were sent to Burma in 1847; others were despatched to Freemantle in Australia in 1854. In the course of twenty-two years the Congregation grew from one to some forty houses. In 1852 the motherhouse had been moved again, to Marseilles, where it remains. All this effort owed much to the determination of the indefatigable Emily.

Emily's achievements came about in spite of the hernia that always plagued her—the result of a charitable action in her youth. From 1850 it became increasingly serious, and it hastened her death on 24 August 1856. She was canonized in 1951.

See C. Testas, *La vie militante de la Bse Mère Emilie de Vialar* (2d ed. 1939); E. de Guérin, *The Idol and the Shrine* (Eng. trans., 1949); G. Bernoville, *Emilie de Vialar* (1953).

St Mary Michaela Desmaisières, *Foundress* (1809-65)

María Micaela Desmaisières was born in Madrid in 1809, lost her mother in childhood, and resisted all attempts to make her marry. She had the title of viscountess and lived for some years with her brother while he was Spanish ambassador in Paris and Brussels. Because of her position she had to attend banquets, state balls, the theatre, and so on. Strictly pious people at that time thought this scarcely compatible with holiness of life. Whether as a protection against the presumed temptations of the world she moved in, or to punish herself for being in it at all, Mary not only received Communion every day but wore what the sources call "instruments of penance" (anything from very uncomfortable clothing to painful bracelets) beneath her dress. (We cannot know what really prompted this self-torture; then, at any rate, it was thought to promote sanctity). Thus fortified she devoted the rest of her time to good works: teaching the ignorant, rescuing prostitutes or defenceless women who might have to take to the streets, and charity to the sick and poor.

When she returned to Spain she started more than one organization for work of this kind and met with various difficulties. Eventually she founded the Congregation of the Handmaids of the Blessed Sacrament and of Charity to care for prostitutes. She was elected its mother general in 1859. The Holy See approved the Institute for five years during its foundress' lifetime and granted it permanent recognition shortly after her death. In the meantime it had spread widely. In 1865 Mother Michaela had set out for Rome in connection with this final approval, when cholera broke out in Valencia. She went there to help her Sisters who were looking after the victims. Though she had survived previous outbreaks she succumbed on this occasion, on 24 August. She was canonized in 1934.

See *A.A.S.* 17 (1925), pp. 292-6; A. R. di S. Teresa, *La Beata Maria Michelina del Sacramento* (1925).

R.M.

St Tation, martyr in Isauria under Diocletian (second/third century)

St Aurea, martyr cast into the sea at Ostia, on the Tiber (second/third century)

St Yachard of Kincardineshire, Scotland, bishop and missionary to the Picts (fifth century)

St Eptadus, priest at Nevers, France (sixth century)

St George Limniota, monk on Mount Olympus, martyr under the Emperor Leo (*c.* 730)

St Herman, hermit at Rinchnach, Germany (1326)

Bd Andrew Fardeau, martyr under the French revolution (1794)—see 2 Jan.

25

ST LOUIS OF FRANCE (1214-70)

Louis (or Lewis) IX, king of France, spent much of his life trying to be the ideal Christian prince. He succeeded in this aim and was canonized as an exemplary monarch who bore adversity without complaint. Certainly he was both a captivating figure in a romantic-historical sense and an impressive actor on the national and, in a sense, the world political stage, for he was much concerned with the affairs not only of France and the Latin West but also of the three great complexes of Byzantium, Islam, and the Mongol (or Tartar) Empire as they went through various stages of decline or self-assertion. (The immensely successful Genghis Khan, for many then and since not only the anti-Christ but the "anti-Louis" of that era, died in 1227). Louis' actions and policies, supported by his legend, have affected the self-conception of French—and other—rulers over the centuries.

The national consequences, of course, have been more obvious. The Bourbon monarchy exalted Louis as a Christian autocrat, whereas the Third Republic praised him as an embodiment of moderation, peace, and justice. Figures as diverse as Louis XIV and Napoleon, De Gaulle, and Pétain have been seen as incorporating many of Louis' virtues but also his defects as a French leader. His attitude to Islam remains one of the components of the immensely complicated present-day relations between Western and Muslim nations. Yet Louis IX's personal integrity, humility, and restraint have always made his holiness as an individual, rather than the sanctity of his office or the factual outcome of his time-bound attitudes, a controlling force in his powerful myth.

Louis was the son of Louis VIII and of Blanche of Castile, his half-English queen, daughter of Alfonso of Castile and Eleanor of England. He enjoyed the protection of the economic wealth accumulated by his grandfather, Philip Augustus, and of prosperous royal domains. He was born (or baptized) at Poissy on 25 April 1214. His father died when he was twelve, on 8 November 1226, and his mother was regent of France until he reached his majority. He was crowned at Reims on 29 November 1226.

Between 1227 and 1234 some barons instigated a revolt against the monarchy, but by 1234 unforeseen deaths, withdrawals by the most powerful, and astute manoueuvring by the queen regent and the king's advisers assured Louis as secure a rule as could then be wished. He scarcely kept in the background himself, for in 1230 alone, when only fifteen, he led three campaigns in the field: two in the west against the Count of Brittany and his associates and one in Champagne, in the east.

He married Margaret, the eldest daughter of Raymund Berenguer, count of Provence, at Sens on 27 May 1234, when she was thirteen and he was fourteen and considered to have attained his majority. The French monarchy had thus reached the shores of the Mediterranean. The marriage also made Henry III of England, married to Raymund's second daughter, Eleanor, Louis' brother-in-law. Louis and Margaret had eleven children: five sons and six daughters. The first child was born in 1240, six years after the marriage. We do not know if there were stillbirths or deaths of other children before then. He was consecrated in 1235 and began to govern the kingdom, though his mother remained influential.

In 1239 Louis joined the lands of Macon to the royal domains. In 1242-3 he defeated Raymond VII of Toulouse and various southern lords and was able to consolidate the royal dominion over Nîmes-Beaucaire and Béziers-Carcassonne after the peace of Loris. He is said to have detroyed the Cathars as a threat to national unity, but the erosion of their power was due more to the efforts of the Church and the Inquisition and even more to the inevitably self-limiting effects of Cathar doctrine. Some historians insist that in reality Louis brought the benefits of long-lasting peace to the south after cruel campaigns and intolerable dissension.

Soon after Louis' majority Hugh of Lusignan, count of La Marche, whose estates were a fief of Poitou, refused to pay homage to the count of Poitiers, Louis' brother. Hugh's wife, Isabel, was the mother of Henry III of England. Henry decided to embark for France to support his stepfather and tried to win back the Angevin lands in western France. Louis defeated him on 21-2 July 1242 at Taillebourg and at Saintes. Henry fled to Bordeaux and in 1243 returned to England, having arranged a truce with the French.

In the 1240s Europe was threatened by powerful enemies of Christendom and, therefore, of Christianity. In March-April 1241 the terrible ravages of the Mongols in central Europe were taken as a warning of imminent catastrophe. In October 1244 the Christians of Palestine were disastrously trounced by the Muslims near Gaza. In December of that year, when sick (probably of dysentery and apparently mortally), Louis made a fateful decision and vowed to lead a Crusade to the Holy Land. His councillors and nobles were against the project, but Louis was resolute. To finance the Crusade he spent some years collecting additional taxes from ecclesiastical benefices and on 12 June 1248 embarked for Cyprus. He disembarked there on 18 September, and two hundred English knights led by the earl of Salisbury joined his forces. A typical insight into Louis' many-sidedness, his desire to balance and consolidate, is that in December he took time off from marshalling his forces to meet the Dominican André de Longjumeau at Nicosia on his return from a voyage to central Asia. He also received two Mongol ambassadors, and in January despatched André and an embassy with rich gifts to the Great Khan.

Islam, however, was an immediate menace. Louis captured Damietta in the

Nile Delta in June 1249 and entered the city walking barefoot but preceded by the papal legate. He ordered inquiries into crimes committed by the Crusaders, especially theft, and decreed that restitution should be made. He decreed that no Muslim was to be killed if he could be taken prisoner. Of course there were too many opportunities to satisfy greed, and Louis' measures did not prevent appalling plunder, violence, and rapine. All this was difficult to reconcile with Louis' emphasis on the high seriousness of the Crusade as a pilgrimage of homage to the tomb of Christ, crucified at Jerusalem. All his enthusiasm could not help the Crusaders, who were wasted by disease and enfeebled by corruption. They were defeated at Mansourah on 5 April 1250, and Louis was taken prisoner. During his captivity he recited the divine office every day with two chaplains, and he refused to hand over the castles in Syria in spite of threats of torture. Eventually he surrendered Damietta, paid a huge sum to ransom himself and the surviving Crusaders (the sick and wounded had been ruthlessly massacred), and was released on 6 May. Far from abandoning the Christian enterprise in Palestine, he went to Acre in Syria from May 1250 to May 1251 to strengthen the Crusaders' territories there. From May 1251 to May 1252 he visited whatever Holy Places he could reach in Caesarea, and he spent May 1252 to June 1253 in Jaffa, not omitting in December to send a Franciscan ambassador to the Mongol prince Sartaq.

He stayed at Sidon from June 1253 to February 1254. When he heard of his mother's death (she had acted as regent) he returned to France, on 17 July 1254 (together with a number of converts from Islam and their families, whom he supported for the rest of their lives), and began a series of long-planned national reforms in his realm, which he had made sure was neither weakened nor suffered episodes of anarchy during his long absence. The most important decree was the Great Ordinance of December for the reformation of the kingdom of France, which between 1254 and 1270 introduced various measures to establish a moral order. Louis decided to compensate for the lost Crusade by preserving the body and soul of the kingdom of France. A complex structure of new decrees urged a new responsibility for social life, monitored by frequent reports on the conduct of the governors and officers of cities, towns, and provincial lands and, above all, of Paris. From 1236 to 1263 Louis issued his monetary ordinances, and asserted the rights of "good"—that is, the royal—coinage against any other ("bad") money. One of his actions defining due and proper coinage was in fact a wise—and very modern—recognition of necessity, for it devalued the coinage in response to growing inflation. Most of Louis' monetary measures were also assertions of the power of the monarchical state against financial divisions and individual enterprise and formed part of his eschatological vision. The *renovatio monetae* (renewal of money) was a pious and sacred act.

As measures of consolidation, in 1255 he married his daughter Isabella to Thibaud V, count of Champagne and king of Navarre; in 1256 he brought peace to Flanders by regulating the succession question there; and in May 1258 he signed the treaty of Corbeil with the king of Aragon and that of Paris with Henry III (ratified in 1259), by which England gained the Limousin and Périgord while Henry renounced all claims to Normandy, Anjou, Maine, Touraine, and Poitou. To critics of his concessions, Louis replied that his main intention was to cement a lasting peace between England and France. The Hundred Years' War was to show how far this was only a pious hope.

Between 1258 and 1265 Louis acted as a somewhat ineffectual if well-intentioned arbitrator between Henry III and his barons; the arbitration of Amiens, which he had thought so successful, failed on 24 March 1264.

The sultan Baibars took Caesarea in 1265. As the Muslim depredations and threats continued, and not having learned the lessons of his previous disastrous expedition, Louis planned another Crusade in 1267. His resolve was confirmed when Baibars took Jaffa in 1268. Louis set sail on 1 July 1270 and landed at Tunis in North Africa, but on 25 August, worn out by illness and austerity, he succumbed to dysentery, probably the result of typhus (which also attacked his son Philip). As he lay dying he received the Last Sacraments, called for the Greek ambassadors to urge them to promote the reunion of Orthodoxy with Rome, and finally achieved what he himself had called a form of martydom. When the Tartars invaded Christendom, he told his mother, "We shall either repel them or, if we are defeated, we shall come before God as confessors of Christ or as martyrs." He had told his companions on his first Crusade that the Christians slain by the Saracens before Sidon were "martyrs and in paradise." Yet Louis' attitude to Muslims, viewed in the past as a positive element of his role as a defender of Christendom, has earned the recent judgment that in the present-day world his "aggressivity toward Islam" and his "western pre-colonialism" (Le Goff) are not merely characteristics of a closed period of history but remain fatefully effective aspects of his heritage.

Louis was a complex man of great charisma from whom a special virtue was thought to flow. His contemporaries wanted to see and to hear but also to touch him. Historians have found him both admirable and detestable. His sensibility and his aims and the means he used to accomplish them were those of more than seven hundred years ago and sometimes are, or appear to be, offensive in the light of modern preferences. Even then, his remains an appreciable personality with which one can empathize and even sympathize.

He was very devout and much more austere than his station customarily permitted, yet dominating in his attempts to make his household, court, and nation similarly rigorous. Unable to follow in their practice of poverty (unless symbolically) Christ and the hermits he so admired, he emulated their humility and made emphatic penitence a constant feature of his life. He scourged himself methodically to curb his strong (and well-attested) appetites for sex, food, and pleasurable talk. He wore a hair shirt under his splendid robes and might prefer suddenly to sit on the ground without, it was said, the slightest affectation, yet insisted on the prestige of his dynasty, denying his wife certain privileges essentially because she did not belong to the royal lineage. He enjoined piety on his family, yet flew into a rage when Margaret tried to arrange a pilgrimage on her own initiative. He was famous for his honesty, especially in observing the stipulations of treaties and agreements, but also for his political astuteness. His impartial justice was unusual for the times, as when he allowed the death sentence for a Flemish count who had hanged three children for hunting rabbits in his woods, then commuted it to mere confiscation of most of his estates, or when he appointed a special commissior of inquiry to examine royal abuses of power.

He was said to have the eyes of a dove and was renowned for his measures to promote peace, as when he proscribed private wars between feudal lords, and when not only prelates and barons but foreign kings asked him to judge and arbitrate. His generosity and almsgiving were exceptional, as when he founded a hospital for three hundred impoverished blind men, or regularly gave food-hampers to the poor at his gates, often serving them in person. He kept lists of the needy whom he helped in every province of the kingdom. But he was also famous for the magnificent banquets at which he entertained the nobility of France. He was celebrated for his mercy to rebels, as when, with the words "A son can't refuse to obey his father!" he refused to execute the son of Hugh de la Marche, implicated in his father's insurrection. He was feared for his correction of vanity but admired for his practical shrewdness, as when he told his courtiers, "Dress well, as your rank demands, so that your wives will find you all the more attractive."

The extended universities, such as the theological institute that became known as the Sorbonne; the fine cathedrals and the monastic foundations, such as Royaumont, Vauvert, and Maubuisson; and the general culture of his reign were admired throughout Europe. He was known especially for the Sainte Chapelle, Paris, his major monument and one of the glories of medieval art and architecture. Austere yet brilliant like Louis himself, it was built in 1245-8 as a private chapel for the king and his family but above all to house the supposed crown of thorns obtained in 1239 from Baldwin II, the Latin emperor at Constantinople. Its position as a central rather than ancillary sacred enclosure in the palace and its dedication to the suffering of God emphasized Louis' conception of sacrifice as the very ethos of kingship.

He was devoted to the Church and its ministers. He enjoyed the company of intelligent priests, whom he consulted to inform his conscience. On more than one occasion he invited the retiring St Thomas Aquinas (28 Jan.) to discuss weighty affairs of State and recorded his table-talk. He also thought that profundity needed intervals of grace and light, but in due measure, of which he was the arbiter. He entertained a fashionable friar noted for improving discourse, found it too heavy for his taste, snapped, "There's a time and a place for everything!" and switched the conversation to an easier topic. His biographers often cite his laughter and his jokes, which he nevertheless withheld on Fridays for solemnity's sake, expecting others to do the same.

As his reign progressed, Louis became more exacting and more determined to impose an ideal moral order on his subjects. In 1230 he forbade usury and would not allow even Jews—hitherto exempt—to practise it. He would not permit obscenity or swearing at court and was so fierce against blasphemy that he ordered all offenders to be branded; he had the sentence carried out on a rich and important citizen of Paris, saying that he, Louis, would suffer the same punishment if he could stop the crime in that way.

Louis was genuinely in favour of peace as a source of national unity and concord and, more importantly, of economic prosperity. He was reluctant to make war but did not hesitate to do so if he thought it necessary. If the peace of the Christian realm was threatened, war was justifiable. He was determined to secure the State and administrative power of France and thus to unify the country. He has been seen as one of the founders not only of the modern French State but even of State centralism in the modern world.

He was even more inclined to enter into conflict against the enemies of Christendom, both external and internal, than against those of national unity. He saw the supreme objective of a Christian monarch as the maintenance of a seamless Christianity, a simultaneously natural and mystical body that ultimately dared not tolerate the presence within it of inimical forces once they threatened that unity. There were many such enemies in his eyes—above all, Muslims, Jews, heretics, homosexuals, even lepers—and he was always ready to assess the degrees of danger that they represented and to act against them when danger was imminent. He used integration but also extirpation as instruments for achieving his ends. He conceived of the desired wholeness of the realm as analogous to that of the body—itself emblematic of the soul. He applied to the body politic the typically medieval imagery of uncleanness, of different modes of soiling what should be all beautiful within, so that political autonomy, the Jewish scriptures, and so on were seen as forms of incurable disease, rotting, maiming, and eventually destroying the national soul. Along with other actual yet mythic figures he influenced subsequent conceptions of unified government.

Louis was prepared to act as the secular arm of the Church against heresy, as when the Inquisition set about eradication of the Cathars, though here too his sense of fairness and due equilibrium inclined him to favour conversion rather than repression, under the probable influence of those Dominicans who followed the policy of St Dominic (8 Aug.) himself. With regard to the Jews he preferred the same policy and veered between correction and protection; in the end, however, he became their fanatical persecutor. There were palliative measures, as when he extended the decree against usury to Christian usurers (from Lombardy). Of course he did not share the ideas of "race" and "blood" essential to modern anti-Semitism, and he thought of himself as condemning usury, not those who practised it. Louis saw Judaism as a perfidious religion and did not think of the dispersed Jews as a nation. He acted as godfather to a number of Jewish converts, as justice demanded. In 1240 a public controversy regarding the Talmud was held with some Jews in the presence of Louis and Blanche. In 1242, however, and again in 1244, when the Inquisition developed into a formidable presence in France, the Talmud was burned publicly. Throughout his reign, with certain exceptions such as the punishment of the instigators of a local pogrom and temporary minor relaxations, the decrees of confiscation, taxes, manual labour, and expulsion became increasingly cruel. In 1269, the same year in which he issued his ordinance against blasphemy, Louis made all Jews wear a distinctive red badge on their chest and back, a precursor of the yellow star they were forced to bear in the Vichy period. "The Jews," he said, "are subject to me under the yoke of servitude. . . . They must give up usury or leave my country immediately to preserve it from corruption by the filth they void."

His body was chopped up and boiled in wine to separate the flesh from the bones, which, together with his heart, were taken back to France and buried at Saint-Denis in 22 May 1271. Miracles were reported at an ever-increasing rate along the route and in the presence of the relics thereafter.

The legend of Louis IX was raised to a new level when Geoffrey of Beaulieu wrote his Life as early as 1272-3, showing how Louis' saintly humility contended with understandable manifestations of royal superbia, or pride, to make him a true follower of the Christ who was both Suffering Servant and King. Louis' contemporaries certainly thought him holy not so much for his achievements in war and politics as for his equable, modest, and uncomplaining behaviour and attitude under trial: while sick, as a captive, and when he lost his wife and son. Pontifical inquiries into his fitness for canonization were ordered in 1273, 1278, and 1282. The reports were solemnly read to Pope Honorius IV in 1285. Pope Boniface VIII canonized Louis at Orvieto on 6 August 1297. In 1298 the casket of bones was exhumed and elevated before Philip the Fair and an assembly of nobles and prelates. In 1308 Philip divided the bones and gave them as relics to important people and churches. Those enshrined in the abbey church of St Denis were scattered at the Revolution. Louis' entrails eventually reached Sicily. To protect them from Garibaldi's troops they were carried off by the unsavoury Bourbon ruler Francis II, who in 1894 willed them to Carthage Cathedral, where they now lie, not so far from where Louis died. In 1309 Joinville presented the future Louis X with his great *History of St Louis*, in which he idolized his friend but made him speak the vernacular as a real person (a major reason for the myth's impact) while regretting that Louis had not been numbered officially among the martyrs: "If God died on the cross, he did the same, for he was crucified when he died at Tunis."

See J. de Joinville, ed. N. de Wailly, *Histoire de Saint Louis* (with nineteenth-century French trans., 1874); *idem*, ed. J. Monfrin, with a useful introduction and modern French translation, *Vie de Saint Louis* (1995); and M. R. B. Shaw, *Chronicles of the Crusades* (1963) for Jean de Joinville's contemporary Life. There are Lives by Geoffrey of Beaulieu and William of Chartres in *AA.SS.*, Aug., 5 (1741), pp. 275-758; Life of *c*. 1305 by William of Saint-Pathus, ed. H.-F. Delaborde (1899); P. B. Fay (ed.), *La vie et les miracles de Saint Louis* (1932); *B.H.L.*, 2, pp. 747-50; L. S. Le N. Tillemont, ed. J. de Gaulle, *Vie de Saint Louis*, 6 vols. (1847-51); H. Wallon, *S. Louis et son Temps* (1975); M. W. Labarge, *St Louis of France* (1968); J. Richard, *Saint Louis, roi d'une France féodale, soutien de la Terre sainte* (1983); J. Le Goff, *Saint Louis* (1996), an exhaustive study which supersedes or corrects previous biographies. See also Louis' instructions for his son, *Les Etablissements de saint Louis*, ed. P. Viollet, 4 vols. (1881-6); D. O'Connell, *The Teachings of Saint Louis. A critical text* (1972); J. Le Goff (ed., with valuable prefaces), *Les Propos de Saint Louis* (1974). On the canonization see L. Carolus-Barré, *Reconstitution du procès de canonisation de Saint Louis, 1272-1297* (1995); and on his crusades, S. Runciman, *History of the Crusades*, vols. 1-3 (1951-4); R. I. Burns, "Christian Islamic Confrontation in the West: The thirteenth-century dream of conversion," in *American Historical Review* 76 (1971), pp. 1386-434; W. C. Jordan, *Louis IX and the Challenge of the Crusade* (1979); P. Alphandéry and A. Dupront, *La Chrétienté et l'idée de croisade*, 2 vols. (2d ed., 1995). On statesmanship, etc., see J. R. Strayer, *Medieval Statecraft and the Perspectives of History* (1971); M. Kerner (ed.), *Ideologie und Herrschaft im Mittelalter* (1982); A. J. Duggan (ed.), *Kings and Kingship in Medieval Europe* (1992); W. C. Jordan, *The French Monarchy and the Jews from Philip Augustus to the Last Capetians* (1989); B. de Jouvenel, *Du Pouvoir* (1947), pp. 11-25 and *passim*. On art see R. Branner, *Manuscript Painting in Paris during the Reign of Saint Louis* (1977).

Louis is the patron of (linen-) drapers because he gave them shops to display their goods in the rue de la Lingerie, Paris. His attributes are a crown of thorns, the three nails of the crucifixion, the cross, a crown, a sword, and a fleur-de-lys. He sometimes holds a model of the Sainte-Chapelle. The rush foundation of Jesus' supposed crown of thorns survived the Revolution and is in Notre Dame. Louis gave away some of the thorns mounted in golden reliquaries, and one of these is in the British Museum. Throughout the centuries it was customary to portray Louis with the features of the reigning monarch, which has led to some iconographical confusion.

There are many grandiose images of Louis: he appears with Augustine in Tiepolo's model (1737-8; National Gallery, London) for the altarpiece once in S. Salvatore, Venice. A simple, effectively austere wooden statue of 1250 from the retable of the Sainte Chapelle, Paris, shows him holding the book of laws. There are several scenes from his life in the stained glass of the Sainte Chapelle, Paris. One miniature (*c*. 1235; Pierpoint Morgan Library, New York) shows him aged twenty with Blanche of Castille. He appears in stone in the vault of the choir of the chapel of St Germain-en-Laye (1238). In a thirteenth-century bas-relief in Notre Dame, Paris, he is on his knees. A drawing (Corpus Christi College, Cambridge) by the English chronicler Matthew Paris (d. 1259) shows him during his final sickness being presented with a cross-reliquary by his mother. In a miniature from the Imperial Bible (Austrian National Library, Vienna) the bearded Louis, penitent but wise, appears enthroned and holding a richly illuminated Bible. A poignant early drawing (Inguimbertine Library, Carpentras, France), based on the lost frescoes his wife ordered for the church of the Cordeliers at Lourcine, portrays the king as a follower of the Man of Sorrows, his head bent in penitence. Various superb miniatures (in the Bibliothèque nationale, Paris) show (1334) Louis on his way to the coronation at Reims, (1250) being crowned, (*c*. 1300) reading a Book of Hours while riding, and praying before relics of the passion. On his royal seal (National archives, Paris) Louis wears a robe decorated with the fleur de lys. The young Tintoretto's portrait (1557; Academy, Venice) shows him aged and penitent, with Jerome and Andrew. A thirteenth-century Bible illustrated by order of Louis is now in the Morgan Library, New York.

ST JOSEPH CALASANZ, *Founder* (1556–1648)

Joseph Calasanz founded the Clerks Regular of the Christian Schools. He came from an aristocratic family. The youngest of five sons of Don Pedro Calasanz and Doña Maria Gastonia, he was born in his father's castle near Petralta de la Sal in Aragon, Spain. He was educated at Estadilla and at the universities of Lérida (where he was awarded a doctorate in law) and Valencia. He is said to have transferred to Alcalá to study theology because of the unwelcome attentions of a young kinswoman. He decided not to marry and was ordained priest in 1583 by the bishop of Urgel. He held administrative posts in Spain, first as vicar general of the Trempe district. He was sent to try to restore a sense of their religious duties among the clergy in the valleys of Andorra, where the bishop of Urgel was joint ruler. He carried out an arduous visitation of the remote area, then returned to Trempe and was made vicar general of the whole diocese.

He had a strong interest in improving the education of the poor in towns and cities. In 1592 he resigned his office and benefices, divided his patrimony between his sisters and the poor, endowed a number of charitable institutions, kept a reasonable income for himself, and went to Rome There he enjoyed the patronage of the Colonna family, for Cardinal Ascanio Colonna had been a friend of his at Alcalá. Together with his friend St Camillus de Lellis (14 July), he cared for the sick and dying during the 1595 plague. His interest in good works led him to a special concern for the education of homeless and abandoned children, whom few religious Orders looked after. None seemed to provide full-time education for them.

He became a member of the Confraternity of Christian Doctrine, which taught children and adults on Sundays and holy days, and came face-to-face with the appalling conditions of the poor and disadvantaged. He asked the parish schoolteachers to admit children without fees. They refused to do so unless their salaries were raised; the Roman Senate rejected this proposal. Joseph asked the Dominicans and Jesuits to help, but they were fully committed elsewhere, so he decided to open a school himself. He was responsible for the establishment of the first free school in Rome, which he set up with three other priests in November 1597 in two rooms provided by Don Antonio Brendani, parish priest of Santa Dorotea, who joined Joseph in his work. After a week a hundred children were receiving instruction. The numbers increased rapidly; in 1599 new premises had to be found as well as unpaid teachers from among the unbeneficed Roman clergy. Joseph obtained Cardinal Ascanio's permission to leave the Colonnas and live on the school premises with the other teachers. They led a quasi-community life and Joseph acted as the superior of what eventually became the Piarist Order. In 1602 there were seven hundred pupils, and a new house was found at St Andrew della Valle. Pope Clement VIII made a grant toward the rent. The school took in some pupils from "good" families, and complaints were made about so-called disorders. The pope ordered a visit of inspection and took the Institute under his personal protection. In 1606 Pope Paul V doubled the grant. Complaints of one kind or another continued, but the school flourished. In 1612, with papal approval and help, Joseph transferred the work to the Torres Palace, next to the church of S. Pantaleone. Joseph was superior; there were several priests; and the pupils now numbered 1,200, including some Jews whom Joseph invited to attend. He spent his remaining years there. Other schools were established, and the Institute was formally recognized as a religious Congregation, of which Joseph became superior general. He used what time he could spare from his duties to care for the sick and needy outside the school. He helped an English convert and his family, refugees from the penal laws, and obtained a pension for them from the pope.

When Joseph was sixty-five one of his priests, Mario Sozzi, who had been admitted to the Institute in Naples and had proved an unsatisfactory provincial in Tuscany, where he had worked independently of the superior general, encouraged rival interests in the Congregation to make unjust accusations against Joseph to the Holy Office. Sozzi had some extraordinary influence with the ecclesiastical authorities. To vindicate Joseph, Cardinal Cesarini ordered Sozzi's papers to be seized; they were found to include some documents of the Holy Office, but Joseph, strange to say, was blamed for this. He was arrested by the Holy Office and paraded through the streets. Only the intervention of Cardinal Cesarini saved him from imprisonment. Sozzi plotted to gain control of the Institute, claiming that Joseph was senile. He was suspended from his office after further calumnies from Sozzi and replaced by an apostolic visitor favourable to the scheming priest. They ran the Institute together. The authorities refused to listen to the truth, and Joseph was constantly humiliated. Sozzi continued to denounce him until his own death in 1643, when Fr Cherubini was appointed to run the Institute. He treated Joseph in the same way. Joseph did not regain his authority in the Institute until 1645, when a committee of cardinals examined the affair and recommended his reinstatement. This was delayed by other plotters, including a female relative of the pope. In 1646 Pope Innocent X made the Cogregation a society of priests under diocesan bishops.

Joseph was now ninety. He suffered all this persecution patiently, saying: "The Lord gave and the Lord hath taken away. Blessed be the name of the Lord." Eventually Cherubini was convicted by the auditors of the Sacred Rota of maladministration of the Nazarene College, for which he was also responsible. He withdrew from Rome in disgrace but returned the next year to ask Joseph's forgiveness before dying. Joseph himself died in Rome on 25 August 1648. The Congregation was restored with simple vows only in 1656 and did not become the religious Order known as the Clerks Regular of the Christian

Schools—or the Piarists, or Scopoli—until 1669. It spread through Spain, Italy, and South America. In 1728 Cardinal Lambertini (later Pope Benedict XIV) referred to Joseph before the Congregation of Sacred Rites as "a perpetual miracle of fortitude and another Job." He was beatified in 1748 and canonized in 1767. In 1948 Pius XII made him patron of Christian schools. His feast-day was formerly 25 August.

See *Letters*, ed. L. Picanyol , 9 vols. (1950-6); *B.T.A.*, 3, pp. 413-6; *Bibl. SS.*, 6, 1321-30; Lives by U. Tosetti (1753; rp. 1917); J. Timon-David, 2 vols. (1884); W. E. Hubert (1886); J. C. Heidenreich (1907); G. Giovannozzi (1930); C. Santoloci, *Giuseppe Calasanzio: educatore e santo* (1948); C. Bau, *Biografia Crítica de S. José de Calasanz* (1949); F. Giordano, *Il Calasanzio* (1960); C. Bau (1967); G. Grimaldi, *Giuseppe Calasanzio* (1997). See also special issue of *Revista Calasancia* 3, no. 12 (1957), esp. bibliography, pp. 695-721.

The most popular scene from his life in art is the saint's last Communion. There is a seventeenth-century painting of the subject by Valdés Leal and an eighteenth-century sketch by Maulbertsch (Germanic Museum, Nuremberg). The most impressive portrayal (San Antonio, Madrid) is that of the same scene by Goya (1746-1828), with Joseph worn and unassuming, which intentionally recalls the *Last Communion of St Jerome* by Le Dominiquin and that of Francis of Assisi by Rubens.

St Genesius of Arles, *Martyr* (*c.* 303)

Genesius was said to be a catechumen and by profession a public notary, that is, he made a record of judicial proceedings for the public archives. One day the clerk of the court at Arles read out an imperial edict of persecution against the Christians. Genesius could not bring himself to trace the words with the stylus on his wax tablet. He stood up, flung his registers at the judge's feet, and resigned. He fled from town to town and requested Baptism from the bishop, who is said to have thought him too young or the risk too great. He refused to confer the sacrament and said that only as a martyr could Genesius receive baptism. His pursuers caught up with him eventually, and he was beheaded on the banks of the Rhône during the persecution of Maximian and Diocletian.

He has no connection with the wholly fictitious Genesius the Comedian, formerly commemorated as a separate martyr on the same day. The actual Genesius became very famous, eventually being proclaimed patron of the city of Arles. His cult was adopted in Rome and spread to Africa, Narbonne, and elsewhere. A church was built to him in Rome; later his body was said to be buried there. He was transformed into a Roman martyr. A pleasing fiction soon (at least as early as the sixth century) turned him into an actor. He was said to have made fun of Christian rites before the emperor but to have been suddenly converted by divine inspiration, as the mocking words in his mouth were rendered true, and human irony became sacred irony.

Genesius is mentioned by Prudentius, Venantius Fortunatus, Hilary, Gregory of Tours, and others and is included in the *Hieronymianum*. See *AA.SS.*, Aug., 5; *C.M.H.*, pp. 463-5; S. Cavallin, *S. Genès le Notaire* (1945).

St Mennas, *Patriarch* (552)

Mennas (or Menas) had the misfortune to be an important cleric during the time of Justinian and Theodora—a reign of the Byzantine era of which it might justly be said that it was one of the most Byzantine. Formulas, anathemas, and edicts came thick and fast, and a dogmatic letter or visit in response had to be very nicely judged in order to play for time, which could mean job security and even life. This was still the era when, in Gibbon's words, "the road to paradise, a bridge as sharp as a razor, was suspended over the abyss." The following is a necessarily reductive summary of immensely complicated and always murky proceedings.

Mennas was a native of Alexandria in Egypt. He was a priest in Constantinople until, in 536, he was appointed patriarch there. He had to sign an expanded *Formula of Hormisdas* before consecration by Pope St Agapitus I (22 Apr.), who was in the city at the time as an envoy of the Ostrogothic king Theodhad and in order to assert his primatial rights. Mennas set about redressing problems caused by his predecessor Anthimus, an undercover Monophysite who had been variously bishop of Trebizond, an ascetic in one of Theodora's palaces, and one of her church pawns, also used, then discarded, by Justinian and tucked away again by Theodora to evade a special council Agapitus wanted to decide his fate. Agapitus died in Constantinople on 22 April 536, but the council met anyway, on 2 May, under Mennas' presidency. It condemned and degraded the wisely absent Anthimus and anathematized the moderate Monophysitist Severus of Antioch, who had been staying in Constantinople at the emperor's invitation with a very large company of monks of the same persuasion, housed here and there at Theodora's expense. But Justinian had changed his mind, probably because for the moment, as Agapitus had maintained, winning good opinions in Italy was more important than touchy Monophysites in the East. Severus and the Severans prudently left the city in March. Agapitus' deacon, Pelagius (later Pope Pelagius I), remained in Constantinople as the emperor's adviser and would seem to have enjoyed more power over church issues than Mennas. Mennas also had to deal with a number of difficult members of sects sheltering under the name of Origen, especially the Palestinian *Laura* movement of the monk Sabas from Cappadocia (d. 532), who in 494 became archimandrite of all the anchorites of Palestine, and the New *Laura* splinter group. Mennas was ordered to obtain influential signatures on a new anti-Origenist edict from Justinian in the form of a theological treatise and a conciliar decree at the beginning of 542. Mennas managed to persuade first the clergy of Constantinople, then other patriarchs and the pope himself to sign the edict.

In 544 the emperor Justinian, who not only engaged in high and low level ecclesiastical intrigue but fancied himself a theologian, tried to conciliate his Monophysite subjects by condemning some writings called the Three Chapters. These included works of the Nestorian Theodore of Mopsuestia (who died before Nestorius was condemned), the writings of Theodoret (whose orthodoxy was acknowledged at Chalcedon), and a letter from Bishop Ibas (read at Chalcedon and pronounced orthodox). By making these works anathema Justinian did not reject Chalcedon but seemed to reduce its authority. The essential issue was not a definition of faith but expediency. Justinian ordered all his bishops to sign the lengthy condemnation. Mennas was the first to obey, though reluctantly. He said he would cancel his own signature if the Bishop of Rome did not agree, but in the end he did not withdraw. Western bishops recognized that the writings were heretical in part but objected to the condemnation because it seemed to compromise the Council of Chalcedon.

The reigning pope, Vigilius, was a scoundrel, if not the worst of the unworthy occupants of the see of Rome. Before he became pope Vigilius had promised to favour the Monophysites, ingratiated himself with the empress Theodora, and replaced the deposed pope, Silverius, who had been a Gothic choice. After Silverius' banishment the improperly reigning Vigilius and his slaves took Silverius to the island of Palmaria, worked him over, and extorted a valid resignation. Vigilius did not keep all his promises to Theodora and was duly arrested in a church in Rome and carried off to Sicily for ten months. Although some obviously Monophysite letters are attributed to Vigilius, he did affirm the Chalcedonian principles but then vacillated, though not endlessly, for in 551 he refused to accept Justinian's edict. Having been summoned to Constantinople by the emperor (always a dangerous sign in matters ecclesiastical), he took over a year to get there in the hope that things would sort themselves out, finally arriving in January 547 accompanied by several Italian bishops.

Vigilius' fears were justified. He sought sanctuary in St Peter's church in the palace of Hormisdas. Justinian's troopers tried to drag him from, it is said, the altar, and at one point of unseemly struggle the pope kicked himself free but brought the altar down on top of himself. However, in his *Judicatum* of Holy Saturday 548 he condemned the Three Chapters. Western opposition became very firm, and an African council formally excommunicated the pope. Vigilius then cancelled his *Judicatum* but sent Justinian a private letter in which he promised to do everything possible to get the Chapters condemned. Later the emperor published this letter.

In July 551 Justinian issued another edict against the Chapters. Vigilius protested and had to escape from Constantinople over the housetops. He took refuge in St Euphemia's at Chalcedon. He promptly excommunicated Mennas and others who had signed the decree. Mennas assured Vigilius that he had not deviated from the acts of the Council of Chalcedon. Vigilius returned to Constantinople. The question of the Three Chapters was referred to an ecumenical council, summoned by Justinian. On 4 May 553, the day the ecumenical council met, Vigilius issued his *Constitutum*, in which he condemned sixty extracts from Theodore's writings, though not Theodore himself, and defended the orthodoxy of Ibas' letter. The council (essentially one of Oriental bishops) condemned the Three Chapters, held that Ibas' letter was not the one read at Chalcedon, and excommunicated Vigilius. After six months in gaol, in a letter of 8 December 554 and in his *Judicatum* of 23 February 554, Vigilius gave way and retracted his *Constitutum* because, he claimed, he had been misled by the devil. He condemned the Chapters and even accepted the council's untruth about Ibas' letter. Vigilius was then allowed to leave Constantinople. He died of an attack of the stone at Syracuse, on his way back to Rome. His capitulation has been called the greatest humiliation in the history of the papacy.

Mennas did not live to see this council. He died on 24 August 552, after Justinian had forced him to apologize to Vigilius as a sop to the vanquished pope. Mennas managed to keep his office in difficult times and deserves some kind of commendation for the particular sagacity this required. A patriarch of Constantinople had supported a policy eventually confirmed by a general council against a feeble pope whose judgment and actions were variously swayed by the conflicting views of Western bishops and Eastern emperor. Pope Gregory I declared the 553 council valid. Mennas was named as a saint in the Roman Martyrology.

See *AA.SS.*, Aug., 5; F. Savio, *Il Papa Vigilio* (1904); *D. T.C.*, 11, 1574-88; E. Duffy, *Saints and Sinners: The History of the Popes* (1997), pp. 42-4; P. N. Ure, *Justinian and His Age* (1951); R. Browning, *Justinian and Theodora* (1971); Jedin-Dolan, 2, pp. 445-9, 452-3.

St Ebba, *Abbess* (683)

This Ebba (or Ebbe) is sometimes called "the Elder" to distinguish her from Ebba ("the Younger"), also abbess of Coldingham, said to have been killed by the Danes about the year 870. She was the daughter of Ethelfrith, king of Northumbria, and the sister of St Oswald (9 Aug.) and Oswy. When her father died she fled to Scotland, in 616. Oswy wanted her to marry the king of the Scots. When she refused and received the monastic habit from St Finan of Lindisfarne (19 Jan.), he gave her a piece of land on the Derwent, where she founded the monastery of Ebbchester. She later moved to Coldingham on the Berwick coast, where she established a double monastery resembling St Hilda's at Whitby. The promontory on which it was built is still known as St Abb's Head. St Cuthbert (20 Mar.) visited her there; St Etheldreda (23 June; separated from her husband, King Egfrith, in 672 after refusing to consummate the marriage) was a nun under her before becoming abbess of her own monastery at Ely. Ebba gained a reputation for unusual wisdom.

Ebba's personal sanctity must have been very considerable to earn her any reputation worth having, for she was a very inefficient abbess, though possibly this was the result of old age and extended devotions. Bede says severely: "The Coldingham monastery of nuns was burned down through carelessness. But everyone who knew the facts was quite well aware that it happened because its members were so wicked, especially those who were supposed to be in authority. But God in his mercy gave them a warning of their punishment. If only they had followed the Ninevites' example and fasted, prayed and wept, they could have averted the just anger of the Almighty." Bede tells us that St Adamnan (23 Sept.), a monk at Coldingham, had a vision in which a stranger told him that the monastery would be destroyed by fire because its monks and nuns were slack and frivolous:

> I have visited every part of this monastery and been into all the buildings and dormitories. I have found no one except yourself worried about their eternal salvation. All of them, men and women, are either sound asleep or awake only to do evil. Even the cells, built for prayer and study, have been converted unto places for eating, drinking, gossip or other amusements. In their leisure moments, the nuns vowed to God abandon the propriety of their vocation and spend their time weaving fine clothes. They use these to their souls' peril, either to dress up like brides or to get attention from strange men. Because of all this a harsh and well-deserved punishment, in the form of a terrible fire, will soon hit this place and its people.

(It has been suggested that Adamnan knew very well what was going on and, when he just had to say something, prudently cast his remarks in vision form. On the other hand, miracles and uncannily accurate predictions are common in Bede.) When Ebba, quite reasonably, asked why Adamnan had not told her earlier, he said: "Well, I hesitated because of my respect for you. Perhaps you can take some kind of comfort in the fact that it won't happen while you're abbess." When the news spread, the community was alarmed for a few days and changed its ways. But after Ebba's death "they relapsed into their earlier sins. Indeed, they were even more wicked than before. Just when they thought everything was all right, the predicted punishment happened and caught them out." Bede says that his informant about all this was his fellow-priest Edgils, who was living at Coldingham at the time: "When most of the inhabitants had left the ruined monastery, he stayed for a long time in our own house and died there. I thought it was a good idea to include this event in my history to warn readers of the ways of God and how terrible he can be in dealing with human beings. Let us beware of indulging in the pleasures of the flesh."

Given all this, it is hardly surprising that there is not much trace of an early cult of Ebba, in spite of her lineage, though the lessons in the *Aberdeen Breviary* and the Durham and Winchcombe calendars testify to later commemoration. Her relics were discovered in the eleventh century and she became popular in southern Scotland and northern England in the twelfth. The relics were divided between Durham and Coldingham. A well-known church and street in Oxford are named after this Ebba.

For Capgrave's Life of Ebba, partly based on Reginald of Durham, see *AA.SS.*, Aug., 5. See also Bede, *H.E.* (n.e. 1990), pp. 251-3; B. Colgrave, ed., *Two Lives of St Cuthbert* (1940), pp. 79-80, 189-90, 318; idem, *Eddius' Life of St Wilfrid* (1927), p. 79; *N.L.A.*, 1, pp. 303-7; *D.C.B.*, 2, pp. 22-3.

St Gregory of Utrecht, *Abbot* (*c.*707-75)

Gregory was born in Trier (now in Germany) about the year 707. One day when he was fifteen his grandmother, abbess of Pfalzel near Trier, asked him to read to the nuns. St Boniface (5 June), apostle to the Germans, had stopped off at the abbey on his way from Friesland to Hesse and Thuringia. Gregory was asked to explain the reading to those without Latin, but the task of exposition was beyond him. Boniface stood up, elucidated the passages, and added a homily on the need for and benefits of an apostolic and virtuous life. This so impressed and moved Gregory that on the spot he decided to follow Boniface, who became his instructor and is said to have loved Gregory as his son. The boy accompanied him on his journeys and helped him in his missions. Shortly before his death, Boniface sent Gregory to Utrecht, now in the Netherlands, to govern a monastery. It was a recent foundation dedicated to St Martin (11 Nov.). Boniface was martyred in 754, as was St Eoban, who had been in charge of the see of Utrecht since the death of St Willibrord (7 Nov.). Gregory administered the diocese for twenty years, though he was never consecrated (the previous Roman Martyrology erroneously titled him bishop).

St Martin's abbey became a great missionary centre under Gregory. Candidates came there from all neighbouring countries, including England. Among them were St Ludger (26 Mar.), who wrote Gregory's Life, St Lebuin (12 Nov.), and St Marchelm (14 July). All three were associated with England, the last two as natives and Ludger as a student at York. By his preaching and judicious administration Gregory made the diocese a fitting environment for the abbey. Ludger praises his prudence, almsgiving, and forgiveness. For the last three years of his life he suffered from gradual paralysis, which he bore patiently. He died at Maastricht on 25 August, about the year 775.

Ludger's Life is our main source of information. See *AA.SS.*, Aug., 5; *M.G.H.*, *Scriptores*, 15. See also H. Timerding, *Die christliche Frühzeit Deutschlands*, 2 (1929); J. A. Coppens, *Kerksgeschiedenis van Noord-Nederland* (1902), pp. 62-70.

R.M.

St Geruntius, bishop of Italica, Spain, who died in prison (? fourth century)

St Severus, abbot at Agde, France (fifth century)

St Aredius, abbot who founded a monastery at St Yrieix, Haute-Vienne, France (591)

St Gurluesius, first abbot of the abbey of Ste Croix at Quimperlé, Brittany, France (1057)

St Thomas of Hereford, bishop (1282): his entry can be found in this edition on 3 October, the traditional date of his commemoration in England.

BB Michael Carvalho, Peter Vasquez, Louis Sotelo, Louis Sasanda, Louis Baba, roasted to death at Simabara, Japan (1624). See "The Martyrs of Japan," 6 Feb.

26

St Tarsicius, *Martyr* (Third Century)

All we know of Tarsicius is that he carried the Blessed Sacrament in Rome at a time of persecution and was killed taking it to the sick or to prisoners. Perhaps he was a deacon, for a deacon's special office was to administer Communion in certain circumstances and to carry the Sacrament from one place to another; but he could have been a layman, and of any age. He was possibly buried in the cemetery of St Callistus (14 Oct.). His grave has never been positively identified, but San Silvestro in Capite claims his relics.

A fourth-century poem by Pope St Damasus (11 Dec.) describes a Tarsicius killed by a mob with sticks and stones rather than "surrender the divine Body to rabid dogs" and bears witness to an early cult. From the sixth century onward Tarsicius was represented as an acolyte whose task it was to take Communion to Christian prisoners, victims of the persecution of Valerian. Pagans met him on the Appian Way and asked him what he was carrying. He thought it shameful to cast pearls before swine. They beat him with clubs and rocks until he was dead. When they turned over his body all trace of the Sacrament had vanished from his hands and his clothing. Christians buried the martyr's body with honour in Callistus' cemetery. Cardinal Wiseman further embellished the story in his ineffably tedious novel *Fabiola* (1854), once almost required reading among young English Catholics, and helped to make Tarsicius the "boy martyr of the Eucharist." Accordingly, he became a patron of altar-servers and of a Confraternity of the Blessed Sacrament.

See *A.A.SS.*, Aug., 3 (1737), p. 201; J. Wilpert, *Die Papstgräber und die Cäciliengruft* (1909), pp. 92-8; O. Marucchi, "La questione del sepolcro del papa Zeffirino e del martire Tarsicio," in *Nuovo Bulletino de archaeologia cristiana*, 116 (1910), pp. 205-25; *B.T.A.*, 3, p. 174.

St Maximilian, *Martyr* (295)

The Passion of St Maximilian, a conscientious objector, is accepted as an essentially authentic, minimally embroidered account of the trial and death of an early martyr. In the third century most Roman soldiers were volunteers, but veterans' sons were obliged to serve. As in our own age, Christians held conflicting views on the permissibility of military service. Maximilian presumably considered all military service to be against God's law. (A famous case for comparison in the twentieth century is that of Franz Jägerstätter, an Austrian Catholic who consistently refused military service under the Nazis already condemned by the Church because their cause was evil. His priest and bishop tried unsuccessfully to convince him that he ought to serve.)

In the consulate of Tuscus and Anulinus, Fabius Victor was brought before the court with Maximilian, at Theveste in Numidia. The public prosecutor, Pompeian, demanded that Maximilian, a conscript and Victor's son, should join the armed forces. The proconsul asked the young man his name. He said that it was pointless to reply for he was a Christian and could not enlist. He persisted in his refusal:

Dion: You have to join up or you'll die.

Maximilian: I'll never do it. You can cut off my head but I'm one of Christ's soldiers and can never be a soldier of this world.

Dion: Who put these ideas in your head?

Maximilian: My conscience and the One who rightfully drafted me.

Dion: Fabius Victor, tell your son his duty.

Victor: He knows his own mind. He won't change it.

Dion: Join up and take the emperor's badge.

Maximilian: No, I can't. I'm already wearing Christ's identity-disk.

Dion: I'll send you to your leader at once.

Maximilian: Do it as soon as possible. That will be real glory.

Dion: Recruiting-officer, give him his badge.

Maximilian: I won't take it, I tell you. If you insist, I'll deface it. I'm a Christian and not allowed to wear any other badge of service than Christ's sacred sign. He is the living God whom you do not recognize. He suffered for us. God sent him to us to die for our sins. All we Christians serve Christ. We follow him as the Lord of life and source of our salvation.

Dion: Join and accept the badge, or you'll perish. It's a very nasty way to go.

Maximilian: I shan't perish, for my God already knows my name and has numbered me in his ranks. I refuse to serve.

Dion: You're a young man. Soldiering is just the right thing for someone of your age. Join the army.

Maximilian: My army is God's army. I can't fight for this world. I'm a Christian, I tell you.

Dion: Christian soldiers serve our rulers Diocletian and Maximian, Constantius and Galerius.

Maximilian: That's their business. I'm a Christian too and I can't serve.

Dion: What sort of wrong do soldiers do?

Maximilian: You know very well.

Dion: If you refuse to do your national service I shall sentence you to death for contempt of the army.

Maximilian: I shan't die. If I leave this earth my soul will live with Christ my Lord.

Dion: Put his name down. You're disloyal. That's why you won't do your

255

military service. You'll be punished as a warning to others. The sentence is: "Maximilian has refused the military oath because of disloyalty. He is to be beheaded."

Maximilian: God lives!

Maximilian was twenty-one when he died. He told his father to give the cloak prepared for his service to the court official. Almost at once his head was cut off. A lady named Pompeiana obtained his body and had it taken on her litter to Carthage, where she buried it close to St Cyprian (15 Sept.), not far from the palace. Victor went home rejoicing and followed his son not long after.

See *AA.SS.*, Mar., 2; T. Ruinart, ed., *Acta Primorum Martyrum Sincera et Selecta* (1689), pp. 309-11; H. Delehaye, *Les passions des martyrs et les genres littéraires* (1921), pp. 104-10. Theveste is possibly a copyist's error and he was actually martyred near Carthage. The old Roman Martyrology named him Mamilianus and erroneously gave the place of martyrdom as Rome. On miliary service see St Victricius (7 Aug.) and St Martin of Tours (11 Nov.); A. Harnack, *Militia Christi* (1905), pp. 114-7; C. J. Cadoux, *The Early Christian Attitude to War* (1919), pp.149-51; G. Zahn, *Franz Jägerstätter* (1965).

St Anastasius the Fuller, *Martyr (c. 304)*

All we know is that a Christian named Anastasius, perhaps a fuller, was probably martyred at Salona, or Split, in Dalmatia.

His more than doubtful Acts say that Anastasius was born at Aquileia of a good family. He heeded Paul's advice to the Thessalonians to do "your own business and work with your own hands," became a fuller, and practised his trade at Salona. During the Diocletian persecution he refused to conceal his Christianity. Indeed, he painted a cross on his door to advertise it. He was arrested and brought before the governor. He refused to sacrifice and was thrown into the sea with a stone tied round his neck. Asclepia, a matron of the city, promised to free any of her slaves who recovered the body. They eventually came upon some "blacks" (presumably African slaves, though the narrative is obscure on this as on other points) who had found it in the water. Asclepia's men told the "blacks" that they would be accused of having murdered Anastasius if they did not surrender the body, which they promptly did. Asclepia's slaves took it back to their mistress. She buried it in her garden, which later became a Christian cemetery with a basilica. The narrator does not find the behaviour of Asclepia's slaves odd or dishonourable.

The old Roman Martyrology named one St Anastasius, martyr at Aquileia, on 7 September, and another, martyr at Salona and said to be the converted officer mentioned in the Passion of St Agapitus (18 Aug.) on 21 August. The second one is almost certainly fictitious. The new draft Martyrology transfers the Anastasius of 21 to 26 August and identifies him as the fuller.

See *C.M.H.*, pp. 467-8, 492.

St Adrian, *Martyr* (? Third Century)

All we can be sure of is that there was an early and very considerable cult of an Adrian, martyr of Nicomedia, both in East and West. The new draft Roman Martyrology commemorates such a saint on this day without further comment. The rest is confusion and conflation, supposition and legend.

The Bollandists and the old Roman Martyrology proposed the existence of two different Nicomedian Adrians, who both suffered there but under different persecutions and whose remains were taken to Argyropolis. The following is a summary of those narratives.

One Adrian is said to have been a pagan officer at the imperial court at Nicomedia. He saw twenty-three Christians scourged and ill treated and declared he too was now a Christian and wished to join them. He was imprisoned. His young wife, Natalia, a Christian to whom he had been married for thirteen months, was told of this. She hurried to the prison, kissed his chains, and pronounced him blessed. He sent her home, promising to let her know what happened. When he knew he was to be executed, he bribed the gaoler to let him go home to say goodbye to his wife. She thought he had saved his life by apostasizing and slammed the door in his face. He explained that the other prisoners were hostages for his return. They went back together. Natalia dressed the prisoners' wounds and looked after them for a week. Adrian was brought before the emperor but refused to sacrifice. He was scourged and re-imprisoned. Other women had followed Natalia's example; the emperor forbade them to enter the prison. Natalia cropped her hair, put on men's clothes, and bribed her way into the gaol in the usual way.

The martyrs were sentenced to have their limbs broken. She asked for her husband to suffer first so that he would be spared the distressing sight of the others' agony. She disposed his limbs on the block; knelt there while he was crushed and dismembered; and hid one of his hands in her clothes. When the martyrs' bodies were burned, she had to be stopped from jumping in with them. Rain put the fire out, and Christians gathered the relics. They were taken to Argyropolis, on the Bosphorus near Byzantium, and buried. An imperial official was pestering Natalia with offers of marriage, so she took the hand to Argyropolis and died peacefully not long after her arrival. Nevertheless, she was accounted a martyr by association, for her body was buried with the others' remains.

This obvious fiction proved very appealing, and Adrian in this manifestation was a great popular martyr of the past. Several paintings elegantly, sometimes magnificently, record his sufferings and Natalia's interventions. He was a patron of butchers and soldiers and invoked against the plague. The former Roman Martyrology gave 4 March as the day of Adrian's death, 1 December as that of Natalia's, and 8 September as that of the alleged translation of their relics to Rome. The joint feast of SS Adrian and Natalia, martyrs, was 8 September. Yet another Adrian (5 Mar.), recorded by Eusebius as a martyr at

Caesarea under Diocletian, sometimes confused with the present Adrians(s), has a more reliable and quite separate tradition.

The other supposed Adrian is said to have suffered at Nicomedia under Licinius. He was a son of the emperor Probus and upbraided Licinius for his persecution of the Christians. The emperor duly ordered him to be executed. His uncle Domitius, bishop of Byzantium, buried his body in the suburb of the city called Argyropolis. The old Roman Martyrology assigned Adrian in this manifestation to 26 August. The narrative is equally untrustworthy though less captivating than the other.

See *AA.SS.*, Aug., 5, pp. 808-11; Sept., 3; S. Salaville, in *Dictionnaire d'Histoire et de Géographie ecclésiastiques*, 1, 608-11; *B.T.A.*, 3, pp. 507-8.

A colourful painting of the northern French school, *c.* 1480 (Metropolitan Museum, New York), shows two executioners intently breaking Adrian's limbs, while finely dressed and mounted courtiers look on.

St Fillan of Glendochart, *Abbot* (Eighth Century)

Fillan (Foelan, Fulan, Phillane, or Phelen) appears in nearly all Scottish and Irish martyrologies and calendars, including the important martyrology of Oengus (804). He was one of the most celebrated of the ancient Scottish saints, symbolic of endurance, protection, and succour and of course a holy figure of legend more than of history, for all that is said of him, including his foundations, is highly speculative. He is one of the many saints whose importance is derived entirely from their reception rather than from any ascertainable life.

According to the account in the Aberdeen Breviary Fillan's Irish parents, Feriach and St Kentigerna (formerly 7 Jan.), daughter of Cellach, prince of Leinster, inspired him with their own piety. In one account Kentigerna fled to Scotland with her children and St Comgan, her brother (13 Oct.), to escape a tribal conflict in Ireland. Although he could have expected a privileged life, Fillan received the monastic habit when young (perhaps in Ireland) and spent many years in a cell some distance from a monastery near St Andrew's in Scotland, which he had to leave when elected abbot. He was very efficient in this office but resigned it after some years to withdraw to a mountainous part of Glendochart, in Perthshire. Together with seven others he built a church there, at Killin, and served it for several years. (Comgan is suposed to have done the same at Lochalsh, but seven is a magical-sacred number.) Fillan is said to have buried his uncle on Iona and to have built a church in his honour.

Fillan was a well-known figure in pre-Reformation piety and folklore. Many delightful legends were told of him. For example, it is said that immediately after his birth his father threw him into a lake; he stayed there a whole year attended by angels. When he was building his church, a wolf killed the ox used to drag the materials to the spot; Fillan started praying and the wolf returned and pulled the cart itself.

After the death of her husband Kentigerna left Ireland and consecrated herself to God in a religious way of life. The *Annals of Ulster* say that she died on 7 January 734. A famous parish church bears her name on Tuch Cailleach, in Loch Lomond, a small island to which she retired some time before her death.

Fillan himself died on 9 January, probably early in the eighth century. He was buried in Strathfillan, where his relics were preserved and honoured for many years. Many miracles of healing were attributed to his intercession. More importantly, as a saint without any English associations, he belonged to the pantheon of guardians and guarantors of the Scottish national consciousness. King Robert the Bruce had a special lifelong devotion to Fillan, a saint with a suitably royal lineage who had nevertheless dedicated himself to God's cause and could intercede for the community of the realm, which was Bruce's guiding notion. After the defeat at Methven, when he fled to the mountain country between Perthshire and Argyll, Bruce put himself under the protection of St Fillan of Glendochart, whose sanctuary he had thereby entered. He venerated the saint's arm bone and other relics in the charge of Abbot Maurice of Inchaffray on the eve of the battle of Bannockburn (though he would not, as is sometimes claimed, have taken them into the conflict with him): "As gude king Robert in that samin nicht / Befoir the feild, at his devotioun / Walkit that nicht, into his orisoun / To Sanct Phelen most speciall of the laif / Becaus the Scottis was wont to haif / His richt arme bane into ane siluer cace . . ." (Boece/Stewart). According to Hector Boece (1527) the priest in charge of the relic had forgotten to put it in the case but it reappeared miraculously. Before and after the battle the Bruce attributed his victory over the English to the saint's intercession. On 26 February 1317/18 he granted Fillan's main church (Killin) and chapel of St Fillan in Glendochart (Strathfillan) to the Augustinian canons of Inchaffray Abbey, intending a daughterhouse to be founded at Strathfillan, and endowed the daughterhouse with land in Glendochart. A charter of 28 October 1318 made the chapel a priory. The king's natural son, Robert Bruce of Liddesdale, gave the then-considerable sum of twenty pounds Scots to the fabric of St Fillan's church. On 16 July 1414 the pope confirmed the presentation of a prior by Inchaffray to Strathfillan. In the mid-sixteenth century it is described as the monastery or chapel royal of Strathfillan.

The new draft Roman Martyrology assigns Fillan to 26 August but seems erroneously to suggest that he was one of two Fillans who founded two monasteries separately in the same century. He was "equivalently" canonized on 11 July 1898. He is associated with the cause of unjustly oppressed peoples deprived of their rights and nationhood.

See *K.S.S.*, pp. 341-6; *L.I.S.*, 1, pp. 134-44; *AA.SS.*, Jan., 9. See also W. Stewart (ed. W. B. Turnbull), *The Buik of the Chroniclis of Scotland: A metrical version of the History of Hector Boece*, 3 (1858), pp. 227-31; G. W. S. Barrow, *Robert Bruce and the Community of the Realm of Scotland* (1965), pp. 226-7, 437; I. Finlay, *Celtic Art* (1973), pp. 169-70; I. B.

Cowan and D. E. Easson, *Medieval Religious Houses in Scotland* (2d ed., 1976), p. 98; *Angels, Nobles and Unicorns: Art and Patronage in Medieval Scotland* (1982), pp. 10-1, 55-8.

The National Museum of Scotland in Edinburgh, possesses a bell, crozier, and shrine formerly believed to have belonged to Fillan. The quadrangular and lipped design of "St Fillan's bell," however, is almost certainly of the twelfth century. It is said to have lain on a gravestone in the old churchyard of Strathfillan where it was used as a magical cure for diseases until 1798, when it was taken to England. It was returned to Scotland in 1869. (Since remote antiquity, bells have been reputed to drive away evil spirits).

The "Quigrich," or St Fillan's crozier, is one of the great treasures of Scotland; its history of association with the saint's cult is well substantiated. It is a magnificently elaborate fourteenth/fifteenth-century silver-gilt shrine made as a crook and bearing a crystal and the image of, presumably, St Fillan. Stars representing the house of Murray were added in the late fifteen or early sixteenth century. They stand for the house of Murray, for John Murray was prior of Strathfillan at that time. The shrine was known as the "Quigrich" (from the Gaelic *coigreach*, "a stranger") because it was carried to a distant place as a kind of intercessory divining-rod for the recovery of stolen property, especially, of course, sheep (by association with its assistance in the recovery of a stolen realm). Within the Quigrich was another (eleventh-century) Irish or Scottish bronze crook, the saint's supposed pastoral staff; the head could possibly also accommodate a fragment of an arm bone. The whole double crozier and staff shrine was kept at Eyich near Crianlarich for several centuries, by the hereditary guardians of the shrine, the Dewars of Glendochart, who took over this duty from the traditional custodians of the staff, the priors of Glendochart, who held it as their "coarb," or symbol of office as successors of Fillan. Faithful to his charge, the last Dewar custodian took it to Canada. Eventually, it returned to the nation whose ancient liberties it symbolizes, for in 1876 he made it over to the Society of Antiquaries of Scotland, which placed it in the National Museum.

Bd Herluin, *Abbot* (994-1078)

Herluin (or Herlouin), founder of one the great ecclesiastical centres of learning, is commonly given the title "Blessed" and appears as such in both the old and the new draft Roman Martyrologies. Yet he received no known cult, and the Bollandists do not include him in their *Acta Sanctorum*.

He was born at Brionne in Normandy in 994. About 1034 he left knightly service to become a monk. Some five years later he founded the abbey of Bec, which was to become one of the most famous and influential intellectual centres of the Middle Ages. Through Lanfranc (also often called Blessed), St Anselm (21 Apr.), its first and second priors, and others, it had an important effect on the ecclesiastical history of England, to which it sent more of its monks than any other foreign abbey. They wore a grey variety of the usual monastic habit of the "black monks" and were known sometimes as an Order. The son of Herluin's overlord founded the great house of Clare, and he and his family founded two Bec priories, Stoke-by-Clare (Suffolk) and St Neot's (Huntingdonshire), and were patrons of Goldcliff (Monmouthshire). Bec eventually owned about forty manors throughout England from Warwickshire southward. Small groups of monks were established at three manors: Cowick (Devon), Steventon (Berkshire), and Wilsford (Lincolnshire). At first the remainder came under two monk-bailiffs, at Ruislip (Middlesex) and Ogbourne (Wiltshire), which were nominal priories. Tooting Bec in south London was a manor of Bec, as was Weedon Beck (Northamptonshire).

The abbots of Bec controlled this scattered organization by a special vow of obedience, visitations, summons to the annual chapter, and paying a small pension to each priory. Stoke-by-Clare and St Neot's are Bec subsidiaries recorded as resisting a tax levied in the thirteenth century for a common house of studies at Oxford. The ties were weakened from the end of the reign of Edward I onward and gradually broken under Edward II, though Cowick remained under the abbot of Bec until the mid-fifteenth century.

Herluin, a rough Norman soldier who desired only to serve God under the Rule of St Benedict (11 July), died on 26 August 1078. His abbey was despoiled at the French Revolution, but it was refounded by monks in 1948.

Two lives of Herluin appear in the Acts of the Benedictine saints collected by J. Mabillon and J. L. d'Achéry (9 vols., 1668-1701). The earlier *Vita Herluinii* is by Gilbert Crispin, abbot of Westminster (d. ?1117), a contemporary who had himself been a monk of Bec. See also M. M. Morgan, "The Abbey of Bec-Hellouin and its English Priories," in *Journal of the British Archaeological Association* 3 (1940), pp. 33-61; D. Knowles, *The Religious Orders in England*, 2 (1955), pp. 162, 165-6.

St Elizabeth Bichier des Ages, *Foundress* (1773-1838)

Jeanne Elisabeth Marie Lucie Bichier des Ages was born at the Château des Ages, at Le Blanc, between Poitiers and Bourges in France, in 1773. Her father was Antoine Bichier, lord of the manor of Ages and a public official, and her mother Marie Augier de Moussac, whose father also held public office. She was a shy and sensitive child. When she was ten she was sent to school at a convent at Poitiers. Her maternal uncle was vicar general at Poitiers, the superioress of the convent was a relative. Elizabeth's favourite game was building sand castles; in later life she remarked that building was obviously meant to be her trade.

When she was nineteen her father died. In February 1792 the National Assembly issued a decree against the property of those who had left France to escape the Revolution. Elizabeth's brother was such a refugee. Since her mother was old and ill, Elizabeth asked her uncle to teach her something about property law and accounts. She defended her brother and family in a long lawsuit eventually decided in their favour.

In 1796 Elizabeth and her mother left the château for La Guimetière, outside Béthines in Poitou. Elizabeth led a life of prayer and good works for the poor. The local parish had a "constitutional" priest, one who had taken the oath to maintain the civil constitution required by the National Assembly in 1790. Many had done so out of genuine conviction and in good faith; the constitution and oath were condemned by Pope Pius VI, which caused great trouble for many French clergy. Elizabeth did not agree with the oath, so every night she

assembled local peasants at the house for prayers, hymns, and spiritual reading. She heard of a priest, Fr Fournet (now known as St Andrew Fournet; 13
May) at Maillé, where he had reopened a church in a barn. Elizabeth became a
frequent visitor there. Andrew devised a rule of life for her and dissuaded her
from joining the Trappistines. She continued to visit the sick and needy and to
teach infants. Two friends, Madeleine Moreau and Catherine Gascard, helped
her in the summer.

In 1804 her mother died. With Andrew's approval she dressed in coarse
peasant's mourning clothes. This offended her relatives, and Andrew was rebuked by the vicar general. Andrew thought that a community of nuns was
needed for good works in that area and suggested that Elizabeth should head it.
She went first to the Carmelites at Poitiers, then to the Society of Providence,
to learn something about the religious way of life. After six months Elizabeth
was in charge of a community consisting of Madeleine, Mary Anne, and two
other young women. In May 1806 they moved into the Château de Molante to
teach children, shelter the sick and aged, and make reparation for the excesses
of the Revolution. In 1811 the community, now of twenty-five nuns, moved to
a bigger house in Maillé itself. Five years later the diocesan authorities approved their Rule, and they took the name of Daughters of the Cross.

In 1815 Elizabeth had to go to Paris for surgery after an accident with a
vehicle. She was received at the Tuileries by the new king, Louis XVIII. When
she returned, Andrew had become rather cold and said she was removed as
superioress. Perhaps there was malicious talk when she was away; perhaps he
thought her reception in Paris would go to her head. Elizabeth was a determined woman: within a week she had redressed the situation and was restored.
She was indefatigable, the Order's work was invaluable in unsettled times and
especially after the depredations of revolution and the Napoleonic campaigns.
Thirteen new convents were opened in 1819-20, and between 1821 and 1825
fifteen houses were founded in a dozen dioceses. The bishop of Bayonne invited them to the south and they spread to the Béarn, the Basque country,
Gascony, and the Languedoc. By 1830 they had sixty convents.

When the Basque house of Igon was opened, a young curate named Fr
Garicoïts (St Michael Garicoïts; 14 May) was appointed spiritual director.
Elizabeth encouraged him in his foundation of the Priests of the Sacred Heart
of Bétharram. When Andrew Fournet died in 1834, Michael Garicoïts became
a second Fr Fournet to the nuns of the Basque convents.

In 1836 Elizabeth's health began to fail. She was exhausted, the effects of her
previous accident caught up with her, and she suffered from severe facial
erysipelas. In 1838 the condition became serious and she became subject to
delirious fits. She died on 26 August.

Elizabeth was a very active figure in the first phase of the extraordinary
expansion of French religious Orders in the nineteenth century and in their
concern with what would now be called social services. In 1789 there had been

only about 35,000 nuns in France; by 1877 there were about 128,000, largely employed in work similar to that undertaken by Elizabeth's Sisterhood. She was canonized in 1947, after the doubtful breathing-space of the wartime period and the mutual support between the collaborationist Vichy régime and retrograde elements in Catholicism. The French Church had entered a hopeful period of rejuvenation and expansion, and the equally self-assertive Communist party was making a serious bid for power. Elizabeth was a model of successful resistance to anticlericalism and of achievements under momentous changes of régime.

See the Lives of Elizabeth and of St Andrew Fournet by L. Rigaud (1885) and that of Elizabeth by E. Domec (1947). See also E. Keller, *Les Congrégations religieuses en France. Leurs oeuvres et leurs services* (1880); H. Marc-Bonnet, *Histoire des ordres religieux* (1968).

Bd Mary of Jesus Crucified (Mary Baouardy) (1846-78)

Born Mariam Baouardy, she was a person of lowly origin who is recommended to us as an exemplar of humility. She was obviously an unusual woman, the complexity of whose personality developed in spite of, yet necessarily in and through, the extreme social constraints but also the sometimes banal pieties of her time and place. She faced her world with courage and acted on it with peculiar determination.

Mariam was born into a family of Uniate (and therefore Catholic) Greek-Melkite-rite Christian Arabs on 5 January 1846 at Abellin (Zabulon), between Nazareth and Mount Carmel in the Holy Land, then part of the Turkish Empire. Her parents, George Baouardy and Mariam Chahyn, had lost twelve male infants. They made a pilgrimage on foot to Bethlehem to ask the Infant Jesus for a daughter and promised to give her his mother's name, and she was duly named Mariam (or Mary) during the Melkite rite of combined Baptism and Confirmation. Her parents died within a few days of each other when Mariam was two. An uncle adopted her. After a number of pleas, she made her First Communion when she was almost eight. In 1854 she was taken to Alexandria, Egypt. When she was twelve, but without her knowledge, her uncle betrothed her to his wife's brother, whom she then refused to marry. She cut her hair off when she discovered that the marriage was imminent. For this she was punished physically and mentally. She asked a former servant in her uncle's house who was about to leave for Palestine to take a message to her brother in Nazareth, but the servant tried to persuade her to convert to Islam. She is said to have replied: "I am a daughter of the Catholic, apostolic and Roman Church. With God's grace I hope to persevere until death in my religion, which is the only true one." Perhaps what the child actually said was somewhat less pompous but amounted to that. At any rate the response was a violent kick and a serious scimitar wound to her neck. The unconscious Mariam was wrapped in a cloth and left in a back street. She came to in a grotto where, she said, a nun dressed in blue restored her to life and foretold her future. Thereafter she remained convinced that she had been saved by Our Lady in person.

When she had recovered, a Franciscan helped Mariam, by then thirteen, to become a servant in Christian families, first in Alexandria, then in Jerusalem, and later in Beirut. She made a vow of perpetual chastity at the Holy Sepulchre. She arrived eventually at Marseilles, aged seventeen and still a servant. She tried to join the Daughters of Charity, but her employer persuaded them not to take her. In 1865 she succeeded in entering the novitiate of the Sisters of St Joseph of the Apparition, who would not allow her to take vows because of a sequence of odd visions, trances, and on 29 March 1867, the experience of the stigmata, all of which Mariam treated as sickness rather than any kind of divine intervention. The novice-mistress' strong disapproval banished the phenomena, but only for a year. When twenty-one, still virtually illiterate and intent on her vocation of humble service, referring to herself as a "little nothing," Mariam became a Carmelite at Pau in south-western France, taking the name in religion of Sr Mary of Jesus Crucified. She was content to cook, wash dishes, scrub, and so forth.

In 1870 she accompanied a small group of Carmelites as a missionary to Bangalore, India. Mariam rejoiced at the extreme poverty of the first Carmel in India, for it enabled her to feel close to the despised Untouchables. From 1871 her stigmata bled copiously from Wednesday evening to Friday morning. She tried to hide her "illness," which she thought was catching, but it prevented her from carrying out her menial tasks as efficiently as before. She took her vows on 21 November 1871 but had to return to France, largely because of growing physical difficulties and a feeling that she was possessed by the devil. She was happy to be back in the Pau community, where she experienced a new sensation of love, which, she said, "burns and consumes me."

In 1872 she told her superiors that Jesus wanted her to found a Carmelite convent at Bethlehem. She managed to overcome all opposition, and with powerful helpers (even, eventually, with the personal intervention of Pope Pius IX) she and eight other nuns dedicated themselves at Lourdes and arrived in Jerusalem on 6 November and in Bethlehem five days later. She chose the design and oversaw the construction of the Carmelite house. The building was sufficiently finished for the Carmelites to start using it on 21 November 1876. There she continued her vocation as a "little sister to everyone." The strange quasi-mystical phenomena apparent throughout her life now took the form of "persecution" under the "torments" of divine love.

She planned another house at Nazareth and made an exhausting pilgrimage in preparation for the work. She suffered from bad circulation in the summer heat and could scarcely sleep at night, yet she appeared every morning on the building-site. She was hardly able to stand from weakness and also entered a new phase of spiritual torment in the belief that God had withdrawn his presence, though this did not weaken her determination or her constant encouragement of the workmen building the convent. On 22 August 1878, when bringing them two buckets of water, she fell and broke her arm, which soon turned gangrenous, causing her extreme agony in the heat. She was thirty-three when she died on 26 August 1878. She was beatified on 13 November 1983 as an example of desire for unity and reconciliation and as a self-effacing person who believed that holiness did not mean "prayer, visions or revelations . . . but humility." She had a special devotion to the Holy Spirit: "O Holy Spirit, source of peace and light, enlighten me. I am poor, make me rich. I am the most ignorant of human creatures, let me understand Jesus!" Presumably a desire to ensure the representation of Christian Arabs among the beatified favoured the choice.

N.S.B., 2, pp. 220-5.

St Teresa of Jesus, *Foundress* (1843-97)

Teresa de Jesús Jornet e Ibars was born at Aytona, Catalonia, Spain, on 9 May 1843. She became a teacher and tested her vocation as a Carmelite tertiary and then with the Poor Clares at Briviesca. She was noted for her resolute devotional life and humility and for the determination which enabled her to found, in 1872, the Little Sisters of the Abandoned Aged. She established the Sisterhood first in Valencia, then in Zaragoza, and built it up throughout Spain and later elsewhere, including America. She covered vast distances and travelled widely to supervise the fast-growing Order, whose work has served as an impressive example of care for neglected and sick old people. She died at Liria on 26 August 1897. She was beatified by Pius XII on 27 April 1958 and canonized on 27 January 1974.

N.S.B., 2, pp. 45-7.

R.M.

St Victor, martyr, slain by the Moors in Spain (third-fourth century)

St Alexander, martyr, a soldier of the Theban legion beheaded at Bergamo, Lombardy (third-fourth century)

St Eleutherius, bishop, at Auxerre (sixth century)

Bd Margaret Faventina, abbess of the Vallombrosan Order in Florence (*c.* 1330)

Bd John of Sagittario in the Campania (1339)

Bd John Bassand, priest and monk of the Celestine Order (1445)

27

ST MONICA (*c.* 331-87)

Monica (or Monnica) was the mother of St Augustine of Hippo (28 Aug.). Married women saints are usually honoured because they were the mothers of canonized saints or illustrious Christian monarchs and exemplified some other "objective virtue" outside the married state. Monica has always been classified as a widow. Almost everything we know about her comes from the *Confessions*, *Dialogues*, *De Beata Vita*, and letters of Augustine, on whose life she had an immense influence: "I do not have sufficient words to express the extreme affection she had for me"; "She had a woman's weak body but a man's strong faith, the composure appropriate to her years, a mother's love for her son, and a Christian's devotion." He sees her from the viewpoint of his own development and often expresses contradictory opinions, which of course make the account more credible than any hagiography. She did not tell her own story. Nevertheless, because Augustine's is her narrative we learn much more about her than about very many other saints. Other accounts are interpretations of what Augustine says, legends, or speculation.

She was probably born at Thagaste in North Africa. She had a highly-disciplined Christian upbringing (unlike Augustine, who regretted this); her family was devout. She was named after the North African goddess Mon, which may indicate her family's earlier religious allegiance. She and her sisters were largely raised by their rather severe nurse, who forbade water even between meals in case it led to wine-bibbing later. Wine was considered to be a major erotic stimulant and therefore especially dangerous for adolescent girls. Yet Monica is not portrayed as perfect. Augustine represents her as someone who, by the grace of God, had to develop and grow in spiritual intensity and in the virtues of a Roman matron: *gravitas*, *pietas*, and *severitas* (seriousness, devoutness, and discipline). In spite of the nurse's precautions she did become fond of wine as a girl. She was responsible for drawing the wine for her parents at mealtimes. She took a few sips herself and soon was drinking a cup a day. A slave called her an alcoholic and she repented at once. Wine here is also a metaphor for passionate impulses. (Augustine, however, stole pears and took years to repent.)

Her parents arranged a marriage for her with Patricius, an equally, though differently, determined person, who perhaps belonged formally to the Christian community. He is often said to have had an uncontrolled temper and to have been violent, but in fact only once had some gossipy servants beaten when his mother asked him to do this because they were causing trouble between her and Monica, for her cantankerous mother-in-law lived in the same house (she later became a Christian under Monica's influence). Patricius never beat Monica, but he was unfaithful. Eventually he became a full Christian, for he was baptized in 370. Augustine says that he was unusually kind and made sure that his son had a good education (Monica, too, wanted her son to have as good a classical education as possible). With difficulty, not long before he died he got the money together to send Augustine to Carthage. In general, Augustine is cold about his father and regrets that he did not tame his son vocally and physically. This lack of understanding for Patricius may have something to do with his mother's acceptance of her primary duty of affection for and obedience to her husband. Monica lived happily with Patricius. In the manner of the times she regarded the marriage contract as a promise to obey her master. He died in 371, when Monica was forty, and she wanted to be buried with him in the tomb she had built for him.

She had at least three children: Augustine, the eldest; Navigius; and Perpetua. She possibly had another boy and another girl. We learn very little about the other children from the *Confessions*, because Augustine presents his relationship with his mother as a central and all but exclusive development. He is telling the story of his heart's progress and how his mother both provided a certain security and brought out in him an understanding through feeling of the feminine and maternal aspect of God (and the Church) that mitigated the stern fatherhood he also longed for. We learn, however, details about Monica that summon up a contradictory, and therefore real, person; she was, for instance, a peacemaker, yet she could also be quite sarcastic. She was the channel for God's love, yet there was a kind of "unspiritual desire" in her affection for her favourite son.

Monica breast-fed Augustine, which was rather unusual in a family like theirs, though he probably also had wet-nurses. With her milk, he says, he imbibed God's guiding generosity. She had Augustine entered as a catechumen, but he was not baptized; this was common at the time. She was perhaps excessively fond of him: "She liked to have me with her, as mothers do, but far more than most mothers." Monica did not arrange an early marriage for Augustine because she was concerned for his professional training. He held this against her: "My family did nothing at all about saving me by marriage from my fall. They were worried only about my learning how to speak eloquently and how to persuade other people by what I said." She was disturbed by Augustine's unsettled and licentious way of life. He despised her admonitions as the mere "advice of a woman." She prayed for his conversion. When he became a Manichee she would have nothing to do with him until she was reassured by a dream that he would eventually share her faith fully. She was standing on a beam when a radiant being told her she should dry her eyes, for "your son is with you," as indeed he was. She told Augustine about this, and he said that they could easily be together if she gave up her faith. She retorted: "He didn't say that I was with you. He said that you were with me!" She also bothered a former Manichean bishop about persuading Augustine in the right direction, but her adviser got rid of her with the remark that Augustine was perceptive enough to see through the rival doctrine in the end. He then said: "Please go away now. A son you spend so much time lamenting about certainly won't perish."

When Augustine went to Italy in 383, she decided to follow him there. He was accompanied by his female companion of many years and their son, and he decided to leave his mother at a shrine in Carthage, pretending to have to say goodbye to a friend: "You allowed my own desires to take me away on a voyage that would put an end to them, and you used her excessively jealous love for her son as a scourge of sorrow for her just punishment." She went to Rome, but he had left the city. She followed him to Milan, where Augustine had settled and where she was befriended and influenced by St Ambrose (7 Dec.). She was so obedient to him that she gave up her habit of taking meal-cakes and bread and wine to saints' shrines on their feast-days. The holy bishop forbade it because it might be an occasion for drunkenness and was similar to pagan rites for the dead. When the Arian queen mother, Justina, persecuted Ambrose, Monica made long vigils on his behalf and was ready to die with him or for him. She was a regular Christian worshipper.

Monica had tolerated Augustine's relationship for fifteen years but decided that it was now her duty to make sure that he was married for his career's sake and to be admitted to Baptism. She set about arranging a suitable marriage with an heiress and instigated Augustine's dismissal of his companion. All this was quite acceptable, for it would indicate moral progress on Augustine's part. Nevertheless, Monica accepted his decision not to marry. She withdrew with Augustine and others to his friend Verecundius' villa at Cassicacum. She ran the household but was able to take part, though diffidently and not at a high level, in the theological and other learned discussions in Augustine's circle in Milan. His and his friends' wives and companions were too busy with children and domestic affairs to do so. She would seem to have known her Bible, but Augustine tried to get her to study philosophy. He came to prize the wisdom she had gained through practice at her own level, which helped to change his own attitude to the supposed supremacy of philosophy. He eventually encouraged her to pray even more intensely. She was overjoyed at her son's conversion and Baptism in 387: "She saw that you had granted her much more than she had asked for in her tears, prayers, plaints and lamenting." She set out with Augustine when he decided to return to Africa but died, aged fifty-five, at Ostia, on the way there. Before that she shared with him an unusual spiritual, even quasi-mystical, experience of ascent toward ultimate truth in which they passed "even beyond their own souls." This is known as the "vision at Ostia." Augustine was grief-stricken at his mother's death, but, now resolutely stoical and intent on self-control, he would not allow either himself or his son the full release of tears in public and even asked God to wipe out his feelings. Eventually he gave way to sorrow in his own room and hoped that Monica would "rest in peace with her husband." Even then he did not accept that she was perfect but prayed for her sins.

The cult of Monica is late and developed in the late Middle Ages. In 1162 Canon Walter of Arrouaise took part of her body home with him, and the Augustinians there celebrated her feast on 4 May. In 1430 Pope Martin V transferred her reputed relics from Ostia to Rome, where they are claimed by the church of S. Agostino.

Her feast-day was formerly 4 May, but 27 August in recent times. Various associations of Christian mothers have taken Monica as their patron. In art she wears a black or grey habit appropriate to a widow or a nun and is often veiled.

See *AA.SS.* for 1 May (1680), pp. 473-92; Augustine, *Confessions*, esp. bks. 5 (ch. 8), 9, in any good modern translation; Lives by E. H. Bougaud (Eng. trans., 1894); F. A. M. Forbes (2d ed., 1928); E. Procter (1931); H. Leclercq, in *D.A.C.L.*, 9, pt. 2 (1934), 2232-56; L. Cristiani (1959). See also P. Henry, *La Vision d'Ostie: Sa place dans la vie et l'oeuvre de S. Augustin* (1938); P. Brown, *St Augustine of Hippo* (1967); L. C. Ferrari, "The Dreams of Monica in Augustine's *Confessions*," in *Augustinian Studies* 10 (1979), pp. 3-18; J. K. Coyle, "In Praise of Monica: a note on the Ostia experience of *Confessions* IX," in *Augustinian Studies* 13 (1982), pp. 87-96; B. Shaw, "The family in late antiquity: the experience of Augustine," in *Past and Present* 115 (1987), pp. 3-51; S. Dixon, *The Roman Mother* (1988); D. G. Hunter, ed., *Marriage in the early Church* (1992); K. Power, *Veiled Desire* (1995). See also bibliography to St Augustine under 28 Aug., below.

The iconography of Monica is rich but late. She is frequently shown with St Nicholas of Tolentino but more often with Augustine. In Michael Pacher's Neustift retable (*c.* 1490) they appear together (Bavarian National Museum, Munich). Filippo Lippi's fifteenth-century portrait places her on a throne surrounded by twelve Augustines (S. Spirito, Florence). The most effective joint portrait is Antony van Dyck's great essay of the Counter-Reformation, *St Augustine in Ecstasy* (1628; Art-historical Museum, Antwerp, Belgium), where her own intensity of mind and body complement her son's, as is proper for a record of the incident in which they had discussed the mystery of eternity to such a degree that they forgot their physical existence (the "vision at Ostia"). Van Dyck has conflated the episode with Augustine's thinking on the Trinity in *De Trinitate*, a much later work.

St Marcellus of Tomi and Companions, *Martyrs* (? Fourth Century)

The new draft Roman Martyrology differs slightly from the previous version in referring to these martyrs as Marcellinus; his wife, Mannea; their children, John and Babyla; Serapion the priest; and Peter, a soldier; and it gives the place of martyrdom as Tomi in Moesia, on the Black Sea.

The hagiographer says that seventeen members of a Christian congregation of a place, perhaps Oxyrynchus, were denounced to the governor of the Egyptian Thebaïd as opposing the imperial decree and refusing to worship the gods. They were the tribune Marcellus, his wife, Mammaea, and their two sons; a bishop and three clerics; a soldier; seven other laymen; and a woman. They were brought before the governor in chains at Thumis. He tried to persuade them to obey the law, but they refused and were condemned to be thrown to the wild beasts in the arena. He made a last attempt to save them the next day in the amphitheatre. "Aren't you ashamed," he cried, "to worship a man put to death and buried years ago by order of Pontius Pilate, whose records, I am told, are still in existence?" This appeal did not influence the Christians. According to the author of their Acts the bishop, Miletius, made a confession of faith in the divinity of Jesus (clearly inspired by the definitions of the Council of Nicea in 325). They were then beheaded, for, the account says, the bears when let loose would not touch them, and no fire could be lit to burn them.

See, for the text of the Acts, *AA.SS.*, Aug., 6, pp. 14-5. See also *Anal.Boll.* 38 (1920), pp. 384-5; P. Franchi de' Cavalieri, *Studi e testi*, 65 (1935). Delehaye is of the opinion that the martyrs really belonged to Moesia and that the hagiographer transferred them to Egypt.

St Poemen, *Abbot* (Fifth Century)

Poemen was a celebrated Desert Father. He withdrew to the Egyptian desert of Skete with one elder and several younger brothers. In 408 Berber raids drove them from their first settlement, and they took refuge in the ruins of a temple at Terenuthis. Anubis, the eldest, and Poemen governed the community by turns. Of the twelve night hours, four were allotted to work, four to singing the office, and four to sleep. In the day they worked until noon, read until three in the afternoon, and then went to gather firewood, food, and other necessities.

Often, it is said, Poemen passed several days and even a whole week without eating. But he told others to fast moderately and to take sufficient nourishment each day. He said no monk should ever drink wine or deliberately gratify the senses in any way. Poemen feared the least occasion that might interrupt his solitude and on one occasion refused to see his mother. It is said that he surrendered the pleasure of a meeting then so that they might enjoy it more in the afterlife. He is chiefly remembered for his pithy, almost proverbial sayings, such as: "Silence is no virtue when charity demands speech." He also encouraged frequent Communion. When Anubis died, Poemen took over complete control of the community. He returned from Terenuthis to Skete, but raiders drove him out again. The Byzantine liturgical books call him the "lamp of the universe and pattern of monks."

AA.SS., Aug., 6, has a short Greek Life.

St Caesarius of Arles, *Bishop* (470-543)

Caesarius was born in 470 at Chalons-sur-Saône in Burgundy, into a Gallo-Roman family. He was a scholarly youth well instructed in traditional grammar and rhetoric by Pomerus, a teacher of African origin, and determined to become a priest. At eighteen he asked to enter Holy Orders. Two years after taking minor orders he withdrew to the monastery of Lérins, noted for its learning. The abbot made him cellarer, but the monks found him too scrupulous, so he was allowed to devote himself to contemplation and penance. His health suffered, and he was sent to Arles to recover. He became very worried about Christian clerics reading pagan authors. Caesarius himself had imbibed a traditional secular culture maintained in certain parts of Gaul among senatorial and similar families. The new, austere idea was that the Christian culture of the future should be established on the basis solely of the Christian message; the names of Christ and Jupiter should not pass the same lips.

The bishop, Eonus, a kinsman of Caesarius, supported the new rigour and found Caesarius' scruples promising. He wrote to the abbot suggesting that Caesarius should become a bishop. He was ordained deacon and priest and put in charge of a neighbouring monastery where the discipline was too lax. Caesarius gave the monks a Rule, governed them for three years, and brought them up to scratch. On his death-bed the bishop of Arles recommended him as his successor. The thirty-three-year-old Caesarius fled in an access of humility and hid among the tombs. He was discovered and had to agree to election by clergy and city. He presided over the church at Arles for forty years.

Caesarius was frugal and pious; he was a highly-serious and responsible pastor determined to codify the structures of worship and penitence so that there could be no excuse for error. He organized his diocese on quasi-monastic lines. He regulated the singing of the divine office, which he ordered to be celebrated publicly, not only on Sundays, Saturdays, and solemn festivals as was the Arles custom, and modified the office to suit laypeople. He stressed congregational singing and memorizing the Bible and wanted laymen to be involved in administering church funds. He taught the faithful to pray from the heart. He preached on all Sundays and holidays and often on other days, in the morning and in the evening. If he could not, he ordered homilies to be read, and always after Matins and Vespers. He favoured a plain and natural style and disliked studied addresses. He was very intent on inculcating a fear of purgatory for venial sins and the need for daily penance to get rid of them. He spoke on prayer, fasting, alms, forgiving injuries, chastity, and doing good works.

He is celebrated as the first "popular" preacher. His sermons were packed with homely allusions and examples and rarely exceeded fifteen minutes. He also stressed the value of corporate worship duly celebrated. He placed great emphasis on the wide diffusion of his sermons: "Whoever may receive this collection of sermons I pray and beg very humbly to read it attentively, and not only to hand it on to others so that they can read and recopy it, but to require them to read it." The diffusion of his sermons reached well outside the bounds of Arles, for his earliest Life says that books were sent to France (northern Gaul), Gaul, Italy, and Iberia. His influence can be traced as far as Fulda in Germany. Some of his works—attributed then to Augustine, Ambrose, and others—were diffused even more widely than once seemed to be the case.

Caesarius did not claim to be an innovator. As Vincent of Lérins had instructed him, the aim was to communicate "the same Catholic faith defined by the Holy Fathers." The main thing was instruction in the "true Catholic faith, which is to be held firmly and inviolate." He made visitations far and wide throughout his diocese and travelled far beyond it.

Caesarius was very insistent on what was then frequent Communion and on worthy reception. He insisted: "Those are good Christians who, when any great feast draws near, in order to ensure that they communicate properly, remain chaste with their own wives for several days beforehand." He laid down strict requirements for long periods of continence. The life of a penitent was the proper model for the laity and presaged even stricter innovations in the future. He required the laity to communicate not only on major feast-days but on the feast of St John the Baptist and on particular Provençal saints' days. In accordance with conciliar thinking at the time, Caesarius believed that certain sins, such as false accusations or apostasy, demanded lifelong exclusion from the Christian community, or allowed only one reconciliation in a lifetime. His list (based on the Ten Commandments) of mortal sins was comprehensive: sacrilege (apostasy and superstitious practices), murder (including abortion), adultery and concubinage, false testimony, theft, pride, anger, calumny, and so forth. He included a number of what would now be considered venial sins. Sexual intercourse between married people was sin if entered into solely for pleasure even if the possibility of conception was not excluded; it was mortal if they used contraceptive measures. He listed in detail the good works that were sufficient to make reparation for minor sins: almsgiving, visiting the sick and prisoners, prayer and fasting, forgiving one's enemies. In most cases a bishop could only encourage penitence, but in certain cases—murder, false witness, and some cases of inadequate penance—he could demand it. Repentance was a fearsome and solemn matter. Like other bishops, Caesarius often recommended that repentance should be left until later in life, for recidivism could ruin a person's chances of salvation.

He founded a monastery for young women and widows of southern Gaul who wanted to devote themselves to God, first at Aliscamps among the Roman ruins and then inside the city walls. He called the monastery St John's initially, but later it became St Caesarius, and he put his sister Caesaria in charge of it. He spent much time devising a Rule for the nuns. It emphasized stability and the completeness and permanence of enclosure. He drew up a Rule for men on the same lines and imposed it throughout his diocese; it became popular elsewhere. He was metropolitan of a number of suffragan sees and presided over several synods, such as that at Orange in 529. This council pronounced against heretics who said that God had predestined some people to eternal damnation. It also affirmed that God by his grace breathes into our souls our first desire for his faith and love and that he inspires our conversion.

At that time Arles was subject to Alaric II, king of the Visigoths. Alaric was told that Caesarius, born a subject of the king of Burgundy, was trying to bring the territory under his rule. This was untrue, but in 505 Alaric banished him to Bordeaux. When he found out the truth, Alaric recalled Caesarius, ordered the accuser to be stoned, but pardoned him at Caesarius' intercession. When the Burgundians besieged Arles and many prisoners were brought into the city, Caesarius supplied them with food and clothes and drew on his church treasury to help them. He stripped off silver and melted down censers, chalices, and patens, remarking that Jesus celebrated his last supper on earthen dishes.

After the death of the king of the Visigoths, Theodoric the Ostrogoth, king of Italy, seized the Visigoth dominions in the Languedoc. He had Caesarius brought under guard to Ravenna. Caesarius saluted him and Theodoric returned the courtesy. He discussed the state of his city with the bishop and said that he could not believe that so angelic a person could do any harm. He released Caesarius and sent him a silver basin, three hundred pieces of gold, and the message, "Receive the offering of the king, your son, and look on it as a token of friendship." Caesarius sold the basin to ransom captives. He went on to Rome, where Pope St Symmachus (19 July) confirmed the metropolitan rights of Arles, recognized Caesarius as apostolic delegate in Gaul, and conferred the *pallium* on him. He was the first bishop in western Europe to receive it.

Caesarius returned to Arles in 514. When the city was taken by the Franks in 536, he largely retired from public life and spent much time at St John's convent. He made a will in favour of the nuns there. He died in 543, on the eve of the feast of St Augustine.

See *M.G.H., Scriptores Merov.*, 3, pp. 457-501, for two early Lives, one by St Cyprian of Toulon and others. *Works*, ed. G. Morin (2 vols., 1937-42). For his testament, ed. G. Morin, see *Revue Bénédictine* 16 (1899), pp. 97-112. For the sermons, see Eng. trans. by M. M. Mueller, in *Fathers of the Church*, 21, 67 (1956ff.), and the excellent French version *Sermons au peuple*, ed. M.-J. Delage (3 vols., 1971-86); for the *Rule of Nuns*, see the Eng. trans. by M. C. McCarthy (1960). See also *B.T.A.*, 3, pp. 418-21; the relatively modern Life by A. Malnory (1934); J. Le Goff and R. Rémond, *La France religieuse*, 1 (1988), pp. 85-111.

There is a finely-decorated seventh-century manuscript of collected Sermons by Caesarius in the Royal Library, Brussels. Others survive from the eight and ninth centuries.

Bd Roger Cadwallador, *Martyr* (1610)

Roger Cadwallador (or Rogers) was born at Stretton, near Sugeres (or Sugwas), Herefordshire. He was the eldest son and heir of a yeoman "of substance." He was a learned child with, it seems, an early vocation to the priesthood. Eventually his father allowed him to go to Reims, where he was ordained deacon on 24 February 1592. In August 1593 he went to the new English College at Valladolid, Spain, was ordained priest, and in 1594 was sent on the English mission. He ministered in Herefordshire for sixteen years and gained a reputation as a zealous priest who usually went about on foot and made many converts, especially among the poor and working people. He was a noted scholar with a particular facility in Greek.

On 5 November 1602 Elizabeth issued a proclamation which seemed to promise that Catholic clergy who showed sufficient allegiance to her as their lawful queen would be granted some kind of tolerance. It was evoked by an offer almost certainly devised by Fr William Watson (see St Margaret Ward, 30 Aug.), the main contact with the government. It was made on the part of some prominent Catholic secular priests, the Appellants, probably including Roger, who would take an oath "to be the first that shall discover . . . traitorous intentions against us and our state, and . . . the foremost by arms and all other means to suppress it." Roger was involved in the long-drawn-out dispute—the Archpriest Controversy—between secular clergy and, primarily, the Jesuits about the organization of the Catholic presence in England. He was certainly one of the Appellants who, later that month, and not long before the queen's death, drew up another declaration known as the Protestation of Allegiance of 30 January 1603. They acknowledged Elizabeth as their true and lawful sovereign, and promised to obey her in temporal matters as divine law ordained, to reject plots and conspiracies against her, and to defend her and her realm against invasions, "notwithstanding any excommunication denounced or to be denounced against her Majesty." Nevertheless, the signatories also declared their allegiance to the Bishop of Rome as divine law demanded and that they were resolved to lose their lives rather than "violate the lawful authority of the Catholic Church of Christ." Thirteen eminent secular priests, including Roger, signed the declaration. The document was not accepted; the deputies who presented it were imprisoned; and the anti-Catholic campaign did not stop as a result, though none of the subscribers would seem to have been persecuted during the remainder of Elizabeth's reign.

At first, James VI/I, with a Catholic wife, was more tolerant than Elizabeth in some respects. But from 1604 onward and especially after the Gunpowder Plot of 1605, he so identified Catholicism with what we call "terrorism" that he wore specially padded clothes and would allow no drawn sword in his presence. Initially, recusancy fines were no longer collected, and even later it was easier to escape them. There were certainly fewer executions of Catholics during James' reign in England, but in 1606 a new Oath of Allegiance, said to have been prepared by Sir Christopher Perkins, a former Jesuit, was imposed on them. The wording—which had implications of conscience scarcely detectable now—seemed chosen to divide and alienate Catholics. It compelled them to abjure and detest, as "damnable, impious and heretical," the notion that a monarch deposed by a pope could be "deposed or murdered" by his or her subjects. There was widespread acceptance of the oath among the gentry. Some priests on the mission, such as George Blackwell, the archpriest in England (himself promptly deposed), took the oath, but most refused it, and Pope Paul V expressly prohibited it in two Briefs to the Catholics of England.

It was in James' reign on Easter Sunday 1610 that Roger was captured by under-sheriff James Prichard at the house of a Catholic widow, Mrs Winifride Scroope. He was examined first by the high sheriff, then by Robert Bennet, bishop of Hereford, whose questions he answered skillfully. He acknowledged his priesthood, which he supposed could hardly be held against him: "For, my Lord, either you must yield yourself properly to be a priest, or I can safely prove that you are no bishop." When the bishop replied that Christ was the only sacrificing priest of the New Testament, Roger retorted: "Make that good, I pray you, my Lord, for so you will prove that I am no more a priest than other men, and consequently no traitor or offender against your law." He refused to take the Oath of Allegiance and was sent to Hereford gaol to be put in unusually heavy irons. He was forced to wear shackles when he was sent on foot to Leominster gaol in Herefordshire. To one visitor he said, shaking them and comparing them to the bells on the high priest's robe in the Old Testament: "Hear, O Lord: these are my little bells."

His health suffered terribly. Though in a fever he was brought out for a second disputation with the bishop and others, yet is said to have defeated their arguments. He was tried as a priest and condemned to death. After that, for some months he was chained every night to the bedpost. On the morning of his execution he put on a new suit of clothes sent him by a friend, sent money to the porter, and made sure he had some with him for the man who led the horse for his hurdle. Several times, on the way and at the scaffold, he was offered his life if he would take the oath. He was forty-three when he was hanged, drawn while still alive, then quartered at Leominster on 27 August 1610. He and Bd Robert Drury (26 Feb.) were the only signatories to the 1603 Protestation who were eventually executed. Roger was beatified by Pope John Paul II on 22 November 1987.

See *M.M.P.*, pp. 293, 299-306; Gillow, 1 (1880), pp. 369-70; "Roger Cadwallador," in *D.N.B.*; J. Bossy, *The English Catholic Community, 1570-1850* (1975), pp. 35-48. Cadwallador translated from the Greek and published *Philotheus, or the Lives of the Fathers of the Syrian Deserts*, by Theodoret, bishop of Cyrus (n.d.), still in print in Challoner's day.

St David Lewis, *Martyr* (1616-79)

David Lewis (alias Charles Baker) was born in Monmouthshire, the son of Morgan Lewis, a Protestant member of a recusant family, and Margaret Prichard, a Catholic, a niece of the spiritual writer Augustine Baker, O.S.B. Their nine children were raised as Catholics, with the curious exception of David. He lived at Abergavenny and was educated at the Royal Grammar School. He was to become a lawyer, and at the age of sixteen he entered the Middle Temple. After three years in London he went abroad as tutor to the son of Count Savage and probably rejoined the Church while in Paris. He returned to Abergavenny for two years and in 1638 began his studies at the English College in Rome. He was ordained priest in 1642 and two years later became a Jesuit novice. In 1646 he was sent on the English mission, but his reputation was so strong in Rome that almost immediately he was recalled to Sant'Andrea to be made spiritual director of the English College. In 1648, however, he was sent back to Wales. His base was at the Cwm, Llanrothal, an obscure hamlet on the Herefordshire-Monmouthshire border. A large farm-house there sheltered the College of St Francis Xavier, which was the Jesuit centre for the west of England and a refuge for priests from 1625 to 1678. David worked in the border country for the next thirty-one years and earned the title of "father of the poor."

In 1678 the "popish conspiracy" was revealed by Titus Oates, and Catholics were pursued everywhere. When the panic reached Monmouthshire, the Jesuits prepared to leave the Cwm and covered their tracks only just in time before it was sacked by the sheriff's men (the greater part of the library was given to Hereford Cathedral). By then David was in hiding at Llanfihangel Llantarnam. Dorothy Lewis, wife of a servant of David's and an apostate Catholic like her husband, said publicly that she "would wash her hands in Mr Lewis' blood, and would have his head to make porridge of, as a sheep's head." Mrs James had a special grudge against Fr Lewis, for she had tried to get some money from him on false pretences. Her husband discovered where the priest was hidden and denounced him. Six dragoons arrested him early on Sunday morning, 17 November, just as he was going to celebrate Mass. He was taken to Abergavenny and then committed to Monmouth gaol, where he remained until 13 January, when he was removed to Usk.

At the March assizes he was condemned to be hanged, drawn, and quartered, mainly on the Jameses' evidence, though the judge exonerated him of the lying charge, circulated in a pamphlet, that he had cheated a woman of £30.

On 27 August 1679 on or near the site of the present Catholic church at Usk, he made a speech in Welsh from the scaffold: "I died for conscience and religion, and dying upon such good scores, as far as human frailty permits I die with alacrity, interior and exterior." The official executioner and his assistants had disappeared, and the hangman was a bungling amateur. The crowd (not, presumably, out of pity, but because they demanded proficient entertainment) threatened to stone him. He ran off, and a blacksmith was bribed to take his place (the sources claim that no one would ever use his services afterwards). David's body was buried in the churchyard nearby, where his grave remains a place of pilgrimage. Very soon, a handkerchief dipped in his blood was reputed to have worked miraculous cures. In 1970 he was canonized by Pope Paul VI.

Lewis' account of his arrest, imprisonment, and trial and his prepared speech from the scaffold are available and have appeared in various forms: see, e.g., *Tryal of David Lewis, a Jesuit, at Monmouth Assizes, for High Treason* (1679). See also *M.M.P.*, pp. 557–61; Gillow, 4 (1880), pp. 205–9; T. P. Ellis, *Catholic Martyrs of Wales* (1932), pp. 129–40; *Publications of the Catholic Record Society* 47 (1953), pp. 299–304; J. Stonor, *Six Welsh Martyrs* (pamphlet, 1961). There is an engraved portrait by Alexandre Voet in Fr M. Tanner's *Brevis Relatio* (n.d.), p. 71.

Bd Dominic of the Mother of God (1792-1849)

Domenico Barberi was born the last of eleven children into a peasant family near Viterbo in Italy on 22 June 1792. He taught himself to read and write, entered the Passionists, and was ordained priest at Rome in 1818. He became the provincial of the Order and in 1840 founded a province in England, which amounted to four houses in his lifetime. From the earliest years of his life as a religious he entertained a fervent desire to dedicate his ministry to work in England, where as yet the Passionists had not established any house and, indeed, the Order was generally thought to be inappropriate to the English mentality and way of life. In 1814, when he was still a novice, he wrote, "One day at the end of October or at the beginning of November, at midday, when praying before the altar of the Blessed Virgin, I had a revelation of the date when, as an ordained priest, I would begin my ministry and where among dissident Christians I would work: in north-western Europe, and England in particular." He also attributed to Jesus a prophetic remark in one of his published ascetic works composed before his missionary work had begun: "England, dear England, over whose fate you, devoted soul, have wept so often, is now ready once again to return to my fold. The time is not distant when you will see a rebirth there of the fervent belief of the first faithful."

He was attached to a parish at Lane End, Staffordshire, and began preaching missions. This was a time when both Catholic and Protestant missions were not shy of evoking hell-fire and the sinfulness of their listeners, designed to bring personal testimonies of repentance. It was this "excitable approach to sin and grace" (Heimann) rather than new Italianate devotions that marked the approach of new Orders such as the Passionists. At first he was ridiculed for his broken English and far from elegant appearance, which earned him the nickname "Paddy-Whack." But people, especially the poor, were soon impressed by Dominic's voluntary poverty and his Christ-like response to the persecution that came his way, as on one occasion when he picked up stones thrown at him and kissed them. He even developed a reputation for miraculous powers, and stories circulated, such as one in which a shoemaker who had met him went home, drew a cross on the wall of his house and hurled things at it, mocking Dominic the while; suddenly his arm withered in front of the horrified gaze of his family. Soon people were falling silent as he passed in the street; children knelt to receive his blessing, and mothers held their babies out to be blessed. He himself attributed his success rather to the example of poverty that he gave and to the fact that despite his poverty he was endlessly giving alms.

Dominic was an early ecumenist who thought that a more Christian life among Catholics was the best inducement to unity. He received John Henry Newman into the Church at Littlemore on 8 October 1845. This made the hitherto obscure Dominic suddenly famous—infamous, indeed, for many people imagined, unsurprisingly, that the priest was a sinister Italian sent from

Rome to ensnare Newman by some cunning and "Jesuitical" pseudo-argument ending in a triumphant conversion. The truth, as Newman described it in his *Apologia pro Vita Sua*, after perhaps the most enthralling and intellectually scrupulous description ever published of a long-drawn-out and utterly personal process of change in religious thinking, was very different:

> One of my friends at Littlemore had been received into the Church on Michaelmas Day, at the Passionist House at Aston, near Stone, by Father Dominic, the Superior. At the beginning of October the latter was passing through London to Belgium; and, as I was in some perplexity what steps to take for being received myself, I assented to the proposition made to me that the good priest should take Littlemore in his way, with a view to doing for me the same charitable service as he had done to my friend.
>
> On October the 8th I wrote to a number of friends the following letter:—
>
> "Littlemore, October 8th, 1845. I am this night expecting Father Dominic, the Passionist, who, from his youth, has been led to have distinct and direct thoughts, first of the countries of the North, then of England. After thirty years' (almost) waiting, he was without his own act sent here. But he has had little to do with conversions. I saw him here for a few minutes on St John Baptist's day last year.
>
> "He is a simple, holy man; and withal gifted with remarkable powers. He does not know of my intention; but I mean to ask of him admission into the One Fold of Christ. . . ."

Dominic died at Reading on 27 August 1849. He was beatified on 27 October 1963.

Newman's remarks on his reception and on Father Dominic are taken from the second edition of the *Apologia*, which contains largely the final text and was published as *History of my Religious Opinions* (1865); see *Newman: Prose and Poetry*, ed. G. Tillotson (1957), p. 753. See also M. Heimann, *Catholic Devotion in Victorian England* (1995), esp. pp. 159–61; A. Wilson, *Dominic Barberi: Supernaturalized Briton* (1967).

R.M.

St Rufus, martyr at Capua (? third–fourth century)

St Licerius, bishop of Lerida in Tarragona (*c.* 540)

St John of Pavia, bishop (*c.* 825)

St Gebhard, bishop of Constance (995)

St Guarinus, bishop of Sion (1150)

St Amedius, bishop of Lausanne (1159)

Bd Angelo of Foligno, Augustinian prior at Foligno (1312)

Bd Luke Chiemon, Japanese catechist beheaded at Nagasaki (1627)—see "The Martyrs of Japan," 6 Feb.

28

ST AUGUSTINE, *Bishop and Doctor* (354-430)

Augustine stands for perplexity and assurance, for the restless body and questing mind, and for the rule and system that enable them to work effectively if transiently in a tumultuous and confusing world. He is one of the great figures of Western civilization, in relation to whose thought and personality many important ideas and individuals have been and still are defined. He had a profound ability to understand and connect impulses, experiences, reading, and insights psychological, emotional, sexual, religious, mystical, philosophical, and political, in powerful images and concepts that have fired countless other spirits to adopt, amplify, or reject them fruitfully.

He was born at Thagaste, then in Roman North Africa (now Algeria), forty-two years after Constantine's conversion and twenty-four years after the seat of the empire was transferred from Rome to Constantinople. A new Greek Christian civilization was coming into being there; the old Latin culture in the West was weakened by barbarian incursions but here and there was revivified by new ideas from the East. The once-prosperous province of Africa had passed its prime, and the powerful African Church was beset by controversies and schisms. Augustine's father, Patricius, was a civic councillor and a pagan (he was baptized shortly before his death in 371); his mother, Monica, was a Catholic Christian. His father taught him to admire the Latin classics (his knowledge of Greek was always limited) and fired his patriotic spirit. His mother was the initial inspiration for his moral ideals and sensitivity, and—though much later—for his understanding of the Church as a universal authority. He was raised as a Christian and registered as a catechumen but was not baptized; a common practice of the time and place reserved Baptism for adulthood.

Augustine went to Carthage toward the end of 370. He was to become a lawyer and studied rhetoric at Carthage University from 372 to 375. He is said to have learned very little from his teachers but was deeply affected by his reading of Cicero and especially of the master's *Hortensius* (now known only by title and theme); by his wrestling with the nature of happiness and evil; and by his search for truth. It took him years to discard (though not in some philosophical works) rhetorical devices that could hamper both the urgent baring of his soul to God and humans and the prophetic intensity with which he thought aloud for others. The Latin style he developed does not rely on predictable if beautiful order and balance. It is like a methodical upturning of dull earth and crumbled rock but with flashes of mica that do not lie there for admiration but spark a sudden illumination of the whole terrain. It is thought en route, always anticipating but never at the point where "everything will be lovely in its form, and lovely in motion and in rest, for anything that is not lovely will be excluded. And we may be sure that where the spirit wills there the body will straightway be; and the spirit will never will anything but what is to bring new beauty to the spirit and the body" (*City of God*, 22:30).

He soon gave up any thought of the law as a vocation but ran his own schools of rhetoric and grammar at Carthage for nine years. He abandoned the socially admirable academic career that could lead to an important political post. He concentrated instead on philosophy and theology, study and teaching. Augustine was essentially a self-educated man. Plato as interpreted by Plotinus seemed vaguely attractive from an early stage, but he was deeply impressed by Manicheism and the dualist understanding of the nature of things (crudely describable as a division of all that is into the opposed realms of light and dark, good and evil). The religion of the force of light appeared immensely superior to orthodox Christianity with its banally human God, and from 373 to 382 he was a devotee of the persuasion. It also offered a fascinatingly elaborate physics that could accommodate many of the sciences in which he was interested, from psychology to astrology. In 383 he went secretly (lest his mother stop him) to Rome to open a school of rhetoric but disagreed with the scholars' custom of frequently changing their masters to cheat them of their fees.

Augustine was also a highly sensual young man, as captivated by the excitement of sex as by the vitality of ideas. For fifteen years he lived with a woman in the widely-tolerated state of concubinage, which excluded any lifelong commitment. In 372 they had a son, Adeodatus (given-by-God). In 384 Augustine went to Milan, where he was appointed professor of rhetoric and public orator. His final emotional and intellectual disillusionment with the Manichees took hold of him in 385 when by chance he started reading Latin translations of Neoplatonic works by Plotinus and Porphyry and set off on a new search for the ultimate. It now seemed necessary to accept the existence of God as a necessary condition for cognition, in the sense of rational knowledge.

His mother arrived in Milan and, with the force of her own development of mind and spirit, renewed her emotional influence on him. In 385 he dismissed the companion to whom he had been faithful for so many years; she returned to Africa. His newfound religiousness was stronger, so it seems, than any thought of regularizing the union. His mother wanted him to marry, but he was not interested. Bishop Ambrose of Milan (7 Dec.) showed him that it was possible and permissible to interpret the Bible allegorically so that it fitted the Platonic ideas that he found increasingly beguiling. It was through Ambrose, fluent in Greek, that Augustine probably acquired much of his knowledge of Eastern theology. The Platonists certainly provided fascinating ideas about God and the Word, or *Logos*, but in them he missed the overpowering personal experience of the process of conviction (rather than mere arrival at a convincing formula) that seized his mind, imagination, and will when he began to tease out the implications of "the Word became flesh and dwelled among us": "He who was God was made human to make gods those who were humans" (*Sermons*, 192, 1:1). Unlike the God of classical teaching, an impersonal, immobile, unchanging power and truth, the threefold Christian God was creative Love making and remaking humans and inviting their choice to love in return. The Bible was the necessary testimony that enabled Augustine to bring together the insights of knowledge and experience: to love God for his own sake, and people for God's sake. He was impressed by the examples of those Neoplatonists and, above all, of the Egyptian monks he had seen in Milan, who surrendered their positions to lead ascetic lives because they followed Christ as man in order to reach Christ as God: "The God Christ is the home where we are bound; the man Christ is the way we go there. We go to him and by him. Why should we fear to go astray?" (*Sermons*, 123, 3:3). Yet in the midst of all this speculation, one of the great conflicts of thought and attitude in world history and thought took place and is recorded in the *Confessions*: "The health of my soul could not be healed save by believing, and refused to be healed that way for fear of believing falsehood. . . . 'How long, how long shall I go on saying tomorrow and again tomorrow? Why not now, why not have an end to my uncleanness this very hour.' Weeping in the most bitter sorrow of my heart I suddenly heard a voice from some nearby house, a boy's voice, or a girl's voice, I do not know: but it was a sort of sing-song, repeated again and again: 'Take and read, take and read'" (8, 12). This struggle has become a model for descriptions of what, in the twentieth century, is best-known as existential *Angst*, or personal anguish about the human condition.

In September 386 Augustine retired to a country house at Cassiacum, near Milan, which his friend Verecundus lent him. His mother, his fifteen-year-old son (who died not long afterwards), his brother Navigius, and several friends went there with him. Augustine devoted himself to penance and prayer in preparation for his new life: "I have loved you too late, Beauty so ancient and so new. I have loved you too late. You were with me but I was not with you. I was away from you, running after the beauties which you have made. The things which exist only through you kept me far away from you. You have called, cried out and pierced my deafness. You have enlightened me, and my blindness is banished by your brightness. I have tasted you and I am hungry for you. You have touched me and I am on fire with longing to embrace you" (Confessions, 10, 27). He was almost thirty-three when he was baptized by Ambrose in Milan on Easter Eve 387. He soon left for Ostia, where he is said to have shared with his mother the "vision at Ostia," a quasi-mystical experience, or a form of sacred enlightenment, already sensed in pre-conversion "ascents of the mind" at Milan. It is generally agreed that these and other personal religious experiences reported by Augustine cannot be classed as mystical contemplation, for he did not separate that, as an extra-intellectual process, from cognition. For Augustine, love came first but required the operations of the mind in order to focus on its object. Monica died in the autumn of 387. He returned to North Africa in 388 to lead a near-monastic life with a group of like-minded people in his house at Thagaste: "Nothing can be better, nothing sweeter for me than to gaze at the divine treasure without noise or hustle" (*Miscellanea*, 1).

Augustine started writing against the Manichees, emphasizing the goodness of creation and the freedom of the human will. His arguments were quasi-philosophical but also biblical—a tendency that increased with the years, for he saw the Bible as a special form of revelation that supplied the faith and therefore the true understanding that the philosophers and reason could not offer. Faith in Christ was a necessary condition for a proficient understanding of the world and the place and function of humans in it: "Understanding is the reward given by faith. Do not try to understand in order to believe, but believe in order to understand" (*On the Teacher*, 11, 37).

He was ordained priest in the seaport of Hippo Regius in 391 and was forced to enter into the controversies that then beset the Church. He spoke at an important council in December 393. In 395 he became coadjutor to Bishop Valerius of Hippo and succeeded him the next year, remaining in the post until his death. He was now a spokesman for the North African Church. He led a modest and frugal life and insisted that the clergy who lived with him should renounce property, eat at the same table, and wear clothes from the common stock. The only silver used in his house was for spoons; the dishes were of earthenware or wood. The amount of wine at meals was carefully regulated.

Many of Augustine's influential writings, such as his sermons on the Gospel and his *On the Trinity*, came out of his agile wrestling with often beguiling concepts now classifiable as theological but associated then with many areas of life and thought. Between 393 and 412 he was involved in controversy with the Donatists and defended the uniqueness and unity of the universal institution— the Church—as its essential, God-given characteristics. There was no salvation outside the Church, whose members were joined together by the sacraments of unity derived from Christ himself. It was Augustine's and all pastors' duty to correct sinners, heretics, and schismatics in order to ensure their salvation. The emperor Theodosius issued an edict against heretics in 392, and in writings in 400 and 408 Augustine supported anti-heretical legislation by the State and what seemed due persecution of those without the Church. He was to become one of the main authorities for later notions of the State as the executive arm of the Church. Coercion in this life was better than damnation in the next.

It would be mistaken, however, to think of Augustine as a largely cerebral and, when practical, condemnatory pastor. He was an active and caring bishop in an era of terrible wars and invasions, social conflicts, and clashes of political and material interests that affected and convulsed the lives of rich and poor, of cities and empires. In an era remarkably like our own he was deeply concerned with the care of the impoverished and unfortunate, the due administration and use of church property, the fair assessment of ecclesiastical and civil litigation, and all sorts of instances in which the right expression of the overarching divine order had to be discovered urgently and applied immediately. Having used his own inheritance, he drew on his church revenues for the destitute, insisted that his flock should clothe the poor of each parish once a year, and did not hesitate to contract considerable debts for distressed people. Possidius tells us that he sometimes melted down parts of the sacred vessels to redeem captives.

He founded a community of religious women to whom, on the death of his sister, the first "abbess," he addressed a letter on the general ascetic principles of the religious life. This letter, together with two sermons on the subject, comprises the Rule of St Augustine, which is the basis of the Constitutions of many canons regular, friars, and nuns. Day by day acute, ingenious, witty, homely, yet learned, profound, and so passionate (we are told) that he could move an entire town to tears, unwinding and remaking a recalcitrant text until its point and place in the whole infinite structure of things seized his hearers, he preached and meditated publicly on the Gospels and psalms. He advised numerous people, from close friends to local grandees. His dinner guests included pagans but never openly sinful Christians. He observed Ambrose's three rules: Never make matches for people in case they go wrong; never persuade anyone to be a soldier; and never dine out in your own city in case you get too many invitations. He conducted an immense correspondence. Around 397 all this experience went into the writing of the *Confessions*, which became not only a record of many years of self-analysis but a dramatic exploration of the nature of human motivation and potential, of the longing for perfection and fulfillment, and of its inevitable disappointment.

On 24 August 410 Alaric the Visigoth sacked Rome. Pagans suggested that adoption of the new religion had angered the gods and brought this disaster on the empire. Augustine wrote *The City of God* (411-26) on the two ideal societies, Jerusalem and Babylon, the eternal City of God and the pagan empire of this earth whose citizens were oriented to Christ or the devil. The fall of Rome was a predestined event in the divine plan for the human race. Humanity was directed to the heavenly city, yet was bound by original sin. In such a state Christian rulers could help the Church by disciplining fallen humankind.

In 396 Augustine had replied to a set of questions from an old friend, the future bishop of Milan, and defined his position on the problem of evil. Human free will was insufficient for salvation without divine grace. Augustine himself had been involved in precisely this struggle between the stubborn will of the individual and the grace of God; the latter eventually won out. Grace was necessary to fight the lustful tendencies in humans. Human freedom was not a marvellous ideal but largely illusory. The deleterious effects of habit seemed to demonstrate constraint rather than liberty. Throughout his life in Africa, Augustine refined his understanding of the various manifestations of evil not as expressions of a mysterious, magical force but as inappropriate choices of negative possibility as against positive potential; of love deflected from growth and fulfillment to deficiency and failure. The house of impulse needed constant refurbishment if fatal habit were not to grip and maim the human spirit, doomed, for reasons unknown but glimpsed at, to function within it. Yet: "A picture may be beautiful when it has touches of black in appropriate places; in the same way the whole universe is beautiful, if one could see it as a whole, even with its sinners" (*City of God*, 11:24).

With the fall of Rome the heretic Pelagius and his disciple Celestius arrived in North Africa as refugees. Pelagians, broadly speaking, believed that humans could reach perfection by freedom of choice. In *On the Spirit and Letters* (*c.* 415) Augustine maintained that it was rather freedom to understand and search for God and perfection under God's supernatural grace that defined and opened up the road of effective liberty. Baptism was necessary for salvation; unbaptized infants could not inherit the fullness of eternal life. In 418 Pope St Zosimus (26 Dec.) condemned Pelagian teachings.

Over a period of about twelve years Augustine reworked and developed his thinking on grace and predestination, not without some influence from the Manichean dualism that he had embraced when a young man first in search of a universally explanatory and supportive system. The Fall became more important as a fateful determinant of present human life. Sin was inherited by the human race. The *Confessions* demonstrated this inheritance in the author's own life. The actual and symbolic instance of the possibility of sinning generated in and by all human beings, and of the sin behind all human suffering, was surely sex, and in particular the sexual act. For Augustine symbol became allegory, and his own unforgettable surrender to impulse one with the great drama of the Fall of humankind. The struggle was between flesh and spirit, between the self-loving human body-and-mind as it is and existence as it ought to be. The ongoing process of understanding and reconstruction of intimate personal experience in the setting of the divine plan anticipated freedom of will in the heavenly City: "It will remember even its past evils as far as intellectual knowledge is concerned; but it will utterly forget them as far as sense experience is concerned" (*City of God*, 22:30).

Much of what Augustine wrote burns the centuries to ashes with the fire of its relevance; much of his thinking was inescapably time-bound and coloured by his own experience. He saw sex as a divinely-created force and married love as conducive to completion and wholeness, and he asserted the right of women as well as men to refuse marriage and choose virginity in spite of the demands of family and society. Undeniably, however, he thought of women as subordinate, dangerous, and a source of pollution, and in his writings "women, sex, sin, shame and death are intimately connected" (Power). But the bad marks for this should not be awarded—anachronistically—to Augustine, but to those who still think that way. His understanding of predestination and his thinking on sex were influential throughout the Christian centuries. They were certainly partly responsible for what now seem unjustifiable physical and mental cruelties. In the last hundred years what may seem to be Augustine's main emphases in these respects have been criticized, modified, or rejected totally in all the main Christian Churches. It would be difficult now to find a respectable theologian who agreed that an unbaptized child must be damned for all eternity or that a sexual union, even in marriage, is somehow inherently sinful unless directly procreative. On the other hand, the notion that women are inherently unfit for a sacerdotal role remains powerfully effective in the Christian Churches.

Augustine was aware of most present-day objections to his arguments and deductions, though as they were presented in the categories of his times; and that cannot be said of all great theologians and moralists. It is not simply a matter of bringing him up to date by enlightened surgery, which does not cure, though it may expose, the essential problems of being which he faced too. His notion of predestination has to be seen together with his development of such ideas as that of the Mystical Body of Christ and the unity of all true believers, of all good thoughts and emotions tending to one good end, one of his great lasting concepts in which he drew together gospel imagery and the implications of Plotinus' Ideal Form, which "grouped and coordinated what from a diversity of parts was to become a unity; it rallied confusion into cooperation; it made the sum one harmonious coherence" (*Enneads*, 1, 6:2). In all sincerity, within the scope of a brilliant intellect and fine sensibilities, Augustine was trying not to resolve but to accommodate what remains unresolved but must still be accommodated: pain with pleasure, evil with good, the pointlessness with the purposiveness of all that is. Now as then, any such reconciliation must either redefine this or that aspect of each side of the dualism and reassign it to the other, or ignore it as beyond the ever-shrinking confines of ecclesiastical and even of moral judgment, as outside, perhaps, the capacities of language and thought and therefore of the speculative intellect altogether. But even the brash young Augustine never chose this last way out: "I wanted to be as certain of things unseen as that seven and three make ten. For I had not reached the point of madness which denies that even this can be known" (*Confessions*, 6, 4).

Toward the end of Augustine's life, the regent Placidia became wrongly suspicious of Count Boniface, who had been the imperial general in Africa. Boniface incited Genseric, king of the Vandals, to invade the African provinces. Augustine wrote to Boniface to remind him of his duty, and a reconciliation was attempted, but it was too late to stop the invaders. People were slaughtered, cities ruined, churches burned, and the clergy reduced to beggary. Augustine died in August 430 during the Vandals' fourteen-month-long siege of Hippo, flooded not only with refugees—including Boniface—from terror and devastation far away, but now even with the field labourers whose chanting the bishop had celebrated as a sign of ultimate peace and concord: "Harvesting, picking grapes, in any work that absorbs them totally, they start by showing their pleasure in words, but are soon so contented that they can no longer say how happy they are, but discard syllables in order to strike up a wordless chant of joy" (*On the Psalms*, 2 [Ps. 32:8]).

Augustine was a person of great integrity and consistency. In him, these virtues at times approached the condition of arid and unrelenting legalism but also guaranteed his ability to withstand each new onslaught on the human spirit and community: "If justice be absent, what is a kingdom but a crowd of gangsters? And what is a gang but a minor kingdom?" (*City of God*, 2, 21). Augustine's thinking throughout his life was scarcely detached from events, for each major stage in his thought can be attributed to a decisive personal experience. In that sense not merely his writings but his emotional attitudes, activities, and achievements have profoundly influenced the theology and moral suasions of the Latin Church (and its separated heirs) in particular, from the popular version propagated by the writings of Pope St Gregory the Great (3 Sept.), Anselm, and Bonaventure, through Aquinas, to Luther and Calvin, to Barth and Niebuhr, and of course the whole Catholic tradition since the Reformation, but also secular ethics in general.

His wrestling with a number of problems produced decisive changes in, and was an essential part of, the transition from the thinking of classical antiquity to that of Christianity proper, before the "Dark Ages" obscured for centuries the subtlety of Augustine's investigations. For instance, his account of the powers of memory, understanding, and will as the reflection of the Trinity in humankind involves a highly-refined discussion of cognition of the mental storage of sense-impressions in images and abstractions and their subsequent sorting, assignment, and accessing; of the difficulties of distinguishing between facts observed and the observing self, that remains relevant. His distinction between the "three times, a present of things past, a present of things present, a present of things future," that is, of creation, existence in time, and uncreation at the end of time, constantly recurs in other words.

Even now, many aspects of, say, feminist theology and feminism are defined by comparison with and in rejection of aspects of Augustine's ethical teaching, which also means his own psychology. The development of introspective and analytical or "depth" psychology in the early twentieth century was deeply indebted to the literary tradition of close observation of human behaviour, and especially of the connections between inward battles of the mind and emotions and outward actions, which began with him: "If you do not wish to fear, probe your inmost self. Do not just touch the surface but go down into yourself and reach into the farthest corner of your heart" (*Sermons* 348, 2). Indeed, many touchstones of Western culture (not only such immediately connected works as Rousseau's *Confessions*, Kierkegaard's *Either-Or*, and Newman's *Apologia* but those as seemingly disparate as Dostoevsky's *Crime and Punishment* and *The Brothers Karamazov*, Freud's *Civilization and its Discontents*, Joyce's *Portrait of the Artist as a Young Man* and *Ulysses*, and Proust's *In Search of Time Lost*) may be thought of as variations on the theme of Augustine's *Confessions*. They embark on the same journey into "the vast recesses, the hidden and unsearchable caverns, of memory, that inward place which is yet no place." Newman was neither the first nor the last to testify that "a mere sentence, the words of St Augustine, struck me with a power which I had never felt from any words before." A century later, Ludwig Wittgenstein, perhaps the most tortured and exacting philosopher of our own times, started his *Philosophical Investigations* with a quotation from the *Confessions* because "the conception must be important if so great a mind held it."

There is an immense number of works on every aspect of Augustine's life and times, thought and influence, and many English translations of the *Confessions* (see those by R. S. Pine-Coffin [1959] and H. Chadwick [1991]), *The City of God* (see H. Bettenson's version [1972] with an excellent introduction by D. Knowles) and the *Letters* (see *Select Letters*, Loeb Classical Library). The controversial writings are to be found in *The Works of St Augustine* (1870-2). E. Przywara, *An Augustine Synthesis* (1945), remains a well-ordered first tasting of the works. Recommended biographies include the early Life by Possidius, Eng. trans. in F. R. Hoare, *The Western Fathers* (1954); G. Bardy, *Saint Augustine, l'homme et l'oeuvre* (6th ed., 1946); G. Bonner, *St Augustine of Hippo: Life and Controversies* (1963); P. Brown, *Augustine of Hippo: A Biography* (1967; still by far the best life and commentary in English); D. Bentley-Taylor, *St Augustine* (1980); A. Mandouze, *Augustine of Hippo* (1987). See also *AA.SS.*, Aug., 6, pp. 213-460. On the thought in general and particular see J. H. Newman, *Apologia pro Vita Sua*, ch. 3 (2d ed., 1865); H. Marrou, *Augustin et la fin de la culture antique* (1938); S. Burleigh, *The City of God: A Study of St Augustine's Philosophy* (1950); E. Gilson, *History of Christian Philosophy in the Middle Ages* (1955); G. Pouler, *Studies in Human Time* (1956); P. Courcelle, *Les Confessions de Saint Augustin dans la tradition littéraire* (1963); R. R. Ruether, *Religion and Sexism: Images of Women in the Jewish and Christian Traditions* (1974); P. Brown, *Society and the Holy in Late Antiquity* (1982); G. Lawless, *Augustine of Hippo and his Monastic Rule* (1987); P. Brown, *The Body and Society: Men, Women and Sexual Renunciation in Early Christianity* (1988); H. A. Meynell (ed.), *Grace, Politics and Desire: Essays on Augustine* (1990); K. Power, *Veiled Desire: Augustine's Writing on Women* (1995). On his spirituality see J. F. Anderson, *St Augustine and Being* (1965). On the theology and controversies see J. Burnaby, *Amor Dei: A Study of the Religion of St Augustine* (1938); H. Puech, *Le Manichéisme: son fondateur, sa doctrine* (1944); G. G. Willis, *St Augustine and the Donatist Controversy* (1950); J. O'Meara, *The Young Augustine* (1954); F. van der Meer, *Augustine the Bishop* (1961); R. F. Evans, *Pelagius: Inquiries and Reappraisals* (1968); R. A. Markus, *Saeculum: History and Society in the Theology of St Augustine* (1970); W. H. C. Frend, *The Donatist Church* (2d ed., 1971).

Augustine's usual attribute is a fiery heart, which may be pierced by an arrow. It stands for the flames of his devotion and love of God. He often appears in episcopal vestments and carries a book and a pen.

The cult of St Augustine began at an early stage. King Liutprand of the Lombards translated his relics from Sardinia to Pavia, Italy. He would seem always to have been a favourite subject in ecclesiastical art, and his life, actual and legendary, has provided subject matter for many great painters. The earliest known image is in a fresco of the sixth century in the Lateran library, Rome. The Brixen altarpiece by Michael Pacher (1486; Alte

Pinakothek, Munich) shows him as a Doctor of the Church. There is a cycle of scenes (early 14th c.) by Balduccio and Campione at Pavia. The most sublimely individual portrait is Andrea dei Verrocchio's in his *Baptism of Christ* (c. 1470-80; Uffizi, Florence). Botticelli's fresco (1480) of the saint in his cell, often imitated, never surpassed, is in All Saints church in Florence. The solemn attendant figures in Gozzoli's version of the departure from Rome for Milan (in a series, 1463-7, on his life; St Augustine, San Gimignano, Italy) emphasize the importance of the occasion. For Taddeo di Bartolo (late 14th c.) he is a solemn teacher (Isaac Delgado Museum of Art, New Orleans, Louisiana). In one (1625-30; private collection, Barcelona) of his several portrayals of Augustine, Zurbarán makes him vulnerable, perplexed, and contemplative. *St Augustine in Ecstasy* (1628; Art-historical Museum, Antwerp) by Antony van Dyck is one of the most powerful portrayals of the saint's complexity; here an immensely energetic body as well as mind contemplates the Trinity in a conflation of the Vision at Ostia with Augustine's later treatise on the Trinity. The saint's penitence appears in his portrayal with Mary Magdalen by Andrea del Niccolo (c. 1470-80; Siena Gallery), and his humility appears in Bernardo Strozzi's *Augustine washing Christ's Feet* (c. 1620-5; Academia Ligustica, Venice). The nineteenth-century notion of the saint is best seen in Ary Scheffer's *St Augustine and Monica* (1854; National Gallery, London). There are many representations of legends; François de Nomé's (1623; National Gallery, London) illustrates one (based on a forgery, alas): in a vision the saint saw a child on the shore trying to empty the sea into a hole. Augustine said it was impossible, and the child answered that Augustine was engaged in the equally impossible task of explaining the Trinity.

No impressive image survives in the British Isles, though the choir stalls of Carlisle cathedral offer a series of paintings on his life, interesting because they are still there.

St Hermes, *Martyr* (? Second Century)

There is satisfactory evidence of the martyrdom of Hermes at Rome and of his early cult there and elsewhere. He appears in the *Depositio martyrum* of 354, in the martyrology of Jerome, and in pilgrims' itineraries. His Passion, however, is as unreliable as the Acts of Pope Alexander I, in which it is recorded. He was buried in the Basilla cemetery on the Old Salarian Way, where the remains of a large basilica were found over his tomb. Fragments of an inscription erected by Pope St Damasus (11 Dec.) bear the martyr's name. The cult spread in western Europe after Pope Leo IV gave some spurious relics to the emperor Lothair I in 850. They became an object of pilgrimage to the church of Renaix in Flanders, where they are still kept. He is the titular saint of three churches in Cornwall.

See *AA.SS.*, 4; *C.M.H.*, pp. 472-3; *D.A.C.L.*, 6, 2303 ff.; G. H. Doble, *St Hermes* (1935).

St Pelagius, *Martyr* (925)

Little St Pelagius is retained in the new draft Roman Martyrology, and many churches throughout Spain have been dedicated in his honour. He is one of those child martyrs so popular in the Middle Ages and may serve as an example of the problems that make them worthless as models but valuable as warnings. Most of them are inventions whose actual origins are lost in time but whose notional bases are reconstructible. They are usually victims of adherents of another religion, a witch, or if their persecutor is a Christian, of his or her evil tendency. Exemplary child victims of the extra-human world, like Bd Augustine Novello (19 May), attacked by a wolf while playing by the city gates yet saved by St Augustine's miraculous intervention, are rare. Even then, a wild animal, though more akin to a capricious demon, is like a Moor, a Jew, a sorcerer, a heretic, or an uncontrollably lustful Christian in that it exists outside the due order of orthodoxy. To point up the wickedness of Judaism, Islam, and so on, the child must evoke tender feelings and parental solicitude; yet it is also a small adult: it is perfectly devout but has chosen to be so as commendably as the Jew or Muslim has willfully persisted in his or her wickedness. This is understandable, for the modern idea of childhood as a highly-complex process of development dates only from the late-eighteenth-century Enlightenment and Romanticism, assisted by the speculations and findings of twentieth-century psychology and genetics. Alive or dead, most infant martyrs of the Middle Ages are magical tropes. The best-known instance is Little Hugh of Lincoln, who, though dead, sang the *Alma Redemptoris Mater* from the drain where he had been thrown and showed the way to his supposed Jewish murderers.

When aged ten, Pelagius, or Pelayo, was left with the Moors as a hostage by his uncle. This was when a great part of Spain was under Islamic domination and Abd-ar-Rahman III was ruling at Córdoba. After three years the ransom had not arrived and Pelagius was a handsome, spirited boy wholly uncorrupted by his prison associates. Abd-ar-Rahman sent for the boy and told him he would be freed and have horses to ride, fine clothes to wear, money to spend, and honours to enjoy if only he would renounce his faith and acknowledge the prophet Mohammed.

But Pelagius replied: "All that means nothing to me. I have been, am and shall remain a Christian." Accounts of his execution vary: one says that he was racked on the iron horse and swung up and down till he expired; another that he was suspended from the forked gallows reserved for slaves and criminals and then dismembered, his limbs being thrown into the river Guadalquivir. His remains were rescued by the faithful and preserved in Córdoba until 967, when they were translated to León. In 985 the relics were removed for safety to Oviedo.

See *AA.SS.*, June, 7, for the short Latin Passion and a far from perceptive discussion of the cult. In 962 the German poet Hroswitha, abbess of Gandersheim, told the story in Latin verse (Eng. trans. by C. St John, 1923). See also J. Trachtenberg, *The Devil and the Jews. The Medieval Conception of the Jew and its Relation to Modern Antisemitism* (1943); P. Senac, *L'Image de l'Autre: l'Occident médiéval face à l'Islam* (1983); P. Ariès, *Centuries of Childhood* (1962).

St Julian of Brioude, *Martyr* (? Third Century)

One of the most famous martyrs of Gaul, also known as Julian of Auvergne, his cult was well established at an early date. His unreliable Passion says that he was a virtuous soldier. When Crispin, governor of the province of Vienne, started to persecute Christians, Julian took refuge in the Auvergne. When he heard that the persecutors were looking for him he gave himself up near, it is said, Brioude (near Clermont-Ferrand), and said: "I have been too long in this bad world. I want to be with Jesus." They beheaded him immediately. Later a church was built at Brioude to hold his relics and became a great pilgrimage centre. St Gregory of Tours (17 Nov.) promoted his cult, which became very strong; Julian was invoked for healing and a number of other causes, and many miracles were reported in each category. Other churches were erected at Tours, Reims, and Paris—St Julien-le-Pauvre opposite Notre Dame. The historian Gibbon's magisterial reply to critics of his account (in *Decline and Fall of the Roman Empire*) of early Christian soldier martyrs and of inconsistencies in their reported motivation and behaviour is relevant to the story of Julian.

See *AA.SS.*, Aug., 6; Gregory of Tours, "De virtutibus Sancti Juliani," in *M.G.H. Scriptores rerum meroving.*, 1, pp. 562-8; Delehaye, *Les Origines du Culte des Martyrs*, p. 357; Lord Sheffield (ed.), *Gibbon's Miscellaneous Works* (1837), pp. 750-70; J. M. W. Hadrill, *The Frankish Church* (1983), pp. 75-93.

St Alexander of Constantinople, *Patriarch* (340)

The few facts recorded about Alexander of Byzantium have been embellished to enhance his importance. The accounts vary considerably. He was already seventy-three years old when he was elected patriarch of Constantinople. He held the office for twenty-three years during the struggle against the Arian heresy. Soon after his election the emperor Constantine ordered a conference between Christian theologians and some pagan philosophers. All the philosophers tried to talk at the same time. Alexander suggested that they choose the most learned among them to express their views. While one of them was speaking, Alexander said: "In the name of Jesus Christ I command you to be silent!" The scholar was said to have been struck dumb until Alexander decided otherwise. In 336 Arius arrived in triumph at Constantinople with an order from the emperor that Alexander should receive him into communion. Alexander shut himself into the church and asked God to remove him or Arius. The night before the day of his solemn reception, Arius died. This seemed to be a divine intervention in answer to Alexander's prayer, formerly recorded thus in the Roman Martyrology: ". . . a renowned old man, by the power of whose prayer Arius, condemned by the judgment of God, burst asunder and his entrails gushed out."

AA.SS., Aug., 6.

St Moses the Black (*c.* 405)

The story of Moses reads as if the outline of an uplifting conversion narrative had become mixed up with an early picaresque novel. Palladius' *Historia Lausiaca* and some early church historians mention him, and he appears in the new draft Roman Martyrology.

Moses is said to have been an Ethiopian servant or slave in the house of an Egyptian official. He was dismissed for general immorality but above all for constant theft. He decided to become a brigand. He was big, strong, and fierce and was soon boss of a gang that terrorized the district. On one occasion a sheep dog barked and ruined an important raid. Moses swore he would kill the shepherd. To get at him he had to swim across the Nile with a sword between his teeth. The shepherd had hidden himself by burrowing into the sand. Moses could not find him so he killed four rams, tied them together, and towed them back across the river. He flayed the rams, cooked and ate the best parts, sold the skins for wine, and walked fifty miles to join the gang.

When next heard of he had been converted and occupied a cell at the monastery of Petra in the desert of Skete. It has been suggested that he hid among the hermits to avoid the law and other pursuers and was moved by the exemplary lives of the Desert Fathers. At Petra he was attacked in his cell by four robbers—a reversal of fortune typical of invented narrative. Moses overpowered them, tied them together, slung them across his back, and dumped them on the floor of the church, saying to the astonished monks: "I'm not allowed to hurt anyone, so what do you want me to do with them?" Of course the robbers reformed their ways and became monks too. But Moses found it difficult to combat his violent passions and consulted St Isidore of Pelusium (4 Feb.) about the problem. The abbot took him up to the roof of the house at dawn. "Look!" he said, "It takes some time for the light to drive away the darkness. The soul is no different." Moses worked very hard to bring himself into line: by physical labour, waiting on his brothers, mortification, and constant prayer. He did so well that Archbishop Theophilus of Alexandria heard of his virtues and ordained him priest. Afterwards, as the new priest stood in the basilica anointed and vested in white, Theophilus remarked: "Now, Father Moses, the black man has become white!" Moses smiled ruefully. "Only outside! God knows that I'm still black inside," he replied.

He was seventy-five years old when Berbers threatened to raid the monastery. Moses would not allow the monks to defend themselves but made them take to their heels before it was too late: "Those that take to the sword shall perish by the sword!" He stayed behind with seven of the monks. The infidels murdered all but one of them. Moses was buried at the monastery of Dair al-Baramus.

Palladius, *The Lausiac History*, contains the earliest Life: see p. 67 of the trans. in *Ancient Christian Writers*, 34 (1964). See also *AA.SS.*, Aug., 6, for a Greek Life (said to have been written by Laurence, a monk in Calabria, Italy) with a commentary. B. Ward (trans.), *Sayings of the Desert Fathers* (1981), contains twenty-one possib y authentic sayings by or about Moses.

Eight London Martyrs (1588)

The defeat of the Spanish Armada at the end of July 1588 was followed by a severe persecution of Catholics. Whether they were enthusiastic patriots or not, they were now generally identified as members of a fifth column, potential or actual, of spies and assassins anxious to follow papal recommendations, remove the usurper Elizabeth from the throne, and subject England to a combined papal and Spanish tyranny. Government propaganda required exemplary victims, and the first martyrs perished in London on 28 and 30 August. To increase fear and terror six new gallows were erected in various parts of the city. Hurdles and quartering were dispensed with.

The first post-Armada victim was William Dean, who was hanged at Mile End Green. He was a Yorkshire man born at Linton in Craven in the West Riding. He was a very learned convert minister who had been curate at Fryston Monk. He went to Reims in 1581, was ordained at Soissons, sent on the English mission in January 1582, imprisoned in Newgate in February 1584 in the Marshalsea, and banished in January 1585 on pain of death should he dare to return. He returned in November 1585, was in the Gatehouse prison by March 1588, was condemned to death on 26 August, and died at Mile End Green on 28 August. Anti-Catholic feeling had been so successfully aroused and was so fanatical that when the cart reached the place of execution and William began, as was usual, to address the crowd and to justify his faith and innocence, "his mouth was stopped by some that were in the cart, in such a violent manner, that they were like to have prevented the hangman of his wages." Henry Webley, a layman who had befriended William, died with him.

William Gunter was a Welshman from Raglan, Monmouthshire, who went to Reims in 1583 and was ordained there only the year before his death. He was arrested on 30 June 1588, imprisoned at Newgate, condemned on 20 August, and hanged at Holywell Lane, Shoreditch, outside the theatre.

Robert Morton was hanged in Lincoln's Inn Fields. He was born at Bawtry, in the West Riding of Yorkshire. He left England around 1568 on a mini-Grand Tour, and stayed three years with a priest-uncle in Rome, being there when the process for Elizabeth's excommunication started and the Bull was issued. He studied at Douai in 1573 but returned home on the death of his father in 1574-5. He married Ursula Thurland of Gamston in Nottinghamshire. In 1578 they decided to emigrate, and he sold all his goods and lands. They were captured on board ship by Richard Topcliffe, recusant- and priest-hunter extraordinary. By 18 July 1578 Robert was in the Gatehouse prison, and Ursula was petitioning for his release. Bishop John Aylmer of London, the lieutenant of the Tower, and the recorder of London interrogated Robert particularly rigorously, for one of his uncles had helped to ensure the excommunication of Elizabeth in 1570 and another had been prominent in the 1569 Northern Rebellion. Nevertheless, friends at Court obtained his release, but Ursula died. Robert fled to Rome and entered the English College on 5 April 1586. He was ordained priest at Reims on 14 June and sent to England on 2 July 1987. Topcliffe pursued him from one refuge to another and arrested him in London. He was condemned at Newgate on 26 August 1588.

Hugh More, a layman only twenty-five years of age, was also hanged in Lincoln's Inn Fields. He was born at Grantham in 1563, within the borders of the present Catholic diocese of Nottingham. He was brought up a Protestant, educated at Broadgates Hall, Oxford, and then entered Gray's Inn. He was reconciled to the Church by Fr Thomas Stephenson, S.J., and went to Reims to study for some time at the seminary there. When he returned to England, he was arrested and given the chance to preserve his life if he attended the established church. He refused and was sentenced to death.

Thomas Holford (alias Acton and Bude) was born the son of a Protestant minister at Aston in Cheshire in 1541. He was appointed tutor in the household of Sir James Scud(a)more at Holme Lacy in Herefordshire. There, about 1582, he was converted by Fr Richard Davi(e)s, who wrote an account of him. Thomas went to Reims on 18 August 1582, was ordained at Laon on 9 April 1583, and sent to England on 4 May. He ministered in Cheshire and London, with many narrow escapes, until May 1585, when he was caught at Nantwich. He was imprisoned in West Chester Castle and examined by the bishop of Chester, and he admitted to being a priest. The bishop sent a copy of his examination to London with a description of Thomas' rather snappy attire: ". . . a black cloak with murrey lace open at the shoulders, a straw-coloured fustian doublet laid on with red lace, the buttons red, cut and laid under with red taffeta, ash-coloured hose laid on with biliment lace, cut and laid under with black taffeta. A little black hat lined with velvet in the brim, a falling band and yellow knitted stockings." Two pursuivants took Thomas to London, and all three put up in an inn. He escaped when they were in a drunken stupor and is said to have run eight miles barefooted to the Bellamy house in Harrow. In 1588 he was caught by a pursuivant at Nantwich after celebrating Mass at the house of St Swithin Wells (10 Dec.). He was condemned on 26 August and hanged at Clerkenwell.

James Claxton (or Clarkson) went to Reims from Rome in 1580, was ordained at Soissons on 9 June 1582, and sent to England on 24 July. He was banished from York in 1585 but returned. He was condemned at Newgate Sessions on 26 August 1588 and was hanged at Isleworth, or between Brentford and Hounslow, with Thomas Felton. They were taken from Newgate on horseback, their hands pinioned behind them and their feet tied under the horse's belly. Thomas was a Minim friar, the son of Bd John Felton (8 Aug.). He was only twenty years old and not yet a priest. His sister, Mrs Frances Salisbury, left an account of him. This says that he came to England to recover his health; he was about to return to his monastery when he was arrested and imprisoned for two years. He was twice released and re-arrested. In the Bridewell prison he was put to hard labour and tortured in the hope that he would reveal priests' names. At Newgate, after the Armada, he was asked if he would have sided with the queen or with the pope and the Spaniards. He replied: "I would have taken part with God and my country." He is said to have been condemned for denying the queen's title as head of the church: "I have read divers chronicles, but never read that God ordained a woman should be supreme head of the Church." Other accounts say that he was sentenced for being reconciled to Catholicism after embracing Protestantism.

These Armada martyrs were beatified in 1929.

See *M.M.P.*, pp. 133-46, 150-1; Gillow, 1-5, *passim*; *L.E.M.*, 1, pp. 351-430, 508-36; Publications of the Catholic Record Society, 5, pp. 150-9; Anstruther, 1 (1968), pp. 78, 100, 140, 170-2, 238-9.

St Edmund Arrowsmith, *Martyr* (1585-1628)

Edmund Arrowsmith would seem to have been the only Catholic priest executed in England in the fifteen years before Parliament was recalled in 1640. He was born in 1585 at Haydock, near St Helens, Lancashire. His parents were Robert Arrowsmith, a yeoman farmer, and his wife, Margery, a Gerard of Bryn, both from families which had already suffered for their Catholicism. Though baptized Brian, he took the name Edmund when confirmed. The Arrowsmiths were often plagued by house searches for priests. One night the father and mother were taken to Lancaster gaol, leaving four small children alone. His mother was a widow in 1599 and was fined for her recusancy. When his father died, Edmund's mother put him under the care of an old priest who had him educated. He went to Douai in December 1605. Ill health prevented his ordination, at Arras, until 1612; he was sent on the English mission the next year. He worked very effectively in Lancashire for ten years, gaining a reputation not only for sincerity and industry but as an enthusiastic if sometimes too daring controversialist.

In about 1622-3 he was arrested and examined before the bishop of Chester. At that time James VI/I was interested in finding a Spanish wife for his son; he ordered all priests in custody to be released to make a good impression on the Spanish king. Edmund decided to become a Jesuit. In 1623 he went into retreat for some months and, as Edmund Bradshaw, entered the Jesuit novitiate at Clerkenwell instead of becoming a novice abroad; he was admitted to the Society in England. Five years later he was betrayed by a young man named Holden, whose lax behaviour he had criticized. He appeared at the Lancaster assizes in August 1628, was indicted as a priest and a Jesuit and for persuading the king's subjects to become Catholics, and was sentenced to death. A pardon was applied for and granted, but local interests seem to have prevented it reaching him in time. The judge ordered Edmund to be manacled and put in a cell so small that he could not lie down. Passing through a courtyard on his way to execution, he saw St John Southworth (28 June), who had been temporarily reprieved, at a window and received absolution from him before, it is said, a vast crowd. Until the last moment he was offered his life if he would conform to the established church. "Tempt me no more," he replied, "I will not do it, in no case, on no condition." He was allowed to die before being drawn and quartered. His last words were: *Bone Jesu!* ("O good Jesus!"). The church of St Oswald at Ashton-in-Makerfield preserves what is said to be a hand of the martyr, and miraculous cures have been ascribed to this relic.

He was beatified in 1929 and canonized by Pope Paul VI in 1970.

See H. More, S. J., *Historia Provinciae Anglicanae* (1630); *A True and Exact Relation of the Death of Two Catholicks who suffered for their Religion . . . at Lancaster, in the Year 1628* (1737; various editions, largely based on the foregoing; modern English version, 1960); *M.M.P.*, pp. 362-73; Gillow, 1 (1880), pp. 62-3; B. Camm, *Forgotten Shrines* (1910), pp. 183-201; G. Burns, S.J.,*Gibbets and Gallows* (1944). There is an engraved portrait in the 1737 *True and Exact Relation.*

Bd Juniper Serra (1713-84)

Junipero Serra was born on 24 November 1713 at Petra-Mallorca (Majorca), Spain. He became a Franciscan in 1730 and was ordained priest in 1737. After teaching for a time, in 1749 he went to America. He was a missionary to the Indians of Texas and Mexico, then worked on the Californian missions. He is proposed as an example of Christian virtue and of the courage, patience, perseverance, and humility essential to the missionary spirit, and as one always intent on preaching the gospel to the native peoples of America so that they might be "consecrated in the truth." As far as his times and origin allowed, Juniper worked for the authentic development of the local peoples, spoke up against the abuse and exploitation of the poor and weak, and stressed their importance as individuals created and redeemed by God. He remains a model in the Serra Clubs of certain countries, which seek, among other things, to encourage vocations to the missionary priesthood. He died at Monterey on 28 August 1784 and was beatified by Pope John Paul II on 25 September 1988.

Osservatore Romano (French version, no. 39, 27 Sept. 1988), pp. 1-2.

Bd Joachima de Mas, *Foundress* (1783-1854)

Joaquina de Mas y de Vedruna, the foundress of the Carmelites of Charity, was born in Barcelona in 1783. Her father was Lorenzo de Vedruna, a member of a noble family of Catalonia; her mother, Teresa Vidal. They had eight children, of whom Joachima was the fifth. Her childhood was uneventful except that aged twelve she went to a Carmelite convent and demanded to be admitted.

In 1783 she met her future husband, Teodoro de Mas, a young lawyer, who had thought of becoming a Franciscan. He is said to have been uncertain which of three Vedruna daughters to marry, so he called at the house with a box of sugared almonds. Two of them turned up their noses at such a childish gift. Joachima accepted the box with delight, and Teodoro chose accordingly. They were married in 1799 when Joachima was sixteen. A few days later she was depressed at the thought that she had betrayed her true vocation. Her husband said that once any children had been launched in life, Joachima and he could become religious. She found this consoling. They had eight children, and Joachima is said to have been a devoted mother. When her second daughter wanted to become a nun, Joachima said firmly: "No, God wants you to marry. Two of your sisters will be nuns." This is exactly what happened, though one, Teodora, could become a Cistercian nun only after a disappointed young man had lost a breach of promise action against her in the episcopal court.

Teodoro died suddenly when Joachima was thirty-three. For the first seven years of her widowhood Joachima devoted her time to children, prayer, and waiting on the sick in the local hospital. She dressed in a Franciscan tertiary habit and led a life of mortification and poverty. Some people thought she had been driven crazy by her husband's death. In 1823 two of their children, José and Inés, were married, and José and his wife took the two youngest into their home.

In 1820 Fr Stephen of Olot, a Capuchin, told Joachima not to enter any existing convent as she was destined to belong to a new Congregation devoted to teaching the young and visiting the sick. Six years later she was clothed with the religious habit by the bishop of Vich. He had approved the foundation of a new community with those objects and put it under the invocation of Our Lady of Mount Carmel. The new Order was called the Carmelites of Charity. It was supported by an influential layman, José Estrada. The community started in Joachima's big house with six members, but they were very poor in material resources. Within a few months, however, they had opened a hospital at Tarrega.

The new Congregation continued to spread through Catalonia. During the Carlist wars the Sisters cared for the sick and wounded of both sides, but some Carmelites of Charity had to seek refuge in Perpignan in France. In the autumn of 1843 they returned to Spain. The foundress and the senior nuns made their final profession early in 1844. In 1850 Joachima felt the first signs of the paralysis that eventually struck her down. In 1851 she resigned the leadership of the Congregation to a priest, Fr Stephen Sala, and later to a Benedictine monk, Dom Bernard Sala. The foundress had to become a simple Sister. The paralysis took four years to affect her completely. When she died aged seventy-one from an attack of cholera, on 28 August 1858, she had founded convents with schools and hospitals all over Catalonia. She was beatified in 1940.

See J. Nonell, *Vida y virtudes de la ven. M Joaquina*, 2 vols. (1905); E. Federici, *La Beata Gioacchina de Vedruna v. de Mas* (1940).

Bd Gabra Michael, *Martyr* (1855)

The history of Catholic attempts to establish missions in Ethiopia is to some extent a story of Roman ineptitude in supporting or appearing to support various European powers (above all, Portugal and Italy) anxious to colonize that long-independent country and in denigrating its ancient Christian Church. In the mid-nineteenth century new attempts, under Italian influence, to establish Catholicism in Ethiopia did produce a small Uniate Church which lasted for a few years.

Not long after Bd Justin de Jacobis (31 July), who became first prefect and then vicar apostolic of the Vincentian mission at Adua, arrived in Ethiopia in September 1839 he met Abba Gabra Michael (Gabra Mika'el, Michel Ghèbrè: servant of Michael), a monk of the Ethiopian Coptic Church, one of the oldest in Christendom. Gabra Michael was renowned for holiness and learning; he was not a priest but had studied theology and went from one monastery to another teaching and learning. He was a member of the deputation from Ethiopia to Egypt and Rome accompanied by Justin. The group went to ask the Coptic patriarch of Alexandria to appoint a monk as primate of the Ethiopian Church, where the only episcopal see had been vacant for twelve years. They asked Justin, whom they respected, to support them. This, however, was an awkward function for a Catholic priest, so he insisted that the ruler of the Tigrai province give him a letter urging union with the Catholic Church and that the party should go on to Rome as a deputation to the Holy See. The Coptic patriarch refused to have anything to do with the Holy See, but Gabra Michael and others defied him and continued to Rome with Justin. They were warmly received by Pope Gregory XVI, went to Mass in St Peter's, and returned home impressed. Eventually, in 1844, Justin received Gabra Michael into the Catholic Church.

The Ethiopian helped Justin train local candidates for the Catholic priesthood. Together they composed a catechism adapted to local needs, translated a work of moral theology into Amharic, and founded a college at Guala in 1845. Gabra Michael was put in charge of it. Salama, a young monk whom the patriarch in Egypt had appointed *abuna*, or primate, of the Ethiopian church, resented this rival activity. He had Justin and Bishop William Massaia (sent from Rome in 1846) banished to the island of Massawa. In 1848 Massaia consecrated Justin and gave him faculties to administer the sacraments according to the Ethiopian rite wherever necessary. Justin returned secretly to Tigrai province and ordained the sixty-year-old Gabra Michael in 1851. A brief period of successful conversions (or "reconciliations") followed. By 1853 there were twenty Ethiopian Catholic priests and, it was said, five thousand other faithful. For a time, Gabra Michael reopened the college and seminary at Alitiena.

The Ethiopian commander Kedaref Kassa had designs on the throne. He started a rebellion which eventually made him Negus Neghesti (King of Kings)

Theodore II. Kassa promised Abuna Salama that he would banish all Catholic clergy. Persecution began again. Justin was arrested, sent to the frontier, and eventually arrived at Halai in southern Eritrea. On 28 August 1855 he wrote to his superiors to announce his escape. In his absence Gabra Michael and four other Ethiopian converts were imprisoned and threatened with torture but refused to recant. Over a period of nine months they were dragged before Theodore and Salama for interrogation. They were lashed with a giraffe's tail (which had the effect of steel wire) and tortured in other ways. Gabra Michael reminded Salama that it was by his intervention that Salama had been exiled rather than executed some years before. In March 1855 Theodore set out on an expedition against the ruler of Shoa. He took Gabra Michael with him in chains. On 31 May a last attempt was made to make him revert to the Ethiopian Church. He refused and was sentenced to death. Among those present was the British consul, Walter Chicele Plowden, who had supported Theodore's usurpation of the throne. He asked the king to reprieve Gabra Michael. His request was granted but Gabra Michael was condemned to be a prisoner for life. He sent a verbal message to the other prisoners at Gondar encouraging them to remain steadfast. For three more months, decrepit with age and ill treatment, he was dragged from place to place as a kind of trophy while the king made his triumphal progress through the country. He caught cholera and recovered; he gave away his small food ration to other sufferers and earned his guards' respect. On 28 August, as Justin was writing his letter from Eritrea, Gabra Michael lay down by the roadside and died.

Italian attempts to take over Ethiopia began in earnest in the late nineteenth century. Gabra Michael was beatified as a martyr in 1926, three years before the signing of the Concordat and Lateran Treaty between the Italian government and the Holy See. In 1936 Italy annexed Ethiopia after a murderous campaign using modern weapons such as bombers. For the next eight years the Church extended its influence in the country.

With due regard to the times of writing, see the Life in French by J. B. Coulbeaux (1902), and in Italian by E. Cassinari (1926). See also D. Attwater, *The Book of Eastern Saints* (1938), pp. 136–47. On the Church and Ethiopia see other works listed under Agathangelo and Cassian, 7 August, above.

R.M.
St Vicinius, first bishop of Sarsina, near Ravenna, Italy (fourth-fifth century)
St Vivian, bishop of Sanctes, France (fifth century)

29

THE PASSION OF ST JOHN THE BAPTIST

John (Yohanan="Yahweh is gracious") was the "Fore-runner of Christ." All we know of his life comes from the Jewish historian Josephus and from the New Testament, where he is not only an actual person but also one who becomes mysteriously challenging in the context of his encounters with Jesus. He is also a symbolic and mythic figure. The last-named aspect has predominated, so that everything else forms part of his reception and may be variously assigned to theology, speculative exegesis, art, literature, legend, folklore, and popular religion. As a result there are "several" Johns who sometimes impinge on and merge with one another, for all these areas are rich with matter regarding the Baptist that can only be touched on here but is very important in deciding what he means, which is also, for the most part, "who he was."

In scripture much that we are told of John is a portent. "There appeared a man named John," who came to "testify to the light" (John 1:6-7). He is a great witness to the truth: a burning and shining lamp lighting the way for Christ, the Man of Fire himself (John 5:33-6; 10:41; Acts 1:5; 11:16; 13:24ff.). The narrators introduce miraculous elements into the setting of his birth and infancy, but they are suitably restrained and not of the cosmic order appropriate to Jesus, on whom a dove descends to symbolize his inward endowment with the Holy Spirit, and whom a voice from heaven once again designates as the Son of God, as we are told in the first sentence of Mark's Gospel.

John was the son of Zechariah, a priest of the Temple, and of the aged Elizabeth, who was related to Mary, the mother of Jesus. The *topos* of an aged and often explicitly sterile mother is used for a number of the holiest figures in scripture and later hagiography: Isaac, Jacob, Samson, Samuel, Mary, St Remi, St Rita, and so on. It suggests an element of the miraculous and minimal involvement of the world of flesh and blood in conception. John's kinship with Jesus may be genuine tradition rather than enhancement of the narrative. His birth was announced by an angel (Gabriel) who told Zechariah to call him John but struck him dumb because he disbelieved the message (Luke 1:20ff.). There are various echoes of the stories of Abraham, Isaac, Samson, and Samuel. One New Testament narrator assumes that Zechariah was deaf and dumb after his vision in the Temple. When the boy was named, his father, in accordance with his inspiration by the Holy Spirit, pronounced the *Benedictus*, a prophetic song of praise and possibly a existing hymn with biblical echoes adapted by the author and styled after the Greek Old Testament. It was very unusual to name a child on the eighth day (usually the time of circumcision) and odd for parents to agree on a name never used in the family. Before appearing in the dramatically appropriate because austere wilderness (the mountainous desert area beginning below the Mount of Olives and extending to the Jordan valley below), John spent a long period of ascetic preparation "in the wilds," away from sophisticated religion and politics (Matt. 3:1-10; Mark 1:4-6; Luke 3:1-9). He preached on the banks of the Jordan in about the year 27. He was a moral teacher and was addressed as "Master." He asked people to feed and clothe the needy and give up cheating and injustice (Luke 3:10-14). Unlike his contemporaries he accepted soldiers and tax-gatherers, but he warned them of their particular temptations. Above all, he required everyone to repent and receive baptism because the kingdom of God was at hand and because, therefore, the state of things was about to change totally, God would rule, and all humankind would live willingly as God intended.

John's baptism was something quite different from the usual Jewish ritual cleansing. It took place in the wilderness, symbolically removed from the conventional places of Jewish worship. It demanded a new conception of religion: a morally sincere state of thinking and inward being as well as moral actions. The coming judgment would fall equally upon the élite of the Pharisees and Sadducees, who thought they were somehow removed from it and who seem to have attended scenes of John baptizing as observers. Normal religious practice was not sufficient for the new order, which demanded confession and cleansing. Accordingly, part of John's missionary work foreshadowed Christ's. He dressed (in skins) and ate (locusts and wild honey) as befitted the last of the Old Testament prophets, which is the intended impression (Matt. 17:13; Mark 9:13). He fulfilled the Jewish belief that Elijah (who had worn "a garment of hair cloth and a leather belt"; 2 Kgs. 1:8) would return before the Messiah (Matt. 17:13; Mark 9:13). Large numbers of people listened to him; many, including Jesus himself, were baptized by him. John was not absolutely sure that Jesus was the one he was expecting, and his doubt continued later. The answer to the question "Are you the one who is to come?" was ambiguous. Jesus is shown as the one who asks awkward questions and leaves John, like others, to work out the answers for themselves. John recognized Jesus' unusual quality (Matt. 3:15ff.; Mark 1:19-36; Luke 3:21ff.), yet the sinless Jesus accepted his baptism "for the forgiveness of sins." It has been suggested that this was to endorse the rite for his followers thereafter, but it is one of the paradoxical elements in the whole Baptist interlude that both presage and form part of the problem of what exegetes call Jesus' "self-consciousness," or how exactly Jesus saw himself. This, of course, lies at the very heart of the challenge repeated through the Gospels: "Who do you say that I am?" (see Joseph of Arimathaea and Nicodemus; 31 Aug.). Some people imagined that Jesus was John returned from the dead (Matt. 16:14; Mark 8:28; Luke 9:19).

There is a truth in the account that is deeper than the outlying symbolic framework and ultimately eludes allegorical and symbolic analysis. Jesus himself tells us what is most significant about John. He acknowledges John, not himself, as a type of Elijah; but his characterizations, as so often, are everfruitful riddles, gnomic sayings intended to provoke thought, which they have done ever since. John is important, "yet the least in the kingdom of heaven is greater than he," perhaps because in the kingdom all our conventional classifications are useless: the first shall be last and the last first, or because those (unlike John) who will know that Jesus has died for our offences and is raised again for our justification will know something more profound. Jesus also says, even more enigmatically, "Ever since the coming of John the Baptist the kingdom of heaven has been subjected to violence and violent men are seizing it," possibly referring to Jesus' overzealous followers or to his and their unmerciful enemies. There are more similar remarks, culminating in "Yet God's wisdom is proved right by its results," again, perhaps, reinforcing the point that John and Jesus were not exactly what people expected them to be, yet were acting in accordance with God's plan.

In the scriptural drama John is very much a foil to Jesus. In a sense he is what Jesus might be taken as: a prophet preparing the way, yet he allows Jesus precedence. What this greater significance consists of is then revealed, but mysteriously, for those with eyes to see and ears to hear, in a dialogue which John serves to provoke but in which he remains a reference figure. John is not the Messiah: it is suggested that Jesus is, but certainly not the Messiah you might expect him to be. The second part of the Baptist's narrative, his own passion, is a complementary action "off-stage," which reflects Jesus' own suffering and death yet also points up its uniqueness.

John condemned the Jewish ruler Herod Antipas for his marriage, which was technically both adulterous and incestuous. This criticism offended Herod, but his new wife resented it even more. Herod was married ten times in all. He had been tetrarch of Galilee and the Transjordan (Peraea) since 4 B.C. He divorced his first wife to marry Herodias. She was not only his niece but his brother's wife and had by her first marriage a daughter of about twenty named (Josephus tells us) Salome. It was against the strict Jewish law to marry a niece but above all one's brother's wife while the brother (Herod Philip) was still alive. At Herodias' insistence, Herod imprisoned John (Matt. 4:12; Mark 1:14; Luke 3:19ff). While in gaol John sent his own disciples to ask Jesus directly whether he was the Messiah (Matt. 11:2-6; Luke 7:18-23). Matthew and Mark assume that this is the point at which Jesus appeared in Galilee. According to Josephus, Herod executed John for political reasons, but the New Testament gives a more vivid account of John's passion, which is also quite compatible with Herod's known character. During a banquet which amounted to a drunken orgy Salome danced (wantonly) before (the lascivious) Herod. He rashly promised to grant her whatsoever she wanted (Matt. 14:1-12; Mark 6:14-28; Luke 9:7-9). Herodias took revenge on John by telling her daughter to ask for the too-censorious prophet's head on a dish. Herod was distressed at this but kept his oath. John was beheaded. There are some similarities to the myth of Orpheus, who was dismembered by Maenads or Thracian women and whose head then floated singing on his lyre to Lesbos or Thrace to be reverently gathered up by a Thracian girl. Images of Orpheus are found in the catacombs, and early Christians are thought to have taken him as a figure of the Prince of Peace (Isa. 2:2-4; 9:1-6; 11:1ff.) and thus as a forerunner of Christ. It is more probable, however, that the analogy was drawn when the myths of antiquity were revived during the Renaissance.

The story of John's death has gripped the imagination of writers, visual artists, and composers ever since, so that the relationship between John and Herodias and that between John and Salome have been elevated to the category of myth in their own right and have been amplified and interpreted in accordance with the literary and cultural fashions of different ages. Over the centuries the Baptist has often taken second place to Salome, who evoked visual interpretations from Leonardo, Dürer, Ghirlandaio, Rubens, Luini, Stanzioni, Titian, and many others. The most elaborate versions of the tale have been devoted to Salome's dance and her contemplation of the Baptist's head. Whereas medieval artists might show Salome doing an acrobatic handstand, by the late nineteenth century her dance had become a highly-nuanced performance of evil entice-ment, and in Flaubert's *Hérodias* it is her mother who dances on her hands. In Heine's poem Herodias is condemned to carry the severed head for ever. In the paintings of Gustave Moreau, the drawings of Aubrey Beardsley, in the prose of Huysmans and Flaubert, in the verse of Laforgue, in Mallarmé's *Hérodiade*, and in Oscar Wilde's play *Salome* the daughter is everything bet-ween the epitome of the *femme fatale* and the spirit of all that is unnatural: "*la déité symbolique de l'indestructible Luxure*" (the symbolic goddess of everlasting lust; Huysmans). She wants John's head out of unrequited love, which turns into sheer perversity.

In Salome's company, as it were, John the Baptist left the relatively secure world of tradition and entered the realm of *fin de siècle* irony: the anteroom to the ambiguities of the modern age. Now Salome and John are almost mysti-cally perverse and doom-laden figures, for as Wilde remarked: "All excess, as well as all renunciation, brings its own punishment." Not only Herod but John is profoundly attracted by, but of course rejects, Salome. Yet in this way the literature of the Decadence may be said also to have assisted the biblical image of John as a reflection of and foil to Jesus by providing the missing parallel to Christ's temptation by the devil. The now unfashionable demonization of woman was scarcely novel but a heightened version of a persistent feature of Christian tradition. There was also an interest in John the Baptist as an attractively ascetic young man who rejected the advances of women and was thus included in the pantheon of saints favoured by homosexuals, along with St Sebastian (20

Jan.), SS Serge and Bacchus, and others. This aspect was encouraged by painters who, from Leonardo to Moreau, represented John somewhat androgynously.

The Acts of the Apostles offer evidence of John's disciples' survival as a particular group even in Ephesus and of his influence twenty years after his death (Acts 19:3). Apollos, an Alexandrian converted to Christianity at Ephesus, knew only the baptism of John (Acts 18:25). At Antioch of Pisidia, Paul mentions John's witness to Jesus (Acts 13.24ff). The quasi-Gnostic Mandaeans greatly honour the Baptist, and it has been suggested that their respect for him may have some connection with his original disciples.

Josephus refers to John, his popularity, and his murder, and he records his imprisonment and death in the fortress of Machaerus by the Dead Sea. Tradition says that he was buried at Sebaste (Samaria), where his supposed tomb was honoured in the fourth century. It was probably desecrated in about 362 by Julian the Apostate, who was said to have had the relics disinterred and publicly burned to discourage the cult of the Baptist; the remains were divided. Many churches claim to possess them, especially his head.

The texts found at Qumran suggest that if John preached in the Jordan valley near the Dead Sea, he must have known and could have been associated with the Qumran community and baptized some of its members. Perhaps he came into contact with it during his time "in the wilds." The Qumran rites place a stress similar to John's on baptism as part of the process of repentance. Qumran was similarly hostile to priestly and scribal circles and influence.

Some of the Fathers (Origen, Ambrose, Jerome, and Leo the Great) say that when Mary visited Elizabeth, John was given a special pre-natal grace. The feast of his Nativity (celebrated with the Epiphany, then, from the late fourth century on 24 June, supposedly six months before Christ's birth) was long considered to be more solemn than his *dies natalis* (his passion, death, or "Decollation"), celebrated on 29 August from about the fifth century. The mention of John in the Canon of the Mass and in the *Confiteor* of the traditional (Roman) rite is evidence of a very early cult. Countless customs of popular religion are associated with the Baptist, whose feast was an especially propitious time for invoking the saint for cures and for gathering medicinal herbs but also for hiring servants. At Magdalen College, Oxford, until the eighteenth century an annual John the Baptist sermon was preached from a stone pulpit in the quadrangle, which was fenced round with green boughs to resemble the wilderness.

The various rites celebrated on St John's Vigil (*i.e.*, the eve of his Nativity) are derived from festivals of Mithras and Vulcan but also from much earlier pagan practices for the summer solstice. There have been very many of them, such as the distribution of spices, the gathering of ferns, and the purifying waters or baths of St John; the decoration of houses and doors with fennel, birch, and flowers; and lamps burning throughout the night, but the most persistent are the Fires of St John. The justification was that fire is seen from afar and signifies that John was a lantern of light to the people. In centuries past every town in France and each quarter of Paris had its own fire. They are still popular in many places, particularly in Alsace and Burgundy. The barbaric custom of animal sacrifices, especially the burning of supposedly diabolical cats (very much favoured by King Charles IX) but also foxes, wolves, and bears, on St John's Eve continued in France until the seventeenth century, when it was forbidden by Louis XIII. Horses' heads were burned in Ireland. St John's Fires survived in Britain, especially in the north, into the late nineteenth century. They are relics of ancient solar rites found in many places throughout the world in antiquity and which honour fire as the principle of the sun rather than the Baptist. At one time a wheel was rolled about to signify the sun and the custom of leaping over the fires prevailed as a remnant of rites of ordeal to prove innocence. It is doubtful that the new Christian symbolism, even that of the baptism of fire that was to follow John's, was or remains in the minds of those who take part in the ceremonies. A vast number of proverbial and other popular sayings to do with weather, health, and so on cite John the Baptist.

Numerous churches and, of course, baptisteries are dedicated to the saint. The high point of his popularity was in the Middle Ages, when at least 496 churches in England alone were named after him. He was patron of the Knights Hospitallers. John's attribute is a lamb (which he usually carries and which may bear the words "*Ecce Agnus Dei*," from John's Gospel 1:36: "John looked towards him [Jesus] and said, 'There is the Lamb of God.'"), a slender cross of reeds, or a banner bearing a reed cross. He sometimes has a scroll with the words "*Vox clamantis in deserto*" ("A voice crying in the wilderness"). Sometimes he carries a baptismal cup. A dish with his own head on it may appear elsewhere in the picture, and occasionally the locusts and honeycomb or wild honey he ate are shown. In accordance with scripture he is often unkempt and wears a rough camel's hair garment, or a tunic of animal's skins and a leather girdle, but as often rich raiment appropriate to the court of heaven. In Byzantine art he may have angel's wings to indicate his function as a messenger. If accompanied, he appears mainly with Zechariah and an angel, John the Evangelist, Zenobius and other patrons of Florence, Cosmas and Damian, Julian the Hospitaller, Sebastian, or patrons from the Medici family (of Florence).

See *AA.SS.* for 4 June (1707), pp. 698-705; *D.T.C.*, 8 (1924), 646-56; D. Buzy, *The Life of John the Baptist* (1947); C. H. Kraeling, *John the Baptist* (1951); C. H. H. Scobie, *John the Baptist* (1964); J. Daniélou, *Jean-Baptiste, témoin de l'Agneau* (1964); W. Wink, *John the Baptist in the Gospel Tradition* (1968). See also J. Péladan, *Leonardo da Vinci* (1910), p. 308; A. van Gennep, *Manuel de folklore français contemporain*, 3 vols (1937); M. Praz, *The Romantic Agony* (Eng. trans., 2d ed., 1951), pp. 289-321; G. B. de l'Isle, *Vieux Dictons de nos Campagnes*, 1 (1952), pp. 447-95; P.-L. Mathieu, *Gustave Moreau* (Eng. trans., 1977), pp. 121-9; R. Ellmann, *Oscar Wilde* (1987), pp. 316-43; J.-P. Albert, *Le sang et le Ciel* (1997).

John is one of the saints most often represented in Christian art. He became especially popular as a subject during the Renaissance, above all in Florence, for he is patron saint of the city. There are several surviving English images of John; the most interesting is that on the seventh-century Ruthwell Cross. From the late Middle Ages his head may be shown alone on a charger. This image was thought to have a medicinal effect, as were the alabaster heads produced, e.g., at Nottingham in the fifteenth century.

A typical portrayal of the *Birth, Naming and Circumcision of John the Baptist* is that of the Master of the Life of St John the Baptist (National Gallery of Art, Washington). An early Tintoretto (1518-94) is one of the loveliest portrayals of the saint's nativity (St Zachary, Venice). Titian (*c.* 1489-1576) shows him as a child with Mary and Jesus (National Gallery, London), as does Andrea del Sarto (1486-1530) (National Gallery, London; and Hermitage, Leningrad) and, sublimely, Leonardo da Vinci (1452-1519) in the cartoon *The Virgin and Child with St Anne and St John the Baptist* (National Gallery, London). In Leonardo's *Saint-Jean* (Louvre, Paris) he is "spiritually androgynous . . . the sex becomes enigmatic" (Péladan). He is gaunt and ascetic in Ercole Roberti's (*c.* 1450-96) version (Berlin Museum). Domenico Veneziano (active 1438-61) makes him a comely youth, naked in the desert (National Gallery of Art, Washington), and portrays him with an emaciated face as part of a sacred conversation piece (*c.* 1442-8; Uffizi, Florence), whereas for Benedetto Bembo (15th c.) he is worn yet solid with experience as he preaches (Columbia Museum of Art, Columbia, South Carolina). In Parmigianino's altarpiece (1527) he is strong and comely (National Gallery, London). Donatello's wonderful marble sculpture (1434-40; National Museum, Florence) makes him very young, slight yet visionary. In a superb mosaic in the Cappella Palatina, Palermo, Italy, John in an almost electrically vibrant hair shirt baptizes Christ in water that responds appropriately. John is light, almost ethereal in Piero della Francesca's *Baptism of Christ* (*c.* 1460; National Gallery, London).

A medieval mosaic in St Mark's, Venice, is a fairly early version of the presentation of John's head in a dish, one of the favourite scenes of his life in art. Benozzo Gozzoli's (1420-97) *Beheading* (National Gallery of Art, Washington) shows Salome as a young Florentine maiden in a flowing robe, a vision of captivating youthfulness. (She is always minimally—if diaphanously—covered, though she almost certainly danced naked).

Bronzino's *Baptist* (c. 1550; Borghese Gallery Rome)is an assured and physically powerful Renaissance man, but the most sublime portrait is probably Raphael's (*c.* 1505; National Gallery, London), which shows him with Nicholas of Bari before the Virgin and Child.

By the late nineteenth century the adoption of the Baptist by symbolist art and literature, and his incorporation into its treatment of sin, sex, and death are evident in Puvis de Chavannes' (1824-98) *The Beheading of St John the Baptist* (National Gallery, London), in which the novelist Anatole France, cast by the Church as a rationalist enemy, appears, it seems, as Herod. The supreme image of the period occurs in Gustave Moreau's series of Salome paintings: *Salome Dancing before Herod* (1876; Los Angeles County Museum of Art, Calif.), *Salome in the Garden* (1878; priv. coll., Paris), and so on, and especially *The Apparition* (1876; Fogg Art Museum, Cambridge, Mass.), in which John's head rises up from the platter to confront Salome. Aubrey Beardsley's monochrome drawings for Oscar Wilde's *Salome* (1894) present John poised between attraction and resistance to evil.

There is no scriptural warranty for many of the scenes in which John is shown in art. They are based on the vast number of legends about the Baptist, and include John as an infant playing with the infant Jesus; Mary seated on the floor holding John after his birth; Herodias piercing the dead Baptist's tongue with a knife or pin; the Baptist's bones being burned.

St Sebbi (*c.* 694)

Sebbi (or Sebbe) began his reign over the East Saxons (Essex, Hertfordshire, and London) in the plague year 664. He was co-king of the region with Sighere, who thought the plague was a sign of the gods' anger at his conversion to Christianity. He returned to the old religion with many of his people. Bishop Jaruman came from Mercia to reconvert them. St Bede (25 May) says he was a good man and successful in his mission. The bishop was supported by Sebbi, who was a wise ruler and so pious that he was more suited to be a bishop than a king. He is said to have built the first monastery at Westminster.

When he had reigned for thirty years, he resigned his crown. He had wanted to do this for some time, but his queen refused to allow a separation. She agreed only because her husband's ill health seemed to show that he would die soon. Sebbi received the monastic habit from Waldhere, successor of St Erconwald (13 May) as bishop of London, whom he asked to distribute his personal estate among the poor. When he felt death was close, he summoned the bishop and asked that only he and two attendants should stay with him, for he was afraid that pain and weakness might make him say or do something unworthy. He reported a dream in which "three men in bright robes visited him. One sat down in front of his pallet while his companions remained standing and asked about the condition of the sick man they had come to see. The first man replied that his soul would leave his body without pain in a splendour of light and that he would die in three days' time. Both of these things happened as he had learned in the vision." He was buried against the north wall of old St Paul's Cathedral; Bede says that the too-short sarcophagus miraculously accommodated itself to Sebbi's body. The liturgical cult of Sebbi is relatively modern. Cardinal Baronius entered him in the Roman Martyrology in the sixteenth century.

See Bede, *H.E.*, pp. 200, 216, 222-3.

St Medericus, *Abbot* (*c.* 700)

Medericus (Merry in French) was born at Autun in France in the seventh century. When still very young he entered a local monastery (probably St Martin's, Autun) of fifty-four exceptionally pious monks. He was chosen abbot against his own will and offered his already ultra-penitential brothers an "example of true virtue." He was so holy that he was constantly asked for advice. Fear of vanity made him resign and withdraw to a forest four miles from Autun where he remained hidden for some time, satisfying all his needs by his own work. Eventually his retreat was discovered, and he was sick, so he had to return to the monastery. He strengthened his brothers' faith and left them in old age to make a pilgrimage to the shrine of St Germanus (28 May; also a native of Autun) in Paris. He lived with a companion (St Frou or Frodulf) in a small cell adjoining a chapel dedicated to St Peter in the northern suburbs of the city. He patiently suffered an illness which lasted for the next two years and nine months. He died happily about the year 700.

AA.SS., Aug., 6. The church of Saint-Merry in the Marais district of Paris now has a prominent social mission to the poor.

BB John of Perugia and Peter of Sassoferrato, *Martyrs* (1231)

Among the Friars Minor whom St Francis of Assisi (4 Oct.) sent to Spain to preach the gospel to the Moors were Brother John, a priest of Perugia, and Brother Peter, a lay brother from Sassoferrato in Piceno, Italy. They lived in cells near St Bartholomew's church while preparing for their work. They were admired for their poverty and humility. They went on to Valencia, then completely under Moorish rule, and resided quietly at the church of the Holy Sepulchre. When they tried to preach in public, the Muslims turned against them. They were arrested and brought before the emir on 29 August 1231. He asked them why they were there. John said that they had come to convert the Moors from the errors of Islam. They were asked to choose between apostasy or death. When they chose death they were sentenced to lose their heads. They were beheaded directly in the emir's garden while, it is said, they prayed aloud for the emir's conversion.

Seven years later King James I of Aragon drove the Moors from Valencia with the help of English and other mercenaries. The emir, it is claimed, became a Christian and gave his house to the Franciscans as a friary, saying: "When I was an unbeliever I killed your brothers from Teruel. I want to make reparation for my crime. Here is my house, consecrated already by the blood of martyrs." The bodies of the two brothers had been taken to Teruel, where miracles were reported at their tomb. A church was erected in their honour at the new friary in Valencia. They were beatified in 1783.

See *Analecta Franciscana*, 3, pp. 186-7; *AA.SS.*, Aug., 6, for their story as related by St Antoninus of Florence.

Bd Richard Herst, *Martyr* (1628)

Richard Herst (or Hurst, or Hayhurst) would seem to have been the only member of the Catholic laity executed in the fifteen years before Parliament was recalled in 1640. He was probably born at Broughton, near Preston in Lancashire. He was a yeoman farmer "of considerable substance" and a recusant. In 1628 the bishop of Chester sent Norcross, a pursuivant, and two men, Wilkinson (a ruffian for whose imprisonment the local constable held a warrant) and Dewhurst, to arrest Richard. He was ploughing a field, with a youth leading the horse. Norcross handed him the warrant and Wilkinson hit him with a stick. A girl at work in the field fetched her mistress, who came with a farm-worker and a man named Bullen. Wilkinson knocked both of them down, whereupon the girl promptly hit Dewhurst on the head. The process servers ran off, but Dewhurst—who was probably pursuing Wilkinson—fell and broke his leg on the ploughed land. He solemnly admitted that his fall was quite accidental and that neither the girl nor Herst was responsible, but he died from a complicated fracture thirteen days later. Richard was indicted and sentenced for murder before Sir Henry Yelverton, even though the coroner's jury offered contrary evidence and the criminal jury was unwilling to declare him guilty. The judge told the foreman in private that Richard had to be sentenced as an example. The day after the sentence, Richard refused to go to church and was dragged there by order of the high sheriff. He threw himself on the ground and put his fingers in his ears to close out the sermon.

A petition was sent to King Charles I asking for a reprieve. It was supported by Queen Henrietta Maria, but strong anti-Catholic interests were at work. Nevertheless, Richard was offered his life if he would take the Oath of Allegiance, condemned by the Holy See. Three letters from Richard to his confessor survive. In one he wrote: "I pray you remember my poor children, and encourage my friends about my debts; and let it appear that my greatest worldly care is to satisfy them as far as my means will extend." On his way to the gallows he looked up and saw the head of St Edmund Arrowsmith (28 Aug.), the only priest executed in the same period, on show above the castle. He remarked that it was the head "of that blessed martyr whom you have sent before to prepare the way for us." When a minister continued to question him, he replied, "I believe according to the faith of the Holy Catholic Church." After praying at the foot of the scaffold he noticed the hangman fumbling with the rope and called up to him, "Tom, I think I must come up and help thee." He was again offered his life if he took the oath but refused as it was incompatible with his religion. He was hanged. He left behind seven children, one still unborn. Richard was beatified in 1929.

See H. More, S. J., *Historia Provinciae Anglicanae* (1630); *A True and Exact Relation of the Death of Two Catholicks who suffered for their Religion at the Summer Assizes held at Lancaster . . .*, 1628 (1737; based largely on the foregoing); *M.M.P.*, pp. 362-73. There is an engraved portrait of "Ricardus Herst" in the 1737 *True and Exact Relation*.

Bd Edmund Ignatius Rice, *Founder* (1762-1844)

Edmund Rice, the founder of the Irish Christian Brothers (C.F.C.) and the Presentation Brothers (F.P.M.) was born at Westcourt near Callan in Co. Kilkenny on 1 June 1762. His parents, Robert and Margaret Rice (née Tierney), were prosperous tenant farmers who had leased 180 acres from Lord Desart, an amenable Protestant landlord. Edmund was the fourth of seven brothers. He had two stepsisters, Joan and Jane Murphy, from his mother's first marriage.

Ireland had just passed through a period of anti-Catholic persecution by the English that had more to do with political allegiances and the hunger for land than with Catholicism. By 1762 the threat to the English throne from the exiled Stuarts had passed, and the harsher Penal Laws were being relaxed. Enterprising Irish Catholics began to improve their position. Some, like Edmund's father, leased farms from the more kindly disposed landlords. Others became traders, merchants, and shopkeepers. This tiny Catholic middle class also supplied vocations to the priesthood. Most Catholics, however, were still illiterate, unskilled workers.

Edmund Rice received an education denied to the majority of his co-religionists. He first attended a "hedge school"—an illegal pay-school set up by a travelling teacher for those whose parents could afford the fees. His religious education was provided by his parents and by an Augustinian friar, Patrick Grace, who, in spite of the Penal Laws, travelled freely around the locality. Later, until he was seventeen Edmund received a practical and classical education at a commercial academy in Kilkenny. This would help him later in his business career and as founder of schools for poor boys.

In 1779 Edmund joined his uncle, Michael, in the port of Waterford to learn at first hand the family business of victualling and ship-chandling, which thrived. The uncle signed it over to his nephew. The laws against Catholics were more relaxed by this time, and Edmund invested heavily in land and property. Eventually he owned over a thousand acres, two inns, and a fleet of merchant ships.

At twenty-four Edmund was well adjusted and likeable. He loved dancing, singing, boating, and riding and dressed with style. He fell in love with Mary Elliott, the daughter of the owner of a tanyard. They married and settled in fashionable Arundel Square. But the young mother-to-be died in January 1789, some say in a fall from a horse. A daughter, Mary, born prematurely, survived her mother but was retarded and had to be nursed for the rest of her life. Years afterwards Edmund referred to this period as "the dregs of misery and misfortune."

Like many Catholic merchants, Edmund was involved in moneylending to poorer Catholics, who dared not go to the city banks. He prided himself on his strict justice in business. He was appointed trustee of many charities but did not dispense charity coldly. He called on the poor and restored debtors from prison to their families. He visited prisoners and was often at the gallows on John's Bridge praying for an unfortunate about to be executed for violating some harsh law.

Edmund was convinced that "something else was yet wanting of him." A chance encounter in 1793 with a friar who spent the night in prayer affected him deeply. Three years before he had approved of his brother's decision to become an Augustinian. Was this the life for him? He considered selling his property, which would now be worth more than a million pounds. Then his direction changed.

One afternoon he and a friend of his, Fr John Power, heard a group of youths shouting and cursing as they fought and fell in the roadway. The priest's sister said: "Well, Mr Rice, you are thinking of burying yourself in a monastery on the Continent. Will you leave these poor boys uncared for?" Now he knew how he would spend the rest of his life. Handouts of food or clothing were not enough. Mentally, morally, and religiously, young people had to be equipped to be independent. The society that made them poor had to be changed. The ruling classes would find this difficult programme dangerously radical.

Edmund was inspired by Nano Nagle's Presentation Sisters, whom he introduced to Waterford in 1798 to cater for the educational needs of poor girls. Edmund now provided an education of sorts for the street boys of Waterford, first in one of his stores after work and then, in 1802, in a converted stable in New Street. Bishop Hussey supported his efforts, but when Edmund began to use his considerable fortune to build a permanent school his business friends doubted his sanity. Edmund persevered. In 1803 he built his first permanent school and residence at Mount Sion in Waterford. He and two companions began to rise early, go to morning Mass, eat sparingly, pray often, and spend most of the day teaching the "roughs and toughs" of the city basic literacy and religion. This was the blueprint for generations of Presentation and Christian Brothers.

Edmund's example and experience attracted well-educated and successful men, who joined the Congregation in increasing numbers. It was mainly their personal generosity that sustained the schools in their first three decades, as education was offered free. Ignatius drew up a detailed timetable: lessons were from 9 A.M. to midday and from 1 to 3 P.M., reading was taught from a History of the Old and New Testaments, and there was great emphasis on the catechism and general moral instruction. The boys received Communion once a month and confessed four times a year. Outside the school they were not allowed to play with other boys. Examinations were fairly constant with the results determining where boys sat in class and the type of further work they did. Corrections were gentle, and corporal punishment was not allowed "except for some very serious fault, which rarely occurs." (Later generations of pupils were to fnd this rule more honoured in the breach than in the observance.) The behaviour of the young boys soon improved, and their parents asked for evening classes for themselves. Edmund established a library, from which boys were allowed to take books home at weekends to read to their illiterate parents. Edmund established a bakery to feed the boys and, often, their families. He set up a tailoring department to provide new suits for the pupils' First Communion and Confirmation. Many pupils were studying vocational subjects, such as bookkeeping, architectural drawing, and navigation, and he provided a new suit for each pupil as he left school to give him a good start in the workplace.

Soon the number of Edmund's followers increased. At first most of them were mature men from all over Ireland who had done well in business. New schools were opened in Carrick-on-Suir and Dungarvan. In 1808, with the bishop's approval, Edmund and his eight companions took religious vows according to the Rule of the Presentation and began to wear religious dress in their houses, now designated monasteries. The Brothers, or monks, constituted a diocesan Congregation with the bishop as their superior. Edmund became known as Brother Ignatius, after St Ignatius of Loyola.

Soon other dioceses wanted "monks' schools," and up to 1820 schools and communities were established in Cork, Limerick, Thurles, and, especially, Dublin. There were never enough Brothers. Encouraged by Archbishop Murray, Edmund procured a copy of the De La Salle Rule. This allowed for the election of a superior general and the easier transfer of Brothers from diocese to diocese, since the local bishop would no longer be the Brothers' superior. Edmund held a meeting of all the Brothers in 1817 to ask if they would choose the new centralized style of government. The majority were enthusiastic; others felt that their basic loyalty was to their own diocese. This was particularly true in Cork, where the bishop would not even allow the Brothers to attend the exploratory meeting. After an appeal to Rome, on 5 September 1820 Pope Pius VII approved the new centralized Congregation of Christian Brothers. The new way of life was accepted by the majority, and Edmund was elected first superior general.

In Cork the community was divided. Some members slipped away to Mount Sion and took their vows as Christian Brothers. The remainder, who were close friends of the bishop, were given a new school and residence where the original Presentation Rule continued, with Bishop Murphy as superior. Years later the Presentation Brothers obtained a superior general. Today both orders look to Edmund as their founder.

Schools were founded in most towns in Ireland. Overseas, schools were established in England, beginning in Preston, Manchester, London, and Liverpool. In 1829 Catholic emancipation was granted, and although Catholics rejoiced, Edmund and his Brothers faced suppression because a clause against male religious had been inserted into the act to soothe Protestant susceptibilities. The penalty for receiving new members could be banishment to the colonies for life. Daniel O'Connell came to the Brothers' defence. The clause became a dead letter unless relatives challenged a bequest left for the charitable work of the Brothers.

In 1828 Edmund had moved the Christian Brothers' headquarters to Dublin, where they were spreading rapidly under the enthusiastic patronage of Archbishop Murray. In 1831 Edmund withdrew his schools on a matter of principle from the National Schools, and the archbishop's support faded. For years to come, the Brothers depended on the pennies of the poor and the proceeds of an annual charity sermon.

In 1838 Edmund retired as superior general, to the regret of most Brothers. There was no obvious successor. In a split vote, Br Paul Riordan, one of Edmund's former critics from Cork, became superior general.

In 1841 Edmund was refused admission to a chapter of the order he had founded. His critics felt that his mere presence would be contentious. In 1842 he was confined to his room suffering from senile dementia. In his lucid moments, his favourite prayers were "Praise be to you, O Christ" and the *Memorare*. He liked having the Bible read to him as well as the Annals of the Congregation for the Propagation of the Faith, which narrated the lives of heroes on the foreign missions. He was not to know that his Brothers had established foundations in India, Australia, and America in the short period before his death. Edmund died at Mount Sion on 29 August 1844, aged eighty-two. He was widely mourned, especially by the poor.

Ireland was emerging from the legacy of the Penal Laws, and canonization was not uppermost in people's minds. The Great Famine of 1847, during which a million died and another million emigrated, overtook events. Edmund's memory was kept alive by his two Congregations of Brothers and by the people of Ireland. The people of Callan, his birthplace, and Mount Sion, his final resting place, hoped that Edmund would be publicly honoured by the Church. They had to wait a long time. His cause was first put forward in 1910, but the archdiocese of Dublin undertook the preparation of his cause only in 1962, the bicentenary of his birth. Edmund was beatified on 6 October 1996. His Congregations celebrate his feast-day on 5 May, accepted as a compromise date on which the maximum number of pupils in both hemispheres would be at school.

Edmund's Brothers today, though fewer in number than they were in the 1960s when they reached over four thousand, are on every continent, working to improve the educational and social condition of hundreds of thousands of people, especially the young. In recent years there has been a great impetus in the Brothers' missions to Africa, India, South America, and the West Indies, and to the inner cities of the First World: in Dublin, Cork, Liverpool, Sydney, Melbourne, New York, Chicago, and Miami, where, as in Edmund Rice's Waterford, poverty hides behind opulent structures. Today, there is a much greater awareness of the Brothers' working in partnership with co-workers, associates, other religious, and people of good will.

The driving force of Edmund's life is best summed up in a letter to a business colleague in 1810: "Let us do ever so little for God, we will be sure he will never forget it, nor let it pass unrewarded. . . . Were we to know the merit of only going from one street to another to serve a neighbour for the love of God, we should prize it more than Gold or Silver."

See: Congregation for the Causes of Saints, Rome, *Positio super Virtutibus* (1988); *Filiis Suis: Decree of Heroic Virtue* (1993); *Positio super Miraculo* (1994); *Decree of Beatification* (1996). Also, D. S. Blake, *A Man for our Time* (1996); W. B. Cullen, A. L. O'Toole, *Steadfast in Giving* (1975); David Fitzpatrick, *Edmund Rice* (1945); D. C. Hurley, *Edmund Ignatius Rice: A Story of Compassion* (1982); P. B. Jacob, *Edmund Ignatius Rice* (1979); F. Keane, *Blessed Edmund Rice* (1997); D. Keogh, *Edmund Rice, 1762-1844* (1996); W. M. McCarthy, *Edmund Ignatius Rice and the Christian Brothers* (1926); M. C. Normoyle, *Dublin: A Tree is Planted* (1975); *idem, Companion to "A Tree is Planted"* (1977), *Roman Correspondence* (1978), *Memories of Edmund Rice* (1979); A. L. O'Toole, *Spiritual Profile of*

Edmund Ignatius Rice, 2 vols. (1984–5); D. Rushe, *Edmund Rice: The Man and His Times* (1981; n.e., 1995); A. Shanahan, *A Quiet Revolution* (1985).

Bd Mary of the Cross (Jeanne Jugan) *Foundress* (1879)

Jeanne Jugan, in religion Sister Mary of the Cross, was a Breton woman born on 25 October 1792 at Cancale, Ille-et-Vilaine, France. In 1839 she founded the Little Sisters of the Poor, and she lived a life of exemplary and heroic evangelical charity. She identified with and begged for the impoverished and abandoned, especially the aged. She said, "It is so wonderful to be poor, to have nothing, and to expect everything from God's bounty." Joan relied entirely on God's providence but did not allow this confidence to dampen her enthusiasm in working for the neglected aged or to curtail her devotional life, which was based on long periods of silent prayer, frequent Mass-going and Communion, and meditation on the mysteries of the rosary and the Stations of the Cross. She overcame many difficulties in establishing her Sisterhood, and four years after its foundation she went through an especially harsh period of critical abuse from members of the Order outside her particular circle of friends. She agreed to step down as superior and shortly afterwards went into retreat at the motherhouse. Without any protest she accepted humbly—indeed heroically, for it lasted twenty-seven years—her retirement from the work which she so treasured. She is recommended not only as a model of brave humility but as one whose message of concern for old people is as vitally needed today as in her own century of almost universal neglect of the aged poor. Joan was aware of the special longing of old people for respect and love, their need to be wanted, and their desire for a degree of privacy and freedom; and she tried, within the constraints of her time, to provide something approaching family homes where their physical, emotional, and spiritual needs could be met more appropriately than in not only the few almshouses of those times but also in the state relief systems of our own era. When she died there were some 2,400 Little Sisters in ten countries. Today there are some 4,400 working in thirty countries and five continents. Mary of the Cross died on 29 August 1879 at La Tour Saint-Joseph. She was beatified by Pope John Paul II on 3 October 1982.

N.S.B. 2, pp. 192–4.

R.M.
St Sabina, martyr (date unkown)
St Basilla of Smyrna (third/fourth century)
St Philonidis, bishop and martyr in Cyprus (*c.* 303)
St Adelf, bishop of Metz, France (fifth century)
St Victor the Hermit (*c.* 610)
Bd Bronislava, Norbertine solitary in Poland (1259)

30

SS Felix and Adauctus, *Martyrs* (*c.* 304)

Felix was a priest in Rome who was arrested in the early days of the Diocletian persecution. He was tortured and sentenced to lose his head. A Christian, so the story goes, was so moved by the sight of Felix on his way to execution that he cried out: "I confess the same faith and the same Jesus Christ as this man. I too will sacrifice my life in the cause of Christ!" The magistrates had him seized, and the martyrs were beheaded together. Christians called the anonymous yet courageous stranger Adauctus ("the one added") because he was joined to Felix in martyrdom. "Felix and Adauctus, in the cemetery of Commodilla on the Ostian Way," are recorded in the 354 *Depositio martyrum*, which is sure evidence of their early cult, further confirmed by the Leonine Sacramentary and many other sources. The story, however, is a much-embellished derivation from an inscription of Pope St Damasus (11 Dec.): "You were truly and rightly named Felix, or happy, for you kept the faith, despised the prince of this world, confessed Christ and sought the heavenly kingdom. Remember too, Christians, the truly precious faith by which Adauctus also sped, a victor, to heaven. At the command of his ruler Damasus, the priest Verus restored the tomb, adorning the thresholds of the saints." There is also an inscription from the pontificate of Siricius. A church built over the tomb of Felix and Adauctus in the cemetery of Commodilla was uncovered in 1905.

See *AA.SS.*, Aug., 6 (1743), pp. 545-51; *B.T.A.*, 3, p. 446; *Anal. Boll.* 16 (1897), pp. 17-43; *C.M.H.*, pp. 476-8.

St Pammachius (410)

Pammachius was a Roman citizen, a member of the house of the Furii, a senator and a learned man. He is sometimes described as a priest, but there is no evidence of this. He was a friend of St Jerome (30 Sept.), with whom he had studied when young and remained in contact all his life. In 385 he married Paulina, the second daughter of St Paula (26 Jan.), another great friend of Jerome's. Pammachius was probably one of the religious men who denounced Jovinian to Pope St Siricius (26 Nov.). Jovinian supported several heresies, including the proposition that all sins and their punishments are equal. Pammachius certainly sent copies of Jovinian's writings to Jerome, who answered them in a long treatise. Pammachius wrote to Jerome to say that he found the master's language too strong and his praise of virginity and depreciation of marriage excessive. Jerome replied in two letters thanking him but defending his own views. Jovinian was condemned in a synod at Rome and by St Ambrose (7 Dec.) at Milan. Nothing more is heard of him except that Jerome wrote a few years later that he had "belched rather than breathed out his life amidst pheasants and pork."

Pammachius' wife died in 397, and Jerome and St Paulinus of Nola (22 June) both wrote letters of sympathy. Pammachius devoted the rest of his life to study and charitable works for the blind, lame, and destitute. Together with St Fabiola (27 Dec.) he built a large pilgrims' hospice at Porto especially for the poor and sick coming to Rome. This, known as a *xenodochium*, was the first institution of its kind, and its site has been laid bare. Jerome praised it warmly. Pammachius and Fabiola spent much time there looking after their guests.

Pammachius was very upset by the argument between Jerome and Rufinus. He helped Jerome with his controversial writings but was unable to temper their language, which he continued to find exaggerated. He wrote to the people on his estates in Numidia urging them to abandon the Donatist schism and return to orthodoxy. This action elicited a letter of thanks from St Augustine (28 Aug.) at Hippo in 401. Pammachius had a church in his house on the Coelian hill. The site of the *titulus Pammachii* is now occupied by the Passionist church of SS Giovanni e Paolo, beneath which remains of the original house have been found. Pammachius died in 410 at the time when Alaric and the Goths captured Rome.

See *AA.SS.*, Aug., 6; F. Cavallera, *Saint Jerome* (2 vols., 1922); I. d'Ivray, *Saint Jérôme et les Dames de l'Aventin* (1938); J. N. D. Kelly, *Jerome* (1975).

St Fiacre (*c.* 670)

Fiacre (or Fiachra) is not in earlier Irish calendars yet appears in the new draft Roman Martyrology. He entered Irish martyrologies in the late twelfth century. He is largely a figure of folk-religion with devotees from more elevated circles in the seventeenth and eighteenth centuries. He is said to have been born in Ireland and to have gone to France to find greater solitude. He arrived at Meaux, where the bishop, St Faro (28 Oct.), offered him a solitary dwelling in a forest which he owned at Breuil in the province of Brie. One legend says that Faro told Fiacre that he could have as much land as he could turn up in a day and that the wily Irishman did not use a plough. Instead he turned the top of the soil with the point of his staff; similar tricks are to be found in very many folk-tales in different cultures.

Fiacre cleared the land of trees and briars, made a cell with a garden, built an oratory in honour of Our Lady, and erected a travellers' hospice, which became the village of Saint-Fiacre in Seine-et-Marne. He received kindly all those who came for advice, as well as the poor who asked for help, and served all comers in his hospice. Miraculous cures were reported in his lifetime. He would never allow a woman within his hermitage enclosure. In 1620, it is said, a Parisian lady who thought her rank excused her from this prohibition entered the oratory and became insane on the spot. In 1641 Anne of Austria, queen of France, made a pilgrimage there on foot but sensibly stayed outside the door and prayed with the other pilgrims. She attributed to Fiacre's intercession the recovery of Louis XIII from a dangerous illness as well as the successful birth of Louis XIV. Fiacre remained popular with the French royal family. Before Louis XIV underwent surgery, the great court preacher Bossuet, bishop of Meaux, began a special novena of prayers at Saint-Fiacre. St Vincent de Paul (27 Sept.) also resorted to his intercession. Fiacre's relics were translated to Meaux and were visited there for a range of afflictions, especially sexually-transmitted diseases, and this last specialism is ascribed to his supposed attitude to women. He is still invoked for cures. He is also a patron saint of gardeners, market gardeners, and the cab drivers of Paris. French taxicabs were for a long time known as *fiacres* because the first firm to hire out coaches, in the mid-seventeenth century, was in the rue Saint-Martin near the Hôtel Saint-Fiacre.

See *AA.SS.*, Aug., 6, 598-620, for a Latin Life of doubtful historical value. See also L. Pfleger in *Zeitschrift für die Geschichte des Oberrheins* (1918), pp. 153-73; L. Gougaud, *Les saints irlandais hors d'Irlande* (1936), pp. 86-92, and (Eng. adaptation) idem., *Gaelic Pioneers of Christianity* (1938), pp. 135-7; *N.L.A.*, 1, pp. 441-3.

St Margaret Ward, *Martyr* (1588)

Margaret is one of the very few women among the known Catholic martyrs of the British Isles acknowledged by beatification or canonization. She is described by the sources as a gentlewoman born at Congleton, Cheshire. She lived in London, where she was in the service—perhaps as housekeeper or companion—of another gentlewoman, Mrs Whitall (or Whittle). Margaret decided to help William (some sources say Richard) Watson (alias Colpepper), an embarrassingly odd secular priest in the Bridewell prison, and became involved in an adventure with bizarre, even farcical, twists and all-too-fatal consequences. A summary account will illustrate some harshly ironic realities of penal times too often glossed over in martyrs' lives in and out of which Watson so often flits.

Reports of Watson's behaviour as maverick priest differ considerably, yet some probabilities emerge from his own *braggadocio* and the contumely of almost all other parties. He was born in Durham in 1558, went to Oxford aged ten (not, as he said, as a student, but as a servant) and to the Inns of Court at fourteen, and was at Reims twice, when aged sixteen and twenty-six. He was ordained and sent on the English mission in 1586. He soon became notorious for controversy inside and outside Catholic circles. He was imprisoned and brutalized in the Marshalsea, protested against the Catholic Anthony Babington's plot to murder Elizabeth and release Mary, Queen of Scots, agreed to attend a Protestant church, was released for eventual banishment, received absolution from another priest, dramatically interrupted a service in the Bridewell church, was retaken, put in irons in a dungeon of the Bridewell prison, almost starved to death, moved to an attic, constantly interrogated, and required to attend Protestant services yet again, until he became a nervous wreck. Hearing of this, Margaret visited him regularly with gifts of food. She obtained the confidence of the gaoler's wife and smuggled a nicely calculated length of rope to Watson, having engaged two Catholic watermen to wait on the river between two and three in the morning. Hoping to take the rope with him, Watson doubled it, bungled his drop from the roof, fell on to a shed and broke an arm and a leg. The watermen promptly carried him off and rowed him to safety. (Bd) John Roche (see below), an Irishman, was either Margaret's young servant, who changed clothes with the priest to delay the gaolers, or more probably one of the watermen who did so later. He was arrested as a result. The rope, left hanging by Watson, was found and traced to Margaret, the obvious culprit, just as she was leaving for other lodgings.

Margaret was put in irons for eight days, suspended by her hands and cruelly beaten, then brought to the bar. She and John were charged with helping not only a prisoner but a traitor to get away. They refused to say where the priest was hiding. Their interrogators offered to release them if they asked the queen's pardon and agreed to attend the established church. Margaret and John said they had done nothing to offend the queen's majesty. Margaret told the judges that if Elizabeth herself "had the bowels of a woman" and had seen Watson she would have rescued him and that to attend the State church was against their conscience. The martyrs could be made to seem guilty of a criminal act in assisting the escape of a prisoner on, as it were, remand. Presumably they would have argued that the legislation under which Watson and they were arraigned was unjust (especially as Watson had been re-arrested before the time allowed him to leave England was up). Nevertheless, their "fault" was technically if not substantially different from that of many other martyrs. Yet in the end, it seems, they were condemned for disobeying an obligation (which Watson himself had both accepted and refused) under what was, essentially, a religious test act. They were hanged at Tyburn on 30 August 1588.

Watson was possibly recognized, re-imprisoned and escaped, spent two years in Liège, went to Ireland, then back to England, acted as chief appellant on behalf of the secular (and largely anti-Jesuit) clergy trying to arrange an acceptable oath with the Privy Council, and was reimprisoned three times, writing his racy autobiography during one stay in gaol, escaping twice, and winning his freedom on the death of Elizabeth in 1603. He obtained an audience with James VI/I and tried to negotiate another special Catholic oath of allegiance. His always fanatical anti-Jesuitism became an obsession; he publicly opposed a supposed Jesuit conspiracy to put the Spanish *infanta* on the throne, collaborated in several polemical works, and wrote one of his own against the Society. He conspired in more than one plot and then with other Catholics in an attempt to kidnap King James VI/I and force him to replace Protestant with Catholic ministers. By now, perhaps, megalomania had set in, for Watson appointed himself lord chancellor in the new government. Fr Garnet, the Jesuit superior, and Fr Blackwell, the archpriest, revealed the plot to the government. On Catholic evidence, therefore, Watson was arrested yet again, and put in the Tower to foil his escaping ability. At his trial he engaged in some delightful exchanges with the equally cranky King James. He was executed before the end of the year, having asked the Jesuits' forgiveness. It is difficult to know whether Watson's behaviour was mentally unbalanced or a brave eccentric's apt response to a crazy world, and exactly what Margaret thought of him or he of her: her conduct of his escape and her loaded remarks about Elizabeth suggest that, to a certain extent, they could have been kindred spirits.

Margaret was beatified in 1929 and canonized by Pope Paul VI in 1970.

See *M.M.P.*, pp. 141-5; *Publications of the Catholic Record Society*, 5, pp. 150-9; L. E. Whatmore, *Blessed Margaret Ward* (1961); "William Watson," in *Dictionary of National Biography*; T. F. Knox, *The First and Second Diaries of the English College, Douai* (n.d.), pp. 175, 209, 211; C. Devlin, *R. Southwell* (1956), pp. 175-8; Anstruther, 1, pp. 572-4.

BB Richard Leigh, Edward Shelley, Richard Martin, John Roche, and Richard Lloyd, Martyrs (1588)

After the defeat of the Spanish Armada at the end of July 1588, the persecution of Catholics became more intense and severe (see "Eight London Martyrs," 28 Aug., above).

On 30 August five martyrs were hanged at Tyburn. They included a priest, Richard Leigh (alias Earth). He was born in London in 1561 and educated at Douai. He went to Reims in 1581 and to the English College in Rome in 1582. He was ordained priest in 1586 and sent on the English mission. He was betrayed by one Anthony Tyrrell and is said to have been banished in the same year, returning almost at once, though this is doubtful, for no banishments are recorded after September 1586. He was a "learned priest." He was arrested and committed to the Tower on 4 July 1588 for offering to answer difficult questions on matters of controversy put to a Catholic gentleman reluctant to risk interrogation by John Aylmer, the bishop of London. The bishop did not accept the challenge but called Richard a popish dog and traitor and ordered him to be arrested so that his mouth might be "stopped with a halter." He was sentenced for his priesthood and died aged about twenty-seven.

Edward Shelley, Richard Martin, and Richard Lloyd (or Floyd or Flower) were condemned for harbouring or assisting priests. Edward Shelley was a gentleman of Warminghurst, Sussex, hanged for "receiving, aiding and comforting" Bd William Dean (28 Aug.). Richard Martin was born in Shropshire and educated at Broadgates Hall, Oxford; he and Richard Lloyd, a Welshman of twenty-two from Anglesey, had paid sixpence for a supper and a quart of wine for Bd Robert Morton (28 Aug.) and had harboured Fr William Horner (alias Forrest; ordained at Douai and sent to England in 1579) in the parish of St Dunstan. John Roche was an Irish waterman or servant hanged on the same day for helping a priest to escape (see St Margaret Ward, 30 Aug., above). Fr Ribadeneira wrote that all these martyrs were forbidden to speak to the crowd from the scaffold because their persecutors were afraid that they would impress people with their constancy, "but the very death of so many saint-like innocent men (whose lives were unimpeachable), and of several young gentlemen, which they endured with so much joy, strongly pleaded for the cause for which they died." They were beatified in 1929.

See *M.M.P.*, pp. 133-45, 150-1; Gillow, 1-5, *passim.*; Anstruther, 1, pp. 175, 208.

Bd Juvenal Ancina, *Bishop* (1545-1604)

Giovanni Juvenal Ancina was born in Fossano in Piedmont, Italy, on 19 October 1545, the first child of Durando Ancina, from a distinguished Spanish family, and his wife, Lucia. He was baptized Juvenal in honour of St Juvenal of Narni (7 Aug.), patron of Fossano. Though pious he did not intend to take Orders or become a religious. When Juvenal was fourteen, his father sent him to Montpellier University in France to read medicine. He then went to study at Mondovi in Sicily and, after his father's death, at Padua University. He was a brilliant student. When only about twenty-four he received a doctorate in philosophy and medicine at Turin. He was appointed to the chair of medicine there in 1569. He treated the poor free of charge. He never took part in games or recreations but played chess and wrote Latin and Italian verse, especially on State affairs. He publicly declaimed an ode on the death of Pope St Pius V (30 Apr.) in 1572. He composed verse and hymns all his life and wrote two epigrams on St Thomas More (22 June). When attending a Solemn Requiem Mass in a church at Savigliano he was overwhelmed by the message of the *Dies Irae* and decided that God required something more from him than a blameless life. He spent more time in prayer and meditation and resigned his Turin post when Count Frederick Madrucci, ambassador of the duke of Savoy to the Holy See, asked him to be his personal doctor.

Juvenal arrived in Rome in 1575 and lodged near the church of Ara Coeli, which was near the prisons, the hospital, the poor quarters, and the prison for young criminals. He began to study theology seriously. He received minor orders and put himself under the direction of St Philip Neri (26 May), who advised him to accept a benefice in Piedmont, which he gave up almost immediately. A leading lawyer at Turin had just become a Carthusian; Juvenal and his brother, John Matthew, wanted to do the same. St Philip Neri recommended his recently-founded Congregation of the Oratory. The brothers were admitted on 1 October 1578.

After four years at the Oratory Juvenal was ordained priest. In 1586 he was sent to the Naples Oratory. The exacting Neapolitans admired his sermons. He made some sensational conversions, including that of Giovannella Sanchia, a singer known as "the Siren"—not only, it was said, on account of her voice. She vowed to sing only sacred songs in future. Juvenal liked music and was a stickler for precise plainchant at the Oratory. He wrote devout words to the latest popular airs and published a hymn book with melodic lines, called *The Temple of Harmony*. One of the Oratorians, Fr Borla, became chaplain at the long-neglected hospital for incurables. Juvenal supported him and formed a confraternity of Neapolitan ladies to help the hospital. He was noted for his charity and had an account with a barber to whom he sent poor men who seemed to need a trim or shave. "Put it down to Fr Juvenal!" he would say.

About 1595, after nearly ten years in Naples, he was thinking of the contemplative life when the Roman Oratory invited him to fill the place left vacant by Baronius, who had become a cardinal. After a year three episcopal sees fell vacant, and Juvenal hid, then fled from Rome in case he was appointed to one of them. He spent five months wandering from place to place and then was ordered back to Rome.

In 1602 the duke of Savoy asked Clement VIII to fill two vacant sees for him; the pope ordered Juvenal to accept consecration as bishop of Saluzzo. When he went to take possession of the see he found that he was embroiled in a controversy between the duke and the Church. To avoid offending one or the other he withdrew to Fossano, where he wrote a pastoral letter for his diocese and devoted himself to local good works. After four months the problem concerning the rights of the Church was resolved and he went to his diocese. Toward the end of 1603 he set out on a visitation. Before going he applied his disconcerting gift of foretelling people's deaths to his own.

He had been back in Saluzzo a few weeks when he heard that a friar in the town was having an affair with a nun. Juvenal warned them that if they continued he would have to act firmly. On the feast of St Bernard he went to officiate for and dine with the Conventual Franciscans on the name-day of the church. The friar took the opportunity to poison the bishop's wine. He was taken ill before Vespers, and by the dawn of 31 August he was dead. The cause of his beatification was introduced at Rome in 1624, but it was not until 1869, when the first Vatican Council had just assembled, that it was finally achieved.

The earliest Life is by F. Bacci (1671). See C. Bowden, *The Life of Bd John Juvenal Ancina* (1891). There are other Lives, in French, by Ingold (1890), Richard (1891), and Duver (1905).

Bd Ildefonsus Schuster, *Abbot and Bishop* (1880-1954)

Cardinal Schuster was archbishop of Milan, the largest archdiocese in Italy, during the Fascist régime, the Second World War, and the difficult period immediately following the war, when he was for a time effectively governor of Milan. His public career, inevitably involving him in the political arena, raises questions with regard to his beatification that can perhaps be resolved only by accepting that this has more regard to his personal qualities than to his public activities and in recognizing the extraordinary range of his services to the Church.

He was born in Rome on 18 January 1880 and christened Lodovico Alfredo Luigi but was known as Alfredo. His origins were humble; his father Giovanni made uniforms and badges for the Papal Swiss Guards. He entered the Benedictine novitiate in November 1898, taking the name Ildefonso in religion. He was ordained priest by Cardinal Respighi in the basilica of St John Lateran on 19 March 1904.

His letters over the next few years bear witness to his studies in the fields of history—he worked on a history of Farfa in his holidays—liturgy, archaeology, and art as well as his determined quest for holiness. He was novice-master from 1908 to 1916.

His reputation for learning and dedication grew, and in 1910 he was given the first of many teaching posts, lecturing in liturgy at the Higher School of Sacred Music. His passionate interest in the subject made him a leader of the liturgical movement in Italy and the author of a massive *Liber Sacramentorum*, the first volume of which appeared in 1919; it was to go through nineteen editions and be translated into eight languages, including English. From 1913 he taught church history at the Benedictine faculty of Sant Anselmo; in 1914 he was appointed liturgical consultant to the Congregation for Rites; in 1917 a new post teaching liturgy at the Pontifical Oriental Institute, just opened by Pope Benedict XIV, was added to his existing duties.

Within the Order, tasks and offices also multiplied. He was secretary to the general chapter of the Cassinese Congregation held in 1915, then procurator general of the Congregation; in December 1915 he was elected prior of St Paul's. When the abbot of St Paul's died in 1918, Ildefonsus was the obvious choice to succeed him, and he was elected unanimously. As abbot he opened the monastery at weekends to groups of students and retreatants, one regular group being led by Giovanni Battista Montini. Pope Benedict XV valued him highly and in this was followed by Pope Pius XI, who in 1920 appointed him president of the Papal Commission on Sacred Art and sent him as apostolic visitator throughout Italy. In 1926 he was placed in charge of overseeing the seminaries in the ecclesiastical province of Milan.

The then archbishop of Milan, Cardinal Eugenio Tosi, died in January 1929, and the papers pointed to Schuster as his obvious successor. He was consecrated in the Sistine Chapel in July. He was promptly created cardinal and presented himself to King Victor Emmanuel III to swear an oath of loyalty to the State—the first Italian bishop to do so, as required under the terms of the new Concordat, signed the same year—and took up his post in September, bringing to an end thirty years of monastic life. He took over the largest archdiocese in Italy, covering five provinces, with three mill on inhabitants served by almost two thousand priests, at a time when the Concordat promised a new era of cooperation between Church and State. The State was in the grip of the irresistible rise of Fascism under *Il Duce*, Benito Mussolini, but Milan had a strong left-wing industrial tradition: only some 15 per cent of the workers supported Fascism, and only eight of the clergy were known sympathizers.

He was received with huge popular enthusiasm—though the Fascist press soon stopped reporting his activities. He started a series of pastoral letters, the first being on the subject of seminaries, Catholic journalism, and the liturgy. Placing himself publicly in the tradition of his predecessors St Ambrose (7 Dec.), St Charles Borromeo (4 Nov.), and Bd Andrew Ferrari (2 Feb.), Ildefonsus embarked on a rigorous course of pastoral visits. With nine hundred parishes, to one of which he dedicated every non-feast-day, the complete visitation took a minimum of over three years and up to six; he was on his fifth round when death finally overtook him. He visited the city parishes in winter and those outside in the other seasons; in mountainous regions the only possible means of travel were foot or mule. Sometimes he covered fifty miles on foot in three days.

His message was rigorous, too, denouncing "profane" reading, cinemas, theatre, dancing—in the manner of a latter-day Curé d'Ars. He was ruthless in denouncing "sin" as the only reason for the decline in religious observance and for the sufferings of the people. He shored up structures such as Catholic Action (under attack from the State). In the name of liturgical purity he emphasized the centrality of the Eucharist. He insisted that his clergy should not just preach the word of God but live up to its demands in every respect: those whom he judged to fail in this he removed from their posts.

His ceaseless pastoral activity still left him time to write on the history of St Ambrose's diocese. Preparations for two great occasions occupied his attention: the fourth centenary of St Charles Borromeo and the sixteenth of St Ambrose. He started two monthly reviews, one dedicated to studies of each saint.

He took the 1918 Code of Canon Law as a basic instrument for reform in the archdiocese. He reinstated the diocesan synods started by St Charles Borromeo but in abeyance since 1914. Used to living by a Rule, he tried to apply the principles to his vast diocese. At his first synod, he established four "pillars" on which the diocese should rest: the divine office, St Thomas Aquinas, the Code of Canon Law, and the Bible as the ultimate underpinning of all. His second synod, in 1935, concentrated on the liturgy; the third, in 1941, reaffirmed the principles of the first; the fourth, in 1946, as he came to the end of his third round of pastoral visitation, concentrated on the Eucharist—Milan had held a triumphal Eucharistic Congress. His fifth and last was held in 1953 and was his final testament to the archdiocese, concentrating on the pastoral spirit that had to inform the mass of legislation: "Fewer laws and more observance." The synods were backed up by pastoral letters to his clergy at the rate of one a month from 1930 to 1940. He still found time to reform Milan's "own" liturgy, the Ambrosian rite. He then turned his attention to the reform of church art. He summed up the aims of all his reforms in a "memorial" addressed to his parish priests in 1939, on the tenth anniversary of his accession.

Like the majority of Italian Catholics, he welcomed the Concordat of 1929 as "giving Italy back to God and God back to Italy" (Pius XI). His monastic background also led him to see all legitimate authority as in some sense sacred. His relations with the régime varied during its course: the years 1929-38 can be seen as those of general agreement; 1938-43 as a process of distancing himself; followed by outright opposition as he saw the results of the war. In the early years he oscillated between fulsome praise of Mussolini and actions that belied this: he refused to say Mass for a Blackshirt rally and to officate at the opening of Milan's new railway station—hailed as a Fascist triumph—in 1931, which probably made the king stay away as well. The low point of his career came in October 1935, when he enthusiastically supported the invasion of Abyssinia (Ethiopia), which he simplistically saw as a crusade taking the gospel back to a country that had known it long ago but turned its back on it. He described the war as a "national and Catholic mission for good." A year later he hailed the Italian intervention in the Spanish civil war, which he saw as caused by Bolshevism renewing an attack on Catholic Spain started by the Moors in the eighth century.

He was, however, by no means a wholehearted believer in Fascism. At a meeting with Mussolini in 1936 he asked *Il Duce* to use his influence with Hitler to modify his policies, to which Mussolini replied that he would try but was powerless. But he hailed the members of the Blue Division killed in Spain as martyrs. In 1939 he defended his relations with the régime as an attempt to Christianize Fascism, asking, "If the Church in Italy could not do so . . . what could?" In the end he was forced to recognize this as an impossible utopia.

In 1938 Jews began fleeing from Germany and large numbers appeared in Milan asking to be baptized for safety. Schuster dissuaded them from this baptism under duress and found refuges for them in parishes and religious houses. In the autumn he delivered an address to his priests (prudently not published until 1951) in which he roundly attacked the doctrine of racism as "an international menace no less than that of Bolshevism." Pius XI openly supported him. When Italy opportunistically entered the war, he declared this "treachery against France" and refused to bless soldiers leaving for the front. When the Fascist régime fell in July 1943, he accused it of having betrayed Italy. In the confused situation that ensued he concentrated on giving his people practical assistance.

323

He saw the outbreak of the Second World War as a disaster and supported Italy's initial stance of non-belligerence while urging a régime of austerity on his flock. When Italy entered the war he cut down his pastoral visits to spend more time in Milan with his people, and he made a point of visiting the wounded who were soon being brought back to the city. But he also saw the war and the austerities and sufferings it produced as something cleansing, as God's judgment on the immorality of cities. On the practical front, he opened a "wardrobe" for the poor and victims of bombing in the archbishop's residence. When the Germans occupied Italy, he condemned this as "the greatest betrayal in history."

When Mussolini fell from power in Italy, Schuster was away on a pastoral visit and was advised to go straight back to Milan to prevent a popular uprising. He found crowds removing Fascist slogans from the walls and tearing down and smashing statues of *Il Duce*. The bombing of Milan intensified, culminating in a raid by over 480 British and U.S. bombers on the night of 13 August 1944. The cardinal issued a pastoral letter begging God and the Allies not to reduce the helpless population to total despair. He knew the German High Command had a plan to retreat through Lombardy leaving a "scorched-earth" wasteland behind them and using Milan as a final bastion. Milan was caught between Mussolini's Fascist "Republic of Salò," German occupying forces, and the advancing Allies. Attempts to save what was left of Italy's second religious and cultural capital became Schuster's overriding task. He engaged in correspondence with the Allies through Col. Dulles in Switzerland and appealed personally to Mussolini to surrender.

On 25 April 1945 Mussolini and his ministers arrived at the archbishop's residence for a face-to-face meeting, arranged by Schuster, with representatives of the Italian partisans. Schuster implored him to sign a surrender document and prepare himself for a life of penance as a political prisoner. But when Mussolini found that he was being asked to sign a document that had been agreed in advance with the Germans, he declared that he had been betrayed, lost his temper, and stormed out of the meeting. That night he took the Lake Como road, on which he ran into a partisan ambush and was captured and shot. Four years later Schuster publicly confirmed that he had been at the centre of intense multi-party negotiations aimed at sparing Milan further destruction, of which this meeting had been part.

With the war over he returned again and again to the theme that spiritual as well as material reconstruction was needed, blaming the nations involved for not listening to the voice of the Church. He organized a welcome and charitable assistance for returning soldiers, turning more and more of what was left of the archbishop's residence into a food and clothing warehouse. He had to face accusations of Fascist sympathies from many of the people, and the new civil government was relatively hostile: his riposte was that the Church could not take political sides but had to save all, "especially the greatest sinners." He stressed the temporal mission of the Church in favour of the poor and condemned Communism outright as materialistic, totalitarian, and atheistic. He told Catholics they could not vote for it. In this he was to be supported by a declaration from the Holy Office in 1949. For him, the reconstruction of Italian society had to be the restoration of a Christian fabric. But he was wise enough to separate Communist ideology from its practical manifestations in aiming to better the lot of the poor, for which he expressed support. When in 1946 a plebiscite was held on whether Italy should remain a monarchy or become a republic, he enjoined silence on the theology faculty, saying this was a purely political matter in which the Church had no preference and would loyally support whatever legitimate authority emerged from the will of the people.

Cardinal Schuster's fourth round of pastoral visitation—extended in time by the war—ended in late 1946, and he promptly embarked on another, during which he told his priests that the new situation of a massive drift away from church practice required them to be heroic apostles. He had organized a huge and triumphant Eucharistic Congress in Monza in September 1945, which he claimed was attended at one point or another by half the population of the archdiocese. This was followed by an intense course of missions in Milan to "stem the anti-Christian tide." Then came a Marian Congress in 1947.

His ceaseless activity went on: missions to parishes, encouragement of Catholic Action, a diocesan liturgical congress. His most practical endeavours went to promoting a housing fund to build "simple, but welcoming and sturdy" houses for the migrants who were coming from the poor south of Italy in ever-increasing numbers looking for work. He also made sure that funds were available to build a new church on every new housing estate.

As the 1950s dawned, Schuster began to feel his advancing years and became more fearful than welcoming of new challenges. But he was able to voice an incarnational response: "Today, abandonment of the secular world by the Church is not advisable; equally, it is not possible. We need therefore to go to the masses to re-Christianize them." He even suggested the need for a council to tackle this. But he seemed trapped in a traditional response in practice: clerical training, Catholic Action, opposition to Communism and its sympathizers.

His last years were increasingly difficult; he felt he no longer understood the world, the Church, or "what the Lord wanted of him." He saw that a change was needed, even in the archdiocese. The charitable actions of the archdiocese grew ever greater, extending beyond its boundaries, as did his reputation. The Church heaped honours on him. But the Vatican also ordered a thorough inspection of the major seminary, with hints that its teaching was not sufficiently orthodox. Although the seminary passed with flying colours the event depressed him. By early 1954 his health was obviously failing fast. He died in the afternoon of 30 August. His last words were to the seminarians: "You want something to remember me by? All I can leave you is an invitation to holiness."

The news of his death spread rapidly; thousands flocked to the seminary, bringing mountains of flowers, mostly poor people bringing humble country-side flowers. His body was taken to Milan two days later, and his funeral brought the whole city to a standstill, with weeping crowds lining the streets. The first steps toward opening the cause for his beatification were taken by the diocese and the Benedictines almost immediately. A bizarre episode threatened to bring them to grief the following year. The *Folies Bergères* were touring Italy, and Archbishop Mimmi of Naples, informed by a report of the nature of the show, rang the *Osservatore Romano* to protest at its presence and even more so at its proposed transfer to Rome. Someone remembered that it had performed in Milan two years before Schuster's death without any protest from him. This laxity would not help his cause. The matter was referred to Pope Pius XII, whose reaction was to ask if Josephine Baker ("*la Baker*," to him) was still with the show. She was, and he had received her in audience years before and had been delighted with her. The show went on in Rome with minor modifications, and this obstacle to Schuster's cause was removed. In 1977 the then General Promoter of the Faith called for a further in-depth "historical-critical" examination of his relations with Fascism, and in 1983 halted the process on this account. He was ceremonially beatified by Pope John Paul II on 12 May 1996.

See the sober biography by Luigi Crivelli, *Schuster. Un Monaco prestato a Milano* (1996), on which the above notice is mainly based; his correspondence with Roncalli, *Schuster-Roncalli. Nel nome della santità: lettere e documenti*, ed. E. Guerriero and M. Roncalli (1996); a selection of his pastorals and addresses, *Al dilettismo popolo. Parola e lettere all diocesi di Milano* (1996). There is a two-volume biography by T. Lecisotti, *Il cardinale Schuster* (1969). See also A. Majo, *Schuster. Una vita per Milano* (1994), with bibliography. His collected notes on the last days of Fascism, *Gli ultimi tempi di un regime*, made as a justification for his actions, were later edited and published (1995). His efforts to save Milan are recounted in G. Rumi, "Milano, una seconda Roma al Nord?" in A. Riccardi (ed.), *La Chiesa di Pio XII* (1986). His great liturgical work, *Liber Sacramentorum*, was originally published in ten volumes (1919-29). His contribution to Benedictine studies was summed up in "Schuster nella storiografia monastica del novecento," in *Benedictina* 41 (1994). For the incident involving the *Folies Bergères* see D. O'Grady, "The Cardinal and the Showgirls," in *The Tablet*, 11 Jan. 1997, p. 40.

R.M.

Sixty Martyrs of Colonia Suffetulana Sbeitla in Africa (399)

St Agilus, Abbot, near Meaux, France (*c.* 650)

St Bononius, Abbot in Bologna, who first lived as a hermit in Egypt and on Mount Sinai (1026)

St Peter of Trebi in Lazio, confessor (*c.* 1050)

31

SS Joseph of Arimathea and Nicodemus (First Century)

Joseph is mentioned in all four Gospels. He was wealthy ("a man of means" in the Authorized Version) and a "good and a just man" of Arimathea (the town known in Hebrew as Ramathaim, between Jaffa/Tel Aviv and Jerusalem), a councillor (and possibly a member of the Sanhedrin, the supreme council, or of the Beth Din, the lower judgment-chamber) who did not vote against Jesus. He was one of Jesus' disciples. We are told that he was looking for the kingdom of God. After Jesus' death Joseph obtained his body from Pilate, bought fine linen to wrap it in, and buried it in his own unused family tomb in the rock (Matt. 27:57-60; Mark 15:43-6; Luke 23:50-44; John 19:38-42). It has been suggested, however, that Jesus, executed as a criminal, would have been buried not in a family tomb but in the public tomb; the family could collect the bones only after a year. If Joseph was the councillor of the Beth Din in charge of public graves and thus with access to the body, it would have been a fortunate coincidence that he was a Jesus sympathizer. It is important in Luke, and mentioned only in Luke, that Joseph took no part in the council's deliberations. Luke makes a sharp distinction between the people (who respond well to Jesus) and their leaders (who do not); this fact would then be a counter-weight to that. Joseph is not to be confused with one of the "brothers [or brethren] of the Lord" (Matt. 13:55; 27:56), otherwise called Joses.

The foregoing is all we know of him, but he was and remains an extraordinarily potent figure in legends. Some of these are of considerable literary and symbolic power, others tedious, yet others tediously cranky.

Joseph appears in late apocrypha such as the *Gospel of Nicodemus* (or *Acts of Pilate*; no earlier than the fourth century), in which he is imprisoned by "the Jews" in a windowless room which they seal up with Caiphas' finger-ring; later he helps to found the first Christian community at Lydda. In *The Golden Legend* the Jews brick him in a massive wall for continuing to preach the gospel; he is miraculously sustained with light and food from heaven and eventually released. The earliest manuscript of the *Story of Joseph of Arimathea* dates from the twelfth century. In it Joseph is gaoled for begging Jesus' body from Pilate. He is released by Jesus and the good thief and spends three days with them, witnessing John, the beloved disciple's, discomfiture on seeing the thief's elevation as "a king in great might, clad with the cross." In the Assumption (15 Aug.) narrative of Joseph of Arimathea (probably no earlier than the thirteenth century) he is called by Our Lady to witness her death, Christ's removal of her soul, and angels taking up her body.

In the Holy Grail legend Joseph is associated with the cup said to have received Christ's blood on Calvary. The association has proved extraordinarily attractive in literature, art, and music as well as in popular religion. The origins of the Grail narrative are much discussed by anthropologists, etymologists, mythographers, literary historians, and others. Many fanciful lines of descent have been proposed. Among the more respectable twentieth-century theories are those which suggest remote antecedents in pre-Christian Iranian, Egyptian, and Greek antiquity and in Byzantine Christianity. Responsible scholars now generally agree that the legend should be traced to Celtic and, more specifically, Gallic and Irish mythology, and that the Grail was originally one of those magical containers which offer their users inexhaustible nourishment and even immortality. The oldest known version of the tale with its specifically Christian elements is French and was written between 1180 and 1190 by Chrétien de Troyes, who ascribed the story to Philippe d'Alsace, working at a time when French literature was composed on both sides of the Channel. More Christian components were added in various reworkings in the early thirteenth century. The first to mention Joseph was that (*c.* 1215) of Robert de Boron, who lived in England; he added details from an unknown source, possibly Glastonbury. De Boron identifies the Grail as the dish from which Jesus ate the Paschal lamb and in which Joseph collected the Lord's blood at the crucifixion. He took it to England, where his descendants guarded it. The latest of the line was Perceval, whose grandfather was the "Fisher-king."

The original *De Antiquitate Glastoniensis Ecclesiae*, or *Antiquity of Glastonbury*, by William of Malmesbury (*c.* 1130) does not mention the Glastonbury legend. An amplified version a century later says that St Philip the Apostle (3 May) went to Gaul with Joseph and sent the latter to England with twelve clerics under his direction. They tried to convert a king, unsuccessfully, but he gave them the island of Yniswitrin, or Glastonbury, where the angel Gabriel told them to erect a church of wattles to Our Lady, thirty-one years after the passion of Jesus and fifteen years after Mary's assumption (though Glastonbury was probably a seventh-century Celtic foundation which became a Saxon monastery under King Ina in about 708 and was destroyed by Vikings in the ninth century).

In the late twelfth century Glastonbury abbey was for various reasons in competition with other abbeys. It claimed, like Canterbury, to have the relics of St Dunstan (19 May). The legends of Joseph's and King Arthur's associations with the abbey brought considerable benefits. It was important to give the Plantagenet monarchy respectable forebears further back in Christian antiquity than the Capetian rulers of France. The supposed discovery of the tombs of Arthur and Guinevere at Glastonbury in 1191 was mutually beneficial to the court and to the abbey. Glastonbury claimed seniority among Black Benedictine abbeys in England, and at the Councils of Constance (1414-8) and Basle (1434) English delegates claimed that their country was the first in western Europe to receive Christianity.

John of Glastonbury's *History* (*c*. 1400) associated Joseph and Arthur with the abbey, and extracts from it appeared for pilgrims' edification on a large frame, the *magna tabula*, in the abbey. Among John's additions is the information that not only Joseph and the twelve clerics but 150 others were carried over the Channel on the shirt of Josephes, the son of Joseph. Yniswitrin is identified not merely with Glastonbury but with Avalon. The *Lyfe of Joseph of Arimathia* (1502), a verse narrative, amplifies John of Glastonbury's account with tales of miraculous cures worked by Joseph and first mentions the Holy Thorn, said to have sprung from Joseph's staff and to flower at Christmas. (The present claimant is a descendant of the hawthorn cut down by one of Cromwell's soldiers; it flowers twice a year, around Christmas and in May). Joseph's grave was said to be at Glastonbury but was never found. At one time Moyenmoutier abbey in the Vosges, France, claimed to have the relics of Joseph.

Nicodemus, "learned in the law," was a Pharisee, or "ruler of the Jews" (John 3:1), and perhaps therefore a member of the Sanhedrin. The meeting with Nicodemus is important in John's theme of judgment. Throughout the fourth Gospel judgment takes place by the way people react to Jesus. You judge yourself by how you face Jesus. First the disciples at Cana accept him and see his glory, then the Jews at the cleansing of the Temple reject him, then comes Nicodemus with his ambiguous stance. He visited Jesus secretly at night and admitted that his mission was from God. This visit is the framework for the discourse on baptism in John 3:1-20, which re-echoes through some of the greatest spiritual writings and countless works of English literature. Nicodemus is chosen to receive the message of rebirth of the spirit through the Spirit and to personify a certain reaction to it. He is for ever associated with such memorable words as: "Except a man be born again, he cannot see the kingdom of God" and, "The wind bloweth where it listeth, and thou hearest the sound thereof, but canst not tell where it cometh, and whither it goeth," and his question: "How can these things be?" (A.V.). He spoke on Jesus' behalf in the council. He said that the law required the accused to be given a hearing (John 7:50ff.). He helped to bury Jesus and brought a great amount of expensive spices with him to embalm the body (John 19:39-42). We know no more of him. He possibly became a disciple of Jesus. The symbolism of his visit and the ambiguity of his attitude are made clear by Augustine: "Although he came to Jesus, yet because he came by night, he still speaks for the darkness of his own flesh. He understands not what he hears from the Lord, understands not what he hears from the Light. . . . This man knew but one birth, that from Adam and Eve; that which is from God and the Church he knew not yet" (*Gospel of John*, 1, pp. 155-8).

On Joseph see M. R. James (ed.), *The Apocryphal New Testament* (1924), pp. 105, 148, 161–5, 216–8; J. Armitage Robinson, *Two Glastonbury Legends* (1926); T. D. Kendrick, *British Antiquity* (1950); G. Ashe, *King Arthur's Avalon: the Story of Glastonbury* (1957); R. F. Treharne, *The Glastonbury Legends* (1967); J. Frappier, *Chrétien du Troyes et le mythe du Graal* (1972); C. Lévi-Strauss, *Le regard éloigné* (1983), pp. 302–34; *AA.SS.*, Mar., 2. On Nicodemus see J. Mendrer, "Nikodemus," in *Journal of Biblical Literature* 77 (1958), pp. 293–323.

Joseph's attributes are a shroud, the crown of thorns, and nails. He appears in a vast number of paintings of almost all schools. He is shown at the deposition of Jesus, either on a ladder lowering the body or on the ground to receive it, and Nicodemus may appear with him. In pictures of the lamentation and the entombment he and Nicodemus (and sometimes St John the Evangelist) carry Jesus' body on a shroud. In representations of the legends he is most often shown holding the Holy Grail to catch the blood from Jesus' wounds or with two cruets to hold the blood and sweat, as on the rood-screen at Plymtree, Devon, in stained glass at Langport, Devon, and in stained glass at St John's, Glastonbury, but there are many variations, such as William Blake's 1773 engraving of Joseph as a brooding solitary. Nicodemus is shown receiving instruction from Jesus. They may be at a table, usually in candlelight, but Nicodemus may stand before Christ, listening intently.

St Paulinus of Trier, *Bishop* (358)

St Athanasius (2 May) called him a "truly apostolic man," and St Jerome (30 Sept.) said he was "happy in his sufferings" for the faith. He was educated in the cathedral school of Poitiers in France. He was a disciple of St Maximinus (29 May), whom he succeeded as bishop of Trier (now in Germany). Paulinus became one of Athanasius' most enthusiastic supporters during his exile at Trier. At the Arianizing synod of Arles in 353 he defended the Nicaean articles of faith and opposed the papal legates who were prepared to condemn Athanasius. For the same reasons he resisted the intimidation and violence of the emperor Constantius. Paulinus was banished from his see together with St Dionysius of Milan (25 May), St Eusebius of Vercelli (2 Aug.), and Lucifer of Cagliari and sent into exile in Phrygia. He died there in 358. St Felix (26 Mar.), bishop of Trier, brought Paulinus' body back to the town in 396. It was enshrined in the church which bore his name in 402, and his tomb was found in the ruins in 1738. In 1883 archaeologists removed what they presumed was his skeleton, still wrapped in oriental silk, with fragments of an older coffin from its sarcophagus. The evidence seemed to show that stories of the saint's decapitation were untrue.

See *AA.SS.*, Aug., 6, with a ninth-tenth-century Latin Life; P. Diel, *Der heilige Maximinus und der heilige Paulinus* (1875); and on the relics, *Jahrbücher des Vereins für Altertumsfreunden im Rheinlande*, 78 (1884), pp. 167 ff.

St Eanswida (*c.* 640)

St Ethelbert of Kent (25 Feb.) was the first Christian king among the English. He was succeeded by his son Edbald, who became a Christian. He wanted his daughter Eanswida (Eanswyth or Eanswitha) to marry a pagan prince from Northumbria. She said she would do so only if his gods answered his prayer by making a wooden log a foot longer. Edbald allowed her, after training in France, to found a nunnery on the Kent coast near Folkestone, possibly the first in England. She led a life of penance and prayer until she died on 31 August in around 640. The Danes destroyed her convent, but it was refounded for Black Benedictine monks in 1095. When part of this priory collapsed into the sea, it was removed to Folkestone and (on 12 September, *c.* 1140) her relics were possibly deposited in the church her father had built in honour of St Peter. Its successor is now known as SS Mary and Eanswida's, and there, in 1885, a Saxon burial chest containing a young woman's bones was found in the north wall. This could have come from a former shrine of the saint, who appears on the seals of Folkestone. The chronicler Capgrave relates legends regarding Eanswida and her miraculous powers.

R. Stanton, *A Menology of England and Wales* (1892), pp. 429-32; *B.T.A.*, 3, pp. 545-6; *N.L.A.*, 1., pp. 296-9; A. Cockayne, *Leechdoms*, 3, p. 422.

St Cuthburga, *Abbess* (*c.* 725)

She was the sister of King Ine of Wessex and the wife of Aldfrid, who succeeded to the Northumbrian throne in 685. He allowed her to become a novice under St Hildelitha (3 Sept.) at Barking Monastery in Essex. Some time after 705, together with her sister St Quenburga, she founded Wimborne Abbey in Dorset and became its abbess. The abbey's rule of enclosure was said to be so strict that not even prelates on lawful church business were allowed to enter it. Cuthburga is recorded as humble and kind to others but austere to herself, spending most of her time in fasting and prayer. Under her successor, St Tetta, Wimborne sent nuns to help St Boniface (5 June) convert Germany.

See *B.H.L.*, 2033, for an unpublished early Life. See also *Anal.Boll.* 56 (1938), p. 336; 58, p. 100; *AA.SS.*, Aug., 6.

St Raymund Nonnatus, *Cardinal* (1204-40)

There are no early or reliable sources for the life of Raymund Nonnatus (*non natus*, or "not born"). Pope Benedict XIV's commission proposed to remove him from the general Calendar, but he has been retained in the new draft Roman Martyrology. The following is a summary of the traditional narrative.

He was taken from his mother's womb just after her death at Portello in Catalonia. He joined the Barcelona Mercedarians under St Peter Nolasco (25 Dec.). He was sent to Algeria with a large sum of money as an official "ransomer," an office which Peter himself had performed. He redeemed a number of slaves, and when the cash ran out he offered himself as a ransom for others. He was treated cruelly at first. Eventually he was freed from gaol because his captors feared he might die and they would lose the ransom for slaves for whom he remained a hostage.

He used his freedom to comfort Christians and convert some Muslims; he was sentenced to be impaled. The gaolers again raised the matter of the ransom owed, so the governor commuted the sentence to running the gauntlet. Having suffered this punishment, the indefatigable Raymund used his liberty as before, and this time he was tortured, his lips were pierced, and his mouth was padlocked; the governor held the key and issued it only at mealtimes. He was kept in a dungeon for eight months, but eventually, in 1239, St Peter himself arrived with a ransom and insisted that the reluctant Raymund return to Spain. Pope Gregory IX made him a cardinal but he continued to live humbly. He was summoned to Rome. He would travel only as a poor religious and died of a fever on the way at Cardona, near Barcelona. He was buried in the chapel of St Nicholas at Portello, and he entered the Roman Martyrology in 1657.

Many miracles were reported through Raymund's intercession. His supposed preaching to Muslims and the resulting sufferings made him a relatively popular subject, mainly in Iberian but also in Italian devotional art. He became a patron of midwives because of the unusual circumstances of his birth.

See *AA.SS.*, Aug. 6 (1743), 737-46; *O.D.C.C.*, p. 1161; *B.T.A.* 3, 449-50; *Bibl. SS.*, 11, 12-6.

Raymund is shown in a white habit, carrying a book and wearing an elaborate emblem or scapular. The painting by C. Saraceni (1585-1620; S. Adrianc, Rome) shows the saint preaching with baroque fervour to a suitably affected crowd. Zurbarán (1631-40; private collection, Geneva, Switzerland) subordinates his countenance to the overwhelming whiteness of his habit.

Bd Andrew Dotti (c. 1250-1315)

Andrea Dotti was born at Borgo San Sepolcro in Italy in about 1250. He came from a distinguished family (his brother was a captain in the bodyguard of King Philip the Fair) and was raised without any thought of entering a religious Order. When he was seventeen he became a member of the Servite Third Order, a purely secular role. A few years later the Order held a general chapter at Borgo San Sepolcro, and Andrew went to hear the prior general, St Philip Benizi (22 Aug.), preach. The text was, "Any one of you who does not give up all his possessions cannot be my disciple." Philip's eloquence touched Andrew's heart. He asked to become a Servite friar and was accepted. After ordination he entered a monastery governed by St Sostenes (St Gerard Sostegni), one of the Order's seven founders (17 Feb.). He became a successful preacher and accompanied Philip on several missionary journeys.

Some hermits at Vallucola were living what was thought to be a too independent way of life. After the death of the emperor Frederick II and the decline of the imperial party in Italy the popes began a determined campaign to eradicate heretics, mainly Cathars and Waldensians and church reform groups that had enjoyed considerable protection in Italy in the first half of the century. The travelling Cathars, or "Good Men," were often solitaries who made their way from one community to another; and the Waldensians survived for centuries in out-of-the way places. The Vallucola group (as far as one can speak thus of hermits) was dangerously untidy and had to be brought into line. Andrew was commissioned to "prepare" them for affiliation to the Servites and submission to their discipline. He was appointed their superior until he was needed again for preaching and as prior of a number of houses. In 1310 he was present at the death of St Alexis Falconieri, one of the main founders of the Servites, at Monte Senario, which impressed him greatly. He was now sixty and therefore—in the thirteenth century—quite elderly. He asked permission to retire to a hermitage and prepare for his death. He is said to have led a very penitential life, yet he seemed in good health. One day, however, when his fellow-monks went to a favourite rock where he spoke to them regularly they found him kneeling motionless. At first they imagined he was in an ecstasy of devotion but soon discovered that he was dead. He was buried in the church at Borgo San Sepolcro, where miracles were said to occur through his intercession. In 1806 Pope Pius VII approved the ancient cult.

See A. Giani, *Annales Ordinis Servorum B.V.M.*, 1, esp. pp. 2301; *D.H.G.E.*, 2, 1663; M. Lambert, *Medieval Heresy* (2d ed., 1992), pp. 147-71.

R.M.
St Aristides, who preached to Hadrian (*c.* 150)
St John of Como, bishop (seventh century)
St John the Anchorite (946)
Bd Benedict of Arezzo, O.F.M. (1281)

(Names are listed for those saints and blessed who have entries in the main body of the text. Those listed in the RM paragraph at the end of each day are omitted.)